DEDICATION

I dedicate this work with thanks and appreciation to my wife, Millie, and our children, Adam and Aimee, and their families.

-R.C.A.

I dedicate this work to my parents, Gary and Darlene Bell, my husband, Mark McManus and my daughters, Isabella and Elouise, for their love, patience, and persistent belief in me.

–L.M.B.M.

I dedicate this work to my parents, Joseph and Mary McKendree, my husband, Daniel Casciato, and my daughter, Giavanna Grace.

–A.G.M.

BRIEF CONTENTS

CONTENTS

ACKNOWLEDGMENTS

I, Ronald C. Arnett, offer my thanks and gratitude to Duquesne University, the Spiritan community, and my colleagues in the Department of Communication & Rhetorical Studies. I am deeply thankful to Susan Mancino, Senior Graduate Research Assistant, for her outstanding work and her thoughtful attentiveness on this project and so many others. Susan co-authored the instructional materials. I am also thankful to Michael Kearney for his assistance. Additionally, I am sincerely appreciative of Paul Carty, Director of Publishing Partnerships of Kendall Hunt Publishing, for his work and ongoing courtesy to all. I am thankful to Leeanne M. Bell McManus and Amanda G. McKendree for their thoughtful contributions to this project. Finally, I am deeply grateful to my colleague Janie Harden Fritz for her thoughtful comments on the manuscript.

I, Leeanne M. Bell McManus, offer my appreciation to my co-authors and everyone who made this project possible. Ronald C. Arnett (Duquesne University) shared his knowledge, support, and patience throughout this project. Amanda G. McKendree (University of Notre Dame) spent countless hours on the phone listening to every chapter as she offered invaluable suggestions. Janie M. Harden Fritz (Duquesne University) read our manuscript and provided valuable feedback that was extremely helpful. She encourages and supports me in my career and I am forever grateful for her guidance and friendship. Paul Carty, Director of Publishing Partnerships, and Angela Willenbring, Senior Editor, (Kendall Hunt Publishing) both demonstrated patience and offered continual guidance. Susan Mancino (Duquesne University) was very thorough and helpful during every step of the process. My colleagues, students, and academic home (Stevenson University) offered encouragement and unending support.

I, Amanda G. McKendree, offer my deepest gratitude to the University of Notre Dame, the Notre Dame Faculty Research Support Program Initiation Grant, and my colleagues in the Eugene D. Fanning Center for Business Communication in the Mendoza College of Business. I also offer my appreciation to Ronald C. Arnett (Duquesne University) who has modeled what it means to be a teacher-scholar throughout this project and Leeanne M. Bell McManus (Stevenson University) who was an enjoyable research and writing partner. Susan Mancino (Duquesne University) and Janie M. Harden Fritz (Duquesne University) were invaluable to this book project. I also offer thanks to the Notre Dame faculty and students who participated in focus groups and workshops, and provided feedback on the manuscript. Finally, I extend my deepest gratitude to Paul Carty, Director of Publishing Partnerships, and Angela Willenbring, Senior Editor (Kendall Hunt Publishing), who offered helpful insights and encouragement as we completed the book.

ABOUT THE AUTHORS

Ronald C. Arnett (Ph.D., Ohio University, 1978) is professor and chair of the Department of Communication & Rhetorical Studies and the Patricia Doherty Yoder and Ronald Wolfe Endowed Chair in Communication Ethics at Duquesne University. He is the former Henry Koren, C.S.Sp., Endowed Chair for Scholarly Excellence (2010–2015). He is the author/coauthor of eleven books and the recipient of six book awards. His most recent works include *Levinas's Rhetorical Demand: The Unending Obligation of Communication Ethics* (2017, Southern Illinois University Press) and two award-winning works: *Communication Ethics in Dark Times: Hannah Arendt's Rhetoric of Warning and Hope* and *An Overture to Philosophy of Communication: The Carrier of Meaning* (with Annette Holba). He was selected as a 2017 Distinguished Scholar by the National Communication Association.

Leeanne M. Bell McManus (Ph.D., Duquesne University, 2007) is a professor in the Business Communication Department at Stevenson University and the Vice President of the Eastern Communication Association. She has co-authored two books, *Communication Ethics Literacy: Dialogue and Difference* (with Ronald C. Arnett and Janie Harden Fritz) and *Event Planning: Communicating Theory and Practice* (with Chip Rouse and Stephanie Verni). She has published excerpts in *Integrated Marketing Communication: Creating Spaces for Engagement* (with Chip Rouse), *Exploring Communication Ethics: Interviews with Influential Scholars in the Field* (with Ronald C. Arnett and Pat Arneson), and *The Encyclopedia of Social Identity*. Dr. Bell McManus has also published in *Atlantic Journal of Communication, Choice: Current Reviews for Academic Libraries, Communication Annual: Journal of the Pennsylvania Communication Association, Communication Education, Journal of the Association for Communication Administration*, and *Review of Communication*.

Amanda G. McKendree (Ph.D., Duquesne University, 2009) is the Arthur F. and Mary J. O'Neil Director of the Fanning Center for Business Communication and an associate teaching professor of management in the Mendoza College of Business at the University of Notre Dame. Her research examines crisis communication, conflict communication, and the influence of rhetoric on organizational identity. She is published in the *SAGE Encyclopedia of Identity, the International Encyclopedia of Organizational Communication, Business Communication Quarterly, Teaching Ideas for the Basic Communication Course, Journal of the Association for Communication Administration*, and *Review of Communication*.

Chapter One

CONFLICT IN AN AGE OF ETHICAL DISPUTE

So those who had hoped to discover good reasons for making this rather than that judgment on some particular type of issue—by moving from the arenas in which in everyday social life groups and individuals quarrel about what it is just to do in particular cases over to the realm of theoretical enquiry, where systematic conceptions of justice are elaborated and debated—will find that once again they have entered upon a scene of radical conflict. (MacIntyre, 1988, pp. 1–2)

If all of us agreed upon what is ethical, conflict would be limited to discerning the correct answer according to an external objective standard. Alas, if such a world ever existed, it does not represent our contemporary reality. We dwell in an era of multiple ethical positions that constitute contrasting communication and conflict orientations. This chapter's *Spotlight on Leadership* features Bill and Melinda Gates and their work navigating conflict that arises from different ethical positions.

© lembi/Shutterstock.com

Bill and Melinda Gates are responsive to some of the most complex problems facing our world today. The goal of the Bill & Melinda Gates Foundation is to improve the quality of life for individuals around the world by focusing on poverty, health, and economic empowerment. Their foundation partners with NGOs, philanthropists, universities, foundation representatives, partner organizations, and governments in Washington, China, South Africa, and India to achieve its mission.

Dissimilar ethical standpoints generate conflicts as we demand that others conform to our ethical expectations. This book, *Conflict between Persons: The Origins of Leadership*, asserts that no one set of common ethical assumptions shape communication and conflict responses in this historical moment. The ethical functions as a motivating engine framing what is worthy of protecting and promoting as we engage in conflict with others, which often does not conform to what they consider worthy of protecting and promoting.

For example, picking an undergraduate major is often demanding. A 2015 *New York Times* article reported that most people are unsure of what major is right for them. However, majors do not directly determine careers; education is an ongoing journey of discerning interests, values and skills (Gebhard, 2015). As one seeks to discern a career path, one reflects on the opinions of others, who may offer contradictory ethical suggestions. As one selects a major, one often receives conflicting advice. Some people want us to consider a major connected to a trendy job, others simply want us to be a commercial success, and a close friend might remind us to follow our heart. Students should be encouraged to "separate [their] goals from other people's goals for [them]" (Gebhard, 2015, para. 6) and engage in interests that uncover their passions. The struggle to find the right path continues after graduation, where remaining in the same job for a career is now a rarity. Most people change their job an average of 10 to 15 times during their career. Age can also impact the number of jobs held.

In 2015, the Bureau of Labor Statistics released its "National Longitudinal Survey of Youth 1979" findings. This survey included 9,964 men and women aged 14 to 22 at the time of the first interview in 1979, who in the 2012-2013 interview were ages 47 to 56 (Number of Jobs Held, para. 2). The report details that individuals born from 1957 to 1964 held an average of 11.7 jobs. The following chart illustrates respondents' job movement over this time period.

Age Range of Respondents	Number of Jobs Held
18–24	5.5
25–29	3
30–34	2.4
35–39	2.1
40–48	2.4

The Bureau of Labor Statistics tracks how long individuals tend to stay at their place of employment. The median tenure of workers ages 55 to 64 is 10.1 years, while the median tenure of workers ages 25 to 34 years is 2.8 years (Employee Tenure, para. 4). This difference reflects a shifting attitude among younger workers who recognize the value of changing jobs more frequently and the potential downsides of staying in a position for too long. A 2016 *Fast Company* article reported that workers who stay with a company longer than 2 years "get paid 50% less, and job hoppers are believed to have a higher learning curve, be higher performers, and even be more loyal" (Giang, para. 3). When employees intend to stay at a job for a brief tenure, they focus on overachieving or making a maximum impact in that short amount of time.

A *Forbes* essay used the terms "job hopping" and "hit-and-run jobholding" as normative understandings of a contemporary career (Meister, 2012, para. 5). Job shifting often commences with ethical dissatisfaction, with 58% of people taking a 15% cut in pay in order to work in an organization with values more akin to their own (Meister, 2012, para. 17). Ethics matters, influencing our decisions and careers. As we grapple with tough choices, we discover that conflict and the clashing of ethical goods are repeatedly at the center of our judgments, quandaries, and hopes.

INTRODUCTION

We live in an age of ethical disputes, making conflict inevitable as we meet others with contrasting ethical positions and contrary communicative expectations. An ethical position held with conviction frequently generates conflict when one encounters another with a differing ethical standpoint embraced with equal assurance. This chapter, "Conflict in an Age of Ethical Dispute," examines the connection between communication ethics and conflict, asserting a basic presupposition: ethical assumptions provide guiding meaning, direction, and conviction that simultaneously generate conflict when we meet persons with alternative ethical positions. The study of communication ethics does not shelter us from conflict; in fact, it invites conflict, providing clarity about what is important to us and to others.

In "Conflict in an Age of Ethical Dispute," we explore six major sections:

1. **Communication ethics and conflict: The engine for dispute** discusses how communication ethics fuels conflict;
2. **A communicative gestalt** describes the interplay of figure and ground and why understanding the whole as greater than the sum of its parts is necessary for understanding both ethics and conflict;
3. **Goods that matter: Understanding the epicenter of conflict** emphasizes that the more something matters ethically, the greater the likelihood of conflict;
4. **Responsibility for conflict** details the inevitability of conflict and our role in its generation and constructive engagement;
5. **Communicative building and construction** frames our responsibility in nourishing a communicative environment;
6. **Framing communicative leadership: The interplay of ethics and conflict** offers insight into our basic leadership assumption—there is a natural link between ethics and conflict.

The admission of the interplay of ethics and conflict is a pragmatic communicative gesture. **Pragmatism** (James, 1907/2008) is the major American contribution to philosophy (Thayer, 1968/1981), a stance of refusing to engage in lament when existence is not as we demand or expect. Pragmatism focuses on thought that guides communicative actions through experience, ever attentive to the uniqueness of a given moment. The recognition of the pragmatic relationship between ethics and conflict is consistent with the International Communication Association's *The Handbook of Communication Ethics* edited by George Cheney, Steve May, and Debashish Munshi (2010), which announces complexity and difference in ethical positions. The editors shift the conversation from communication ethics as a uniform "set of standards" to learning about differing views of communication ethics (p. 336). *Conflict between Persons: The Origins of Leadership* concurs with Cheney, May, and Munshi's stress on ethical multiplicity and the reality of conflict generated in an era defined by narrative and virtue contention (MacIntyre, 1981).

COMMUNICATION ETHICS AND CONFLICT: THE ENGINE FOR DISPUTE

A number of communication authors have creatively aligned communication ethics with difference (Arnett, Arneson, & Bell, 2006; Arnett, Fritz, & Bell, 2009; Cheney, May, & Munshi, 2010; Johannesen, 1983). Acknowledging that we live in a world of multiplicity and difference affects conflict in everyday life. The decisive conclusion of *Communication Ethics Literacy: Dialogue and Difference* is that conflict is inevitable when we recognize that we live in an era of a "multiplicity of 'goods'" (Arnett, Fritz, & Bell, 2009, p. 9). The authors argue that communication ethics understood in a time of narrative and virtue contention necessitates the pragmatic linkage between communication ethics and conflict study.

Out of respect and thanks to our colleagues (Arnett, 2013), we want to restate that this organic link between ethics and conflict is consistent with the insights of W. Barnett Pearce and Stephen W. Littlejohn (1997). They made this point almost two decades ago in *Moral Conflict: When Social Worlds Collide*. Using the language of W. Barnett Pearce (2007), this project engages what he termed "**appreciative inquiry**" (p. 63), exploring the existential fact that we live in an era of moral conflict, resulting in the colliding of social worlds (Pearce & Littlejohn, 1997). In our judgment, their insights were ahead of normative conversation about the linkage between ethical differences and conflict generation. Their contention, however, now reveals itself locally, nationally, and internationally through financial, political, and social crises. Conflict is the foreground or figure that often emerges from contrasting ethical positions that dwell within differing backgrounds; contrasting ethical backgrounds generate conflict as they collide. Conflict and ethics constitute a communicative gestalt that requires thoughtful communicative engagement.

A COMMUNICATIVE GESTALT

Communication ethics is a background that gives moral weight and importance to foreground conflicts. The relationship between background and foreground in **Gestalt theory** asserts that what we apprehend in the foreground depends upon its background. For instance, consider renovating a house room by room. Renovating one room announces the need for further renovation, revealing the relational nature of the house—its background. One quickly discovers that with the completion of a renovated room, more work is called forth in order to keep the house looking balanced and aligned. Renovations not only change the house, but they also amend the relation between the house and its residents. The interplay of foreground and background in the renovation influences the lives of those living within the house, with persons and change in the dwelling announcing a communicative gestalt, a whole greater than the sum of the parts.

The contemporary concept of gestalt emerged in the 20th century in association with Gestalt psychology, introduced in 1912 by **Max Wertheimer**. The original concept, however, is much older. The origin of the well-known phrase "the whole is more than the sum of its parts" lies in Aristotle's (trans. 1984) *Metaphysics*. Additionally, **John Stuart Mill** (1843/1875), in *A System of Logic: Ratiocinative and Inductive*, stated that gestalt assumes that parts have different qualities than the whole. The parts can stand alone, but when assembled together, they create something unique. For example, the colors yellow and blue are exclusive in their own right, but when mixed, they form the color green. Mill called his approach "mental chemistry," arguing that the mind plays an active role in bringing ideas together (pp. 441–442), with each distinctive part reconstituting the whole.

JOHN STUART MILL (1806–1873)
was a British philosopher and economist who advocated utilitarianism. The basic assumption of **utilitarianism**, founded by Jeremy Bentham, contends that actions prompting happiness for the greater community are right and those that deny happiness are wrong. Mill's writings addressed liberty, logic, utilitarianism, political economics, and political philosophy ("John Stuart Mill," 2013).

As suggested in the previous paragraph, the most popular understanding and use of Gestalt theory is in the early 20th century, with Max Wertheimer as the founder of Gestalt psychology (King & Wertheimer, 2005). Wertheimer (1912/1961) initiated the idea of gestalt in an essay, "Experimental Studies on the Seeing of Motion." He examined the complexity of motion and its impact upon perception. Wertheimer's insight into the reality of gestalt detailed how foreground perception depends upon a background or context for comprehensibility. The notion of gestalt in children's flipbooks uses motion to shape perception as one quickly flips through the pages. This kinesis creates a perception that something is moving even though the illustrations remain dormant on the page. The faster one flips through the book, the quicker the object seems to move. However, if one turns each page individually, the perception of movement is lost. The pages require movement in rapid succession in order to invite the perception of change.

Discussion of the connection between background and foreground continues to influence Gestalt psychology; perhaps every introductory communication student has had a professor display a silhouette with multiple perceptual meanings, each dependent upon the interplay of background and foreground. A common optical illusion that illustrates the interplay of

background and foreground is a drawing that consists of both an old lady and
a young woman with each one dependent
upon the background against which one
perceives the image (Figure 1.1). Once one
has visualized one or the other (old lady
or young woman), it is difficult to switch
from one perceptual scene to the other. If
one focuses on the dark horizontal line, one
visualizes either the mouth of an old lady
or the necklace of a young woman. Our
focus of attention shifts between the old
lady and the young woman as our perspective relocates. Just as it is not easy to alter
perspectives, it is demanding to understand the ethical background of another
that obliges us to perceive differently.

The communicative gestalt of ethics
and conflict is a first step in countering thoughtlessness and routine perceptual engagement, which assumes that the

FIGURE 1.1   An optical illusion that
depends upon foreground
and background.

whole world perceives identically. Examining different foreground and background linkages
can assist in understanding what another is protecting and promoting in a conflict. Gestalt
theory disrupts thoughtlessness that does not take into account the complexity of the texture and connections between background and foreground action, which **Hannah Arendt's**
(1963/2006) classic work suggests.

HANNAH ARENDT (1906–1975)
was born in Hannover, Germany and studied at the Universities of Marburg, Freiburg, and
Heidelberg. In 1941, she came to the United States with her husband, Heinrich Blücher, to
escape the Nazi reign. She became an American citizen in 1951. Her most well-known works
include *Origins of Totalitarianism* (published in 1951, critiquing anti-Semitism, imperialism, and racism), *The Human Condition* (published in 1958, introducing her conception of
the *vita activa*), and her most controversial work, *Eichmann in Jerusalem: A Report on the
Banality of Evil* (published in 1963, reporting the trial of Adolf Eichmann in 1961 for the *New
Yorker*) ("Hannah Arendt," 2013).

In *Eichmann in Jerusalem: A Report on the Banality of Evil*, Arendt (1963/2006) countered the
demand to situate evil solely within **Adolf Eichmann**. Arendt's controversial book framed
the "banality of evil" as the direct result of "thoughtlessness" (p. 288). Her point was that the

long-term consequences of thoughtlessness invite evil; thoughtlessness permits a banality of evil where extreme commonness goes undetected. Arendt suggested that thoughtlessness rests within a basic assumption: there is only one perception of background and foreground that shapes understanding. Thoughtlessness assumes there is only one perceptual gestalt—*mine*.

ADOLF EICHMANN (1906–1962)
was an Austrian citizen who joined the Nazi party in 1932. Eichmann rose within Nazi ranks, assuming the responsibility of overseeing and organizing the logistics and transportation of the Jewish people within occupied Europe. Eichmann was arrested in Buenos Aires, Argentina, in 1960 and then taken to Israel for trial—his sentencing was death by hanging in 1962 ("Adolf Eichmann," 2013).

Eichmann's gestalt centered on concern about strategic career advancement, with no focus on the significance of others. Arendt unmasked a thoughtless background that nourished career advancement that was oblivious to other ethical demands and gave rise to unspeakable atrocities.

Arendt's message reminds us that the partnership between ethics and conflict is not new. Any dominated group of people can attest to the reality of an ethical position imposed by a dominant group that leads inevitably to conflict. The interplay of ethics and conflict is at the heart of acts of oppression whenever a more powerful group implements a good that obliterates another principled perspective. The effort to trump local ethical positions is a historical characterization of "colonialism" and "imperialism" (Arendt, 1948/1994, p. 131). In everyday interpersonal life, this act of domination is the communicative style of the bully (Pörhölä, Karhunen, & Rainivaara, 2006). Oppressed persons throughout history have understood the hegemonic evil of imposed views of the good that destroy another's ethical and moral ground.[1] The notion of gestalt suggests that different realties emerge from contrasting backgrounds that give rise to dissimilar foreground perceptions.

---

1. There are multiple examples from human history that illustrate an imposed dominant ethic that propels conflict against indigenous people, from schoolyard bullies to historical figures such as Adolf Hitler (1889–1945), the leader of the National Socialist (Nazi) Party and chancellor and Führer of Germany from 1933 until the end of World War II and his death in 1945. He was the mass murderer of six million Jewish men, women, and children in concentration camps. Another historical figure of an imposed dominion ethic is Benito Mussolini (1883–1945). Mussolini was the Italian prime minister from 1922 until his overthrow in 1943. He sent approximately 300,000 people to death between invasions in Ethiopia, Libya, and Yugoslavia. A third infamous historical figure of imposed dominion is Joseph Stalin (1879–1953). Stalin was the secretary-general of the Communist Party in the Soviet Union (S.U.) from 1922 until 1953 and the leader of the S.U. from 1941 to 1953. Stalin targeted "uncooperative peasants," arresting them in masses, killing or exiling them, or sending them to concentration camps where they were worked to death ("Joseph Stalin," 2013). Stalin is responsible for up to ten million deaths ("Joseph Stalin," 2013). Each dictator imposed a dominant ethic toward one culture rather than creating diversity, forcing a particular view of the good upon others.

News headlines publicize seemingly endless struggles over differing economic structures, contending religions, competing traditions, and contrasting perspectives on the nature of the individual, announcing dissimilarities in ethical backgrounds. For instance, Arendt (1958/1998) began *The Human Condition* by countering an ethical good implied in celebratory headlines of human entry into space; she critiqued the emphasis on escape from earth (pp. 1–2). She demanded that we take responsibility for existence and cease to glorify flight from accountability for events on earth. Understanding ethics and conflict as a communicative gestalt is the beginning of constructive conflict engagement. Such knowledge does not assure answers or constructive outcomes; however, such awareness assists thoughtful engagement with an era defined by narrative and virtue contention.

GOODS THAT MATTER: UNDERSTANDING THE EPICENTER OF CONFLICT

The link between communication ethics and conflict assumes that ethical positions give moral height and importance to a given content that propels a dispute. **Emmanuel Levinas** (1984/1989), a philosopher known for the phrase "ethics as first philosophy," argued for the priority of ethics (pp. 75–87). Following his lead, we adapt his position: ethics as first principle in the initiation of conflict. Conflict and communication ethics share, in this case, a common

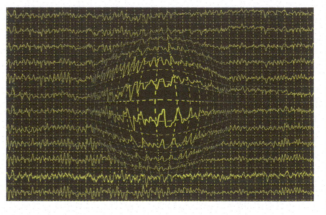

FIGURE 1.2   The epicenter of an earthquake.

© xpixel/Shutterstock.com

conceptual and pragmatic space—"**tainted ground**," which implies a perspective that one holds so tenaciously that one may reject any position that contrasts with one's own (Arnett, 2008a). Conventionally, the notion of tainted ground is a pejorative statement. We contend that all ethical ground is biased; only when we meet a position contrary to our own do we resort to negative assessments—such is the reason that we understand ethics as the good that one seeks to protect and promote.

The 21st century garners a multiplicity of perspectives; this assumption is central to scholarship in this historical moment.[2] The ethical consensus of our time contends that we live in a historical moment of narrative and virtue contentiousness. Such an era calls for a pragmatic turn that seeks to understand another's ethical position as one thoughtfully enters a conflict. The study of communication and conflict in this era requires a pragmatic acknowledgment of the importance of responsibility in understanding our own ethical positions and those of others.

This movement of difference has been termed **postmodernity**[3] (Lyotard, 1984). This era is an ongoing argument about what is ethical and what is of importance and matters (Aronowitz & Giroux, 1991; Audi, 1999; Bloland, 1995). Arnold Toynbee (1946), a British historian, coined the term "postmodern" in A *Study of History*, providing further explication of the postmodern age in volumes VIII and IX of his work (Toynbee 1963a/1954, 1963b/1954). Jean-François Lyotard (1984) brought the term into philosophical literature with the publication of *The Post-Modern Condition: A Report on Knowledge*. Lyotard (1984) acknowledged the breadth of postmodernity in his first footnote to *The Post-Modern Condition* (pp. 3, 85). Lyotard noted an intellectual genealogy that included literary theory, cultural studies, and the sociology of postindustrialism; each perspective provides insight into a changing society where decision-making and the pursuit of truth are temporal and contingent (Peters, 1995). Postmodernity emerged after World War II, marked by the transition from one encompassing grand meta-narrative to various petite narrative structures (Lyotard, 1984).

We argue that postmodernity is a call for celebration as we acknowledge the reality of narrative diversity and multiplicity. Postmodernity deconstructs the myth that conflict is a mere problem requiring correction that necessitates imposing proper, right thinking upon the other. In an era in which individuals no longer share the same perspective on many local and global issues, the hope of a single answer is a dysfunctional myth that ignores a normative lack of consensus. This era no longer functions in a reality of consensus on *right* action, a master ethical standard (Pearce & Littlejohn, 1997). The implications for conflict study are twofold. First,

---

2. Scholars such as Michel Foucault (1926–1984), Jacques Derrida (1930–2004), Hans Baumann (1914–1988), John Caputo (b. 1940) and the ethicist Alasdair MacIntyre (b. 1929) are attentive to a multiplicity of perspectives of what constitutes the good.

3. Postmodernity is a term used by many scholars such as Jacques Derrida (1930–2004), Michel Foucault (1926–1984), Richard Rorty (1931–2007), and Jean Baudrillard (1929–2007).

we must recognize the limits of polar terms, such as good and bad, right and wrong, or even ethical and unethical. Second, we must acknowledge difference as a key to learning as we meet others in a changing communicative environment.

Some scholars are tired of the emphasis on difference and have demanded that we get on to the next stage, stating that postmodernity has become passé (Davis, 2010, pp. 39–41; Mercer, 1995, p. 319). This position, however, announces the recalcitrance of modernity, which attempts to date ideas in a linear fashion with some as young and others as old, wanting something more contemporary and novel than the term "postmodernity." Yet, postmodernity continues to reflect the historical fact that we live in an era of difference, multiplicity, and conflict generated by such recognition (Arnett, 2008b).

FRIEDRICH NIETZSCHE (1843–1900)
was a German philosopher and cultural critic, writing on religion, philosophy, and morality. Nietzsche is associated with nihilism, the will to power, Übermensch (superman), and his famous announcement that "God is dead," made after the secularization of the Enlightenment ("Friedrich Nietzsche," 2013).

The assertion that ethics generates conflict brings forth images of **Friedrich Nietzsche** and the charge of **nihilism,** the unrelenting questioning of authority, religion, and ethics. Nietzsche lived in the 19th century and was a contemporary of Russian novelist **Ivan S. Turgenev,**[4] who wrote *Fathers and Sons* (Turgenev, 1862/1998), which popularized nihilism (See Figure 1.3). The following dialogue is an exchange between the son, Arkady, the father, Nikolai, and the uncle, Pavel, as they express their varied interpretations of what it means for the son's friend, Bazarov, to be a nihilist.

"What is Bazarov?" Arkady grinned. "Do you want me, uncle, to tell you precisely what he is?"

"Please be good enough, nephew."

"He is a nihilist."

"What?" asked Nikolai Petrovich, while Pavel Petrovich raised his knife in the air with a piece of butter on the end of the blade and remained motionless.

"He is a nihilist," repeated Arkady.

"A nihilist," said Nikolai Petrovich. "That's from the Latin nihil, nothing, so far as I can judge. Therefore, the word denotes a man who . . . who doesn't recognize anything?"

---

4. In the introduction to *Fathers and Sons,* Freeborn (1998) describes Ivan S. Turgenev "as the first Russian writer to gain recognition in Europe and America and as a master of the short socio-political novel and the lyrical love-story" (p. i).

FIGURE 1.3 Nihilism

"Say, rather, who doesn't respect anything," added Pavel Petrovich and once more busied himself with the butter.

"Who approaches everything from a critical point of view," remarked Arkady.

"Isn't that the same thing?"

"No, it's not the same thing. A nihilist is a man who doesn't acknowledge any authorities, who doesn't accept a single principle on faith, no matter how much that principle may be surrounded by respect."

"And that's a good thing, is it?" interjected Pavel Petrovich.

"It depends on who you are, uncle. It's a good thing for one man and a bad thing for another." (Turgenev, 1862/1998, pp. 22–23)

This novel highlights the struggles between generations and their differing reactions to laws and institutions. Turgenev left Russia due to the hostile reaction to the novel. The polemical nature of the novel developed themes of social reform in Russian society, revealing contrasts between generations and changing social structures.

Additionally, **Friedrich Heinrich Jacobi**, whom **Martin Buber** (1947/2002) appreciatively cites in his essay "The History of the Dialogic Principle" in the afterward to *Between Man and Man*, was the first to introduce the term "nihilism" to the philosophical vocabulary. "As Jacobi categorically put the point: 'nihilism is the result and goal of all thought'—of all abstract thinking per se" (Ankersmit, 2008, p. 228). Jacobi used the notion of nihilism to disparage both **rationalism** (extreme appeal to reason) and **subjectivism** (extreme appeal to personal experience) (Ankersmit, 2008, p. 230). Postmodernity is not nihilistic; it simply admits that there is no one ground under our feet. Postmodernity recognizes multiplicity of ethical grounds, the importance of difference, and the danger of a single perspective.

MARTIN BUBER (1878–1965)
was a Jewish philosopher whose work focused on dialogue. His most well known work, *I and Thou*, published in 1923, explored dialogue between self and other ("Martin Buber," 2013).

Postmodernity and nihilism require differentiation. Nihilism undercuts all authority; post-modernity recognizes the multiplicity and locality of authority. Postmodernity undercuts the universal assumptions of modernity without rejecting the importance of local practices. The contribution of postmodernity is the recognition that there are differences that shape how we perceive and engage the world. The constructive energy of postmodernity requires us to meet life on its own terms, attending to the historical moment and acknowledging existence—whether approved by us or not. Working from a perspective of multiplicity requires us to admit that one communication ethic does not solve all problems; in fact, an imposed communication ethic is often the instigator of conflict and too often the root cause of serious disputes (Arnett, Arneson, & Bell, 2006).

Alasdair MacIntyre (2016), one of the premiere ethicists of the 20th and 21st centuries, in *Ethics in the Conflict of Modernity*: *An Essay on Desire, Practical Reasoning, and Narrative*, articulates that we live in an era in which goods are in constant conflict. He begins his discussion of ethics in conflict with an emphasis on desire, which is unquenchable—unlike need, which is possible to satisfy. The unquenchable desire for a given good, a given ethic, cannot presuppose that others function with the same desires. Additionally, he recognizes that some desires, ethical positions, and understandings of the good are misdirected, problematic, and wrong. Thus, we live in a historical moment where we often disagree about what is ethical, and we meet people deeply committed to a given perspective that can and often does generate conflict when another propels an opposing or contrary good. We increasingly live in an era where "our deepest moral convictions are expressed in and through our emotions" (p. 68). To quarrel with another, to contend with the goods of another, is to invite contention.

MacIntyre works with the assumption that narratives shape what we consider good. A narrative is composed of practices and a story that informs us of the importance of those practices to which we collectively agree. Where there are different narratives, we find people desiring different goods. The complexity of ethics and conflict does not rest with narrative contention alone. MacIntyre underscores the fact that some scholars argue against narrative itself; they reject narrative for a space beyond restraints, cultures, and provinciality. One finds an ethic tied to the human face, which is central to the work of Levinas cited by MacIntyre (2016, p. 238) and articulated by one of the authors of this project (Arnett, 2017). However, if we are to understand how ethics arise differently, MacIntyre's argument of different narratives, of contrasting practices, held together by dissimilar stories that yield a particular view of the good, is not universal but tied to a unique context and place. MacIntyre gives us insights similar to that of Charles Taylor and Paul Ricoeur. Each frames narrative as ground for practices and stories that tell us what is good; if we change the narratives we situate a life within, we can alter our practices and what we consider good. Ethics are in conflict because we live in an age where there is not one narrative, but many.

RESPONSIBILITY FOR CONFLICT

In this historical moment, understanding and attending to the interplay of ethics and conflict is a first principle of communicative responsibility. Richard Johannesen (1983), one of the major scholars in communication ethics, stated that our responsibility is to promote human freedom (p. 6). Communication ethics scholars Ronald C. Arnett (1990) and Pat Arneson and David R. Dewberry (2009) remind us of the intricate disciplinary connections between ethics and free speech. The connection between free speech and communication ethics is longstanding within the communication discipline: protecting each person's vote and voice, learning from contrary public positions, and supporting public space composed of competing and contending opinions.

The emphasis on responsibility in argument in the public arena is fundamental to **discourse ethics** (Habermas, 1983/1990). Instead of critiquing the denial of vote and voice (the task of free speech), discourse ethics examines questions about abjuration of public access; discourse ethics necessitates communicative entrée into the **public domain**. Although discourse ethics has a number of variations, **Jürgen Habermas** (1983/1990) and Seyla Benhabib (1992) are primary players; each emphasizes the importance of participation in the public domain. Their work has roots in the scholarship of Hannah Arendt (1955/1983), a champion of participation and response in and for the public domain. For Arendt, a healthy public domain requires a responsibility to nourish the "**interspaces**" (p. 31) that permit diverse persons and ideas to be heard and responded to in singular fashion.

JÜRGEN HABERMAS (b. 1929)
is a German philosopher of social and political thought. He received a Ph.D. in philosophy at the University of Bonn in 1954 and studied at the Universities of Göttingen and Zürich. Habermas was the student of Theodor Adorno and Max Horkheimer ("Jürgen Habermas," 2013).

> *The term "public" signifies the world itself...To live together in the world means essentially that a world of things is between those who have it in common, as a table is located between those who sit around it; the world, like every in-between, relates and separates men at the same time. (Arendt, 1958/1998, p. 52)*

Public space does not suggest agreement on a single issue—just as an extended family sitting around a common table cannot presuppose that each person thinks similarly. The public domain is a shared space that brings diverse subjects and ideas into conversation. For Arendt, the public domain is an arena of multiple ideas that denies the viability of a solitary hegemonic voice; communicative responsibility requires diversity of ideas in the public domain.

Arendt (1955/1983) argued that the public sphere becomes unfit, no longer responsible, and void of ethical discourse when it is no longer hospitable to difference; the public domain requires "interspaces," distance between opinions and persons (p. 31). A diminished public domain emerges when there is denial of vote and voice—a *free speech* issue. Additionally, a diminished public domain emerges when there is denial of access and participation—a *discourse ethics* issue. Both free speech and discourse ethics assume universal rationality—a position that contends with assertions from postmodern scholars. However, there is agreement that we have a responsibility to acknowledge difference and learn from contrary perspectives. Pat J. Gehrke (2009) explores this emphasis in *The Ethics and Politics of Speech*, which emphasizes that politics cannot be controlled; clarity of direction is constantly disrupted by otherness, which sometimes meets our approval and often functions in contrast to our limited perspectives.

The free speech tradition contends that sharing one's opinion in public is a universal right. A discourse ethics perspective assumes that procedural access to the public domain is a universal right. Postmodernity, on the other hand, is a movement that questions the reality of a universal standard, privileging difference as the heart of the ongoing story of the human condition. Therefore, whether one works from a postmodern locus defined by differences among narrative and virtue systems or a modern emphasis on universal and procedural rights, there is a major point of agreement—one must acknowledge the reality of difference. Our communicative responsibility is to assist in the construction of a public dwelling composed of interspaces between and among opinions and persons.

We cannot be assured that free speech and a procedural ethics will make discourse possible for all in the public domain, but we can attempt to construct communicative dwellings that invite "keeping the conversation going" (Rorty, 1979) as we encounter different and contrasting ethical positions. Communicative dwellings require communicative responsibility to keep the conversation going, calling for constant construction and maintenance. Deborah Tannen (1998) in her thoughtful explication of the argument culture points to a contrary necessity. Places or communicative dwellings where "the goal is to mediate and diffuse polarization" with an objective of nuancing insight emerge from contrary positions (p. 288). Tannen wants us to learn from difference and cease being hopelessly mired in "an adversarial frame of mind" (p. 3). Just as organizations can find themselves in trouble with deferred maintenance and must begin a regular attentiveness to repair and reconstitution, one must assume responsibility to build and maintain public space that invites diversity of opinion. Multiplicity of interspaces between opinions and persons is at the center of our concern and responsibility. A constructive understanding of ethics and conflict resists the trap of neglected concern for diversity in the public domain.

COMMUNICATIVE BUILDING AND CONSTRUCTION

We contend that unproductive conflict emerges in response to delayed upkeep of the dwelling of the public domain composed of diverse interspaces. Our communicative obligation is to keep the public domain alive with diversity of thought and resistant to colonization by one particular group or idea. Diversity within the public domain requires building and renovation (Arnett, 1999); we must respond to change that emerges from physical decline in structures and answer the desire to connect the dwelling of public space to innovative ideas and insights. A construction perspective on communication and conflict embraces discourse that permits learning from difference; such construction is an expected part of the life of a craftsman who is concerned with careful and thoughtful building and renovation (Sennett, 2008, p. 9).

In social science literature, one finds the language of **social construction** (Berger & Luckmann, 1966/2011). "Social construction" gathered significant public attention from sociological theory and from Berger and Luckmann's (1966/2011) *The Social Construction of Reality*. They stressed social interaction, which assumes a basic presupposition—we negotiate, reinforce, and shift meanings in the process of rubbing shoulders with one another (Berger & Luckmann, 1966/2011).

Berger and Luckmann contended that human meaning is socially constructed through our social interaction. What we understand as common sense is actually the accumulative result of previous negotiations and social interactions that gave rise to agreed-upon ideas and assumptions that became commonplaces (Berger & Luckmann, 1966/2011). The young are born into communicative patterns of common sense socially constructed in an earlier moment. When ideas from an earlier moment of social construction no longer assist, there is an implicit demand for renovation. If renovation does not work, then innovative building and construction must begin anew. The act of conflict emerges when common sense assumptions meet challenge by a newer generation who bring previous assumptions into question through their social interaction.

Changes in social construction explain what some term as the clash between generations situated within differing understandings of the good. Berger and Luckmann gave insight into "taken for granted" (pp. 3, 19, 23) assumptions called common sense that sow the seeds of discontent when these assumptions no longer describe the social interaction of persons in a particular moment or place. This communicative reality of difference can generate conflict. Ongoing building in social interaction gives rise to social worlds that will eventually collide (Pearce & Littlejohn, 2007). We now live in a moment of petite acts of social construction that do not always concur with one another.

A number of scholars have worked within the genre of conceptualizing social communicative interaction. In addition to the notion of "social construction" (Gergen, 1985), some have examined "**constructivism**" (Dewey, 1916; Piaget, 1967; Vygotsky, 1962). Communication scholar W. Barnett Pearce (1995) distinguishes between constructivists and social constructionists:

"Constructivists see communication as a *cognitive* process of *knowing* the world and social constructionists see it as a *social* process of *creating* the world" (p. 98, emphasis in original). Pearce's distinction views constructivists as focusing on perception, while social constructionists focus on social interaction. Using the construction metaphor, a constructivist has a cognitive understanding of social interaction (conceptual plans for building a house) and the social constructionist is interested in how the actual brick and mortar interact in the building of a house. This distinction shapes differences in approaches to communication. Constructivists are interested in the cognitive stories we make up and live within (Pearce, 1995). Communication scholars Delia, O'Keefe, and O'Keefe (1982) describe constructivism as a cognitive theory of human communication that examines how people produce and perceive messages in society. Constructivism focuses on how the mind constructs reality in relation to the external world (Gergen, 1999).

Social constructionists find importance in the stories we make real by our actions. Pearce (1995) notes that social constructionists are interested in knowing how to act so that our communicative choices fit into ongoing, unfinished patterns that contribute to the ongoing negotiation of the meaning of these patterns. Kenneth J. Gergen (1985), in his foundational work "The Social Constructionist Movement in Modern Psychology," views discourse as an artifact of "communal interchange" (p. 266). Social constructionism focuses on discourse as the means by which the self and the world are articulated and acted out (Gergen, 1999).

Our use of social construction in this project moves back and forth between a social constructivist position and a social constructionist position—considering both the cognitive and the social considerations of reality. Our rationale is that both approaches have pragmatic value. When one seeks to describe reality from a particular standpoint, a constructivist perspective renders insight into cognitive processes and perception of the communicative environment. However, when the impulse for change and the need for increased awareness of the resistive nature of a given narrative are present, a social constructionist approach to conflict offers an interactive understanding of the conflict event with pragmatic currency. Our approach to social construction and conflict falls into the philosophical category of pragmatism, with particular attention to moments of communicative description and communicative intervention. We understand a social constructionist view of communication and conflict as a pragmatic necessity. Negotiation and (re)building relationships take place interactively after a collision of ethical positions. Our conception of communicative construction of the dwelling of public space includes both the cognitive and the social dynamics of construction. In basic construction terms, we need thoughtful blueprints and a creative and innovative sense of application. Communication and conflict begin with an ethical commitment to construct public space where difference prospers, conflict is expected, and creative learning becomes the norm.

FRAMING COMMUNICATIVE LEADERSHIP: THE INTERPLAY OF ETHICS AND CONFLICT

When important moral differences are left unexpressed, points of view and perspectives on the world go unheard, and the interests of entire groups become marginalized in the process. (Pearce & Littlejohn, 1997, p. 6)

If we understand a given ethical perspective as an affirmation of a particular ethical good (Arnett, 2008a), then we are left with the reality of competing goods that shape contrasting perspectives on communication ethics and human action. Accepting a given ethical position additionally requires acknowledgment of diversity as central to the understanding and practice of communication ethics. To understand what is ethical, one must watch and observe what good another person protects and promotes. This pragmatic assertion about the multiplicity of ethical positions unites the study and practice of communication ethics and conflict in this historical moment. The test of leadership is not just in conflict, but also in the interplay of ethics and conflict—contention between and among persons who hold clashing ideas and engage in contrasting actions that matter differently to the persons in conflict.

1. Leadership requires knowledge of best practices and thoughtful contemporary theory that offers insight into the issues that shape the historical moment in which an organization must function and prosper.
2. Leadership must attend to theory that provides communicative insight; theory is akin to conceptual eyeglasses that permit us to see what would otherwise go unnoticed.
3. Leadership must understand the theoretical and the practical implications of the unity of ethics and conflict in this era.
4. Communicative leadership:
   a. understands why ethics is often an engine for conflict;
   b. identifies both the communicative implications of the parts and the whole as we meet another in conflict;
   c. recognizes the goods that matter to oneself and others;
   d. accepts responsibility for building communicative dwellings that seek to learn from difference and conflict.

Leadership begins with the study and practice of communication ethics understood as background that carries a sense of a given good that we want to protect and promote. **Communication ethics** is the study of what matters—the ethically weighty and good that invites communicative resistance to contrasting perspectives, giving rise to conflict. Communicative leadership must learn to "frame" ideas within an era of disagreement, moving conflict to increase insight and creative productivity. Gail T. Fairhurst introduced the notion of framing in 1996, with her now classic work within the field (with Robert A. Sarr) and furthered the conversation in her 2011 book, *The Power of Framing*, where she argues, "Through framing, we create the realities to which we then must respond" (p. 27). The next chapter outlines the work of Fairhurst, who states the importance of framing for communicative leadership. We will end each chapter with insights from her work related to the ongoing communicative activity of conflict between and among persons.

REFERENCES

Adolf Eichmann. (2013). In *Encyclopaedia Britannica Online*. Retrieved from http://www.britannica.com/EBchecked/topic/180925/Adolf-Eichmann

Ankersmit, F. (2008). Jacobi: Realist, romanticist, and beacon of our time. *Common Knowledge, 14*, 221–243.

Arendt, H. (1983). *Men in dark times*. San Diego, CA: Harvest Books. (Original work published 1955)

—. (1994). *The origins of totalitarianism*. San Diego, CA: Harvest. (Original work published 1948)

—. (1998). *The human condition*. Chicago, IL: University of Chicago Press. (Original work published 1958)

—. (2006). *Eichmann in Jerusalem: A report on the banality of evil*. New York, NY: Penguin. (Original work published 1963)

Aristotle. (Trans. 1984). *Metaphysics*. In Jonathan Barnes (Ed.), *The complete works of Aristotle: The revised Oxford translation* (Vol. 2) (pp. 1552–1728). Princeton, NJ: Princeton University Press.

Arneson, P., & Dewberry, D. R. (2009). Mapping free speech scholarship in the communication discipline: 1969–2006. In J.A. Aune (Ed.), *Free speech yearbook: 2006–2008* (pp. 200–229). Washington, DC: National Communication Association.

Arnett, R. C. (1990). The practical philosophy of communication ethics and free speech as the foundation of speech communication. *Communication Quarterly, 38*, 208–217.

—. (1999). Metaphorical guidance: Administration as building and renovation. *Journal of Educational Administration, 37*, 80–89.

—. (2008a). Rhetoric and ethics. In W. Donsbach (Ed.), *International encyclopedia of communication* (pp. 4242–4246). Malden, MA: Wiley-Blackwell.

—. (2008b). Pointing the way to communication ethics theory: The life-giving gift of acknowledgement. *Review of Communication, 8*, 21–28.

—. (2013). Carrier of meaning: Adieu to W. Barnett Pearce. *Qualitative Research Reports in Communication, 14*, 1–9.

—. (2017). *Levinas's rhetorical demand: The unending obligation of communication ethics*. Carbondale: Southern Illinois University Press.

Arnett, R. C., Arneson, P., & Bell, L. M. (2006). Communication ethics: The dialogic turn. *Review of Communication, 6*, 62–92.

Arnett, R. C., Fritz, J. M. H., & Bell, L. M. (2009). *Communication ethics literacy: Dialogue and difference*. Thousand Oaks, CA: Sage.

Aronowitz, S., & Giroux, H. A. (1991). *Postmodern education: Politics, culture, & social criticism*. Minneapolis: University of Minnesota Press.

Audi, R. (Ed.). (1999). *Cambridge dictionary of philosophy* (2nd ed.). New York, NY: Cambridge University Press.

Benhabib, S. (1992). *Situating the self: Gender, community and postmodernism in contemporary ethics*. New York, NY: Routledge.

Berger, P. L., & Luckmann, T. (2011). *The social construction of reality: A treatise in the sociology of knowledge*. Indianapolis, IN: Architects, LC. (Original work published 1966)

Bloland, H. G. (1995). Postmodernism and higher education. *Journal of Higher Education, 66,* 521–559.

Buber, M. (2002). *Between man and man* (Ronald Gregor-Smith, Trans.). London: Routledge. (Original work published 1947)

Bureau of Labor Statistics. (2015). Number of jobs held, labor market activities, and earnings growth among the youngest baby boomers: Results from a longitudinal survey. Retrieved from https://www.bls.gov/news.release/pdf/nlsoy.pdf

Bureau of Labor Statistics. (2016). Employee tenure in 2016. Retrieved from https://www.bls.gov/news.release/tenure.nr0.htm

Cheney, G., May, S. & Munshi, D. (2010). *The handbook of communication ethics*. New York, NY: Routledge.

Davis, N. T. (2010). A critique of Richard Rorty and postmodernism. *Macalester Journal of Philosophy, 7,* 36–42.

Delia, J. G., O'Keefe, B. J., & O'Keefe, D. J. (1982). The constructivist approach to communication. In F. E. X. Dance (Ed.), *Human communication theory* (pp. 147–191). New York, NY: Harper & Row.

Dewey, J. (1916). *Democracy and education*. New York, NY: Free Press.

Doyle, A. (2016). How often do people change jobs. *The Balance*. Retrieved from https://www.thebalance.com/how-often-do-people-change-jobs-2060467

Emmanuel Levinas. (2013). In *Encyclopaedia Britannica Online*. Retrieved from http://www.britannica.com/EBchecked/topic/337960/Emmanuel-Levinas

Friedrich Nietzsche. (2013). In *Encyclopaedia Britannica Online*. Retrieved from http://www.britannica.com/EBchecked/topic/414670/Friedrich-Nietzsche

Freeborn, R. (1998). Introduction. In I. S. Turgenev, *Fathers and sons* (R. Freeborn, Trans., pp. vii–xxii). London: Penguin. (Original work published 1862)

Gebhard, N. (2015). Four steps to choosing a college major. *The Balance*. Retrieved from https://www.thebalance.com/how-often-do-people-change-jobs-2060467

Gehrke, P. (2009). *The ethics and politics of speech: Communication and rhetoric in the twentieth century*. Carbondale: Southern Illinois University Press.

Gergen, K. J. (1985). The social constructionist movement in modern psychology. *American Psychologist, 40,* 266–275.

—. (1999). *An invitation to social construction*. London: Sage.

Habermas, J. (1990). Moral consciousness and communicative action (C. Lenhardt & S.W. Nicholsen, Trans.). Cambridge: Massachusetts Institute of Technology. (Original work published 1983)

Hannah Arendt. (2013). In *Encyclopaedia Britannica Online*. Retrieved from http://www.britannica.com/EBchecked/topic/33469/Hannah-Arendt

James, W. (2008). *Pragmatism: A new name for some old ways of thinking*. New York, NY: Longmans, Green, and Co. (Original work published 1907)

Johannesen, R. L. (1983). *Ethics in human communication*. Prospect Heights, IL: Waveland Press.

John Stuart Mill. (2013). In *Encyclopaedia Britannica Online*. Retrieved from http://www.britannica.com/EBchecked/topic/382623/John-Stuart-Mill

Joseph Stalin. (2013). In *Encyclopaedia Britannica Online*. Retrieved from http://www.britannica.com/EBchecked/topic/562617/Joseph-Stalin

Jürgen Habermas. (2013). In *Encyclopaedia Britannica Online*. Retrieved from http://www.britannica.com/EBchecked/topic/562617/Jurgen-Habermas

King, D. B., & Wertheimer, M. (2005). *Max Wertheimer & gestalt theory*. New Brunswick, NJ: Transaction.

Levinas, E. (1989). Ethics as first philosophy. In S. Hand (Ed. & Trans.), *The Levinas reader* (pp. 75–87). Oxford: Wiley-Blackwell. (Original work published 1984)

Lyotard, J. F. (1984). *The postmodern condition*. Minneapolis: University of Minnesota Press.

MacIntyre, A. (1981). *After virtue: A study in moral theory*. Notre Dame, IN: University of Notre Dame Press.

—. (1988). *Whose justice? Which rationality?* Notre Dame, IN: University of Notre Dame Press.

—. (2016). *Ethics in the conflicts of modernity: An essay on desire, practical reasoning, and narrative*. Cambridge, UK: Cambridge University Press.

Martin Buber. (2013). In *Encyclopaedia Britannica Online*. Retrieved from http://www.britannica.com/EBchecked/topic/82688/Martin-Buber

Meister, J. (2012, August 14). Job hopping is the 'new normal' for millennials: Three ways to prevent a human resource nightmare. *Forbes*. Retrieved January 25, 2012, from http://www.forbes.com/sites/jeannemeister/2012/08/14/job-hopping-is-the-new-normal-for-millennials-three-ways-to-prevent-a-human-resource-nightmare/

Mercer, N. (1995). Postmodernity and rationality: The final credits or just a commercial break? In A. Billington, M. Turner, & T. Lane (Eds.), *Mission and meaning: Essays presented to Peter Cotterell* (pp. 319–338). Carlisle, PA: Parternoster Press.

Mill, J. S. (1875). *A system of logic, ratiocinative and inductive: Being a connected view of the principles of evidence and the methods of scientific investigation*. London: Longmans, Green, Reader, and Dyer. (Original work published 1843)

Pearce, W. B. (1995). A sailing guide for social constructionists. In W. Leeds Hurwitz (Ed.), *Social approaches to communication* (pp. 88–113). New York, NY: The Guilford Press.

—. (2007). *Making social worlds: A communication perspective*. Oxford: Blackwell.

Pearce, W. B., & Littlejohn, S. W. (1997). *Moral conflict: When social worlds collide*. Thousand Oaks, CA: Sage.

Peters, M. (1995). Legitimation problems: Knowledge and education in the postmodern condition. In M. Peters (Ed.), *Education and the postmodern condition* (pp. 21–37). Westport, CT: Bergin & Garvey.

Piaget, J. (1967). *Six psychological studies*. New York, NY: Random House.

Pörhölä, M., Karhunen, S. Rainivaara, S. (2006). Bullying at school and in the workplace: A challenge for communication research. *Communication Yearbook, 30*, 249–301.

Princeton Review. (2011). Not a major deal? *Princeton Review*. Retrieved July 26, 2012, from http://in.princetonreview.com/in/2011/02/not-a-major-deal.html

Rorty, R. (1979). *Philosophy and the mirror of nature*. Princeton, NJ: Princeton University Press.

Sennett, R. (2008). *The craftsman*. New Haven, MA: Yale University Press.

Tannen, D. (1998). *The argument culture: Moving from debate to dialogue*. New York, NY: Random House.

Thayer, H. S. (1981). *Meaning and action: A critical history of pragmatism*. Indianapolis, IN: Hackett Publishing. (Original work published 1968)

Toynbee, A. (1946). *A study of history*. Oxford: Oxford University Press.

—. (1963a). *A study of history: Vol. VIII*. New York, NY: Oxford University Press. (Original work published 1954)

—. (1963b). *A study of history: Vol. IX*. New York, NY: Oxford University Press. (Original work published 1954)

Turgenev, I. S. (1998). *Fathers and sons* (R. Freeborn, Trans.). London: Penguin. (Original work published 1862)

Vygotsky, L. S. (1962). *Thought and language*. Cambridge, MA: MIT Press.

Wertheimer, M. (1961). Experimental studies on the seeing of motion. In T. Shipley (Ed. & Trans.), *Classics in psychology* (pp. 1032–1089). New York, NY: Philosophical Library. (Original work published 1912)

Chapter Two

FRAMING COMMUNICATION: CONFLICT AND LEADERSHIP

Ethical codes are communication resources that assist leaders in morally positioning themselves and others as they communicate, whether in crises or everyday matters. When reflected upon, these codes help leaders actively resist the temptation to surrender to self-interest at the expense of other stakeholders whose interests may be every bit as legitimate. There is common ground to discover when we stop thinking, "my interests or yours." (Fairhurst, 2011, p. 6)

"Framing Communication: Conflict and Leadership" acknowledges the contributions of Gail T. Fairhurst's scholarship for this project, *Conflict between Persons: The Origins of Leadership.* This chapter's *Spotlight on Leadership* features Gail T. Fairhurst, whose work serves as the connecting link between the disciplines of communication and conflict and leadership. We attend to insights from her work at the conclusion of each chapter, announcing practical connections between communication and leadership. Our understanding of conflict generated from the clashing of ethical standpoints employs Fairhurst's (2011; Fairhurst & Sarr, 1996) notion of "framing" as a pragmatic communication tool for navigating communicative environments of difference. We allude to Fairhurst's work at the end of each chapter, concentrating on two of her books on framing: *The Art of Framing: Managing the Language of Leadership* published with Robert Sarr (Fairhurst & Sarr, 1996) and *The Power of Framing: Creating the Language of Leadership* (Fairhurst, 2011).

FIGURE 2.1 Gail T. Fairhurst

Courtesy Gail Fairhurst

In "Visual Framing of the Syrian Conflict in News and Public Affairs Magazines," Keith Greenwood and Joy Jenkins (2015) explicate framing. Their essay is particularly helpful in understanding the coordinates of framing. They begin with an emphasis on visual studies, photography, and film. They remind us of crucial words such as *scene angle, image,* or *view* tied to cropping, selecting, and editing (p. 209). They suggest that memorable visual events frame, revealing duration of importance and meaning. They use the framing of the 2011 Arab Spring protests and rebellions to suggest the slanted perspective of news at that time. Headlines, captions, selected photographs, and images suggest that framing is an everyday occurrence and a major carrier of human meaning. They attend to social media as a currently central and pivotal outlet.

In "Strategic Social Media Use in Public Relations: Professionals' Perceived Social Media Impact, Leadership Behaviors, and Work-Life Conflict," Hua Jiang, Yi Luo, and Owen Kulemeka (2017) suggest that public relations officials connected with social media often experience work–life conflict, that framing what is meaningful does not presuppose that all that is meaningful has been framed. As one engages social media to assist a corporate structure, one must find ways to frame a life connected to family, friends, leisure, recreation, and activities outside the workplace. Social media is but one way to frame what is meaningful, not the mode of framing.

Paula Hopeck and Tyler R. Harrison (2017) connect framing to end-of-life issues, suggesting that professionals in health care must engage the inevitable in a manner that assists families in grieving, lament, and goodbye. The work is akin to Victor Frankl's (1963) three major coordinates: what we give to life, what we take from life, and our stand against the inevitable. Framing and reframing at the end of the life assist a family in meeting the inevitable. Such a skill brings hope to families in moments when nonframed information simply pierces the human heart like a sword.

INTRODUCTION

"Framing Communication: Conflict and Leadership" announces the connections between the work of Gail T. Fairhurst and conflict emerging from competing goods. The guiding assumption of *Conflict between Persons: The Origins of Leadership* is that we live in an era of narrative and virtue contention. There are multiple conceptions of the good that divide human communicators, resulting in people protecting and promoting different ethical positions (Arnett, Fritz, & Bell, 2009). The art of framing joins diversity of ethical origins as a pragmatic constituent element of communicative leadership as one engages conflict from contending ethical positions.

In "Framing Communication: Conflict and Leadership," we explore four major sections:

1. **Introducing Gail T. Fairhurst** frames the relevance of Fairhurst's work to this project;
2. **Communication responses to Fairhurst's work** outlines scholarly responses from the discipline of communication to her work;

3. **Fairhurst's scholarship** explores three of her major books and three of her award-winning journal articles;
4. **Framing communicative leadership** identifies relevant connections between Fairhurst's understanding of framing and this project.

Gail T. Fairhurst is a professor of communication at the University of Cincinnati and the author or co-author of multiple peer-reviewed articles, invited publications, book reviews, book chapters, and books. The Organizational Communication Division of the National Communication Association (NCA) bestowed the "Best Book" award on two of her books: *The Art of Framing: Managing the Language of Leadership* received the award in 1997 and ten years later, *Discursive Leadership: In Conversation with Leadership Psychology*. She was the recipient of "Best Article" awards from the same division in 1994 and 2002. Additionally, she received the "Best Article" Award from the International Communication Association in 2005. Her recognized scholarship works within the intersection of communication and leadership.

Fairhurst is the recipient of 20 national and international awards. Additionally, she was a Fulbright scholar at the School of Economics and Management, Lund University, Sweden, in 2009 and the keynote and/or invited speaker at over 70 national and international meetings of management and communication. Fairhurst's work unites the practical, the scholarly, and the popular; she frames the importance of communication for the study and practice of leadership.

We live in an era defined by one privileged term, *difference*. We must learn from others whose perspectives are, at times, in contrast with our own. A pragmatic response to contrasting ethical contentions begins with framing the importance of learning from contradistinction. Refusing to frame creative communicative responses to contrasting orientations misses the existential demands of this historical moment. Throughout our project on conflict, Gail T. Fairhurst functions as a conversational companion; we close each chapter with insights from her work.

COMMUNICATION RESPONSES TO FAIRHURST'S WORK

Patrice Buzzanell (1996), a distinguished scholar of organizational communication and a former president of the International Communication Association,[1] provided an initial look at *The Art of Framing: Managing the Language of Leadership* in *Management Communication Quarterly* (Fairhurst & Sarr, 1996). Buzzanell (1996) admitted that the work has a strong bent toward the practicing professional, which made her reluctant to review the book from

---

1. Patrice Buzzanell served as the president of the International Communication Association from 2008 until 2009.

an academic perspective (p. 243).[2] Fortunately, Buzzanell offered both a practitioner and an academic response, framing for us the reality of two different communicative goods.

Buzzanell stressed that the keys to **framing** are threefold. First, framing is inherently a communication activity (pp. 243–244; Fairhurst & Sarr, 1996, p. xi). Second, framing includes an active grouping of ideas with an objective of constructing a particular meaning that conveys a given direction (Buzzanell, 1996, p. 244; Fairhurst & Sarr, 1996, p. xiii). Third, framing is not a one-time activity; it is an ongoing part of everyday communicative leadership (Buzzanell, 1996, p. 244; Fairhurst & Sarr, 1996, p. xiii). For the practitioner, *The Art of Framing: Managing the Language of Leadership* reminds one of numerous lost opportunities for framing and the importance of weaving framing into everyday communicative leadership. In order to prepare oneself for spontaneous moments of framing, one must reflect carefully in advance, engaging the construction of "mental models," "conversational goals," and consideration of multiple "rhetorical devices" that bring thoughtfulness to what appears to be spontaneous exchanges (Buzzanell, 1996, p. 248).

The art of framing is akin to a jazz musician who follows the direction of others and then offers a creative adaptation of a particular composition. "Jazz is a collaborative music that must accommodate conflict without resolving it. At once highly structured and immediately improvised, intensely cooperative and yet individually expressive, the best jazz respects these opposites yet renders them harmonious" (Clark, 2010, p. 130). From a practitioner's perspective, framing is a thoughtful communicative practice that requires one to adapt ideas on the spot, enacting a communicative act akin to that of a jazz musician who offers creative adaptation that lends new insight.

From an academic perspective, Buzzanell (1996) stated that Fairhurst's clear communication focus connected to leadership was an answer to earlier calls from scholars such as Lee Thayer (1988), who emphasized the importance of bringing communication to the forefront of leadership study and practice. Buzzanell also reminded us that framing is not a neutral activity and suggested that Dennis Mumby's (1987) work assumes that framing is a political activity. In another essay on Fairhurst, Michael W. Shelton (1998) understood Fairhurst's use of framing as a political activity worthy of discussion in a course on "political communication" (p. 174). Buzzanell (1996) concluded her review with a succinct summary of the importance of framing. "*The Art of Framing* defines leadership as the management of meaning but says that, whatever leadership's philosophy, framing is a process to articulate mental models and make them accessible to anyone leadership encounters" (Buzzanell, 1996, p. 253). Also of interest was J. David Johnson's (1997) statement that there is an additional pool of earlier scholarship that links framing to leadership (p. 397).[3] Johnson states that Schön and Rein (1994) offered a contribution of particular interest—the "co-designing" of meaning in preparation for mutual

2. Fairhurst and Sarr initially intended to produce a resource for practicing managers. Surprised by the reception from academics, Fairhurst (2011) included a more scholarly focus in a set of footnotes in the later work, *The Power of Framing: Creating the Language of Leadership* (Gail T. Fairhurst, personal communication, June 4, 2013).
3. The earlier scholarship includes Bolman and Deal's (1991) *Reframing Organizations: Artistry, Choice, and Leadership* and Schön and Rein's (1994) *Frame Reflection: Toward the Resolution of Intractable Policy Controversies.*

framing efforts (Johnson, 1997, p. 398). Additionally, we suggest that the insightful work of W. Barnett Pearce and Vernon Cronen (1980) in *Communication, Action, and Meaning: The Creation of Social Realities* outlined the importance of co-designing of multiple conceptions and levels of meaning through the "coordinated management of meaning." Jolanta Aritz (2012) placed framing within a larger orbit of scholarship and tied it to **Gregory Bateson** (1972) and **Erving Goffman** (1974).

GREGORY BATESON (1904–1980)
was a British-born anthropologist whose primary study areas included cultural symbolism, rituals, and issues related to learning and communication ("Gregory Bateson," 2013).

ERVING GOFFMAN (1922–1982)
was a Canadian-American sociologist whose work focused on face-to-face communication and social interaction ("Erving Goffman," 2013).

Reactions to Fairhurst's (2007) *Discursive Leadership: In Conversation with Leadership Psychology* continued to underscore her ability to link theory and practice in a manner that renders insight and wisdom into communicative leadership applications. Joy L. Hart (2009) stated that Fairhurst's scholarship on discourse has two major strands. First, **discourse** with a "little d" brings persons and context into interaction (p. 185). Second, **Discourse** with a "big D" is a Foucaultian orientation that assumes that the manner in which we discuss a given subject announces a "system of thought" that frames and limits communicative resources available to "communicating actors" (p. 185). Dennis Tourish (2007) contends that there is linkage between Fairhurst's work and that of François Cooren, which makes scholarly sense—they have co-authored seven publications.[4] They understand discourse as a form of materiality witnessed in social contexts. To examine this mutual communicative influence, scholars must explore the "**sequences of interaction**" (Tourish, 2007, pp. 1732–1733), which announce the temporal and embedded nature of communicative leadership.

Sequences of interaction are important in Fairhurst's stress on "conversation analysis," which lends insight into what is occurring in a particular place at a given time (Svennevig, 2008, p. 530). Fairhurst framed a picture of materiality of both discourse and Discourse through a wide variety of perspectives, such as "conversational analysis, interaction analysis, speech act schematics, discursive psychology, Foucaultian analysis, critical discourse analysis, and narrative analysis" (Barclay, 2007, p. 122). In each of the aforementioned frameworks, the common denominator is discerning a discourse pattern within a context and identifying Discourse

---

4. The references at the end of this chapter and in the appendix include Cooren and Fairhurst's co-authored publications.

thought structures that shape "...power relationships within society" (Barclay, 2007, p. 120). Fairhurst rejects a communicative self-conception unresponsive to "social context" (Tourish, 2007, p. 1734). Institutions restrain and constrain discourse; one must unmask the limits of everyday discourse and thought patterns, understood by Foucault as Discourse.

FAIRHURST'S SCHOLARSHIP

This section examines three of Fairhurst's articles and three of her books tied to leadership.

Award-Winning and Seminal Articles

Fairhurst received three article awards. We examine each award-winning article individually, looking first at the two articles that received awards from the National Communication Association and then at the article that won an award from the International Communication Association:

1. "The Leader-Member Exchange Patterns of Women Leaders in Industry: A Discourse Analysis," by Gail T. Fairhurst, published in *Communication Monographs* in 1993, received the 1994 Best Article award from the National Communication Association's Organizational Communication Division;

2. "Discursiveness, Contradiction, and Unintended Consequences in Successive Downsizings," by Gail T. Fairhurst, François Cooren, and Daniel J. Cahill, published in *Management Communication Quarterly* in 2002, received the 2002 Best Article award from the National Communication Association's Organizational Communication Division;

3. "Organizations as Discursive Constructions," by Gail T. Fairhurst and Linda Putnam, published in *Communication Theory* in 2004, received the 2005 Outstanding Article award from the International Communication Association.

4. Additional relevant recent research articles.

1. "The Leader Member Exchange Patterns of Women Leaders in Industry: A Discourse Analysis" (Fairhurst, 1993) examines gender differences in the social construction of Leadership Member Exchange (LMX). Fairhurst (1993) contends that the LMX model of leadership relies upon T. Jacobs's (1971) differentiation between "leadership" and "authority," with the former having a strong interpersonal influence on relationships that permits persons to move "transformationally" beyond their limited "self-interests" (p. 321). At the other end of the scale, authority is management that is "formal," "contractual," "role bound," and defined by "low trust" (Fairhurst, 1993, p. 322). Fairhurst (1993) contends that meaning is not private, but socially constructed (p. 322); she cites the work of Stuart J. Sigman (1987, 1991), who examined micro- and macro-interactional processes which find shape through cultural, social, and contextual engagements (Fairhurst, 1993, pp. 322–323). Relational processes of interaction provide a leader with resources ranging from decision-making "influence," organizational and career "information," "valued task assignments," work "latitude or autonomy," "support" of

worker projects, and "attention" to career and professional growth of workers (Fairhurst, 1993, p. 323). Interactional engagement between employees and leadership sanction these resources, which are relationally connected to one another. Previous studies demonstrated that leadership with controlling tendencies withholds resources. Fairhurst (1993) sought to determine if women in leadership might distribute resources differently; she contended that gender was an unexplored variable in LMX studies.

Fairhurst's study investigated leadership conversations, focusing on discourse patterns of leaders; she discovered typical male and female variability in terms of aggressiveness and support language. She found that multiple aspects of identity confounded communicative transactions—official status and role was confounded with gender, race, and age. Young female leaders needed to clarify their official role with greater acuity (Fairhurst, 1993, p. 246); otherwise, their typical support strategies actually undercut their leadership influence.

> *The young leader must learn that extricating herself from this paradox does not require that she abandon ego massage, face support, or collaborativeness as compliance gaining tactics. They are merely inappropriate when a situation warrants invocation of legitimate authority. (Fairhurst, 1993, p. 346)*

Leaders not only need to frame for others, but must frame their own role with messages, in order to be understood within a given context.

2. "Discursiveness, Contradiction, and Unintended Consequences in Successive Downsizings" (Fairhurst, Cooren, & Cahill, 2002) examined the unintended communicative consequences of frequent downsizing. They investigated a ten-year time period of downscaling at the U.S. Department of Energy; their research was particularly attentive to communicative contradictions and paradoxes that followed the downsizing. The authors worked from a constructionist position (Fairhurst, Cooren, & Cahill, 2002, p. 505), guided by four basic assumptions: (1) individual and collective reflection on institutional actions leads to attributions expressed in conversation about the organization; (2) linguistic distinctions name and rename the identity of a place; (3) contradictions shape the communicative environment as downsizing moves from expressions about lifetime employment to the reality of temporal engagement; and (4) each discursive contradiction is real—it matters (Fairhurst, Cooren, & Cahill, 2002, pp. 505–506). The discursive environment of consistent downsizing was framed by "tension, contradiction, and paradox" (p. 506). Primary and secondary or divertive contradictions emerged in this discourse landscape, revealing "unintended consequences" that surfaced during the downsizing (p. 509).

Through interviews with employees at the U.S. Department of Energy, the researchers witnessed discourse that responded to a moment of traumatic change—807 employees had been "separated" from the plant, with 1,866 remaining to await the eventual elimination of the entire plant (Fairhurst, Cooren, & Cahill, 2002, p. 509). The plant became a symbol of a broken system of promises that fueled cynicism; the remaining workers began to function like "whistle blowers to the Inspector-General" (Fairhurst, Cooren, & Cahill, 2002, p. 513).

Secondary contradictions emerged when the Department of Energy had to recall some workers after discovering that crucial knowledge skills were lacking with the remaining employees. Managerial attempts to manage employee attributions increasingly led to discursive engagement of distrust and anger. The discourse of the workers noted the contradictory nature of managerial expressions uttered to the downsized employees. The workers responded to lost congruence between word and deed. The unintended consequence of the manner of the downsizing was a communicative environment of normative suspicion. Ongoing worker discourse responded to actions from upper-level leadership.

3. "Organizations as Discursive Constructions" (Fairhurst & Putnam, 2004) framed the way discourse shapes an organization as similar to the manner in which construction framing determines the identity of a physical structure. "Following Alvesson and Kärreman, we distinguish between *discourse* that refers to the study of talk and text in social practices and *Discourses* as general and enduring systems of thought" (Fairhurst & Putnam, 2004, p. 7). Discourse frames enduring systems of thought, providing the foundation or horizon for everyday discourse about organizational identity.

The authors examined three different discourse orientations toward organizations, with each uniting a number of related theories: (1) the organization is treated as an already formed object to which actors relate ("object orientation"); (2) the organization is in a continual process of becoming ("becoming orientation"); and (3) the organization exists only insofar as it is relatable to the moment-by-moment goings on of organizational activity ("grounded in action orientation") (Fairhurst & Putnam, 2004, pp. 9–20; Gail T. Fairhurst, personal communication, June 4, 2013). The above genres of discourse in organizations provide a textured communicative examination of an organization—ranging from a solidified organizational identity to an interactive identity based upon continual accounting for what matters. The authors discovered social practices grounded in action, exploring these three different discourse identity orientations that together offer an exemplar of "cross-theoretical thinking" (Fairhurst & Putnam, 2004, p. 23). Such theoretical diversity assists in understanding the "discourses" within an organization, rather than being curtailed by a single Discourse that imposes a monolithic mode of thinking upon an organization (Fairhurst & Putnam, 2004, p. 23).

The essays discussed above by Fairhurst and colleagues offer a number of insights about conflict. For the purpose of this book, *Conflict between Persons: The Origins of Leadership*, there are three issues that assist in the understanding and engagement of conflict. First, *role clarity* is necessary; multiple roles shape leadership responsibility. One must frame one's role for others and for oneself. Second, *contradictions* have unintended communicative consequences, decreasing the ability of others to trust the congruence between word and deed. Third, *cross-theoretical thinking* can offer textured insight that takes one out of a provincial and normative imposition of ideas upon a communicative environment and into a pragmatic, cosmopolitan scholarly perspective.

4. Three of Fairhurst's recent essays are particularly relevant to her ongoing examination of framing and leadership. In a chapter of the *Sage Handbook of Process Organization Studies*,

Fairhurst (in press) offers a chapter on "Leadership Process." In this essay, Fairhurst reminds leaders that the process of leadership is (1) temporal, making one ever attentive to sequential moments and change; (2) relational, calling forth the reality of co-created activity; and (3) contextual, with recognition that places and situations are culturally grounded. In an essay coauthored by Mathew L. Sheep, Fairhurst, and Shalini Khazanchi (2016), titled "Knots in the Discourse of Innovation: Investigating Multiple Tensions in a Reacquired Spin-off," there is an explication of the reality of multiple tensions in narrative accounts within an organization. Such "tensional knots" (p. 468) yield complex paradoxical environments that, perhaps, when creatively engaged can invite "innovation paradoxes" (p. 481). Then in the essay, "Contradictions, Dialectics, and Paradoxes in Organizations: A Constitutive Approach," Linda L. Putnam, Fairhurst, and Scott Banghart (2016) lean into a basic assumption that difference can yield creative insight. In this essay, there is a return to the issue of knotted problems and paradoxes; once again, the advice is not to ignore such a reality but to push off them and utilize them. Leaders need a repertoire of responses willing to engage contradiction, paradoxes, and dialectics (p. 75). Many of us are educated within an Aristotelian framework that A is not B and that this is not that; however, the reality of organizations today and the complexity of narrative differences make the phrase *the unity of contraries* a more apt and useful guiding frame for leaders.

Books on Communication and Leadership

This section examines three of Fairhurst's books in accordance with their respective publication dates. This chronological investigation begins and ends with books devoted to framing.

1. *The Art of Framing: Managing the Language of Leadership*, by Gail T. Fairhurst and Robert Sarr (1996), opens with an assertion that leadership is essentially a "language game" (p. xi). Despite the overly simplistic transmission model of communication that was shared by many organizations and managers at the time, Fairhurst and Sarr (1996) suggested that leaders spend more than 70% of their time communicating, while simultaneously paying too little attention to the importance of the science and art of language (p. xi). Fairhurst and Sarr (1996) did their initial work on framing in an organization devoted to the implementation of **W. Edwards Deming's** Total Quality Management (TQM) philosophy (p. xii). Their investigation of the interplay between TQM and framing centered on processes open to constant improvement and increased productivity.

> **W. EDWARDS DEMING** (1900–1993)
> was an American statistician and educator whose "advocacy of quality-control methods in industrial production aided Japan's economic recovery after World War II and spurred the subsequent global success of many Japanese firms in the late 20th century" ("W. Edwards Deming," 2013). TQM is a philosophy brought forth by Deming that focuses on achieving "efficiency, solving problems, imposing standardization and statistical control, and regulating design" ("Total Quality Management (TQM)," 2013).

Framing is an ongoing activity that defines communicative leadership. The task of leadership takes on the "risk of managing meaning" (Fairhurst & Sarr, 1996, p. 2), which organizes resources and direction. Meaning management is a communicative skill that requires practice; it defines the communicative success of a leader. Framing involves three basic components: "language," "thought," and "forethought" (Fairhurst & Sarr, 1996, p. 7). The authors discuss language in action as "focus" that assists by placing information in categories with "classifications" that amass evidence, making it accessible to "memory," advancing access to both specifics and abstractions via "metaphorical" consideration of a particular topic (Fairhurst & Sarr, 1996, pp. 7–8). Language provides forays into content that requires "thought and reflection" (Fairhurst & Sarr, 1996, p. 8)—thought engages language in reflection. Language in action requires constant thought enacted in reflection and forethought, which is antithetical to thoughtlessness and babble. What appears as sponta-

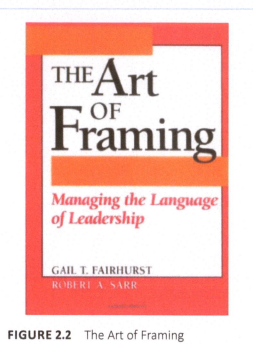

FIGURE 2.2   The Art of Framing

Republished with permission of John Wiley and Sons, Inc., from The Art of Framing: Managing the Language of Leadership, Gail Fairhurst, Robert Sarr © 1996; permission conveyed through Copyright Clearance Center, Inc.

neous framing requires reflection, forethought, and everyday practice (Fairhurst & Sarr, 1996, pp. 10–11). One must consider carefully what matters; communicative leadership contrasts with thoughtlessness. One must take the "initiative" to frame meaning (Fairhurst & Sarr, 1996, p. 14) and lead through framing, engaging language in action that announces values. Framing is not neutral; the organizing of ideas and events and discussion about them is a value-laden task of leadership. Leaders have a position on what direction matters for an organization.

Getting to particular goals requires attentiveness to three different realms of content: "task," "relationship," and "identity" (Fairhurst & Sarr, 1996, p. 23). In other words, the things we do, the people we do them with, and what we think of ourselves and others constitute communicative content that gives rise to goals that determine leadership success. Communicative goals of task, relationship, and identity are global, specific, and both short and long in duration, with attentiveness to the emergent (Fairhurst & Sarr, 1996, p. 28). Goals generate a general ambiance, a background for understanding tasks, relationships, and identity; this background shapes a communicative climate as leadership focuses on more than one goal at a time.

Engaging a multiplicity of goals requires "mental modeling" that considers options prior to a given event (Fairhurst & Sarr, 1996, p. 38). **Mental models** entail thoughtful advance preparation, offering readiness for the unexpected. First, a mental model works from a picture or vision of what one seeks to create or promote. Second, a mental model necessitates a vision driven by the purpose or mission that is larger than the immediate moment. Third, a mental model envisions actions appropriate to and consistent with the mission and core values of an organization (Fairhurst & Sarr, 1996, p. 43). A mental model goes beyond one person's expectations—uniting the mission, vision, and values of a given place.

"**Vision-based framing**" (Fairhurst & Sarr, 1996, p. 50) requires a mental model that assists in understanding what goes unnoticed in everyday looking. **Visions** are leadership responses to challenges that limit an organization. Leaders must know the content, practices, policies, and responsibilities, as well as the programs and strategies that temporally define an organization. In essence, a vision is never about *me* alone. In order to implement a vision that is broader than one's own perspective, three communicative tools assist: "miracle questions," "exception framing," and "continuous benchmarking" (Fairhurst & Sarr, 1996, pp. 66–71). Questions connected with the word "miracle" suggest taking people and an organization beyond their normative expectations. An example of Fairhurst and Sarr's (1996) stress on miracle questions is illustrated in the 2012 movie, *The Big Miracle*, starring John Krasinski and Drew Barrymore, which conveys a story about pragmatic cooperation, bringing together a reporter, a Greenpeace volunteer, the National Guard, oil giant ARCO, a small Alaskan town's community, and two world superpowers. All of these diverse groups must cooperate to save a family of gray whales caught in Arctic Circle ice. The work of this unlikely alliance began with a simple reminder: There is always something we can do to help.

Exception framing takes us beyond the obvious by responding to rhetorical interruptions and freeing us from conventional expectations. Exception framing necessitates continuous benchmarking, not to follow the pack but to fuel innovation. Additionally, one must continuously **benchmark** leadership progress, determining the implementation success of one's own vision.

Visions emerge within a "context" (Fairhurst & Sarr, 1996, p. 80). **Context** is the dwelling where ideas and actions are tested. Context is both local and inclusive of the larger environment. "Context insensitivity" can move a "supposed" leader to decisions that are right in the abstract, but nonsensical in a particular moment and location (Fairhurst & Sarr, 1996, pp. 81–82). Context sensitivity is experiential and situated in continuous study. Mental models attentive to diverse contexts influence leadership decision-making, permitting one to do "proactive framing" (Fairhurst & Sarr, 1996, pp. 93–94) before the fact and "retrospective framing" (Fairhurst & Sarr, 1996, pp. 94–95) after an event has been concluded. Leaders must combine non-stop benchmarking, learning, and framing.

There are multiple ways to offer a vision—some constructive and others void of depth and insight. For instance, "jargon" and "spin" are problematic if overused (Fairhurst & Sarr, 1996, p. 100); they invite a sense of banality. Routine messages with little variation seldom have a major impact, but the use of "metaphors" and "stories" (Fairhurst & Sarr, 1996, p. 100) that announce the unseen and the unexpected contribute constructively to framing of a contextually sensitive vision. Framing moves an organization in a given direction; one must avoid presenting "mixed messages" (Fairhurst & Sarr, 1996, p. 127) that confuse information recipients. Generally,

mixed messages come from the contradiction between what we say and what we do; such discrepancy fuels cynicism. Mixed messages destabilize the veracity of framing, undercutting trust between persons.

One prepares to frame goals "spontaneously" by putting language into action through mental models and contextually sensitive communicative responses. There is an ongoing dialectic between thoughtful goals that one hopes to put into action and spontaneous responsiveness to a given context. One must engage in framing readiness, which requires constant reflection, prior, during, and after the moment, in order to restate a given direction in response to an unforeseen interruption. Most "high impact" moments for framing a given vision come unannounced, requiring immediate "planned" participation.

Framing is a communicative task that requires a high degree of credibility (Fairhurst & Sarr, 1996, p. 170). The "believability" of statements of vision (Fairhurst & Sarr, 1996, p. 171) depends upon personal credibility. One must simplify in the act of framing, moving the abstract and the complex in clear directions—speaking in a manner appropriate to the context. One gains authority with each accomplished vision that is contextually responsive. Success begets a willingness of others to listen to a leader; success frames leadership.

2. *Discursive Leadership: In Conversation with Leadership Psychology*, by Gail T. Fairhurst (2007), announces the importance of communication that involves interactive reflection between persons on the unique significance of a given context. Communication gives viability to discourses within an organization and to Discourse that frames the structure of thought and identity within an organization.[5] Sequential and episodic order matter as one understands discourse—each part informs and reframes the temporal gestalt of organizational identity. The order of discourse and "membership categorization" determine the meaning of a given utterance (Fairhurst, 2007, pp. 50–52).

Fairhurst (2007) countered conventional leadership literature by turning to **Michel Foucault's** understanding of discipline to explain the power of Discourse that historically and culturally shapes the manner in which one thinks about given subjects in a particular

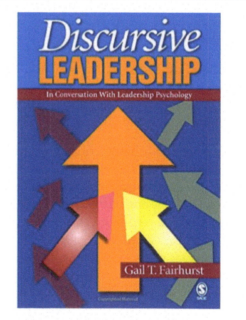

FIGURE 2.3 Discursive Leadership

Republished with permission of SAGE College, from Discursive Leadership: In Conversation with Leadership Psychology, Gail Fairhurst, © 2007; permission conveyed through Copyright Clearance Center, Inc.

5. "Following Alvesson and Kärreman, we distinguish between *discourse* that refers to the study of talk and text in social practices and *Discourses* as general and enduring systems of thought" (Fairhurst & Putnam, 2004, p. 7).

place (p. 75). A Foucaultian perspective rejects the impulse to view the leader as simply an autonomous communicative agent; the structure of a given culture affects leaders. The thought structures of Discourse unknowingly discipline us; the key is to unmask its power. Only through thoughtful examination of disciplined Discourse can one break free from the prison of limited thought and speech. In Shapiro's words and from a Foucaultian perspective, one must "defamiliarize" (Fairhurst, 2007, p. 76) oneself, breaking free from history and culture that imprison and limit thought and speech. No Discourse is an untainted, objective mode of thinking (Fairhurst, 2007, pp. 85–90). In Fairhurst's understanding, identity within an organization emerges from Foucault's view of historical and cultural Discourse that shapes daily discourse within a specified place. One's identity within an organization finds support and contention in the stories told; narratives integrate word and deed. **Narrative,** as practices and stories in action, consists of more than the words of a charismatic leader; actions that involve both human and nonhuman materials that both limit and promote prearranged interactions matter.

MICHEL FOUCAULT (1926–1984)
was a French philosopher who has had a significant influence post-World War II. He studied psychology and philosophy at the École Normale Supérieure, with scholarly focuses on power and power-knowledge ("Michel Foucault," 2013).

In the **praxis** of leadership, one cannot ignore either theoretical or practical examples of meaning in action. In the psychology of persons and place, everyday discourses matter. Discourse shapes our thought and speech historically and culturally, framing the manner in which we understand everyday conversations, common discourses about the materials around us. One must attend to communication ingredients for understanding and doing leadership, first by differentiating discourse and Discourse, and second by understanding their unique impact on a certain place. Credible and enduring communicative leadership frames authority through understanding and influence, not in control and command.

3. *The Power of Framing: Creating the Language of Leadership*, by Gail T. Fairhurst (2011), announces the power of framing in more detail, connecting this communicative construct to the unique realities in which

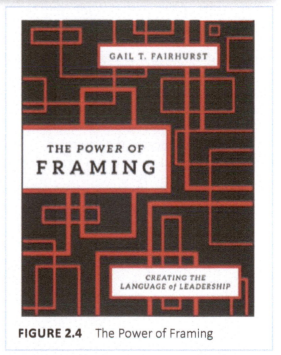

FIGURE 2.4 The Power of Framing

Republished with permission of John Wiley and Sons, Inc., from The Power of Framing: Creating the Language of Leadership, Gail Fairhurst, © 2010; permission conveyed through Copyright Clearance Center, Inc.

leaders find themselves. In *The Power of Framing*, Fairhurst outlines six roles of what she refers to as "reality construction" necessary for framing (p. 2). She admits that leaders cannot control events but must work "to control the context" (pp. 2–3). To activate such authority over the context, leaders must "define the situation" (pp. 3–5). The reality of the context and situation are often in dispute. Leaders must "apply ethics" to articulate a reality with a value dimension (pp. 5–6). Throughout this process, leaders must "interpret uncertainty" (pp. 7–8). They do so by not only defining the context and situation but also by "designing the response" that can be justified ethically in accordance to the context and situation (pp. 8–9). Throughout this process, leaders must control their own spontaneous communication, making sure that framing moves the discourse in an intended direction (pp. 12–14). The explicit discussion of ethics is important for *Conflict between Persons: The Origins of Leadership*—ethical expectations are a vital public part of a mission and code system within an organization. The reality of multiple ethical perspectives requires a leader publicly to articulate and affirm an ethical perspective. As Fairhurst explains, if one works from the perspective of Barbara J. O'Keefe's research on message design logic, one must understand the ethical implications of "**expressive**" communication that reflect *my* position, "**conventional**" communication that attends to the norms of a given place, and "**strategic communication**" that attends to a single event, functioning as an illustration or pathway to a larger and more important destination (Fairhurst, 2011, pp. 17–19). Each framing response must work from a particular design logic while remaining contextually appropriate and adhering to a publicly understood ethic, if leadership is to be accountable and credible.

The skill of framing begins with discernment of the "cultural Discourses" of a given location (Fairhurst, 2011, pp. 36–37). Knowledge of the cultural Discourse of a specific place frames imagination within a unique situation. Without attentiveness to the uniqueness of a distinctive workplace home, the act of framing morphs into unproductive fiction. Fairhurst suggests that core framing tasks work to situate ideas within an identifiable horizon. As one sets collective goals and strategies, the nature of an organization and its projects calls forth ongoing acts of enthusiasm and trust, encouraging flexibility while nurturing a coherent and meaningful organizational identity.

Framing is both a science and an art, requiring the benchmarking of data and results, providing a responsive dance within a definite context. Complexity in framing responds to data that emerge from the context with publicly examined and tested results. The art of framing comes from the practice of thoughtfully uniting goals with a specific context. Leadership framing is a practice that entails discernment, trial and error, and ongoing assessment as one focuses on public ethics of a given place that are fundamental to implementing contextual goals and increasing productivity framed by ongoing assessment.

In the pursuit of productivity, communicative leadership must unite reason and emotion. "Emotionally intelligent leaders" frame with data, information, reason, and emotional sensitivity, ever attentive to context and others (Fairhurst, 2011, pp. 114–117). The tone and emotional shape of words move a smart idea into quicker adoption or into immediate rejection. To be emotionally intelligent obliges one to be sensitive to the context and to others. Emotional intelligence supports the ethical disposition in an organization.

Moral height emanates from one's **ethos**[6] in a given environment. Ethos arises from a congruent connection between publicly stated codes of mission adherence and actions of leaders who represent a given perspective. Leading requires one to know the who, what, when, where, and why of an exclusive situation that must be understood against the backdrop of a larger context. Framing responsively with the assistance of context and background augments leadership ability as one provides ideas and suggestions appropriate to a specific communicative environment.

Fairhurst (2011) concludes *The Power of Framing* with a number of instructive examples. In each example, Fairhurst presents a scenario that demonstrates contextually responsive framing. For instance, she presents an example of a team that continually completes tasks at the last minute, barely meeting deadlines (pp. 197–198). Her advice for framing is directed toward a member who wants to change this behavior and incorporate a more "thoughtful process" that plans ahead (p. 197). Fairhurst offers the following advice tied explicitly to the guiding metaphors of particular chapters: (1) express the "mental model" of the situation of last-minute decision making (Chapter 2); (2) warn the team that their current decision-making practices could lead to "complacency" (Chapter 4); and (3) frame "last-minute success" as "near-failure" (Chapter 3) (pp. 197–198). In each situation, one uses a mental model and a vision to break this unproductive cycle, uniting word and deed in a given context.

FRAMING COMMUNICATIVE LEADERSHIP

> *Leaders must figure out what leadership is in the context of what they do and, through their framing and actions, persuade themselves and other people that they are doing it. (Fairhurst, 2011, p. 158)*

As stated in the introduction of this chapter, Gail T. Fairhurst's work moves theoretically important communicative leadership ideas into practical application. In order for one to lead in a conflict setting, making ideas applicable to a unique context is indispensable.

Fairhurst's work has five major guiding insights for this project:

1. *Praxis*, understood as theory-informed action, must replace unreflective routine;
2. **Differentiating and understanding** discourses and Discourse in a given communicative environment yields concrete, rather than abstract, insight;
3. **Metacommunication about role** within an organization requires one to frame publicly one's responsibilities as a leader;

---

6. Ethos is one of Aristotle's three appeals for persuasion, along with logos and pathos. Ethos refers to the persuasive power of a speaker's credibility from his or her character. Ethos refers to an ethical appeal while logos refers to persuasion using logic and pathos refers to appeals using emotion (Garver, 1994, p. 109).

4. **Framing** necessitates constant reflection, learning, and practice;
5. **Attentiveness** to context that includes local and the larger communicative environments must shape communicative leadership, not one's self-centered aspirations—success emerges as a by-product of focusing on the particularities of context and others.

We apprehend the creative spirit of Fairhurst's work as a form of transactional framing, permitting one to respond to and with the unexpected, framing within a unique context and moment. Thoughtfulness about proactive and retroactive framing makes transactional framing possible; one discovers the content skill of transactional framing through study, reflection, and practice.

We provide an extensive bibliography of Fairhurst's scholarship in the appendix of this book, encouraging readers to examine her material further. Fairhurst does what the communication discipline does best—she unites theory and practice, exemplifying *praxis* as theory-informed practices that thoughtfully direct communicative leadership. We are thankful and appreciative of her ongoing contributions and welcome the opportunity to frame connections between her work and our understanding of conflict fueled by ethics in contention.

As we offer thanks to a colleague for her work on framing, we want to stress one major truism: The constant companion to framing is locality.[7] We frame at a given time, in a given moment, for a given group of people—such action is not akin to the pejorative term *spin* but is the turning of persons to insights that can be understood, engaged, and implemented. The failure to frame manifests itself every time an administrator goes to a conference and returns with the blind ambition to impose a new policy or procedure without asking how it fits here or how it could be modified to make it relevant to this place at this time.

REFERENCES

Aritz, J. (2012). [Review of the book *The power of framing: Creating the language of leadership*, by Gail T. Fairhurst]. *Journal of Business Communication, 49*, 95–100.

Arnett, R. C., Fritz, J. M. H., & Bell, L. M. (2009). *Communication ethics literacy: Dialogue and difference*. Thousand Oaks, CA: Sage.

Barclay, L. A. (2007). [Review of the book *Discursive leadership: In conversation with leadership psychology*, by Gail T. Fairhurst]. *Business Communication Quarterly, 72*, 120–136.

Bateson, G. (1972). *Steps to an ecology of mind*. New York, NY: Ballantine.

Bolman, L. G., & Deal, T. E. (1991). *Reframing organizations: Artistry, choice, and leadership*. San Francisco, CA: John Wiley & Sons, Inc.

Buzzanell, P. M. (1996). [Review of the book *The art of framing: Managing the language of leadership*, by Gail T. Fairhurst and Robert A. Sarr]. *Management Communication Quarterly, 10*, 243–254.

7. The authors would like to thank Diana Hartford, an undergraduate student at Duquesne University, for her thoughtful reflection and participation with the text through her class discussion. Locality matters, and Diana's comments add clarity to this conversation.

Clark, G. (2010). Rhetorical experience and the National Jazz Museum in Harlem. In G. Dickinson, C. Blair, & B. L. Ott (Eds.), *Places of public memory: The rhetoric of museums and memorials* (pp. 113–135). Montgomery: University of Alabama Press.

Cooren, F., & Fairhurst, G. T. (2002). The leader as the practical narrator: Leadership as the art of translating. In D. Holman & R. Thorpe (Eds.), *Management and language: The manager as a practical author* (pp. 85–103). London: Sage.

—. (2004). Speech timing and spacing: The phenomenon of organizational closure. *Organization, 11*, 793–824.

—. (2009). Dislocation and stabilization: How to scale up from interactions to organizations. In L. L. Putnam & A. Nicotera (Eds.), *Building theories of organization: The constitutive role of communication* (pp. 117–152). New York, NY: Routledge.

Cooren, F., Fairhurst, G. T., & Huët, R. (2011). Why matter always matters in organizational communication. In P. Leonardi & B. Nardi (Eds.), *Materiality in organizing: Social interaction in a technical world* (pp. 296–314). Ann Arbor: University of Michigan Press.

Erving Goffman. (2013). In *Encyclopaedia Britannica Online*. Retrieved from http://www.britannica.com/EBchecked/topic/1377872/Erving-Goffman

Fairhurst, G. T. (1993). The leader-member exchange patterns of women leaders in industry: A discourse analysis. *Communication Monographs, 60*, 321–351.

—. (2007). *Discursive leadership: In conversation with leadership psychology*. Thousand Oaks, CA: Sage.

—. (2011). *The power of framing: Creating the language of leadership*. San Francisco, CA: John Wiley & Sons.

—. (In press). Leadership process. In A. Langley & H. Tsoukas (Eds.), *The Sage handbook of process organization studies*. London: Sage.

Fairhurst, G. T., & Cooren, F. (2004). Organizational language-in-use: Interaction analysis, conversation analysis, and speech act schematics. In D. Grant, C. Hardy, C. Oswick, N. Phillips, & L. Putnam (Eds.), *The Sage handbook of organizational discourse* (pp. 131–152). London: Sage.

—. (2009). Leadership as the hybrid production of presence(s). *Leadership, 5*, 469–490.

Fairhurst, G. T., Cooren, F., & Cahill, D. (2002). Discursiveness, contradiction, and unintended consequences in successive downsizings. *Management Communication Quarterly, 15*, 501–540.

Fairhurst, G. T., & Putnam, L. (2004). Organizations as discursive constructions. *Communication Theory, 14*, 5–26.

Fairhurst, G. T., & Sarr, R. A. (1996). *The art of framing: Managing the language of leadership*. San Francisco, CA: Jossey-Bass.

Frankl, V. (1963). *Man's search for meaning: An introduction to logotherapy*. Boston, MA: Beacon Press.

Garver, E. (1994). *Aristotle's rhetoric: An art of character*. Chicago, IL: The University of Chicago Press.

Goffman, E. (1974). *Frame analysis*. New York, NY: Harper & Row.

Greenwood, K., & Jenkins, J. (2015). Visual framing of the Syrian conflict in news and public affairs magazines. *Journalism Studies, 16*, 207–227.

Gregory Bateson. (2013). In *Encylopaedia Britannica Online*. Retrieved from http://www.britannica.com/EBchecked/topic/1365404/Gregory-Bateson

Hart, J. L. (2009). Communicating leadership: Putting organizational discourse at the forefront [Review of the book *Discursive leadership: In conversation with leadership psychology*, by Gail T. Fairhurst]. *The Review of Communication, 9*, 185–187.

Hopeck, P., & Harrison, T. R. (2017). Reframing, refocusing, referring, reconciling, and reflecting: Exploring conflict resolution strategies in end-of-life situations. *Health Communication, 32*, 240–246.

Jacobs, T. (1971). *Leaderships and exchange in formal organizations*. Alexandria, VA: Human Resources Research Organization.

Jiang, H., Luo, Y., & Kulemeka, O. (2017). Strategic social media use in public relations: Professionals' perceived social media impact, leadership behaviors, and work-life conflict. *International Journal of Strategic Communication, 11*, 18–41.

Johnson, J. D. (1997). [Review of the book *The art of framing: Managing the language of leadership*, by Gail T. Fairhurst and Robert A. Sarr]. *Quarterly Journal of Speech, 83*, 397–398.

Michel Foucault. (2013). In *Encylopaedia Britannica Online*. Retrieved from http://www.britannica.com/EBchecked/topic/214682/Michel-Foucault

Mumby, D. K. (1987). Changing the deal while keeping the people. *Academy of Management Executive, 10*, 50–59.

Pearce, W. B., & Cronen, V. (1980). *Communication, action, and meaning: The creation of social realities*. Santa Barbara, CA: Praeger.

Putnam, L. L., Fairhurst, G. T., & Banghart, S. (2016). Contradictions, dialectics, and paradoxes in organizations: A constitutive approach. *The Academy of Management Annals*. doi:10.1080/19416520.2016.1162421

Schön, D. A., & Rein, M. (1994). *Frame reflection: Toward the resolution of intractable policy controversies*. New York, NY: Basic Books.

Sheep, M. L., Fairhurst, G. T., & Khazanchi, S. (2016). Knots in the discourse of innovation: Investigating multiple tensions in a reacquired spin-off. *Organization Studies*. doi:10.1177/0170840616640845

Shelton, M. W. (1998). [Review of the book *The art of framing: Managing the language of leadership*, Gail T. Fairhurst & Robert A. Sarr]. *Journal of the Association for Communication Administration, 27*, 172–175.

Sigman, S. J. (1987). *A perspective on social communication*. Lexington, MA: Lexington Books.

—. (1991). Handling the discontinuous aspects of continuous social relationships: Toward research on the persistence of social forms. *Communication Theory, 1*, 106–127.

Svennevig, J. (2008). Exploring leadership conversations. [Review of the book *Discursive leadership: In conversation with leadership psychology*, by Gail T. Fairhurst]. *Management Communication Quarterly, 21*, 529–536.

Thayer, L. (1988). Leadership/communication: A critical review and a modest proposal. In G. M. Goldhaber & G. A. Barnett (Eds.), *Handbook of organizational communication* (pp. 231–263). Norwood, NJ: Ablex.

Tourish, D. (2007). Themed book reviews: Communication, discourse and leadership [Review of the book *Discursive leadership: In conversation with leadership psychology*, by Gail T. Fairhurst]. *Human Relations, 60*, 1727–1740.

Total Quality Management (TQM). (2013). In *Encylopaedia Britannica Online*. Retrieved from http://www.britannica.com/EBchecked/topic/1387320/Total-Quality-Management-TQM/

W. Edwards Deming. (2013). In *Encylopaedia Britannica Online*. Retrieved from http://www.britannica.com/EBchecked/topic/157093/W-Edwards-Deming

Chapter Three

HUMAN SENTIMENT: FROM ARGUMENT TO CONFLICT

If the same arguments which convince you, convince me likewise, I necessarily approve of your conviction; and if they do not, I necessarily disapprove of it; neither can I possibly conceive that I should do the one without the other. To approve or disapprove, therefore, of the opinions of other is acknowledged, by every body, to mean no more than to observe their agreement or disagreement with our own. But this is equally the case with regard to our approbation or disapprobation of the sentiments or passions of others. (Smith, 1854/2000, p. 15)

"Human Sentiment: From Argument to Conflict" rests on a basic premise: conflict is not synonymous with argument. **Argument** relies on logic, reason, and evidence marshaled with intent to persuade (Putnam & Fairhurst, 2001, p. 106). **Conflict** incorporates perceptions, goals, and values (Putnam & Poole, 1987, p. 552), combined with communicative interactions and context (Ting-Toomey, 1999, p. 198). Conflict involves a complex interplay of all the senses. Argument centers on public evidence and logic. Formal argument is used in the court system and in the high school and college activities of competitive debate and speech. Conflict is not a competitive intellectual event; it resists being situated within a set of rules—conflict is seldom neat and pristine. In *Corporate Communication Crisis Leadership: Ethics and Advocacy*, Ronald C. Arnett, Sarah M. DeIuliis, and Matt Corr (2017) explore the movement between and among issue, argument, conflict, and crisis. At each stage from issue to crisis, leaders have an opportunity to learn from the issues relevant to the social and financial life of a company. This chapter's *Spotlight on Leadership* features Howard Schultz, whose work with innovative employee resources and community outreach programs offers opportunities for personal and professional growth.

© Pe3k/Shutterstock.com

Howard Schultz, the "soul" of Starbucks, established the company's values and vision, driving Starbucks' interactions with employees, customers, and communities home to a local Starbucks store. Starbucks offers benefits to employees and purchases ethically sourced coffee.

The movement from argument to conflict indicates that leaders have ignored signs available to them. Crises do not emerge from a vacuum; there is a history of signs that outstanding leaders discern, preempting problems before they begin to cost time, effort, and ultimately the reputation of a company.

Today's professionals frequently merge their personal and professional lives, inviting conflict in the attempt to respond concurrently to both work and personal obligations (Ashkenas, 2012). Typically, employees arrive at the office early and stay late, working more hours than in previous years (Ashkenas, 2011). The expectation to be accessible 24/7 is a common reality due to easy access to communication technologies that encourage an "always-on" mentality (Ter Hoeven, van Zoonen, & Fonner, 2016). When one's professional life encroaches on personal life, conflict emerges (Gausepohl, 2016; Lee, 2014). Family life and work life conflict is most prevalent in the United States, with 95% of American fathers and 90% of American mothers reporting a lack of work–family balance. Many factors such as extended workweeks, unpaid leave, issues of discrimination, and increased family responsibilities can create these conflicts (Williams & Boushey, 2010). As one seeks to prioritize personal and professional obligations, conflict arises as different ethical goods compete for our time and attention. We are often torn in two directions simultaneously. Human sentiment moves us in multiple directions, giving rise to internal conflict as well as fueling intrapersonal and interpersonal conflict.

INTRODUCTION

Conflict is seldom understandable from a standpoint of pure rational assessment. The communicative environment of conflict is messy; persons are emboldened and sometimes enflamed by human sentiment, manifesting something other than unsullied logic about what matters. Meaning found in statements of formal inaccuracy reveals the power of life outside the limits of clear logic. For instance, there is an exchange from **Fiddler on the Roof** on the subject of tradition between Tevye and Mendel in which we witness Tevye reporting inaccurate information about traditions that still claim his loyalty.

> *Tevye: As Abraham said, "I am a stranger in a strange land…"*
>
> *Mendel: Moses said that.*
>
> *Tevye: Ah. Well, as King David said, "I am slow of speech, and slow of tongue."*
>
> *Mendel: That was also Moses.*
>
> *Tevye: For a man who was slow of tongue, he talked a lot. (Jewison, 1971)*

As Tevye misstates facts, we witness accuracy taking a back seat to the sway of human sentiment.

In "Human Sentiment: From Argument to Conflict," we explore four major sections:

1. **Rationalism, reason, and rationality** announces perspectives from which individuals arrive at particular conclusions;
2. **Argument** unites public evidence and logic in order to display a path that leads to a solution to a given dispute;
3. **Conflict and human sentiment** is a holistic phenomenon that involves the local and larger environment, which engages all the senses;
4. **Framing communicative leadership: Sensing what matters** reveals how one discerns what requires framing at a given point in time.

This chapter paints a caricature distinction between argument and conflict in order to emphasize that conflicts are messy, often illogical, and driven by differing ethical assumptions. Argument relies on public evidence. Conflict, on the other hand, generally finds energy in human sentiment. Conflict often dwells outside the boundaries of what we consider reasonable. In a world of competing ethical goods, we discover clashes between and among views of the good that do not adhere to clean lines and clarity of distinction. Differing human sentiments fuel the unkempt realm of conflict.

RATIONALISM, REASON, AND RATIONALITY

The communicative movement from rationalism to reason to rationality shifts the conversation from the *a priori* to reasoned self-talk and from thinking to an instrumental concern for the public. **Rationalism** assumes that we have innate categories in our minds that guide the thinking process. The sensory extreme to rationalism is **empiricism**, which relies upon concrete experiences that construct categories in our mind; we begin in a state of *tabula rasa*, a "blank slate" open to experiences that become cataloged (Pinker, 2002, p. 5). On the contrary, rationalism assumes that arguments emanate from preexisting cognitive categories. These *a priori* categories shape the cognitive coordinates of knowledge (Setiya, 2007). The importance of experience is lost in rationalism as an abstraction of intellect and ideas driving action, eclipsing the sensory (Malmgren, 2011). Rationalism presupposes universal truth that can be located as long as one ignores the particularities of a given context or environment. Truth, discovered in the method or theory, points to an abstract answer. If one encounters a situation in which a decision is made that prompts the response, "This makes no sense at all for how we actually live our lives," then one has met rationalism in everyday life. Rationalism walks above sensory ground and seeks the correct abstract theoretical answer, which makes universal truth accessible. Rationalism is an absolute commitment to preexisting cognitive categories (Savion, 2010).

The dark side of confidence in rationalism emerges as we witness the imposition of ideas upon others. When one ignores the local context, one is only a step away from inflicting an abstract assertion upon local people and customs (Savion, 2010). When rationalism is imposed on people, they may begin to rebel, giving birth to significant conflict and social upheaval as a result of imposed rationalism. Bruner (2006) believes that rationalism becomes irrational when humans force decisions based on an ideology that circumvents thought.

For the purposes of this chapter, we turn to Lawrence A. Blum's (1982) assessment of rationality tied to the moral. His article, "Kant's and Hegel's Moral Rationalism: A Feminist Perspective," articulates the importance of human emotion. Blum contends that Kant and Hegel frame two different versions of moral rationalism (p. 287). Blum argued that rationalism is disinclined toward "emotional responsiveness" (p. 288). Rationalism assumes that there are concepts and knowledge that trump information from sense experience and emotion. In argument, *a priori* concepts and knowledge provide background from which the rationalism commences. The various theses of rationalism assume an *a priori* proposition that offers an intuitive warrant prior to experience. The *a priori* frames information and is privileged over sense experience.

G. W. F. Hegel and **Immanuel Kant** engage reason differently. Hegel equates reason as a universal concept that constitutes reality played out in history, which makes progress possible. Immanuel Kant (1781/1965) started as a rationalist, but after reading the work of David Hume that attended to the sensatory, he had a spiritual awakening; Kant (1785/1993) began to unite abstract ideas with experience. Kant unites nurture and perception. Rationality is an assumed ontological property of human beings, an ability to use ideas and experience to try to discern truth in a given situation or identify the best solution to a problem.

Reason requires public testing. Rationality is the performative modality of reason, and for Kant, practical reason was vital. Kant's practical reason does not determine Truth, but strives to discern direction for individuals. The ongoing test of practical reason is the "**categorical imperative**" where one should "act only according to that maxim whereby you can, at the same time, will that it should become a universal law" (Kant, 1785/1993, p. 30). Enacting rationality requires the conscious doing of reason. Unlike Hegel, Kant opened reason to common people willing to abide by the discipline of the categorical imperative.

FIGURE 3.1

In communication, reason and rationality refer to a process by which people come to conclusions or make decisions based on evidence and argument (Popper, 1994; Toulmin, 2001). **Reason** is a logical approach to conceptual decision making that supports conclusions and explains facts (Kruglanski & Orehek, 2009). Reason does not determine an end result; it informs us about objects and actions necessary for the achievement of end goals (Hampton, 1992). Reason is the basis of thinking; it is the cognitive process of discernment. Reason allows human beings to make sense of the world and form arguments based on facts and information (Kompridis, 2000). Reason permits us to make sense of the world as we verify information and uncover connecting links between and among given facts and experiences (Kompridis, 2000). Reason contributes to the sophisticated intellective capacity associated with human activities such as philosophy, language, mathematics, and art (MacIntyre, 2001).

GEORG WILHELM FRIEDRICH HEGEL (1770–1831)
was a German philosopher whose works focused on dialectics and history's progression in terms of thesis, antithesis, and synthesis ("Georg Wilhelm Friedrich Hegel," 2013).

IMMANUEL KANT (1724–1804)
was a German Enlightenment philosopher whose works centered on epistemology, ethics, metaphysics, and aesthetics. His most well-known works include *Critique of Pure Reason*, published in 1781; *Critique of Practical Reason*, published in 1788; and *Critique of Judgment*, published in 1790 ("Immanuel Kant," 2013).

Communication scholars have examined the role of reason in various settings, particularly interpersonal and political contexts (Martínez-Ramos, 2009; Rowland, 2011; Yungbluth & Johnson, 2010). Martínez-Ramos (2009) turns to the work of Socrates and **Jacques Lacan** to explore reason and its relation to love—the relationship of *logos* and *eros*. She describes reason as being found within a "temporal frame" (p. 171) that views love as dependent on the particular situation. Yungbluth and Johnson (2010) use reason as a way to differentiate between conflict resolution and conflict management. When we only evaluate the facts to determine what is reasonable in a given conflict, we are focusing on **conflict resolution**. In contrast, **conflict management** privileges a dialogic approach to reason, uncovering the assumptions of what is fair and reasonable (Yungbluth & Johnson, 2010).

JACQUES LACAN (1901–1981)
was a French psychologist known as an "original interpreter" of Sigmund Freud ("Jacques Lacan," 2013) and founder of the Freudian School of Paris (1964–1980). In 1932, Lacan received a medical degree and began practicing psychiatry and psychoanalysis in Paris ("Jacques Lacan," 2013).

The doing of reason engages the instrumental act of rationality. **Rationality** as an instrumental activity has its roots in Aristotle's view of *logos* (logical appeal) and in the systematic process of the scientific method (Toulmin, 2001). Rationality focuses on logical consistencies free from emotional appeals and in accordance with reason (Kruglanski & Orehek, 2009). The liberation of individual thought is the heart of rationality, which is fundamental to the Enlightenment (Hammond, 2007) and to the development of a democratic consciousness (Milojević, 2010). Rationality offers a focus on the rational rather than on the ethical, emotional, or ontological features of an argument (Bruschke, 2004). Rationality, tied to individual freedom, offers a practical avenue toward liberation of thought. Fisher (1989) discusses Chaïm Perelman's (1979) view of rationality as "devoid of passion, detached from considerations of circumstances, time, and place, and serv[ing] the interest of monolithic systems, whether philosophical or political" (Fisher, 1989, p. 131). Popper (1994) understood rationality as a practical method of critical thinking and human problem solving. Theories of rationality focus on beliefs and actions within a system responsive to empirical and conceptual evidence, decision making, and change (Holland, 2006). During the Enlightenment (mid-17th–18th centuries), the emancipatory hope for rationality encouraged individual thought, permitting persons to break free from total dependence upon religious authorities and monarchies; rationality paved the way for the advent of various forms of participatory democracy (Milojević, 2010).

One of the most detailed descriptions of rationality comes from the work of **Max Weber**. Researchers have identified four categories of rationality in Weber's work (Brubaker, 1984; Habermas, 1984; Kalberg, 1980; Levine, 1981): (1) **practical rationality**, which engages everyday affairs with a "methodical attainment of a definitely given and practical end by means of an increasingly precise calculation of adequate means" (Weber, 1958, p. 293); (2) **theoretical rationality**, which permits one to use "precise and abstract concepts" (Weber, 1958, p. 293) to make sense of reality; (3) **substantive rationality**, which involves values that guide people in their daily lives; and (4) **formal rationality**, which is the rational calculation of means to ends based on rules, regulations, and the law. Weber suggests that it was essential for the development of the Western world to adopt these richly different forms of rationality. Each conception of rationality offers a particular freedom for thinking on one's own (Kalberg, 1980), involving everyday experimentation, the use of theory and abstraction, personalized values and understandings of the good, and a recognition of the impersonal forces that shape possibilities. The interplay of reason and rationality make argument possible.

MAX WEBER (1864–1920)
was a German philosopher and political economist who is most well known for *The Protestant Ethic and the Spirit of Capitalism*, published in 1904 and 1905, and his work on bureaucracy ("Max Weber," 2013).

ARGUMENT

Argument requires public display of evidence, revealing a conceptual path that logically articulates a solution to a given dispute. Argument connects evidence, ideas, and experience that propose support for given claims. Argument works within an agreed-upon paradigm with the objective of offering a rational argument on how to proceed in a decision-making context. **Thomas S. Kuhn** (1962/1970) established our modern understanding of paradigm in *The Structure of Scientific Revolutions*. He defined a **paradigm** as an "accepted model or pattern" (p. 23). A paradigm consists of a unified set of coordinates or boundaries that guide inquiry. In an argument, the paradigmatic boundaries are in place, providing opportunity for an argument within agreed-upon coordinates.

THOMAS S. KUHN (1922–1996)
was an American historian and philosopher. He attended Harvard, receiving a B.A. (1943) an M.A. (1946) in physics and his Ph.D. (1949) in the history of science. He taught at Harvard from 1951 until 1956, the University of California at Berkeley from 1956 until 1964, Princeton from 1964 until 1979, and MIT from 1979 until 1991. His most well-known book, *The Structure of Scientific Revolutions*, was published in 1962 ("Thomas S. Kuhn," 2013).

A well-known author on argument was the British philosopher **Stephen Toulmin**. His volume on *The Uses of Argument* (Toulmin, 1958/2003) is a classic, providing a model for understanding argument. His approach is still widely cited today (Harmon, Green, & Goodnight, 2015; Hitchcock & Verheij 2005; Persuit, 2011; Simon, 2008; Whithaus, 2012) as a key understanding of the theory of argument. Moreover, a special issue in *Argumentation* titled "The Toulmin Model Today" (Hitchcock & Verheij, 2005) revealed Toulmin's view of argument as an ongoing communicative roadmap that explains the process of an argument.

STEPHEN TOULMIN (1922–2009)
was an English philosopher and educator. He was educated at Cambridge University and taught at Oxford. He became the department head at the University of Leeds from 1955 until 1959, and the director of the Nuffield Foundation from 1960 until 1964. He moved to the United States in the 1960s, where he taught at Brandeis University, Michigan State University, University of California at Santa Cruz, University of Chicago, Northwestern University, and University of Southern California ("Stephen Edelston Toulmin," 2013).

Toulmin (1958/2003) acknowledges that arguments have many sides; few issues can be understood fully in polar terms of black and white or all right and all wrong. His model focuses on what makes an argument effective via development, analysis, and evaluation, framing six coordinates that shape an effective argument. The following components of conceptual evidence frame Toulmin's view of argument:

1. **Claim** is the statement being argued (p. 90), otherwise known as the thesis to the argument. The claim designates the main point of the argument.
2. **Data** is associated with the facts and evidence that compose the baseline of an argument (p. 90).
3. **Warrant** acts as a bridge that offers a logical rationale uniting data and claim (p. 91).
4. **Qualifiers** strengthen the argument and state the conditions under which the argument gathers significance (p. 93). Qualifiers enhance the claim.
5. **Rebuttals** are counter-arguments used by both parties that state why a particular argument is not true in specific circumstances (p. 93).
6. **Backing** is additional research that supports the warrant (p. 96).

Toulmin offers the following example to illustrate the above coordinates in action (p. 97). When we make the claim that Harry is a British subject, the claim rests upon data that includes the fact that Harry was born in Bermuda. There is an implicit warrant that a man born in Bermuda is a British subject. The warrant connects the claim and the data. The qualifier is both his parents were British citizens. The qualifier ensures the validity of the warrant, which decreases the need for further support or backing to uphold the warrant (p. 97).

Toulmin's method for articulating the importance of argument presupposes examining public evidence through logical structures. His model counters assertions based solely on power and/

or official status. Toulmin's model of argumentation constructs the importance of a public display of evidence; he provides a schema for examining evidence publicly.

An argument presupposes some agreement on the viability of rules for a particular public dispute. Arguments can be a part of a conflict; however, conflicts generated by different ethical positions seldom accommodate an agreed-upon argumentative method for evaluating what is true or correct. Ioana A. Cionea, Amy Janan Johnson, Jacqueline S. Bruscella, and Bobbi Van Gilder's (2015) "Taking Conflict Personally and the Use of the Demand/Withdraw Pattern in Intraethnic Serial Arguments" is a preliminary study of serial, ongoing arguments on a similar theme or topic. The researchers examined differences between and among four different ethnic groups. The first difference pivots on distinctions between individualistic and collectivistic cultures; however, interestingly, within each domain of the individualistic and collectivistic cultures there are variances in which the given person or ethnic group would either demand or withdraw from the conflict. The study implies the theoretical and conceptual danger of reifying the notion of collectivistic and individualistic differences. Our knowledge of culture related to argument should suggest and guide, not dictate, particularly in an era in which many persons are influenced by more than one culture and more than one ethnic background. Conflict propelled by contrary views of the good involves paradigmatic disagreement; the rules in conflict are not as clear as in Toulmin's argumentative model. When contrasting ethical positions generate conflict, we generally find more human sentiment and passion and less logical argumentation. Conflict is often resistant to *a priori* agreed-upon rules of argumentative rationality.

CONFLICT AND HUMAN SENTIMENT

Conflict resists a neat packaging within a single paradigm that organized an agreed-upon set of rules. Conflict overflows, going beyond expectations. Conflict is messy and seldom propelled by evidence alone. When we hear laments about members of Congress not working together, we witness the power of conflict in action. Congress members have paradigmatic differences that result in dismissing the arguments and evidence of those interested in contrary ethical goods. Conflict involves all of our senses, putting us on high alert. We engage human sentiment to discern the moral weight of a given perspective. Returning to Blum's (1982) essay, the stress on rationalism minimized the importance of human sentiment and emotion and missed the contextual complexity of human engaging human. Emotion and human sentiment intimately connect with the goods that we seek to protect and promote. Contrasting characterizations of conflict announce what matters to the participants in conflict.

Multiple definitions of conflict shape the landscape of the communication field. In the *Sage Handbook of Conflict Communication*, Putnam (2006) examined five components of conflict definitions: (1) scope, (2) nature of action, (3) relationship, (4) communication, and (5) context. **Scope** focuses on incompatible interests, goals, needs, desires, values, and beliefs. The **nature of the action** examines expressed struggles, dissonance, tension, and frustration.

Relationship examines the connections between persons and their interdependence. **Communication** includes the distribution of symbols, acts, and exchanges of messages. **Context** examines elements that give rise to conflict, such as limited or scarce resources, which are regulated by one's culture, and differing cultural communities (Putnam, 2006, p. 7). Putnam contends that conceptualizations of conflict generally consider these components instrumental in sorting through a wide array of conflict definitions.

Perhaps the most well-known definition of conflict in our field of communication comes from Hocker and Wilmot (1978/1985);[1] their basic assertion is that conflict is "a dispute over limited resources" (p. 198). They elaborate by stating that conflict is an "expressed struggle between at least two interdependent parties who perceive incompatible goals, scarce resources, and interference from others in achieving their goals" (p. 23). The stress on limited resources and perceived incompatible outcomes is consistent with Mortensen's (1974) definition of conflict as "an expressed struggle over incompatible interests in the distribution of limited resources" (p. 93). Mortensen's emphasis was one of the earliest definitions of conflict underscoring inadequate resources. Most definitions within the field of communication adopt some variation of Mortensen's definition of conflict (Putnam, 2006). Pearce and Littlejohn (1997) suggest that "moral conflict occurs when disputants are acting within incommensurate grammars… or [when] different forms of life overlap" (p. 55). Pearce and Littlejohn's definition aligns with our project; they feature the connection between ethical assumptions and conflict. All of these definitions of conflict announce one basic assumption—conflict begins with difference.

Our understanding of conflict adds the assumption that significant conflict emerges over paradigmatically contrasting ethical goods. Ethics in communication signals that something matters enough for us to mobilize our resources in order to protect and promote a given ethical good. Significant conflict does not happen when things do not matter. François Cooren (2010) emphasizes that our communicative attention shifts to things that "**matter**" (p. 3). The significance of events, people, and projects reflect an existential fact—they matter. We adhere to Cooren's stress on how much things matter throughout this project. People, objects, perceptions, and ideas are things that matter and generate weight in a given conversation. We protect and promote what matters, making the possibility of conflict ever so real when we find another at odds with a good that we understand as bearing significant encumbrance.

As one senses conflict, one feels weightiness within the communicative environment. In such a moment, one feels the conflict expressed in the phrase, "You could cut the tension with a knife." We sense the weightiness of what matters differently, which divides persons. Sensing significance permits one tacitly to comprehend tension in the environment, even when its origin is difficult to grasp. **David Hume** (1740/2008) made the case for the importance of **sensations**; he rebelled against universal confidence in rationality. Sensations and sentiments are defining characteristics of the Scottish Enlightenment ("Scottish Enlightenment," 2013), which was in contrast to the Enlightenment writ large out of France ("Enlightenment," 2013).

---

1. Hocker and Wilmot's *Interpersonal Communication* was first published in 1978. Subsequent editions have continued to be released with the most recent edition being in 2011.

Reason drove the French Enlightenment, and human sentiment shaped the Scottish Enlightenment. Hume (1740/2008) stated that our ideas originate from sensations (p. 3). Impending conflict alerts us to sensations. Sensations about conflict inform us about the weightiness of issues that demand our attention.

DAVID HUME (1711–1776) was a philosopher of the Scottish Enlightenment. His works addressed epistemology, history, economics, empiricism, and skepticism. Hume's most well-known work is *A Treatise of Human Nature* ("David Hume," 2013).

In *De Anima*, Aristotle (trans. 2001) classified what we conventionally term the five senses: sight, touch, smell, taste, and sound. The sensing organs (eye, skin, nose, tongue, and ear) make up our sensory wiring and give shape to our humanness. Sensations alert us to bodily responses to shifts in the environment. Through the senses, we become aware of things that demand attention. Each of us has experienced "chills up and down the spine" that communicate important sensations; bodily sensations alert us to what matters.

Conflict arises when we do not sense what matters to another. If we are to navigate a particular conflict setting well, we must sense what matters within a given place and among a group of people. An inability to detect when a communicative environment changes is an example of failing to sense what matters. For example, not knowing the importance or the significance of a given object might result in tossing an old object into the trash, only to learn that for another person, the item has great merit. Without sensing the preeminence of a given phenomenon, one might go into a family member's room and spend a whole day cleaning only to hear an anguished cry: "Where is my grandfather's watch?" With this question, the communicative atmosphere within the room becomes heavy and uncomfortable with sensations that scream the reality of misperception about what matters.

Sensing the weightiness of things that matter reminds us of a basic fact of life: some things matter more than others, and what is of value to one person may not coincide with what claims the loyalty of another. Failure to recognize this reality of difference opens the door to conflict between persons. Parfit and Scheffler (2011) contend that we have reasons to act on certain ideas based not on subjective ethical theories but because these ideas "matter" to us (p. xxxii). Articulating what is important guides the ability for the other to understand us and for us to understand the other (Magnacca, 2010). We sense what matters by the weight given to the issue and the energy required to protect and promote a specified issue/action.

In the field of communication, "high-context" and "low-context" communication describe how messages are framed and interpreted (Hall, 1976). **High-context communication** is defined as the "internal contexting [that] makes it possible for human beings to perform the exceedingly important function of automatically correcting for distortions or omissions in the messages" (Hall, 1976, p. 117). High-context communicators, when listening to a message, consider the manner in which something accompanies that message. **Low-context communicators** focus on the explicit content of the message, with very little if any interpretation supplied by the listener (Hall, 1976). When responding to the question, "Where is my grandfather's watch?", a high-context communicator would sense the worry and concern about the particular object. The low-context communicator would answer bluntly, providing information alone. A high-context communicator senses changes in a communicative environment. Hall's work continues to inform the communication discipline today, particularly within intercultural communication (Andersen, Hecht, Hoobler, & Smallwood, 2003; Cheng, 2003; Ting-Toomey, 1999). If one fails to sense the communicative environment, one will miss what matters in a unique communicative situation.

When one fails to attend to shifts in a communicative environment, conflict is likely to emerge, demanding that we pay proper attention. Conflict gives shape and clarity to the worth and weight of things that matter; conflict can unmask the reality of a given place—its identity. Conflict is an interruption to routine lives placed on autopilot. All of us have known someone whose life is seemingly incredibly easy and unreflective. The person has seldom had to make a decision about what matters. Conflict is existential communication that alerts us to what matters. Kellett and Dalton (2001) offer dialogue as "an ideal that creates a template" to approach and understand conflict (p. 22). In their book *Managing Conflict in a Negotiated World: A Narrative Approach to Achieving Dialogue and Change*, they look to the work of Cissna and Anderson (1998) to understand how dialogue can represent or create "ideal existential communication" (Kellett & Dalton, 2001, p. 22). They want communicators to sense what matters to another.

Conflict gives us a chance to learn; otherwise, our lives dwell in thoughtless routine, and we miss what is vital to another. The most famous public trial of people who missed the importance of another was the Nuremburg Trials,[2] held from November 20, 1945, until October 1, 1946, after World War II. These trials displayed one defendant after another who stated that he had only followed orders. The Nazis were responsible for the mass murder of six million Jewish men, women, and children killed in concentration camps. The trials centered on calling to account the people who contributed to the atrocities. The normative defense was loyalty and a duty claim, known as the "Nuremburg Defense" (Webber & Feinsilber, 1999, p.

---

2. During the Nuremberg Trials (or Nürnberg Trials), the International Military Tribunal tried 22 former Nazi leaders, including Martin Bormann, who was tried in absentia. They were charged with four counts—war crimes, crimes against peace, crimes against humanity, and a conspiracy to commit criminal acts. Three were acquitted, four sentenced to 10 to 20 years in prison, three to life imprisonment, and 12 sentenced to death. Additionally, two former Nazi leaders never went to trial—one committed suicide and the other was deemed to have "mental and physical conditions" ("Nürnberg Trials," 2013)

388). This repetitive argument of "I was only following orders" and the perverse embracing of Kantian emphasis on "duty" (Arendt, 1963/2006) were the normative defenses and simultaneously the reason for their conviction, imprisonment, and execution. For the defendants at Nuremburg "could hardly claim that they did not know what they did was wrong; rather they could only claim that they did not know a court would punish them for it" (Bassiouni, 2008, p. 287). The Nuremburg Trials served as a public drama against the use of "**blind loyalty**" as a defense (Sabel, 1993, p. 92). The Nuremburg Trials stated what mattered for the Western world—justice for more than six million innocent lives[3] eradicated by thoughtless disregard for the sacredness of human life.

One witnesses this thoughtless adherence to authority in the classic experiment by Stanley Milgram. This controversial study conducted by Milgram (1974/2009) measured the willingness of participants to obey authority figures; the study was motivated by the Nuremberg Trials and the trial of Adolf Eichmann in particular (p. 5). In *Obedience to Authority: An Experimental View*, Milgram explains that the results of his study are consistent with Hannah Arendt's (1963/2006) announcement of the "banality of evil" in her *Eichmann in Jerusalem: A Report on the Banality of Evil* (Milgram, 1974/2009, p. 5). Milgram's (1974/2009) study revealed that persons were willing to give electrical shocks of increasing voltages to another person in obedience to the commands of an authority figure (p. 13). The people in the study did not know that the person supposedly receiving the electrical shocks was an actor feigning pain (p. 3). The ethicality of enacting such a study was questionable (Zimbardo, 2009, p. xiv), but the results are unmistakable. Milgram's (1974/2009) results revealed more than half of the participants were willing to follow rules laid down by a figure in authority and administer electric shocks to someone apparently in pain from those shocks, even if they did not personally condone the action. Milgram recognizes the "the most fundamental lesson" of his experiment: "Ordinary people, simply doing their jobs, and without any particular hostility on their part, can become agents in a terrible destructive process" (p. 6). When abstract commitments trump sensory concern for another, atrocity is invited.

We need to pay attention to sensations that inform us about what matters; slogans of blind loyalty take the responsibility for action out of our hands. Milgram (1974/2009) reminds us of British author C. P. Snow's (1961) warning that "more hideous crimes have been committed in the name of obedience [blind loyalty and routine duty] than have ever been committed in the name of rebellion" (p. 24). Conflict can serve to interrupt thoughtless routine. We are responsible, called to attend to sensations that awaken us from routine and blind allegiance and demand that we attend to discerning what really matters. The rub of conflict is that what really matters does not come from universal concession. In order to engage conflict constructively, we must know what matters to us and to the other.

Barbara Miller Gaither and Lucinda Austin's (2016) essay, "Campaign and Corporate Goals in Conflict: Exploring Company-Issue Congruence through a Content Analysis of Coca-Cola's

---

3. This number reflects the number of lives lost in concentration camps. Numbers range significantly beyond this limited count, which include those who lost their lives in ghettos from starvation, those who were immediately killed, and those whose lives and families were forever devastated.

Twitter Feed," explicates the changes in leadership related to corporate social responsibility (CSR). The sentiment has shifted from engaging CSR as an immediate response to a crisis in which there was a disconnect between what the company did, its primary line of production, and an external corporate social responsibility engagement. With increased emphasis on sustainability and accountability, the disparity between product generation and the CSR task has entered a new era of increasing coherence and connection. The sentiment now driving CSR is the natural connection between what a company does and its contribution to the external environment. The essay explores the pros and cons of Coca-Cola engaging in this alliance of product and contribution to social responsibility. In essence, the sentiment is what one does should have a natural alliance with making the world a better place in a given area of contribution that aligns with the overall mission of a company.

This chapter applauds the use of argument when and where possible, while acknowledging that conflict includes multiple dimensions of the human condition: reason, attentiveness to the power of human senses, and the necessity of attending to sentiment. Conflicts involve human sentiments that alert us to what matters. Conflict has a vital place in the human story as we seek to discern what matters, demanding that we attend to ethical goods protected and promoted in a given communicative environment.

FRAMING COMMUNICATIVE LEADERSHIP: SENSING WHAT MATTERS

The choice was not between tolerance and intolerance, but between the rights of the whole versus those of a part, between the existing mythology and a competing sentiment. (Medhurst, 1982, p. 18)

The first chapter in *The Art of Framing: Managing the Language of Leadership* discusses the importance of framing in everyday conversations. Fairhurst and Sarr (1996) use the term "seizing" (p. 1), which suggests that one senses the proper moment to offer a coherent framed message. The difference between imposing an idea on another and a natural expression rest in one's ability to feel and understand the uniqueness within a given communicative environment. Our attentiveness to sensations alerts us to possibilities that can augment the weight of what we say. At a minimum, a leader needs to understand the difference between argument and conflict and which communicative response is needed to address/frame an appropriate response for a unique situation.

Fairhurst and Sarr state the needed ingredients for preparation for framing:

1. **Forethought** about what matters requires knowing the goods one wants to protect and promote (p. 7);
2. **Mental models** permit one to envision conversations and direction—playing out multiple possibilities before the communication event (p. 10);

3. **Initiative in framing** necessitates meeting the moments that emerge, responding to what is, and limiting laments about events that move contrary to one's expectations and wishes (p. 14);

4. **Framing as co-constructed** requires a leader to respond to context, situation, and uncertainty as one designs an appropriate and ethically reliable direction (pp. 3–8).

A leader is not born, but learns to practice what matters. The first practice in conflict is to identify that human sentiment and emotion must be recognized and acknowledged. Leaders need to practice sensing shifts and changes in a communicative environment. Leaders need to acknowledge that human sentiment often fuels the energy for the "why" of conflict engagement in oneself and the other. Indeed, leaders are not born—they gather wisdom and insight through practice. The practicing of sensing what matters to oneself and others frames a first step to leadership, as conflict works as an everyday teacher reminding one that it is not just me that matters, but the entire communicative environment. Leaders must determine what is important and what is worth fighting to achieve. The first step is attending to what alters and announces changes in a communicative environment. To fail to pay attention to what one senses eliminates potential alerts. We then miss communicative moments capable of providing important sensory direction about what matters.

REFERENCES

Andersen, P. A., Hecht, M. L., Hoobler, G. D., & Smallwood, M. (2003). Nonverbal communication across cultures. In W. B. Gudykunst (Ed.), *Cross-cultural and intercultural communication* (pp. 73–90). Thousand Oaks, CA: Sage.

Arendt, H. (2006). *Eichmann in Jerusalem: A report on the banality of evil.* New York, NY: Penguin Books. (Original work published 1963)

Aristotle. (2001). *Aristotle's* On the soul *and* On memory and recollection (J. Sachs, Trans.). Santa Fe, NM: Green Lion Press.

Arnett, R. C., DeIuliis, S. M., & Corr, M. (2017). *Corporate communication crisis leadership: Ethics and advocacy.* New York, NY: Business Expert Press.

Ashkenas R. (2011, October 18). *Should you stay late or go home?* Retrieved January 22, 2012, from http://blogs.hbr.org/ashkenas/2011/10/should-you-stay-late-or-go-hom.html

—. (2012, October 19). *Forget work-life balance: It's work-life blend.* Retrieved January 21, 2012, from http://www.forbes.com/sites/ronashkenas/2012/10/19/forget-work-life-balance-its-time-for-work-life-blend/

Bassiouni, M. C. (2008). Introduction to international humanitarian law. In M. Cherif Bassiouni (Ed.), *International criminal law, Volume III: International enforcement* (pp. 269–292). Leiden, Netherlands: Koninklijke Brill NV.

Blum, L. A. (1982). Kant's and Hegel's moral rationalism: A feminist perspective. *Canadian Journal of Philosophy, 12,* 287–302.

Bruner, M. L. (2006). Rationality, reason, and the history of thought. *Argumentation, 20,* 185–208.

Brubaker, R. (1984). *The limits of rationality: An essay on the social and moral thought of Max Weber.* London: Allen & Unwin.

Bruschke, J. (2004). Toward reviving rationality in argument: Adding pieces to Johnson's puzzle. *Argumentation & Advocacy, 40*, 155–172.

Cheng, W. (2003). *Intercultural conversation*. Amsterdam: John Benjamins Publishing Co.

Cionea, I. A., Johnson, A. J., Bruscella, J. S., & Van Gilder, B. (2015). Taking conflict personally and the use of the demand/withdraw pattern in intraethnic serial arguments. *Argumentation and Advocacy, 52*, 32–43.

Cissna, K. N., & Anderson, R. (1998). Theorizing about dialogic moments: The Buber-Rogers position and postmodern themes. *Communication Theory, 8*, 63–104.

Cooren, F. (2010). *Action and agency in dialogue*. Amsterdam: John Benjamins Publishing Co.

David Hume. (2013). In *Encyclopaedia Britannica Online*. Retrieved from http://www.britannica.com/EBchecked/topic/276139/David-Hume

Enlightenment. (2013). In *Encyclopaedia Britannica Online*. Retrieved from http://www.britannica.com/EBchecked/topic/188441/Enlightenment

Fairhurst, G. T., & Sarr, R. A. (1996). *The art of framing: Managing the language of leadership*. San Francisco, CA: Jossey-Bass.

Fiddler on the Roof. (2013). In *Encyclopaedia Britannica Online*. Retrieved from http://www.britannica.com/EBchecked/topic/206093/Fiddler-on-the-Roof

Fisher, W. R. (1989). *Human communication as narration: Toward a philosophy of reason, value, and action*. Columbia, SC: University of South Carolina Press.

Gaither, B. M., & Austin, L. (2016). Campaign and corporate goals in conflict: Exploring company-issue congruence through a content analysis of Coca-Cola's Twitter feed. *Public Relations Review, 42*, 698–709.

Gausepohl, S. (2016). 6 ways to improve your work-life balance today. Retrieved from http://www.businessnewsdaily.com/5244-improve-work-life-balance-today.html

Georg Wilhelm Friedrich Hegel. (2013). In *Encyclopaedia Britannica Online*. Retrieved from http://www.britannica.com/EBchecked/topic/259378/Georg-Wilhelm-Friedrich-Hegel

Habermas, J. (1984). *The theory of communicative action, Vol. 1: Reason and rationalization of society*. Boston, MA: Beacon.

Hall, E. T. (1976). *Beyond culture*. New York, NY: Doubleday.

Hammond, K. R. (2007). *Beyond rationality: The search for wisdom in a troubled time*. New York, NY: Oxford University Press.

Hampton, J. (1992). Rethinking reason. *American Philosophical Quarterly, 29*, 219–236.

Harmon, D. J., Green, J. E., & Goodnight, G. T. (2015). A model of rhetorical legitimation: The structure of communication and cognition underlying institutional maintenance and change. *Academy of Management Review, 40*, 76–95.

Hitchcock, D. L., & Verheij, B. (Eds.). (2005). The Toulmin model today [Special issue]. *Argumentation, 19*, 255–320.

Hocker, J. L., & Wilmot, W. W. (1985). *Interpersonal conflict* (2nd ed.). Dubuque, IA: W. C. Brown. (Original work published 1978)

Holland, R. (2006). (De-) Rationalizing the irrational: Discourse as culture/ideology. *Critical Discourse Studies, 3*, 37–59.

Hume, D. (2008). *A treatise of human nature* (D. F. Norton & M. J. Norton, Eds.). Oxford: Oxford University Press. (Original work published 1740)

Immanuel Kant. (2013). In *Encyclopaedia Britannica Online*. Retrieved from http://www.britannica.com/EBchecked/topic/311398/Immanuel-Kant

Jacques Lacan. (2013). In *Encyclopaedia Britannica Online*. Retrieved from http://www.britannica.com/EBchecked/topic/327112/Jacques-Lacan

Jewison, N. [Director.] (1971). *Fiddler on the roof* [Motion picture]. United States: Cartier Productions.

Kalberg, S. (1980). Max Weber's types of rationality: Cornerstones for the analysis of rationalization processes in history. *The American Journal of Sociology, 5*, 1145–1197.

Kant, I. (1993). *Grounding for the metaphysics of morals*. (J. W. Ellington, Trans.). Indianapolis, IN: Hackett. (Original work published in 1785)

—. (1965). *Critique of pure reason* (P. Guyer & A. W. Wood, Eds.). New York, NY: Cambridge University Press. (Original work published 1781)

Kellett, P. M., & Dalton, D. G. (2001). *Managing conflict in a negotiated world: A narrative approach to achieving dialogue and change*. Thousand Oaks, CA: Sage.

Kompridis, N. (2000). So we need something else for reason to mean. *International Journal of Philosophical Studies, 3*, 271–295.

Kruglanski, A. W., & Orehek, E. (2009). Toward a relativity theory of rationality. *Social Cognition, 27*, 639–660.

Kuhn, T. S. (1970). *The structure of scientific revolutions*. Chicago, IL: University of Chicago Press. (Original work published 1962)

Lee, D. J. (2014). 6 tips for better work-life balance. Retrieved from http://www.forbes.com/sites/deborahlee/2014/10/20/6-tips-for-better-work-life-balance/#7a879160dbc9

Levine, D. (1981). Rationality and freedom: Weber and the beyond. *Sociological Inquiry, 51*, 5–25.

MacIntyre, A. C. (2001). *Dependent rational animals: Why human beings need the virtues*. Chicago, IL: Open Court Publishing.

Magnacca, M. (2010). *Grab your audience's attention: First impressions set the presentation on, or off, course*. Upper Saddle River, NJ: Pearson.

Malmgren, A. (2011). Rationalism and the content of intuitive judgments. *Mind, 478*, 263–327.

Martínez-Ramos, D. E. (2009). On rational madness: Love and reason in Socrates and Lacan. *Communication Review, 12*, 162–173.

Max Weber. (2013). In *Encyclopaedia Britannica Online*. Retrieved from http://www.britannica.com/EBchecked/topic/638565/Max-Weber

Medhurst, M. J. (1982). The first amendment vs. human rights: A case study in community sentiment and argument from definition. *Western Journal of Speech Communication, 46*, 1–19.

Milgram, S. (2009). *Obedience to authority: An experimental view*. New York, NY: HarperCollins. (Original work published 1974)

Milojević, M. (2010). Rationality and deliberative democracy. *Theoria, Beograd, 53*, 71–88.

Mortensen, C. D. (1974). A transactional paradigm of social conflict. In G. R. Miller & H. W. Simons (Eds.), *Perspectives on communication in social conflict* (pp. 90–194). Englewood Cliffs, NJ: Prentice Hall.

Nürnberg Trials. (2013). In *Encyclopaedia Britannica Online*. Retrieved from http://www.britannica.com/EBchecked/topic/422668/Nürnberg-trials

Parfit, D., & Scheffler, S. (2011). *On what matters*. Oxford: Oxford University Press.

Pearce, W. B., & Littlejohn, S. W. (1997). *Moral conflict: When social worlds collide*. Thousand Oaks, CA: Sage.

Perelman, C. (1979). *The new rhetoric and the humanities: Essays on rhetoric and its applications*. New York, NY: Springer.

Persuit, J. J. (2011). The universal and particular: Stephen Toulmin's rhetorical theory and the natural law tradition. *Review of Communication, 11*, 51–65.

Pinker, S. (2002). *The blank slate: The modern denial of human nature*. New York, NY: Viking.

Popper, K. (1994). *The myth of the framework: In defense of science and rationality*. London: Routledge.

Putnam, L. L. (2006). Definitions and approaches to conflict and communication. In J. G. Oet-zel & S. Ting-Toomey (Eds.), *Sage handbook of conflict communication* (pp. 1–32). Thousand Oaks, CA: Sage.

Putnam, L. L., & Fairhurst, G. T. (2001). Discourse analysis in organizations: Issues and con-cerns. In F. M. Jablin & L. L. Putnam (Eds.), *The new handbook of organizational communica-tion: Advances in theory* (pp. 78–136). Thousand Oaks, CA: Sage.

Putnam, L. L., & Poole, M. S. (1987). Conflict and negotiation. In F. M. Jablin, L. L. Putnam, K. H. Roberts, & L. W. Porter (Eds.), *Handbook of organizational communication: An interdis-ciplinary perspective* (pp. 549–599). Newbury Park, CA: Sage.

Rowland, R. C. (2011). Barack Obama and the revitalization of public reason. *Rhetoric & Public Affairs, 14,* 693–726.

Sabel, C. (1993). Constitutional ordering in historical context. In F. Scharpf (Ed.), *Games in hierarchies and networks* (pp. 65–122). Boulder, CO: Westview Press.

Savion, L. (2010). *The dark side of rationality.* Dubuque, IA: Kendall Hunt Publishing.

Scottish Enlightenment. (2013). In *Encyclopaedia Britannica Online.* Retrieved from http://www.britannica.com/EBchecked/topic/529682/Scottish-Enlightenment

Setiya, K. (2007). *Reasons without rationalism.* Princeton, NJ: Princeton University Press.

Simon, S. (2008). Using Toulmin's argument pattern in the evaluation of argumentation in school science. *International Journal of Research & Method in Education, 31,* 277–289.

Smith, A. (2000). *The theory of moral sentiments.* Amherst, NY: Prometheus Books. (Original work published 1854)

Snow, C. P. (1961). Either-or. *Progressive, 24.*

Stephen Edelston Toulmin. (2013). In *Encyclopaedia Britannica Online.* Retrieved from http://www.britannica.com/EBchecked/topic/600670/Stephen-Edelston-Toulmin

Ter Hoeven, C. L., van Zoonen, W., & Fonner, K. L. (2016). The practical paradox of technol-ogy: The influence of communication technology use on employee burnout and engagement. *Communication Monographs, 83,* 239–263.

Thomas S. Kuhn. (2013). In *Encyclopaedia Britannica Online.* Retrieved from http://www.bri-tannica.com/EBchecked/topic/324460/Thomas-S-Kuhn

Ting-Toomey, S. (1999). *Communicating across cultures.* New York, NY: Guilford Press.

Toulmin, S. E. (2001). *Return to reason.* Cambridge, MA: Harvard University Press.

—. (2003). *The uses of argument.* Cambridge, MA: Cambridge University Press. (Original work published 1958)

Webber, E., & Feinsilber, M (Eds.). (1999). *Merriam-Webster's dictionary of allusions.*

Weber, M. (1958). *The Protestant ethic and the spirit of capitalism.* New York, NY: Scribner. (Orig-inal work published 1904 & 1905)

Whithaus, C. (2012). Claim-evidence structures in environmental science writing: Modifying Toulmin's model to account for multimodal arguments. *Technical Communication Quarterly, 21,* 105–128.

Williams, J., & Boushey, H. (2010). The three faces of work-family conflict: The poor, the professionals and the missing middle. *American Progress.* Retrieved from https://www.americanprogress.org/issues/economy/reports/2010/01/25/7194/the-three-faces-of-work-family-conflict/

Yungbluth S. C., & Johnson, S. E. (2010). With respect to emotion in the dominion of rationality: Managing conflict through respectful dialogue. *Atlantic Journal of Communication, 18,* 211–226.

Zimbardo, P. (2009). Foreword to the Harper Perennial modern thought edition. In S. Milgram, *Obedience to authority: An experimental view* (pp. i–xvii). New York, NY: HarperCollins.

Chapter Four

CONFLICT ORIGINS: UNDERSTANDING WHAT MATTERS

Conflicts may be the sources of defeat, lost life and a limitation of our potentiality but they may also lead to greater depth of living and the birth of more far-reaching unities, which flourish in the tensions that engender them. (Jaspers, 1963, pp. 226–227)

"Conflict Origins: Understanding What Matters" assumes that conflicts of substance have some general point of origin. Not all conflicts have definitive starting instances; however, our assertion is that the reality of different ethical goods functions as a point of origin, giving birth to significant conflicts. This chapter's *Spotlight on Leadership* features Angela Merkel, a world leader who carefully balances the differing ethical goods associated with diverse views on climate protection and trade policies.

© 360b/Shutterstock.com

Often referred to as the most powerful woman in the world, Angela Merkel receives praise for her public responses to international issues such as Brexit and the migrant crisis. She holds a masters of science degree and a doctorate from Leipzig University in Physical Chemistry.

Differing views of the good can move us into positions of "moral rivalry," a contention central to **Alasdair MacIntyre's** (1990) *Three Rival Versions of Moral Enquiry*. MacIntyre states that contrasting narratives give rise to differing goods and interests. Narratives are value-laden grounds that shape expressions of what matters.

Teamwork in group activity includes the uniting of difference with an agreed upon objective. As people work with others, multiple narratives, goods, and interests create conflict. These conflicts help people confront issues, examine different perspectives, and engage unique opportunities for problem solving (Levine, Resnick & Higgins, 1993). Research suggests that teams make better decisions when disagreement occurs in the early discussions of ideas (Schulz-Hardt, Mayer, & Frey, 2002) and when someone functions as a devil's advocate (Schwenk, 1990). Moreover, Jehn's research (1994, 1995, 1997) discusses the importance of task conflict that allows teams to scrutinize ideas and engage in a deeper understanding of the issues. Conflicts have the potential to foster learning and develop innovative and creative ways of thinking (De Dreu & West, 2001). Take, for example, the relationship between surgeons and nurses. When surgeons and nurses work together in treating a patient, conflict can emerge over the task at hand, the process, and their working relationships (Greer, Saygi, Aaldering, & de Dreu, 2012). These professional groups do not always agree on what matters; different narratives drive their decisions. Conflicts over process occur when professionals work closely together in high-stress scenarios daily (Greer, Saygi, Aaldering, & de Dreu, 2012). At first blush, the fact that there are different narratives and goods in medical work seems problematic, but the patient can actually benefit from the differences, which keep the focus of attention on multiple elements of one's health. Our contention is that multiple narratives, goods, and interests can generate conflict that introduces difference, which results in additional thought and textured insight.

INTRODUCTION

Conflict origins arise from narratives that shape interests, goods, and goals and provide a sense of identity. Our argument is that the origin of conflicts centered on ethical differences rests within contrasting and contending narrative structures. Pragmatically, we must commit ourselves to learning about different narrative frameworks if we are to understand what matters to us and to others. In conflict, narratives support what matters, with power resources assisting in the implementation of issues and actions of importance.

In "Conflict Origins: Understanding What Matters," we explore four major sections:

1. **Narratives, interests, and goals** describes how insights move us and shape conflict;

2. **History and the historical moment as power-laden possibilities** discusses the difference between a chronological view of history and historicity, which is characterized by unique questions that define a given moment and require our responsive engagement;

3. **Engaging power resources: Otherwise than convention** emphasizes the importance of communicative raw materials necessary for implementing what matters (Follett, 1927/1973);

4. **Framing communicative leadership: Story, practices, and meaning** highlights the importance of learning and using knowledge of differences for assisting others and privileging the importance of learning for leadership.

Narratives are generative soil for ethical practices and goods that we are encouraged to protect and promote. The stress on origins begins with narratives but is played out in the *praxis* of everyday life via learning and implementation. The task of learning requires us to attend to the unknown and to alterity. Our conception of learning is a continual return to an origin that begins ever anew (Arnett, 2005, p. 60; Hazell, 2009, p. 6). We understand the experience of conflict as an opportunity to learn; conflict is the meeting of continual origins, reframing clashes into a communicative *praxis* form of education. As we learn about conflict origins that give us reason to protect and promote differing goods, we gather content that assists our self-understanding and knowledge of what matters for others. We reframe the sense of origin from a stable, permanent place to the moment of meeting the unexpected, calling forth learning from differences discovered in conflict between and among persons.

NARRATIVES, INTERESTS, AND GOALS

Narratives, interests, and goals function as guiding action metaphors for understanding what matters to others and to us. **Narratives** are "public and personal stories that we [a particular group of people] subscribe to and that guide our behavior" (Baker, 2006, p. 464). Arnett and Arneson (1999) contend that a story becomes a narrative when the ideas are no longer a product of an individual but "corporately agreed upon" (p. 7). **Collective agreement**, the concurrence of a large number of people within a group, moves a story to a narrative that can offer guidance for communicative action. Narratives are guiding patterns that give meaning and structure to our speech, writing, and visual communication (Jameson, 2001). Narratives are dwellings for what matters, sheltering the "needs, concerns, and desires of individuals or groups" (Bingham & Nabatchi, 2003, p. 106). Recognizing the reality of the multiplicity of narratives is central to learning (Postman, 1995) about what is of interest and importance to others. Narratives frame the manner in which we interpret and assess communicative action. Narratives assist in understanding identity: a person's identity is grounded in multiple narratives that constitute a sense of uniqueness.

The work of **Walter Fisher** (1984, 1985, 1987, 1992, 1994) brought narrative into the common vocabulary of the field of communication. His scholarship focused on "symbolic actions" that create meaning in the world (Fisher, 1987, p. 58). Fisher (1987) contended: "Narratives assist us in understanding the actions of others, as we attend to the stories they [collectively] take seriously" (p. 66). A narrative unites a group of people with a common vision. In addition to Walter Fisher (1984), W. Barnett Pearce (1989) contributed significant insight into the importance of narrative for the study and practice of human communication. He stressed the movement from speech act to speech episodes to the vitality of an integrative story that frames the episodes into a narrative composed of story and practices affirmed by many. It is the work, however, of two ethicists, one a philosopher and the other a theologian, who first conceptualized the difference between narrative and story: Alasdair MacIntyre (2006) and Stanley Hauerwas (1981). MacIntyre underscored the importance of public virtues in the shaping of narratives. Public virtues require the union of story, practices, and corporate agreement on their importance.

WALTER FISHER (b. 1931)
is an Emeritus Professor at the University of Southern California. His work, *Human Communication as Narration: Toward a Philosophy of Reason, Value, and Action*, led to his conception of the narrative paradigm, which presents humans as primarily story-telling creatures ("Walter Fisher," 2013).

Another way to understand narrative is through the notion of the **American Dream**, understood as a story with practices that keep alive the possibilities of financial and social mobility and simultaneously display concern for others. **Alexis de Tocqueville** (1835, 1840/1963) in *Democracy in America* coined the notion of the American Dream as a description of a collective narrative that consists of two basic components or coordinates: first, a commitment to individual success, and secondly, an obligation to the community. The American Dream is a narrative of hope for social improvement that includes individual advancement and care for a community. In *The Epic of America*, **James Truslow Adams** (1931/2012) textured Tocqueville's use of the idea of the American Dream in the early 20th century. Adams described it as "that dream of a land in which life should be better and richer and fuller for everyone, with opportunity for each according to ability or achievement" (p. 308). The advancement of this American narrative includes concern for the community if one is to avoid the pitfalls of individualistic greed and self-concern alone. Conflict emerges when a narrative no longer bonds a group of people, necessitating a realignment of practices within the story or acknowledgement of the need for a new story or stories to vie for narrative status within a given community.

ALEXIS DE TOCQUEVILLE (1805–1859)
was a French political writer. Tocqueville visited America with the task of writing his observations of the American prison system. The emerging work, *Democracy in America*, however, provided a critique and analysis of American life ("Alexis de Tocqueville," 2013).

Interests are expressions of a narrative; they represent what is of importance as we make claims and negotiate conflicts (Kolb, 1989). Philosopher Jürgen Habermas (1971) defined interests as "basic orientations rooted in specific fundamental conditions of the possible reproduction and self-constitution of the human species" (p. 196). Interests are orientations; they give us a sense of direction. Even our individual decisions on various modes, strategies, and styles of communication are based on interests (Ma, 2006, p. 261); therefore, we should expect people to communicate in accordance with their own interests. Within communication literature, we find the notion of interests tied to each dimension of human life: political contexts (Boulianne, 2011; Lasorsa, 2009), the public domain (Craig, 2005; Hagins, 1996; Ryan & Martinson, 1985), commercial activity (Brevini, 2009), corporate life (Lee & Hwang, 2004; Youmans & York, 2012), and self-protection (Clark, 1979). Interests influence what drives us, persuading us about which people and ideas will capture our attention. Interests function as an engine that propels goals.

Charles Berger (1995) defines **goals** as "desired end states toward which persons strive" (p. 143). Austin and Vancouver (1996) define goals as representations of "desired states" that range from the biological to interpersonal (p. 338). Goals span a lifetime and are not understood independently, but are better comprehended in conjunction with other goals (Austin & Vancouver, 1996). Goals are related to desires for attaining or avoiding various outcomes (Monahan, Miller, & Rothspan, 1997).

Goals serve three different functions in interpersonal relationships: (1) propelling action and accomplishing an interpersonal need; (2) defining purposes for interactions and communicative behavior; and (3) providing a standard from which to evaluate communicative behaviors and outcomes in our interpersonal interactions (Dillard, 1990). Lack of clarity in goals invites conflict (Schnake & Cochran, 1985). Martin Buber (1950/2006) stated in pejorative terms that lack of direction is the home of the "demonic" (p. 10). In the field of communication, goals, like the notion of interests, have been linked to a wide range of communicative contexts and approaches.[1] Goals are the foreground center of many conflicts, with background narratives and interests providing rationale for our unique expectations that might clash with those of others.

Conflicts often emerge when another curtails our goals. However, sometimes our later goals are of more assistance than our initial hopes. This view of goal development includes "prospective," "transactional," and "retrospective" goals (Clark & Delia, 1979; Hawes & Smith, 1973; Hubbard, 2001). **Prospective goals** consist of objectives we anticipate doing. **Transactional goals** emerge in the give and take of life—our goals may change in response to what existence presents. **Retrospective goals** become reality as we reflect upon what actually happened that was contrary to an original hope; we now understand the outcome as a goal we did not originally consider.

---

1. Goals and interests are tied to terms such as relational (Cupach, Spitzberg, Bolingbroke, & Tellitocci, 2011; Wrench, Brogan, Wrench, & McKean, 2010), interpersonal (Sunnafrank, 1986; Walther, Van Der Heide, Tong, Carr, & Atkin 2010), primary and secondary (Meyer, 2002, 2004, 2005, 2009), dating (Henningsen, Henningsen, McWorthy, McWorthy, & McWorthy, 2011), argument (Bevan, 2010), and interactional (Burleson & Gilstrap, 2002; Kunkel, 2002; Liu, 2012; MacGeorge, 2001; Miczo, Averbeck, & Mariani, 2009; Wilson, 1990).

Changes in goals often result in internal conflict of who I want to be, what I seem to be, and what circumstances permit. Conflict at the prospective level occurs when someone or something arrests our momentum. Shifting goals emerge from our stumbling efforts to discern direction. Consider, for example, being rejected from a university that one considered just perfect. As one reads the rejection letter there is an abrupt end to a prospective goal. One must consider new possibilities at another university (a transactional goal). After completing two years at a different university, one realizes that all that disappointment and change actually worked out well (retrospective goal). Without conflicts that disrupt our sense of routine and demand that we respond to change, we would miss insights that could offer clarity and direction.

Narratives, interests, and goals allow us to understand and engage conflict with increased practical sophistication. Narratives act as guiding stories for our actions, nourishing interests and encouraging goals. Narratives shelter what matters. Understanding the narratives, interests, and goals of oneself and others announces the practical importance of power for protection of interests and the pursuit of particular goals. Before examining power resources, we turn to the importance of history and the historical moment, which are invitations for communicative action.

HISTORY AND THE HISTORICAL MOMENT AS POWER-LADEN POSSIBILITIES

History offers insight into the chronology and significance of past events, whereas the historical moment announces the reality of unique questions that demand response. Knowledge of the historical mission of an organization requires awareness of past events. Attentiveness to questions that emerge in a historical moment permits the development of communicative practices that can be utilized to further the success of a mission in a particular era. In the international best seller, *Good to Great: Why Some Companies Make the Leap…and Others Don't*, Jim Collins (2001) suggests that the majority of CEOs of "great" companies were promoted from within the corporation. Those coming from outside the corporation, known as "savior CEOs," are "negatively correlated" with the transformation from good to great (p. 31). The CEOs cultivated from within are aware of organizational history and culture and understand the communicative practices that can enhance a company's mission and vision. Knowledge of an organization's history assists with creative response to questions emerging from the historical moment.

History, as described by Cicero, offers an "evidence of time" (Cicero, trans. 1822, p. 118). **Edward Hallett Carr** (1961/2008) contends that history is "an unending dialogue between the present and the past" (p. 35). Various perspectives of history (Carr 1961/2008; Collingwood 1946; Elton, 1967; Gaddis 2002; Hughes 1975) differ in their emphasis on the role of objectivity in interpretation (Novick, 1988), but each approach understands the importance of public evidence in crafting historical arguments as both a science and an art. There are different approaches to understanding what history is and what the historian does (Carr, 1961/2008; Sider & Smith, 1997). The basic agreement of history is that knowledge of the past influences the wisdom of present and future decision making and action.

Miras Boronat (2016) connects us to reflections on utopia and conflicts between antagonistic and ideological structures and regimes. The author reflects on the fall of the Berlin Wall in 1989, the collapse of the Soviet Union, and the 1992 Declaration on the End of History when the USSR and liberalism could no longer end conflict. The basic premise is the movement through history as a dialectical enterprise. The new utopia today is the Internet and all its manifestations—a movement toward instant communication. The basic question is what will challenge this new utopia, dialectically continuing to pursue and develop insights not yet engaged and understood. At best, the conflict rests on the Internet and its manifestations as an unquestioned sense of hope and protagonists generating questions about its appropriate use. Utopias challenged by contrary perspectives function as A-frame houses with each side keeping the other durable and healthy.

One witnesses the notion of dialectic countering a uniform social memory with a celebration of memory locally rooted in Sanz Sabido's (2016) "Local Memories: Conflict and Lived Experience in the Spanish Civil War." Without counteraction memories become totalized and oversimplified, generating a repression of sizable consequence. Only the tension and interplay of the local and the larger social environment disrupt memory from fading into the totalizing grasp of ideological imposition of ideas.

Another way to describe this fashion of utopian clashes and dialectical counters that generate new insight is to uphold the important necessity of argumentation. Interestingly, Xi, Hample, and Wang (2015) show that current Chinese students are more sophisticated in argument than their U.S. peers. Chinese students recognize that the objective is not personal, and they attempt to propel constructive movement from multiple parties. Argument that understands history contributes to the viability of an inclusive history; such argument contends with those seen and only imagined, not just for me.

Not only do unchallenged utopias and ideologically imposed memories become problematic but also negative stereotype images of the other when they are historically internalized. Over time, we can witness multiple minorities situated within a negative internalized history. The essay "Arab Americans: Stereotypes, Conflict, History, Cultural Identity, and Post 9/11" by Semann (2014) examines Arab identity in such a historical moment. Just as utopias require counter narratives, so do negative stereotypes with an emphasis on real acts of patriotism from the very groups vilified by the denial of their assimilation.

Both enduring and temporal conflicts occur within a context of human history, which requires someone to record human events and deeds that shaped a people and a given place in time. Alasdair MacIntyre (1998) stated in *A Short History of Ethics: A History of Moral Philosophy from the Homeric Age to the Twentieth Century*, "History is neither a prison nor a museum, nor is it a set of materials for self-congratulation" (p. 4). History permits us to learn from successes and failures, offering insight into contemporary considerations. MacIntyre suggests the importance of recording great deeds.

This classical connection between history and the recording of important deeds was fundamental to Hannah Arendt's political and cultural criticism of the 20th century (Arnett, 2013). Arendt (1958/1998) stressed how "behavior" or individual action becomes known as "action." A historical story consists of interpreted and recorded behavior. **Action**, understood within human history/story, gives depth and direction to behavior, imbuing it with public clarity about interests and goals. Behavior becomes "action" when situated within human history, a recorded story about significant deeds. History, as a record of significant deeds, reminds us of what mattered at a given time. As the historical moment shifts, what matters changes as well. When we neglect shifts in the historical moment, we struggle on behalf of interests and goals that no longer address the contemporary moment. Our conflicts become human spectacles better understood as lament.

Hans-Georg Gadamer (1976, 1986) discussed the importance of the historical moment as a question that requires understanding and interpretation. His perspective begins with questions that are important for a particular historical moment. Attentiveness to the historical moment requires attentiveness to questions that reflect what is meaningful in a unique moment in time; when questions distinctive to a given moment go ignored, conflict is inevitable. Meaning is historically situated, and as questions shift, so does the historical moment, giving rise to conflicting perceptions. Smola and Sutton (2002) investigated current generational differences that exist in the work values of individuals. In their study, they highlighted various historical events that shape a person's work values. Their findings suggest that work values differ among generations from different historical eras. Acknowledging the differences across generations may mitigate or offer a reason for potential workplace conflicts.

A constructive interpretation of a conflict cannot rest solely upon one's own formation. The guiding framework must be the historical moment, not what one demands the world to be (Arnett, 2001). In conflict, one must pay attention to the changing questions in shifting historical moments. If one dwells solely in the past, one becomes an anachronism—out of place and out of time. Attentiveness to a historical moment requires us to respond to the questions of this time, place, and context. The current historical moment addresses a time when most people carry cellular phones.

FIGURE 4.1   London public telephone box.

The context thirty years ago was quite different. In London, for example, individuals relied on red box telephone booths (Figure 4.1) as the primary option for making a phone call while in public. In that historical moment, there were 80,000 red box telephone booths in the United Kingdom; today there are less than 11,000 red box telephone booths due to the popularity of the cell phone (Cox, 2012, para. 3). The red box telephone booth is now more a part of British tradition than a communicative utility.

The first fundamental power resource in conflict engagement requires us to attend to questions that arise in a given historical moment; history and the historical moment function as background that leads to understanding within a conflict. Understanding the unique questions associated with a given historical moment provides argumentative parameters for engaging the conflict—one must work within the horizon of questions that define a specific era. For instance, in an era of economic crises, struggles over limited resources become routine (Edsall, 2012), as are environmental issues in an era of dramatic climate alterations (Moss et al., 2010). To ignore questions generated in such a moment makes one an anachronism, unable to pay attention to the needs of a given time and place.

The interplay of history and historical moment keeps an organizational mission statement vibrant and alive. **Mission statements** guide an organization's actions and serve as "common corporate reporting tools" (Williams, 2008, p. 94) that offer information on what an organization has historically accomplished.

© marekuliasz/Shutterstock.com

Bartkus, Glassman, and McAfee (2000) define a mission statement "solely as a communication tool" (p. 29). The mission of an organization is a power resource that reminds us of history; a mission statement must be responsive to the historical moment. When history and responsiveness to unique questions unite in the daily practices of an organization, the result is clarity of identity and direction.

Awareness of the unique questions present in a given historical moment provides a power resource that unites reflection on history and questions that define a historical moment. Individuals engaged in conflict must respond to questions generated by a given historical moment in order to discover creative new possibilities. Thoughtful reactions to conflict respond to questions that shape the larger historical background. Ignoring the interplay of history and historical moment invites conflict and action; thoughtful use of power resources in order to move an agenda forward creatively is essential in conflict situations.

ENGAGING POWER RESOURCES: OTHERWISE THAN CONVENTION

Conventional literature on conflict discusses particular power resources that both unite and separate us. Communication scholars discuss the ongoing importance of power within organizational and interpersonal contexts (Coleman, 2006; Pachter & Magee, 2000; Richmond, McCroskey, & McCroskey, 2005; Tedeschi, Schlenker, & Bonoma, 2009); perception and use of power influences engagement in conflict situations. An early pioneer in the examination of power in organizational settings was **Mary Parker Follett** (1927/1973). She defined **power** as "the ability to make things happen" (p. 101); her acuity about conflict centered on implementation of ideas and actions. She countered the misconception that power is only a social weapon against other people (Coleman, 2006); she argued that power is a resource that makes productivity possible. The insights from French and Raven (1959) assume a similar understanding about the use of power resources; their work on power continues to propel the study and practice of this topic more than a half century later.

MARY PARKER FOLLETT (1868–1933)
was an American author and sociologist. Follett studied interpersonal relations and personnel management. Her work continues to influence the study and practice of business administration ("Mary Parker Follett," 2013).

French and Raven framed five categories of power: (1) reward, (2) coercive, (3) legitimate, (4) expert, and (5) referent (pp. 158–163). They considered **reward** a form of power manifested by what one is able to bestow upon another. Reward power permits a person to gain access to material resources for accomplished work; it functions as a base-line incentive (p. 158). When a leader gives someone a raise for good work, we witness reward power in action. **Coercive power** uses fear and punishment to control the behavior of another (p. 158). Consider a guardian who removes certain privileges from a child for inappropriate actions or a leader who threatens to demote an employee for poor performance. These communicative practices display coercive power in action. **Legitimate power** is linked to an official role, which grants one authority for appropriate use of any of the forms of power (p. 159). For example, a police officer has the right to give someone a speeding ticket, just as a leader can assign unwanted duties that must be accomplished to complete a project. **Expert power** combines knowledge and specialized skills (p. 163). Medical professionals diagnose illnesses and ailments because of their publicly and professionally verified expert power. **Referent power** is associated with those who have significant influence over us due to their prestige and our attraction and relational connections to them (p. 162). Respected and trusted leaders have referent power. Those who connect themselves with such persons gather referent power by their professional connections to that person.

Rollo May's (1972) book, *Power and Innocence: A Search for the Sources of Violence*, focuses on five types of power: (1) exploitative, (2) manipulative, (3) competitive, (4) nutrient, and (5) integrative. **Exploitative power** focuses on consuming power by making demands on the other (pp. 105–106); this form of power pressures another to the point of losing a sense of choice. **Manipulative power** seeks control by having power over another without the other's awareness (pp. 106–107); this form of power keeps the other in the dark about what is actually occurring. **Competitive power** engages another person in a power struggle in which only one party will eventually benefit (pp. 107–109); this conception of power assumes life is a zero-sum game. **Nutrient power** cultivates relationships in order to assist others (p. 109); this use of power centers on empowerment of the other—aiding the other with resources needed to be successful. **Integrative power** coordinates a communicative environment, encouraging people to share resources with the objective of enhancing creative productivity for all (pp. 109–110). May's balanced view of power includes nutrient and integrative power that facilitates creativity and productivity. Power is not inherently negative, but it can be, depending upon its use and objectives.

Tying history and the historical moment with power resources sometimes alerts us to conflicts, and when we are fortunate, power assists as a constructive asset. An example of this constructive union dwells in the work of Darell Hammond, CEO and founder of KaBOOM! Inc., an innovative nonprofit company that builds playgrounds. Hammond's life was routinely full of conflict. He was born into a family with eight children; he was the second to the last.

His father left. His mother had a breakdown (Hammond, 2011, p. 2). He became a ward of the state and ended up in a group home (Hammond, 2011, p. xiii). He is dyslexic (Hammond, 2011, p. 17). He dropped out of college in his junior year. He then ended up at an institute at Northwestern University that worked to gather resources in struggling communities and address the issues facing those communities.

Hammond came from a history of conflict and bad breaks. Yet, the background history of his early life and his learning at the Assets Based Community Development Institute prepared him for responding to unique questions that emerged in his historical moment. Hammond (2011) developed his organization after learning of the tragedy involving two young children, a four-year-old girl and her two-year-old brother, who were accidently locked in a Pontiac during a hot summer day and suffocated (p. 39). The *Washington Post* article explained that the children turned to the car as a place to play since there was no playground close to their home (p. 39). Hammond responded to this event, moving from recognition of a tragic conflict to the creation of a national nonprofit that works with communities in need of tools, resources, and guidance for building and renovating playgrounds in the toughest and poorest neighborhoods in North America (Hammond, 2011).

He and his friend, Dawn Hutchison, then incorporated KaBOOM!. Working with nonprofits, they built 38 playgrounds, and two years after they moved to Washington D. C., that number increased to over 2,000. Hammond stated:

We are social creatures. And this is a fact kids first figure out on the playground, where they learn how to cooperate and compete, how to share, how to take turns, and what happens when they don't get these things right. They learn to experience conflict and solve disputes. (p. 110)

Hammond is now a successful CEO, was the recipient of the 2011 President's Volunteer Service Award, and was listed by *Forbes* (Coster, 2011) as a member of the top 30 social entrepreneurs in the United States.[2]

Hammond's contributions demonstrate conflict awakening us to the creative possibilities of the interplay of history, historical moment, and interests and goals shaped by practices and stories that situate one within a meaningful narrative of how one man used his power to transform communities. Hammond's history made him receptive to the question that emerged from a conflict when creative resources for response were not present. His contribution was to bring forth power resources that turn problems and conflicts into opportunities for others. Power resources link responsiveness to history and the historical moment. The moment matters; it opens opportunities for interests and goals lived out in communicative practices to give shape to a narrative contributing to the meaning of a life.

FRAMING COMMUNICATIVE LEADERSHIP: STORY, PRACTICES, AND MEANING

In the forthcoming century, the only thing that is certain to me is that our greatest challenge as a nation will be that of identity. By identity, I mean the process and manner in which individuals, groups, communities, cultures, and institutions define themselves. Whether one chooses to reflect on or dismiss the conversation on identity is unimportant. The fact is that our identities are as constant as the ritualistic rising of the sun and the advent of a new day. (Jackson, 1999, p. xiv)

The second chapter in *The Art of Framing: Managing the Language of Leadership* (Fairhurst & Sarr, 1996) stresses the importance of content in the act of communicative leadership. Conflict emerges when the comments are hollow and limited in substance. The suggestion is that leadership must frame from the "inside out" (Fairhurst & Sarr, 1996, p. 23). We understand the inside as requiring a response to questions central to a given historical moment; replies to a historical situation give identity to interests and goals that frame a narrative. One does not impose a narrative from the outside; if a narrative is to have durability and strength, it must begin from responses to practices and the moment of our work together. A leader begins with what is, not with what he/she wants to force upon a given environment.

---

2. Additionally, in 2011, Stevenson University awarded him the Inaugural Social Entrepreneurship Award as well as conferring upon him an honorary doctorate of Humane Letters.

Fairhurst and Sarr (1996) and Fairhurst (2011) state the needed ingredients for preparation for framing:

1. **The dimensions** (p. 28) of framing content include task, relationship, and identity—reminding us of the dangers of pretentiousness and the necessity of working with the reality before us;
2. **Duration** of content goals vary from the immediate to the long term and are both specific and holistic—content goals must address a historical moment or their duration of utility fades;
3. **Mission, vision, and values** are driven by practices and communicative story that respond to what is needed, not just to what a leader individually demands.
4. **Discourse as background and discourse as foreground** suggest that Discourse (with a capital D) shapes the perimeters and limits of interpretive possibilities while discourse (with a lower d) implements possibilities within a given context. The background of Discourse and the foreground action of discourse both open possibilities and restrain conceptual and practical action (p. 33).

A leader is not born, but shaped in response to history and through attentiveness to the historical moment. One frames from what is and from an imaginative vision of what might be possible.

Leaders seek to understand history that is general to the world, specific to an industry, and tied to one's own life. Such knowledge requires a commitment to reading and learning. Attending to a historical moment requires knowing what has been in order to discover new insights via questions that emerge at a unique time and place. Responding with knowledge and thoughtful skill puts in place appropriate interests and goals that reflect what is needed and required in a particular moment. Leaders frame narratives that emerge through practices and stories constituted by real currency and that make sense to a given people and place. Leaders do not frame their demands for others, but rather respond to the demands of the moment—framing communicative practices and stories that emerge from interruptions to the routine; such interruptions remind us of the gift of conflict that becomes the gist of stories and practices that can reshape a people and a place.

Conflict origins are opportunities to meet, to understand, and to engage a perspective other than one's own, whether articulated by another or in changing demands in the era or industry in which we work. Leadership engages in the understanding of the human history of oneself, of the other, of events, of people, and of organizations, not out of some pristine hope for truth, but out of a pragmatic desire to know what matters. Organizations and people seldom find their identity in prospective demands or in interactional confusion but out of a necessity to make sense out of a life when direction needs to be affirmed and, at times, changed. Our fundamental interest in conflict is that it makes us alert. It is an awakening. It encourages retrospective goals. If we had the ability to wave a wand and eliminate conflict, what a mistake that would be. Human life would lose texture, identity, and clarity about the topology of one's own history about what matters. Communication and conflict about what matters is the nucleus of a narrative written by leadership in responsive action to and with others.

REFERENCES

Adams, J. T. (2012). *The epic of America*. Piscataway, NJ: First Transaction. (Original work published 1931)

Alasdair MacIntyre. (2013). In *Encyclopaedia Britannica Online*. Retrieved from http://www.britannica.com/EBchecked/topic/1725846/Alasdair-MacIntyre

Alexis de Tocqueville. (2013). In *Encyclopaedia Britannica Online*. Retrieved from http://www.britannica.com/EBchecked/topic/597857/Alexis-de-Tocqueville

Arendt, H. (1998). *The human condition*. Chicago, IL: University of Chicago Press. (Original work published 1958)

Arnett, R. C. (2001). Dialogic civility as pragmatic ethical praxis: An interpersonal metaphor for the public domain. *Communication Theory, 11*, 315–338.

—. (2005). *Dialogic confession: Bonheoffer's rhetoric of responsibility*. Carbondale: Southern Illinois University Press.

—. (2013). *Communication ethics in dark times: Hannah Arendt's rhetoric of warning and hope*. Carbondale: Southern Illinois University Press.

Arnett, R. C., & Arneson, P. (1999). *Dialogic civility in a cynical age: Community, hope, and interpersonal relationships*. New York: State University of New York Press.

Austin, J. T., & Vancouver, J. B. (1996). Goal constructs in psychology: Structure, process, and content. *Psychological Bulletin, 120*, 338–375.

Baker, M. (2006). Translation and activism: Emerging patterns of narrative community. *The Massachusetts Review, 47*, 462–484.

Bartkus, B., Glassman, M., & McAfee, R. B. (2000). Mission statements: Are they smoke and mirrors? *Business Horizons, 43*, 23–29.

Berger, C. (1995). A plan-based approach to strategic interaction. In D. E. Hewes (Ed.), *The cognitive bases of interpersonal interaction* (pp. 141–180). Hillsdale, NJ: Lawrence Erlbaum.

Bevan, J. L. (2010). Serial argument goals and conflict strategies: A comparison between romantic partners and family members. *Communication Reports, 23*, 52–64.

Bingham, L. B., & Nabatchi, T. (2003). Dispute system design in organizations. In J. Killian & W. J. Pammer (Eds.), *The handbook of conflict management* (pp. 105–127). New York, NY: Marcel Dekker, Inc.

Boulianne, S. (2011). Stimulating or reinforcing political interest: Using panel data to examine reciprocal effects between news media and political interest. *Political Communication, 28*, 147–162.

Brevini, B. (2009). Under siege by commercial interests? BBC and DR online between the national and European policy frameworks. *Interactions: Studies in Communication & Culture, 1*, 203–215.

Buber, M. (2006). *The way of man and Ten rungs*. New York, NY: Citadel Press. (Original works published 1950 & 1947)

Burleson, B. R., & Gilstrap, C. M. (2002). Explaining sex differences in interaction goals in support situations: Some mediating effects of expressivity and instrumen-tality. *Communication Reports, 15*, 43–55.

Carr, E. H. (2008). *What is history?* New York, NY: Penguin. (Original work published 1961)

Cicero, M. T. (Trans. 1822). *De oratore* (William Guthrie, Trans.). Boston, MA: R. P. & C. Williams, Cornhill-Square.

Clark, R. A. (1979). The impact of self interest and desire for liking on the selection of communication strategies. *Communication Monographs, 46*, 257–273.

Clark, R. A., & Delia, J. (1979). Topoi and rhetorical competence. *Quarterly Journal of Speech, 65*, 187–206.

Craig, R. T. (2005). How we talk about how we talk: Communication theory in the public interest. *Journal of Communication, 55*, 659–667.

Coleman, P. T. (2006). Power and conflict. In M. Deutsch, P. T. Coleman, & E. C. Marcus (Eds.), *The handbook of conflict resolution: Theory and practice* (pp. 533–559). San Francisco, CA: Jossey-Bass.

Collingwood, R. G. (1946). *The idea of history*. Oxford: Clarendon Press.

Collins, J. (2001). *Good to great: Why some companies make the leap...and others don't*. New York, NY: HarperCollins.

Coster, H. (2011 November 30). Forbes' list of the top 30 social entrepreneurs. *Forbes*. Retrieved May 6, 2013, from http://www.forbes.com/sites/helencoster/2011/11/30/forbes-list-of-the-top-30-social-entrepreneurs/

Cox, C. (2012). *God save the phone booth: UK removing famous red phone boxes?* Retrieved January 24, 2012, from http://abcnewsradioonline.com/world-news/god-save-the-phone-booth-uk-removing-famous-red-phone-boxes.html#ixzz2Iv41om9Q

Cupach, W. R., Spitzberg, B. H., Bolingbroke, C. M., & Tellitocci, B. S. (2011). Persistence of attempts to reconcile a terminated romantic relationship: A partial test of relational goal pursuit theory. *Communication Reports, 24*, 99–115.

De Dreu, C. K. W., & West, M. A. (2001). Minority dissent and team innovation: The importance of participation in decision making. *Journal of Applied Psychology, 88*, 1191–1201.

Dillard, J. P. (1990). A goal-driven model of interpersonal influence. In J. P. Dillard (Ed.), *Seeking compliance: The production of interpersonal influence messages* (pp. 41–56). Scottsdale, AZ: Gorsuch-Scarisbrick.

Edsall, T. B. (2012). *The age of austerity: How scarcity will remake American politics*. New York, NY: Anchor.

Elton, G. R. (1967). *The practice of history*. London: Methuen.

Fairhurst, G. T., & Sarr, R. A. (1996). *The art of framing: Managing the language of leadership*. San Francisco, CA: Jossey-Bass.

Fisher, W. R. (1984). Narration as a human communication paradigm: The case of public moral argument. *Communication Monographs, 51*, 1–22.

—. (1985). The narrative paradigm: An elaboration. *Communication Monographs, 52*, 347–367.

—. (1987). *Human communication as narration: Toward a philosophy of reason, value, and action*. Columbia: University of South Carolina Press.

—. (1992). Narration, reason, and community. In L. P. Hinchman & S. K. Hinchman (Eds.), *Memory, identity, community: The idea of narrative in the human sciences* (pp. 307–327). Albany: State University of New York Press.

—. (1994). Narrative rationality and the logic of scientific discourse. *Argumentation, 8*, 21–32.

Follett, M. P. (1973). Power. In E. M. Fox & L. Urwick (Eds.), *Dynamic administration: The collected papers of Mary Parker Follett*. London: Pitman. (Original work publish 1927)

French, J., & Raven, B. H. (1959). The bases of social power. In D. Cartwright (Ed.), *Studies in social power* (pp. 150–167). Ann Arbor, MI: Institute for Social Research.

Gadamer, H. G. (1976). *Philosophical hermeneutics* (D. E. Linge, Ed. & Trans.). Berkeley: University of California Press.

—. (1986). *Truth and method*. New York, NY: Crossroad.

Gaddis, J. L. (2002). *The landscape of history*. Oxford: Oxford University Press.

Greer, L., Saygi, O., Aaldering, H., & de Dreu, C. (2012). Conflict in medical teams: Opportunity or danger? *Medical Education, 46*, 935–942.

Habermas, J. (1971). *Knowledge and human interests*. Boston, MA: Beacon Press.

Hagins, J. (1996). The inconvenient public interest: Policy challenges in the age of information. *Journal of Applied Communication Research, 24*, 83–89.

Hammond, D. (2011). *KaBOOM! How one man built a movement to save play*. New York, NY: Rodale.

Hans-Georg Gadamer (2013). In *Encyclopaedia Britannica Online*. Retrieved from http://www.britannica.com/EBchecked/topic/223269/Hans-Georg-Gadamer

Hauerwas, S. (1981). *A community of character: Toward a constructive Christian social ethic*. Notre Dame, IN: University of Notre Dame.

Hawes, L. C., & Smith, D. H. (1973). A critique of assumptions underlying the study of communication in conflict. *Quarterly Journal of Speech, 59*, 423–435.

Hazell, C. (2009). *Alterity: The experience of the other*. Bloomington, IN: AuthorHouse.

Henningsen, D. D., Henningsen, M. L. M., McWorthy, E., McWorthy, C., & McWorthy, L. (2011). Exploring the effects of sex and mode of presentation in perceptions of dating goals in video-dating. *Journal of Communication, 61*, 641–658.

Hubbard, A. S. E. (2001). Conflict between relationally uncertain romantic partners: The influence of relational responsiveness and empathy. *Communication Monographs, 68*, 400–414.

Hughes, H. S. (1975). *History as art and as science: Twin vistas on the past*. Chicago, IL: University of Chicago Press.

Jackson, R. L. (1999). *The negotiation of cultural identity: Perceptions of European Americans and African Americans*. Westport, CT: Praeger.

Jameson, D. A. (2001). Narrative discourse and management action. *The Journal of Business Communication, 38*, 476–489.

Jaspers, K. (1963). *General psychopathology*. Chicago, IL: University of Chicago Press.

Jehn, K. (1994). Enhancing effectiveness: An investigation of advantages and disadvantages of value-based intragroup conflict. *International Journal of Conflict Management, 5*, 223–238.

Jehn, K. (1995). A multimethod examination of the benefits and detriments of intragroup conflict. *Administrative Science Quarterly, 40*, 256–282.

Jehn, K. (1997). Affective and cognitive conflict in work groups: Increasing performance through value-based intragroup conflict. In C. K. W. De Dreu & E. Van de Vliert (Eds.), *Using conflict in organizations* (pp. 87–100). London: Sage.

Kolb, D. M. (1989). Labor mediators, managers, and ombudsmen: Roles mediators play in different contexts. In K. Kressel & D. G. Pruitt (Eds.), *Mediation research: The process and effectiveness of third-party intervention* (pp. 91–114). San Francisco, CA: Jossey-Bass.

Kunkel, A. (2002). Explaining sex differences in the evaluation of comforting messages: The mediating role of interaction goals. *Communication Reports, 15*, 29–42.

Lasorsa, D. L. (2009). Political interest, political knowledge, and evaluations of political news sources: Their interplay in producing context effects. *Journalism & Mass Communication Quarterly, 86*, 533–544.

Lee, T. T., & Hwang, F. H. F. (2004). Journalistic ideologies versus corporate interests: How Time and Warner's merger influences Time's content. *Communication Research Reports, 21*, 188–196.

Levine, J., Resnick, L., & Higgins, E. T. (1993). Social foundations of cognition. *Annual Review of Psychology,44*, 585–612.

Liu, M. (2012). Same path, different experience: Culture's influence on attribution, emotion, and interaction goals in negotiation. *Journal of Asian Pacific Communication, 22*, 97–119.

Ma, Z. (2006). Negotiating into China: The impact of individual perception on Chinese negotiation styles. *International Journal of Emerging Markets, 1*, 64–83.

MacGeorge, E. L. (2001). Support providers' interaction goals: The influence of attributions and emotions. *Communication Monographs, 68*, 72–97.

MacIntyre, A. (1990). *Three rival versions of moral enquiry: Encyclopaedia, genealogy and tradition.* Notre Dame, IN: University of Notre Dame Press.

—. (1998). *A short history of ethics: A history of moral philosophy from the Homeric Age to the twentieth century* (2nd ed.). Notre Dame, IN: University of Notre Dame.

—. (2006). *The tasks of philosophy*, Vol. 1. New York, NY: Cambridge University Press.

Mary Parker Follett. (2013). In *Encyclopaedia Britannica Online*. Retrieved from http://www.britannica.com/EBchecked/topic/212320/Mary-Parker-Follett

May, R. (1972). *Power and innocence: A search for the sources of violence.* New York, NY: Dell Publishing.

Miras Boronat, N. S. (2016). Utopias in conflict: History, political discourse and advertising. *Critical Discourse Studies, 13*(3), 310–324. doi:10.1080/17405904.2016.1141693

Meyer, J. R. (2002). Contextual influences on the pursuit of secondary goals in request messages. *Communication Monographs, 69*, 189–203.

—. (2004). Effect of verbal aggressiveness on the perceived importance of secondary goals in messages. *Communication Studies, 55*, 168–184.

—. (2005). Effect of secondary goal importance on the anticipation of message outcomes. *Southern Communication Journal, 70*, 109–122.

—. (2009). Effect of primary goal on secondary goal importance and message plan acceptability. *Communication Studies, 60*, 509–525.

Miczo, N., Averbeck, J. M., & Mariani, T. (2009). Affiliative and aggressive humor, attachment dimensions, and interaction goals. *Communication Studies, 60*, 443–459.

Monahan, J. L., Miller, L. C., & Rothspan, S. (1997). Power and intimacy: On the dynamics of risky sex. *Health Communication, 9*, 303–321.

Moss, R. H., Edmonds, J. A., Hibbard, K. A., Manning, M. R., Rose, S. K., van Vuuren, D. P. et al. (2010). The next generation of scenarios for climate change research and assessment. *Nature, 463*, 747–756.

Novick, P. (1988). *That noble dream: The 'objectivity question' and the American historical profession.* Cambridge: University of Cambridge Press.

Pachter, B., & Magee, S. (2000). *The power of positive confrontation: The skills you need to know to handle conflicts at work, at home, and in life.* New York, NY: MJF Books.

Pearce, W. B. (1989). *Communication and the human condition.* Carbondale: Southern Illinois University.

Postman, N. (1995). *The end of education: Redefining the value of school.* New York, NY: Alfred A. Knopf.

Richmond, V. P., McCroskey, J. C., & McCroskey, L. L. (2005). *Organizational communication for survival: Making work, work.* Boston, MA: Ally and Bacon.

Ryan, M., & Martinson, D. L. (1985). Public relations practitioners, public interest and management. *Journalism Quarterly, 62*, 111–115.

Sanz Sabido, R. (2016). Local memories: Conflict and lived experience in the Spanish Civil War. *Catalan Journal of Communication & Cultural Studies, 8*(1), 11–30. doi:10.1386/cjcs.8.1.11_1

Schnake, M. E., & Cochran, D. S. (1985). Effects of two goal setting dimensions on perceived intraorganizational conflict. *Group and Organizational Studies, 10,* 168–183.

Schulz-Hardt, S., Jochims, M., & Frey, D. (2002). Productive conflict ingroup decision making: Genuine and contrived dissent as strategies to counteract biased information seeking. *Organizational Behavior and Human Decision Processes, 88,* 563–586.

Schwenk, C. R. (1990). Effects of devil's advocacy and dialectical inquiry on decision making: A meta-analysis. *Organizational Behavior and Human Decision Processes, 47,* 161–176.

Semaan, G. (2014). Arab Americans: Stereotypes, conflict, history, cultural identity and post 9/11. *Intercultural Communication Studies, 23*(2), 17–32.

Sider, G., & Smith, G. (Eds.). (1997). *Between history and histories: The making of silences and commemorations.* Toronto: University of Toronto Press.

Smola, K. W., & Sutton, C. D. (2002). Generational differences: Revisiting generational work values for the new millennium. *Journal of Organizational Behavior, 23,* 363–382.

Sunnafrank, M. (1986). Communicative influences on perceived similarity and attraction: An expansion of the interpersonal goals perspective. *Western Journal of Speech Communication, 50,* 158–170.

Tedeschi, J. T., Schlenker, B. R., & Bonoma, T. V. (2009). *Conflict, power, and games: The experimental study of interpersonal relations.* Piscataway, NJ: Aldine Transaction.

Tocqueville, A. (1963). *Democracy in America.* New York, NY: Alfred Knopf. (Original work published 1835, Vol. 1; 1840, Vol. 2.)

Walter Fisher. (2013). University of Southern California. Retrieved June 5, 2013, from http://annenberg.usc.edu/Faculty/Communication%20and%20Journalism/FisherW.aspx

Walther, J. B., Van Der Heide, B., Tong, S. T., Carr, C. T., & Atkin, C. K. (2010). Effects of interpersonal goals on inadvertent intrapersonal influence in computer-mediated communication. *Human Communication Research, 36,* 323–347.

Williams, L. (2008). The mission statement. *Journal of Business Communication, 45,* 94–119.

Wilson, S. R. (1990). Development and test of a cognitive rules model of interaction goals. *Communication Monographs, 57,* 81–103.

Winners of the Pulitzer Prize for history. (2013). In *Encyclopaedia Britannica Online.* Retrieved from http://www.britannica.com/EBchecked/topic/483089/Winners-of-the-Pulitzer-Prize-for-history

Wrench, J. S., Brogan, S. M., Wrench, J. D., & McKean, J. R. (2010). The relationship between religious followers' functional and relational goals and perceptions of religious leaders' use of instructional communication. *Human Communication, 13,* 281–302.

Xie, Y., Hample, D., & Wang, X. (2015). A cross-cultural analysis of argument predispositions in China: Argumentativeness, verbal aggressiveness, argument frames, and personalization of conflict. *Argumentation, 29*(3), 265–284. doi:10.1007/s10503-015-9352-8

Youmans, W. L., & York, J. C. (2012). Social media and the activist toolkit: User agreements, corporate interests, and the information infrastructure of modern social movements. *Journal of Communication, 62,* 315–329.

Chapter Five

CONFLICT, WELCOME, AND DIFFERENCE

Conflict occurs in almost all social settings. Most people learn at a very young age that conflicts arise in families, playgrounds, classrooms, Little League fields, ballet centers, scout troops, and cheerleading teams. Even as relationships become more complex and people become involved in more diverse and public settings, conflicts remain remarkably similar to those experienced in childhood. (Folger, Poole, & Stutman, 1997, p. 6)

"Conflict, Welcome, and Difference" examines the importance of communication dwellings, where we learn by negotiating difference together. Conflict emerges when we erroneously presuppose agreement between persons on issues that matter to them. This chapter's *Spotlight on Leadership* features Scott Harrison, founder of Charity Water. Access to clean water is a human necessity. For Harrison, water is an issue that matters.

Scott Harrison is founder of Charity Water, a non-profit organization dedicated to providing clean and safe drinking water to people in developing nations.

© G Holland/Shutterstock.com

We exacerbate unnecessary conflict as we make implicit and explicit demands for common agreement. Communicative dwellings of welcome extend a sense of relational meaning, giving us the stamina and support for attending thoughtfully to opposing ethical goods that invite both conflict and the opportunity to learn. A communicative dwelling of welcome is inclusive in that it supports both parties as they meet the reality of contrasting goods.

FIGURE 5.1   The Martin Luther King, Jr. National Memorial in Washington, D.C.

Bernard Armada (2010) attends to the importance of welcoming difference with regard to the National Civil Rights Museum as a memory site for **Martin Luther King, Jr.** (Figure 5.1). The National Civil Rights Museum was part of a movement to renovate Memphis, which pushed African American communities out of the downtown area (p. 225). These actions initiated a protest from Jacqueline Smith, who was forced out of the neighborhood after the renovation. Smith's protest site was located across the street from the museum with signs reading, "Boycott the National Civil Wrong Museum—9 Million Dollar Tourist Trap" (p. 224). Smith argues that dedicating the funds of the museum budget to empower marginalized populations would serve King's memory better. In 2002, the National Civil Rights Museum underwent a major expansion that acquired Smith's protest site, forcing her to a less visible location. Armada expresses the danger of "institutionalized memory" (p. 231) facing the National Civil Rights Museum from silencing an alternative memory of African American displacement. Even a museum for Civil Rights evokes a contrasting response regarding what we should protect and promote. The very conflict reminds us that actions dismissing the voices of the dispossessed are far from over.

MARTIN LUTHER KING JR. (1929–1968)
was a social activist, Baptist minister, and leader of the civil rights movement. King protested African-American segregation with nonviolent rebellion tactics such as marches and sit-ins. He received the Nobel Peace Prize in 1964. In 1968, James Earl Ray assassinated King in Memphis, Tennessee, at the Lorraine Motel, the current site of the National Civil Rights Museum. Figure 5.1 features the Martin Luther King Jr. National Memorial in Washington, D.C., which opened to the public in August 2011 ("Martin Luther King, Jr.," 2013).

INTRODUCTION

In this historical moment, difference is a pragmatically privileged term. Such an emphasis is an ongoing repetitive reminder that not all human beings function similarly or value the same ideas and actions. The communicative reality of difference is an everyday phenomenon, displayed as you visit the home of a friend whose family engages in communicative practices contrary to your own. The acknowledgement of difference has long-standing actuality in international and culturally diverse engagements; when we travel to new places and meet different people, we become cognizant of the uniqueness of dissimilar communicative practices. This historical moment moves intercultural common sense into the realm of the everyday. We live in an era of minimal social and cultural agreement, even in our own neighborhoods. A constructive conflict consideration acknowledges the normative nature of difference and the importance of social construction of communicative dwellings of welcome.

In "Conflict, Welcome, and Difference," we explore eight major sections:

1. **Environmental communication** stresses the systemic nature of discourse and how relationships connect to a "natural world" in which actions, things, and ideas matter (Cox, 2013, p. 19) and carry moral weight;
2. **Family** discusses how varied configurations now claim our loyalty, with and without biological and proximate connections (Vangelisti, 2004);
3. **Aggregate** depicts a group or body of persons loosely associated with one another;
4. **Community** identifies a people with a commitment to a common task, a common activity that has public significance;
5. **Culture** explains a system of ideas/beliefs about social life that relies upon conventions, assumptions, and a sense of common identity;
6. **Society** gathers together multiple families, aggregates, communities, and cultures, allowing for a sense of diversity and difference;
7. **Face saving** emphasizes the reality of unintended consequences that must be thoughtfully engaged;
8. **Framing communicative leadership: Dwellings of welcome** articulates the importance of context via the insights of Gail T. Fairhurst.

This chapter facilitates a picture of implicit and explicit offerings of welcome that recognize difference and conflict as opportunities for growth, understanding, and learning—not necessarily agreement. The hope of learning from difference emerges when a communicative environment sustains us as we meet differing views of the good within communicative configurations, such as family, aggregate, community, culture, and society. These connections frame social identity; they protect and promote what matters. Conflict dwells in the clashing of goods—communicative dwellings of welcome assist both parties in the meeting of conflict.

ENVIRONMENTAL COMMUNICATION

Environmental communication has significant currency in an era of ongoing concern for climate and natural resources (Corbett, 2006; Hendry, 2010). Cox (2013) defines **environmental communication** as a "pragmatic" and "constitutive vehicle" for understanding how relationships connect to the "natural world" (p. 20). Environmental communication is a practical field of study that applies communication principles to engaging conflicts over wilderness, farmland, and endangered species (Cox, 2013).

Environmental communication expands the complexity of human communication. One of the initial efforts to comprehend the intricacy of environmental life systems came from Ludwig von Bertalanffy (1968); he is a founder of general systems theory, which examines the interconnected nature of a communicative environment. He stressed the notion of a "system" (p. vii) where a change in one part of an environment affects the entire structure. The interplay of part and whole provides a unique perceptual perspective that is akin to a "part" that informs our view (partially) of a system in a unique fashion (p. 213)— to change a part alters the conception of the whole. Consider standing in a valley that blocks and surrounds one's vision; the perspective of one's location makes it impossible for one to see long distances (Figure 5.2). This lack of vision is in contrast to a level field in Northern Indiana where one can see for extensive distances, ending only with the limits of one's own vision (Figure 5.3). On the other hand, one might be hiking in the Blue Ridge Mountains in Virginia, where it is possible to see even farther than is possible on a flat plane (Figure 5.4). Whether one is standing in a valley, on flat land, or on a mountain, one is part of a larger system that shapes perception. Environmental

FIGURE 5.2 Visual perspective from a viewpoint located in a valley.

FIGURE 5.3 Visual perspective from a viewpoint located on a flat plain.

FIGURE 5.4 Visual perspective from a viewpoint located on a mountain ridge.

communication assumes the interplay of part and whole, with each shift in a part altering perception of a given environment.

In order to read a map and understand the topography of a particular geography, we must recognize variations in the terrain. In the human milieu, we are part of the topography of a given communicative environment. The individual is a sign of "moral topography" in **Charles Taylor's** (1989) *The Sources of the Self* (pp. 111–114). Taylor suggests that there are "moral sources" that undergird the self (p. 111); they give rise to an individual person whose identity functions as a form of human topography. Moral sources can be understood based on "what [is] in us, what faculties, or levels, or aspects of our being" (Taylor, 1988, p. 302). Taylor (1989) understands the self as emerging from the ground up, from narratives of importance; the self then becomes a form of topography in the human environment, announcing what matters by actions that protect and promote some ideas, persons, and possessions and neglect others.

Each view of reality that emanates from a single moral topological perspective suggests the limits of our ability to understand an environment in a holistic fashion. Sociologist **William G. Sumner** (1906) coined the term "**ethnocentrism,**" which contends that "one's own group is the center of everything, and all others are scaled and rated with reference to it" (p. 13). Ethnocentrism is a denial of difference in human topography. When we presuppose that one particular view of a unique environment is the only true perspective, ethnocentrism invites conflict propelled by arrogance and ignorance. Ethnocentrism denies the diversity of human topography. Lederer and Burdick's (1958/1999) work *The Ugly American* describes a person traveling abroad who demands that another culture be like his own.

We experience conflict when we are environmentally centric and dismissive of what we do not know and have not previously encountered. The unwillingness to learn is in contrast to semiotician **Umberto Eco's** writings, scholarly works, and novels (Figure 5.5). His most well-known narrative, *The Name of the Rose*, reveals the pragmatic importance of curiosity and interest in the face of difference (Eco, 1980/1983). His novel is a murder mystery set in a medieval Italian monastery with a learned monk operating as a detective. The main character, Friar William of Baskerville, must reject environmental and perceptual centrism in order to think differently than the religious community in which several murders have been committed. William of Baskerville requires detective skills that permit him to see and understand otherwise

FIGURE 5.5   Umberto Eco.

than the local. William of Baskerville, played by Sean Connery in the movie rendition of the novel, brought a dissimilar topographical presence to the communication environment of the Italian monastery. He was able to see what others continued to neglect. Uniqueness of perception can transfer one from ethnocentrism to a particularity of insight that meets and seeks to understand that which is distinctive from the norm. Our uniqueness of acumen begins with sources of the self that constitute a moral topography, commencing with the family.

UMBERTO ECO (1932–2016)
was an Italian novelist, semiotician, and critic. His most well-known novels include *The Name of the Rose* (Eco, 1980/1983) and *Foucault's Pendulum* (Eco, 1988/1989). His most well-known works on communication and semiotics include *A Theory of Semiotics* (Eco, 1976) and *Semiotics and the Philosophy of Language* (Eco, 1984). Additionally, he is the author of three pictorial collections: *On Beauty* (Eco, 2004/2011), *On Ugliness* (Eco, 2007/2011), and *The Infinity of Lists* (Eco, 2009/2011).

FAMILY

Family is an initiator of patterns that unreflectively follow us as we meet conflict. Peter M. Kellett and Thomas G. Matyók edited a 2016 collection on transformative communication in personal, family, and workplace conflicts. The introductory chapter by Linda L. Putnam and Samantha Rae Powers (2016) describes how a transformative approach moves beyond traditional win–win, win–lose, and lose–lose orientations to interpersonal conflict. Putnam and Powers emphasize contradictions, paradoxes, and dialectical tensions as central keys for engaging transformative conflict.

Individuals initially learn how to manage and resolve conflict within their families (Noller, 1995), an experience that continues to influence conflict responses later in life (Canary, Cupach, & Messman, 1995; Dumlao & Botta 2000). Art Bochner (1989) exemplifies the diversity of contemporary understanding of family in the 21st century.[1] His conception of difference in the family is exemplified in the *Handbook of Family Communication*, edited by Anita L. Vangelisti (2004), which also textures our understanding of family with an emphasis on biological, blended, same-sex families, families constructed by adoption, and families formed through friendships. Vangelisti (2004) suggests that each of the above family structures "are based on, formed, and maintained through communication" (p. xiii). What holds diverse forms of family together is communication attentiveness to maintaining a dwelling of support and welcome.

Kantor and Lehr (1975) discussed three different family types: (1) open, (2) closed, and (3) random (p. 160). **Open families** allow new experiences to emerge (p. 126). **Closed families** maintain tight connections, exhibiting skepticism about difference and experiences outside the family unit (p. 119). **Random families** unpredictably encourage all new types of experiences (p. 134) to the point of risking a sense of belonging.

The notion of family, with or without biological or legal ties, announces communicative commitment and relationship. **Family** consists of a relational unit where love triumphs over liking. Rubin (1970) differentiated between liking and loving by suggesting that the former encompasses positive assessment of and respect toward another, whereas the latter entails an enduring feeling of connection and commitment toward another. Loving is described as possessing a more powerful sense of affection and/or affiliation than liking (Sternberg, 1987; Wright, 1999). It is possible to be biologically connected and to have a family that ignores the importance of love over liking, and, on the other hand, those who have no biological or official relationship may form a family where love is consistently privileged over liking. A family welcomes with a depth more profound than temporary enjoyment/liking of the other.

Our base definition of family as a communicative environment where love trumps liking requires us to beware of places and persons who too glibly use the term family. For instance, a business that says it is a family and routinely releases its employees demonstrates the danger of the "banality of evil" (Arendt, 1963/2006)—misusing the notion of family. Each organization has what Jürgen Habermas (1973) termed "particular interests" (p. 111). Organizational interests can encourage the fabrication of family—when in reality there is a lack of support, love, and appreciation aside from their utility. A business is a place of common interaction, not necessarily of common interests. A family rests in stark contrast to an aggregate, a communicative environment composed of relationships bonded by mere happenstance.

---

1. Bochner served as the editor of the *Journal of Applied Communication Research* from 1989 to 1991. The first two issues of his editorship were themed in family communication, for which Bochner (1989) received the National Communication Association's (NCA) Bernard J. Brommel Award for Distinguished Scholarly Contributions to Family Communication in 2005.

AGGREGATE

The term aggregate emerged in the 15th century describing a group or body of units or parts that are loosely associated with one another. The term comes from the Latin *aggregat*— meaning "herded together" (Oxford Dictionaries, 2013). An aggregate reminds us that we are often thrown together by proximity with, at best, a temporal common purpose. An **aggregate**, in the field of communication, is a group of individuals randomly placed together (Pavitt, Braddock, & Mann, 2009) or a group of individuals who work together without conceptualizing the connection that their individual efforts have on the larger whole (Boyd & Waymer, 2011; Contractor & Monge, 2002; Eisenberg, 1984).

An aggregate is often our first group experience outside the family. Temporal common interests and convenience hold an aggregate together. An aggregate is a place of welcome where there is considerable space between persons, permitting a temporary unity of effort that will not continue beyond a limited time frame. We assume when we stand waiting for a light to change that all of us will cross the street in safety together. At a theatre or a sporting event, we assume that people will not interrupt us during significant moments in the drama. In an aggregate, we engage in conflict when there is a violation of the norms that guide our loose association. Conflict can occur when one seeks information from another that is unnecessary for the functioning of the aggregate. Unlike an aggregate, where there is an intentional distance between and among us, a community offers a connection to a "common center" (Friedman, 1988, p. 238; Buber, 1992).

COMMUNITY

The communicative movement from family to community[2] relies upon the reality of aggregates. Family and aggregates function as communicative extremes, taking us from the intimate to the impersonal. The construct of community rests between these bookends. In a family, one can be loved even when one is not liked. In an aggregate, there is minimal connection, just an implicit common agreement that permits collective communicative action. **Community** brings us together in a manner akin to a family, without totally ignoring the importance of distance that shapes an aggregate.

A philosopher known for his work on dialogue, Martin Buber (1992), defines community as a place constituted by a commitment to a "**common center**" worthy of protecting and promoting. Buber (1958) contended that healthy communities require a commitment to a common center that brings people together while preserving the "interspaces" between persons (Arendt, 1968, p. 31). In a community with a common center, there is an incentive to work with people one does not like. Once again, liking falls short. The facilitation of the common center holds people together, trumping liking.

---

2. The theme of community was the guiding topic for the 2012 National Communication Association (NCA) conference.

Maurice Friedman (1983), a principal interpreter of Martin Buber, and Ronald C. Arnett (1986), in *Communication and Community: Implications of Martin Buber's Dialogue*, differentiate between two distinctly different versions of community: (1) a "community of affinity" and (2) a "community of otherness" (Arnett, 1986; Friedman, 1983, p. 136). A **community of affinity** consists of people relationally connected to one another without a common center other than immediate pleasure; the lack of commitment to a common center creates in-groups and out-groups. Communities of affinity have limited life; when human beings disagree, they have nothing to hold them together.

A **community of otherness**, on the other hand, invites unity that recognizes diversity of individuals who contribute to a common center. Buber's notion of a common center suggests that the unique task of community is to gather diverse individuals together. The mission of the nonprofit organization Mothers Against Drunk Driving (MADD) was constituted in an effort to stop drunk driving, support the victims of violent crime, and prevent underage drinking. A diverse group of individuals, including parents who have lost their children to drunk driving tragedies, high school and college students, community leaders, government officials, automotive industry lobbyists, law enforcement officers, and survivors of drunk driving accidents join together under the banner of one common center—enlightening all about the dangers of drinking while driving (Lerner, 2012).

Hans J. Ladegaard and Ho Fai Cheng (2014) exemplify the difficulty of inviting a positive and creative response to otherness, to those who are culturally strange to us, in their essay, "Constructing the Culture 'Other': Prejudice and Intergroup Conflict in University Students' Discourses about 'the Other'." The essay examines university education in Hong Kong and the international relation project there. The project uncovers information that is normative on many campuses. There are negative stereotypes about students coming from different cultural groups. The authors state "it is also an illusion to think that 'getting to know' people from other cultures will guarantee success in intergroup communication" (p. 169). The mere fact that people participate together in the same classroom, dining room, or recreational space does not ensure a willingness to overcome one's own ethnocentric tendencies. Active participation in getting to know the other is essential. Without concerted effort otherness remains an abstract consideration rather than a practical enhancement of learning.

Community is a dwelling place where there is a commitment to a common center that has more moral height than dislike of particular practices of the members. Arnett (1986) states:

> For a community to survive, it must have a story. That story must be one that individuals can relate to, feel a part of, and affirm. It is a communicative vision of where we are going and why that keeps a community vibrant and healthy. Time is needed for people to tell their stories and to retell them. If we become too efficient in time use, we may close the door to a sense of community within our group and our organization. (p. 173)

Drawing on the work of Alexis de Tocqueville (1835, 1840/1963) in *Democracy in America*, Robert Bellah, Richard Madsen, William M. Sullivan, Ann Swidler, and Steven M. Tipton (1985/2008), in *Habits of the Heart: Individualism and Commitment in American Life*, suggest that a "**community of memory**" (p. 159) is developed through an enduring commitment to stories that continue to bring people together around a common center, uniting persons in times of conflict within the community. Arnett (1986) connects community and communication, stressing that (1) community does not rest on feelings alone, but on a commitment to stories that bring people together; and (2) stories guide what matters to the community, not just to individual relationships.

The stress on common center illustrates Stanley Deetz's (2016) conception of generative democracy in practice. Conversations within community begin not with the conflict itself but with the components of the decision-making process. He offers coordinates, each one presupposing pragmatic agreement: (1) ground rules for engagement; (2) recognition of difference; (3) collaborative talk; (4) collective fact finding; and (5) invention of conflict options (pp. 20–22). Together, these steps invite agreement and then implementation between and among the conflict participants.

The notion of common center is also played out by David Derezotes, Sally Planalp, and George Cheney (2016) around the notion of sustainability. The generating unity of the dialogue emerges with collective agreement on events, topics, products, life circumstances, and global climate—all inviting conversation that gathers the participants around one major action metaphor, sustainability. For persons from diverse standpoints to come to work together, discerning an agreed upon common center worthy of preserving invites constructive engagement of conflict from a community perspective.

Community functions as a significant human hope when the notion of family fails, due to lack of proximity or strains in relationships. Community prospers when it is situated in hope that is tenacious and more resolute than **optimism**. Optimism is tied to a consumer culture where we demand that the world conform to our expectations. Optimism creates conflict as one imposes demands on the other and on existence, requiring both to meet our wishes. **Hope**, on the other hand, is resolute and full of courage, willing to support the unlikeable as one works to facilitate a common center within a community (Buber, 1992). Community prospers when situated within a common center (Buber, 1992) that calls for a commitment to something other than ourselves (Arnett, 1986).

CULTURE

Max Horkheimer and **Theodor Adorno** (1944/2002) defined **culture** as "a relatively unconscious system of ideas/beliefs about social life and organization which relies upon conventions, assumptions, and a sense of common identity, shared among social subjects" (Holland, 2006). Cultures are fashioned by numerous unreflective practices that coordinate our everyday activities; one notices the particularity of a culture in moments of violation and comparison. A culture indicates the semantic meaning of symbols and signs, giving us the ability to navigate a communicative environment/context with quickness and clarity without reflection on what something actually signifies. Cultures carry with them defining coordinates that frame the meaningful importance of signs and symbols (Catt, 2011). When a culture begins to atrophy, it ceases to unite a people through unreflective practices and symbols that previously gave a culture identity. Giri (2006) highlights the interplay of culture and one's communication style. Culture provides insight for interpreting the behaviors of others and monitoring one's own behavior in various social situations. In an organizational context, Eisenberg and Riley (2001) discuss the symbolic nature of culture that provides meaning for the construction of various narratives, events, and artifacts that impart identity to an organizational setting.

MAX HORKHEIMER (1895–1973)
was a German philosopher and the director of the Institute for Social Research at the University of Frankfurt from 1930 until 1941 and then again from 1950 until 1958. Horkheimer developed critical theory and was part of the Frankfurt School of philosophical thought ("Max Horkheimer," 2013).

THEODOR WIESENGRUND ADORNO (1903–1969)
was a German philosopher who was a part of the Frankfurt School. In 1934, Adorno moved from Germany to England to escape the Nazi regime. He then moved to the United States in 1938, where he stayed until returning to Germany in 1949. Adorno taught at the University of Oxford and Princeton University and was the co-director of the University of California at Berkeley's Research Project on Social Discrimination from 1941 until 1948. After returning to Germany, Adorno worked with Max Horkheimer to rebuild the Institute for Social Research and the Frankfurt School of critical thought ("Thomas Wiesengrund Adorno," 2013).

Swidler (1986) uses the example of the "culture of poverty" (p. 275) to describe the difficulty of moving fluidly from one culture to another. Individuals within a particular culture acquire habits and skills that curtail facility of movement from one culture to another. Moving out of a culture of poverty requires recognition of the habits, skills, and actions of another culture.

Swidler (1986) defines culture as "a 'tool kit' of symbols, stories, rituals, and world-views" (p. 273). These cultural components outline the behavior of individuals within specific cultures. To navigate other cultures, we must acknowledge their stories, symbols, and worldviews. A culture proposes clues for finding our way within a communicative environment; when these symbols are no longer meaningful, the culture loses its significance and is either transformed or replaced.

Stuart Hall (1989, 1992a, 1992b) stated that the main task of a scholar of culture is to understand how meaning varies from one cultural context to another. Hall (1989) stated that culture emphasizes the exchange of meaning, permitting people of a similar culture to understand one another. Cultures nurture common beliefs (Ting-Toomey, 2010a, 2010b, 2011) and traditions (Canagarajah, 2012, p. 129). A classic theory used to describe human communication and cultural norms is the Sapir-Whorf hypothesis, which reveals the relationship between action and language. **Edward Sapir** (1921, 1949/1985) developed the framework for the theory, and his student, **Benjamin Lee Whorf** (1956), elaborated on the thesis that language and thought are intimately connected. John B. Carroll's (1956) introduction to Whorf's *Language, Thought, and Reality* describes this position as assuming that "the structure of a human being's language influences the manner in which [a person] understands reality and behaves with respect to it" (p. 23). The function and structure of language shapes perception and behavior within a culture.

EDWARD SAPIR (1884–1939)
was an American anthropologist and linguist who is well known for his careful study of Native American languages and for ethnolinguistics, the examination of relationship between culture and language ("Edward Sapir," 2013).

BENJAMIN LEE WHORF (1897–1941)
was the student of Edward Sapir and was an American linguist. Whorf, known for his study of Hebrew, Hopi, and Mexican and Mayan languages and dialects, concentrated on the relationship between language and thinking ("Benjamin Lee Whorf," 2013).

Numerous scholars in the field of communication have differentiated between individualistic and collectivist cultures. Ting-Toomey and Kurogi (1998) suggest that **collectivist cultures** adopt relational, process-oriented conflict strategies. **Individualistic cultures** adopt outcome-oriented strategies. Ting-Toomey (2005) offers a helpful distinction between the two terms, stating that individualism focuses on individual rights, whereas collectivism focuses on group interests (p. 74). Individualistic and collectivistic cultures manifest important diversity within the human community. Acknowledging the reality of cultural diversity on this macro level might decrease actions of unreflective extremes. In the words of Aristotle (trans. 1992), most mistakes are forms of either "excess" or "deficiency," whether stressing the individual or the group to the point that one disregards all contrary perspectives.

Cultures carry communicative practices and symbols identifying their significance. A society can accommodate multiple cultures with minimal communicative practices ratified through public action and law. Laws do not operate in isolation; they have a symbolic and interactional impact on individuals and cultures within a society (Drucker & Gumpert, 1996). Societies accommodate multiple cultures that create space for manifold voices, not just for a dominant group (Moon, 1996). Moon (1996) calls for a focus on intercultural communication that addresses those ignored by the majority of a society. Diversity of voices is cultivated within society when there is intentional room for difference between and among persons.

SOCIETY

Society is a gathering of multiple families, aggregates, communities, and cultures; a society has the chance to nourish diversity and variability. The identity of a society is constituted through communication practices (Castells, 2007) that offer direction without nullifying the reality of increasing difference (Karp, 2012). According to Simmel (1909), one of the founders of conflict theory, society has two distinctive meanings. First, society is doing, finding sustainability through the interaction of individuals. Second, the identity of society is a complex web of interrelationships. Society requires a commitment to "reciprocal relationships" (p. 57). Adam Smith (1759/1875), in *The Theory of Moral Sentiments*, states that difference in society carves a path for understanding what constitutes fair exchange. Society matures with an understanding that goodwill for others is a prudent course of action. For society to function, there needs to be a sense of reciprocal distance and respect for difference. Ideally, society permits diversity of families, aggregates, communities, and cultures to enrich the lives of multiple persons (Coffé & Bolzendahl, 2011), offering distance between persons of difference. It is within a society that protects distance that we can encounter contrary thoughts and ideas with the hope of learning.

ADAM SMITH (1723–1790)
was a Scottish philosopher and economist. Smith is most well-known for the economic system explicated in *An Inquiry into the Nature and Causes of the Wealth of Nations*, published in 1776 ("Adam Smith," 2013).

Conflict emerges when there is a denial of difference and a refusal to learn from what is contrary to the familiar. Creative conflict engagement with others offers a glimpse of a world enriched by differences. All the contexts above, from family to society, can welcome or push another aside. One of the practical skills of welcome rests in communicative face saving.

FACE SAVING

Conflict is often a face-threatening act, requiring us to work carefully with another. Pragmatically, face saving is important in everyday conflict—the majority of those with whom we enter a conflict will continue to have an impact on our daily relationships. **Face maintenance** (Goffman, 1959) works toward upholding a positive sense of face in social interactions. Face is a central issue in elements of dispute. People within all cultures seek to portray a positive presentation of face in social settings (Brown & Levinson, 1978/1987), particularly ones that are conflict driven. Brown and Levinson (1978/1987) write:

> *Thus face is something that is emotionally invested, and that can be lost, maintained, or enhanced, and must be constantly attended to in interaction. In general, people cooperate (and assume each other's cooperation) in maintaining face in interaction, such cooperation being based on the mutual vulnerability of face (p. 61).*

The notion of face is central to face negotiation theory.

Face saving is studied and practiced through face negotiation. **Face negotiation theory** offers insight into how personal and cultural differences inform us about shifts in understanding of narratives, interests, and goals. Face negotiation theory, developed by Stella Ting-Toomey (1985), is a way to manage conflict situations. The theory describes how individuals from different cultures negotiate face and deal with conflict (Ting-Toomey, 1988). Ting-Toomey and Kurogi (1998) suggest that face is "a claimed sense of favorable social self-worth that a person wants others to have of her or him" (p. 187). Ting-Toomey's face negotiation theory is applicable to various cultures including China, Germany, Japan, and the United States (Morisaki & Gudykunst, 1994; Oetzel et al., 2001; Pan, 2000). The theory has been used to study the effects of face maintenance as a major mediator factor in conflict (Ma, 1992), making it a valuable asset to the field of communication and conflict.

Facework describes the "actions oriented toward one's own face as well as the actions oriented toward the other's face" (Lim, 1994, p. 212). Ting-Toomey and Cocroft (1994) summarized the communication literature on facework through five propositions. First, individuals negotiate facework over the need for "face-approval" (p. 327) and "face-autonomy" (p. 325). **Face-approval** suggests that others recognize one's "positive face" (p. 310). **Face-autonomy** conveys independence and freedom from the interference of others. Second, facework strategies have implications for self-face, other-face, and mutual-face. "**Self-face**" protects one's need for inclusion in relationships and is positively associated with being dominant and emotionally expressive (p. 325). The "**other-face**" protects another's need for inclusion and is associated with integrating, obliging, and compromising styles of communication (p. 325). The "**mutual-face**" (p. 323) protects the relationship that exists between various individuals and is also associated with integrating, obliging, and compromising styles (Oetzel, Myers, Meares, & Laura, 2003). Third, individuals typically use facework strategies to "maintain," "mitigate," "threaten," and/ or "honor" self and other (Ting-Toomey & Cocroft, 1994, p. 325). These strategies determine one's need for freedom, space, inclusion, and sometimes disassociation from others (Morisaki & Gudykunst, 1994, p. 53). Fourth, facework negotiation takes place between parties who are directly involved in the interaction. Finally, facework strategies derive their meaning and function from culture (Ting-Toomey & Cocroft, 1994, p. 325). One's culture gives insights into appropriate facework strategies. Ting-Toomey and Cocroft's (1994) propositions demonstrate the "fundamental" (p. 325) value of face in communication and conflict settings. Granted, there is a difference between individualistic and collectivistic cultures on the role of face saving.[3] Our contention, however, is that this research has great salience in an era defined by the norms of narrative and virtue contention.

"Intercultural facework competence" requires diverse knowledge and a commitment to interpret the conflict communication process from various lenses (Ting-Toomey 2004, 2007, 2009); one must attend to the face of the other. In conflict, we must be mindful of what matters to others, which necessitates learning from difference and face negotiation. Conflict within contexts that seek to welcome understands that face saving matters.

FRAMING COMMUNICATIVE LEADERSHIP: DWELLINGS OF WELCOME

> It seems obvious in an everyday sense why we should be interested in caring. Everywhere we hear the complaint "Nobody cares!" ... As human beings we want to care and to be cared for. (Noddings, 1984/2003, p. 7)

The fourth chapter in *The Art of Framing: Managing the Language of Leadership* discusses the importance of framing within communicative contexts. Fairhurst and Sarr (1996) stress the importance of "context sensitivity" (p. 80). Framing does not occur in the abstract, but within a concrete place at a specific time. Attending to particular contexts requires that one's words and actions demonstrate congruence with the needs of a communicative environment. We have all met people who seem to say the wrong thing at the wrong time. A leader cannot even afford to say the right thing (understood as an ideal abstraction) within the wrong context— to do so moves potentially creative and important ideas and initiatives to the side of "missed opportunities" (p. 97).

---

3. Face saving assists in both in "low-context communication," where the message is direct and inattentive to context, and in "high-context communication," which focuses on context and the "code" of the situation (Hall, 1976, p. 72). In a conflict situation, the particularity of a culture matters.

Fairhurst and Sarr state the needed ingredients for preparation for framing:

1. **Contexts** form how we engage another's thinking and actions. Family, aggregates, community, society, and culture are macro-contexts framing how we think. To ignore their importance moves communication from the practical to the problematically abstract. Communication frames with attentiveness to context. As stated in chapter 4, Fairhurst (2011) articulates the importance of attentiveness to background context (Discourse) that both makes possible and limits the potentialities of foreground action (discourse).

2. **Larger environments** frame our interpretation of immediate events. Wherever we are situated, there is another communicative environment within which our engagement must be understood. The stress on environmental communication unites relationships within a larger world. We do not communicate within a private sphere alone. Leadership communication engages a larger public; there is always another influenced by the conversation who is not present during the discourse.

3. **Missteps** are communicative reminders of what we do not know about the larger environment and all the contexts in which we must work. We should never assume we know everything. Communicative leadership works to save the face of others for one prudent reason: all of us err—if not now, then soon.

Dwellings of welcome can include family, aggregate, community, culture, and society. It is, however, concern for the face of the other that moves a house to a home or a cavalier greeting to a genuine welcome. One frames the invitation or the welcome to environments larger than oneself. Through attentiveness to communicative practices, a given place or dwelling is made larger and more responsive to differences that emerge in conflict.

REFERENCES

Adam Smith. (2013). In *Encyclopaedia Britannica Online*. Retrieved from http://www.britannica.com/EBchecked/topic/549630/Adam-Smith

Arendt, H. (1968). *Men in dark times*. New York, NY: Harcourt Brace & Company.

—. (2006). *Eichmann in Jerusalem: A report on the banality of evil*. New York, NY: Penguin. (Original work published 1963)

Aristotle. (1992, Trans.). *The eudemian ethics* (M. Woods, Trans.). Oxford: Oxford University Press.

Armada, B. (2010). Memory's execution: (Dis)placing the dissident body. In G. Dickinson, C. Blair, & B. Ott (Eds.), *Places of public memory: The rhetoric of museums and memorials* (pp. 216–237). Tuscaloosa: University of Alabama Press.

Arnett, R. C. (1986). *Communication and community: Implications of Martin Buber's dialogue*. Carbondale: Southern Illinois University Press.

Bellah, R. N., Madsen, R., Sullivan, W. M., Swidler, A., & Tipton, S. M. (2008). *Habits of the heart: Individualism and commitment in American life*. Berkeley: University of California Press. (Original work published in 1985)

Benjamin Lee Whorf. (2013). In *Encyclopaedia Britannica Online*. Retrieved from http://www
.britannica.com/EBchecked/topic/643026/Benjamin-Lee-Whorf

Bochner, A. P. (Ed.). (1989). Family communication. *Journal of Applied Communication Research*, *17* (1 & 2).

Boyd, J. & Waymer, D. (2011). Organizational rhetoric: A subject of interest(s). *Management Communication Quarterly*, *25*, 474–493.

Brown, P., & Levinson, S. C. (1987). *Politeness: Some universals in language usage*. Cambridge: University of Cambridge Press. (Original work published 1978)

Buber, M (1958). *Paths in utopia*. Boston, MA: Beacon Press.

—. (1992). *On intersubjectivity and cultural creativity* (S. N. Eisenstadt, Ed.). Chicago, IL: University of Chicago Press.

Canagarajah, S. (2012). Postmodernism in intercultural discourse: World Englishes. In C. B. Palston, S. F. Kiesling, & E. S. Rangel (Eds.), *The handbook of intercultural discourse and communication* (pp. 110–132). West Sussex: Wiley-Blackwell.

Canary, D., Cupach, W., & Messman, S. (1995). *Relationship conflict*. Thousand Oaks, CA: Sage.

Carroll, J. B. (1956). Introduction. In J. B. Carroll (Ed.), *Language, thought, and reality: Selected writings of Benjamin Lee Whorf* (pp. 1–34). Cambridge, MA: Massachusetts Institute of Technology Press.

Castells, M. (2007). *Mobile communication and society: A global perspective: A project of the Annenberg Research Network on International Communication*. Cambridge, MA: Massachusetts Institute of Technology Press.

Catt, I. E. (2011). The signifying world between ineffability and intelligibility: Body as sign in communicology. *Review of Communication*, *11*, 122–144.

Charles Taylor. (2013). In *Encyclopaedia Britannica Online*. Retrieved from http://www.britannica.com/EBchecked/topic/939950/Charles-Taylor

Coffé, H., & Bolzendahl, C. (2011). Civil society and diversity. In M. Edwards (Ed.), *The Oxford handbook of civil society* (pp. 245–256). New York, NY: Oxford University Press.

Contractor, N. S., & Monge, P. R. (2002). Managing knowledge networks. *Management Communication Quarterly*, *16*, 249–258.

Corbett, J. B. (2006). *Communicating nature: How we create and understand environmental messages*. Washington, DC: Island Press.

Cox, R. (2013). *Environmental communication and the public sphere* (3rd ed.). Thousand Oaks, CA: Sage.

de Tocqueville, A. (1963). *Democracy in America*. New York, NY: Alfred Knopf. (Original work published 1835, Vol. 1; 1840, Vol. 2)

Deetz, S. (2016). Disarticulation and conflict transformation: Interactive design, collaborative processes, and generative democracy. In P. M. Kellett & T. G. Matyók (Eds.), *Communication and conflict transformation through local, regional, and global engagement* (pp. 3–24). Lanham, MD: Lexington Books.

Derezotes, D., Planalp, S., & Cheney, G. (2016). Transforming conflicts over sustainability through dialogue. In P. M. Kellett & T. G. Matyók (Eds.), *Communication and conflict transformation through local, regional, and global engagement* (pp. 47–70). Lanham, MD: Lexington Books.

Drucker, S. J., & Gumpert, G. (1996). The regulation of public social life: Communication law revisited. *Communication Quarterly*, *44*, 280–296.

Dumlao R., & Botta, R. A. (2000). Family communication patterns and the conflict styles young adults use with their fathers. *Communication Quarterly, 48,* 174–189.

Eco, U. (1976). *A theory of semiotics.* Bloomington: Indiana University Press.

—. (1983). *The name of the rose* (W. Weaver, Trans.). San Diego, CA: Harcourt Brace Jovanovich. (Original work published 1980)

—. (1989). *Semiotics and the philosophy of language.* Bloomington: Indiana University Press.

—. (1989). *Foucault's pendulum* (W. Weaver, Trans.). Orlando, FL: Harcourt Books. (Original work published 1988)

—. (2011). *On beauty: A history of a Western idea.* London: MacLehose Press. (Original work published 2004)

—. (2011). *On ugliness.* London: MacLehose Press. (Original work published 2007)

—. (2011). *The infinity of lists: An illustrated essay.* New York, NY: Rizzoli Press. (Original work published 2009)

Edward Sapir. (2013). In *Encyclopaedia Britannica Online.* Retrieved from http://www.britannica.com/EBchecked/topic/523671/Edward-Sapir

Eisenberg, E. M. (1984). Ambiguity as a strategy in organizational communication. *Communication Monographs, 51,* 227–242.

Eisenberg, E. M., & Riley, P. (2001). Organizational culture. In F. M. Jablin & L. L. Putnam (Eds.), *The new handbook of organizational communication* (pp. 292–322). Thousand Oaks, CA: Sage.

Fairhurst, G. T., & Sarr, R. A. (1996). *The art of framing: Managing the language of leadership.* San Francisco, CA: Jossey-Bass.

—. (2011). *The power of framing: Creating the language of leadership.* San Francisco, CA: John Wiley & Sons.

Folger, J. P., Poole, M. S., & Stutman, R. K. (1997). *Working through conflict: Strategies for relationships, groups, and organizations.* New York, NY: Longman.

Friedman, M. (1983). *The confirmation of otherness in family, community, and society.* New York, NY: Pilgrim Press.

—. (1988). *Martin Buber's life and work: The early years, 1878–1923.* Detroit, MI: Wayne State University Press.

Giri, V. N. (2006). Culture and communication style. *Review of Communication, 6,* 124–130.

Goffman, E. (1959). *The presentation of self in everyday life.* New York, NY: Doubleday.

Habermas, J. (1973). *Legitimation crisis* (T. McCarthy, Trans.). Boston, MA: Beacon Press.

Hall, E. T. (1976). *Beyond culture.* New York, NY: Anchor Press.

Hall, S. (1989). *Ideology and communication theory.* In B. Dervin, L. Grossberg, B. O'Keefe, & E. Wartella (Eds.), *Rethinking communication theory: Vol. 1, Paradigm issues* (pp. 40–52). Newbury Park, CA: Sage.

—. (1992a). *Culture, media, language: Working papers in cultural studies, 1972–79.* London and Birmingham: Hutchinson Centre for Contemporary Cultural Studies, University of Birmingham.

—. (1992b). Race, culture, and communications: Looking backward and forward at cultural studies. *Rethinking Marxism, 5,* 10–18.

Hendry, J. (2010). *Communication and the natural world.* State College, PA: Strata Publishing.

Holland, R. (2006). (De-)rationalizing the irrational: Discourse as culture/ideology. *Critical Discourse Studies, 3,* 37–59.

Horkheimer, M., & Adorno, T. (2002). The culture industry: Enlightenment as mass deception. In M. Horkheimer, & T. Adorno (G. S. Noerr, Ed. & E. Jephcott, Trans.), *The culture industry* (pp. 94–136). Palo Alto, CA: Stanford University Press. (Original work published 1944)

Kantor, D., & Lehr, W. (1975). *Inside the family.* San Francisco, CA: Jossey-Bass Publishers.

Karp, I. (2012). Public scholarship as a vocation. *Arts and Humanities in Higher Education, 11,* 285–299.

Kellet, P. M., & Matyók, T. G. (Eds.). (2016). *Transforming conflict through communication in personal, family, and working relationships.* Lanham, MD: Lexington.

Ladegaard, H. J., & Cheng, H, F. (2014). Constructing the cultural 'other': Prejudice and intergroup conflict in university students' discourses about 'the other.' *Language and Intercultural Communication, 14*(2), 156–175.

Lederer, W. J., & Burdick, E. (1999). *The ugly American.* New York, NY: Norton. (Original work published 1958)

Lerner, B. H. (2012). *One for the road: Drunk driving since 1900.* Baltimore, MD: Johns Hopkins University Press.

Lim, T. S. (1994). Facework and interpersonal relationships. In S. Ting Toomey (Ed.), *The challenge of facework: Cross-cultural and interpersonal issues* (pp. 209–228). Albany: State University of New York Press.

Ma, R. (1992). The role of unofficial intermediaries in interpersonal conflicts in the Chinese culture. *Communication Quarterly, 40,* 269–278.

Martin Luther King, Jr. (2013). In *Encyclopaedia Britannica Online.* Retrieved from http://www.britannica.com/EBchecked/topic/318311/Martin-Luther-King-Jr

Max Horkheimer. (2013). In *Encyclopaedia Britannica Online.* Retrieved from http://www.britannica.com/EBchecked/topic/271792/Max-Horkheimer

Morisaki, S., & Gudykunst, W. B. (1994). Face in Japan and the United States. In S. Ting-Toomey (Ed.), *The challenge of facework: Cross-cultural and interpersonal issues* (pp. 47–94). Albany: State University of New York.

Moon, D. G. (1996). Concepts of culture: Implications for intercultural communication research. *Communication Quarterly, 44,* 70–84.

Noddings, N. (2003). *Caring: A feminine approach to ethics and moral education.* Berkeley: University of California Press. (Original work published 1984)

Noller, F. (1995). Parent-adolescent relationships. In M. Fitzpatrick & A. Vangelisti (Eds.), *Explaining family interactions* (pp. 77–111). Thousand Oaks, CA: Sage.

Oetzel, J. J., Myers, K. K., Meares, M. M., & Laura, E. E. (2003). Interpersonal conflict in organizations: Explaining conflict styles via face-negotiation theory. *Communication Research, 20,* 106–115.

Oetzel, J. G., Ting-Toomey, S., Masumoto, T., Yokochi, Y., Pan, X., Takai, J., & Wilcox, R. (2001). Face and facework in conflict: A cross-cultural comparison of China, Germany, Japan, and the United States. *Communication Monographs, 68,* 235–258.

Oxford Dictionaries. (2013). *Aggregate.* Retrieved February 28, 2013, from http://oxforddictionaries.com/us/definition/american_english/aggregate

Pan, Y. (2000). Facework in Chinese service encounters. *Journal of Asian Pacific Communication, 10,* 25–61.

Pavitt, C., Braddock, K., & Mann, A. (2009). Group communication during resource dilemmas: 3. Effects of social value orientation. *Communication Quarterly, 57,* 433–451.

Putnam, L. L., & Powers, S. R. (2016). Contradictions and dialectics as keys to conflict transformation. In P. M. Kellet & T. G. Matyók (Eds.), *Transforming conflict through communication in personal, family, and working relationships*. Lanham, MD: Lexington.

Rubin, Z. (1970). Measurement of romantic love. *Journal of Personality and Social Psychology, 16*, 265–273.

Sapir, E. (1921). *Language: An introduction to the study of speech*. New York, NY: Harcourt Brace.

—. (1985). *Selected writings of Edward Sapir in language, culture, and personality* (D. G. Mandelbaum, Ed.). Berkeley: University of California Press. (Original work published 1949)

Simmel, G. (1909). The problem of sociology. *American Journal of Sociology, 15*, 289–320.

Smith, A. (1875). *The theory of moral sentiments, or an essay towards an analysis of the principles by which men naturally judge concerning the conduct and the character, first of their neighbors, and afterward of themselves: To which is added, a dissertation on the origins of languages* (D. Stewart, Ed.). London: George Bell and Sons. (Original work published 1759)

Sternberg, R. J. (1987). Liking versus loving: A comparative evaluation of theories. *Psychological Bulletin, 102*, 331–334.

Sumner, W. G. (1906). *Folkways: A study of the sociological importance of usages, manners, customs, mores, and morals*. Boston, MA: Ginn & Company.

Swidler. A. (1986). Culture in action: Symbols and strategies. *American Sociological Review, 51*, 273–286.

Taylor, C. (1988). The moral topography of the self. In S. B. Messer, L. A. Sass, & R. L. Woolfolk (Eds.), *Hermeneutics and psychological theory: Interpretive perspectives on personality, psychotherapy, and psychopathology* (pp. 298–320). New Brunswick, NJ: Rutgers University Press.

—. (1989). *Sources of the self: The making of the modern identity*. Cambridge, MA: Harvard University Press.

Theodor Wiesengrund Adorno. (2013). In *Encyclopaedia Britannica Online*. Retrieved from http://www.britannica.com/EBchecked/topic/6362/Theodor-Wiesengrund-Adorno

Ting-Toomey, S. (1985). Toward a theory of conflict and culture. In W. Gudykunst, L. Stewart, & S. Ting-Toomey (Eds.), *Communication, cultural and organizational processes* (pp. 71–87). New York, NY: Sage.

—. (1988). Intercultural conflict styles: A face-negotiation theory. In Y. Kim & W. Gudykunst (Eds.), *Theories in intercultural communication* (pp. 213–235). Thousand Oaks, CA: Sage.

—. (2004). Translating conflict face-negotiation theory into practice. In D. Landis, J. M. Bennett, & M. J. Bennett (Eds.), *Handbook of intercultural training* (3rd ed., pp. 217–248). Thousand Oaks, CA: Sage.

—. (2005). The matrix of face: An updated face-negotiation theory. In W. B. Gudykunst (Ed.), *Theorizing about intercultural communication* (pp. 71–92). Thousand Oaks, CA: Sage.

—. (2007). Intercultural conflict training: Theory-practice approaches and research challenges. *Journal of Intercultural Communication Research, 36*, 255–271.

—. (2009). Intercultural conflict competence as a facet of intercultural competence development: Multiple conceptual approaches. In D. K. Deardorff (Ed.), *The Sage handbook of intercultural competence* (pp. 100–120). Thousand Oaks, CA: Sage.

—. (2010a). Mindfulness. In R. Jackson (Ed.), *Sage encyclopedia of identity* (Vol. 1, pp. 455–458). Thousand Oaks, CA: Sage.

—. (2010b). Applying dimensional values in understanding intercultural communication. *Communication Monographs, 77*, 169–180.

—. (2011). Intercultural communication ethics: Multiple layered issues. In G. Cheney, S. May, & D. Munshi (Eds.), *The ICA handbook of communication ethics* (pp. 335–352). Mahwah, NJ: Lawrence Erlbaum.

Ting-Toomey, S., & Cocroft, B. (1994). Face and facework: Theoretical and research issues. In S. Ting-Toomey (Ed.), *The challenge of facework: Cross-cultural and interpersonal issues* (pp. 307–340). Albany: State University of New York Press.

Ting-Toomey, S., & Kurogi, A. (1998). Facework competence in intercultural conflict: An updated face-negotiation theory. *International Journal of Intercultural Relations, 22,* 187–225.

Vangelisti, A. L. (2004). *Handbook of family communication.* Mahwah, NJ: Lawrence Erlbaum Associates.

von Bertalanffy, L. (1968). *General system theory: Foundations, development, applications.* New York, NY: George Braziller.

Whorf, B. L. (1956). *Language, thought, and reality.* New York, NY: Wiley.

William Graham Sumner. (2013). In *Encyclopaedia Britannica Online.* Retrieved from http://www.britannica.com/EBchecked/topic/573450/William-Graham-Sumner

Wright, D. E. (1999). *Personal relationships: An interdisciplinary approach.* Mountain View, CA: Mayfield.

Chapter Six

RELATIONAL PERCEPTION IN CONFLICT

There's nothing wrong with standing back and thinking. To paraphrase several sages: 'Nobody can think and hit someone at the same time.' (Sontag, 2003, p. 106)

"Relational Perception in Conflict" recognizes that interactive enrichment requires learning cognizant of long-term relationship attentiveness. Relationships are central to sociality and give rise to conflict when differences emerge. This chapter's *Spotlight on Leadership* features Jeff Bezos, founder of Amazon.com, who is disrupting the relationship individuals hold with traditional brick-and-mortar stores.

© aradaphotography/Shutterstock.com

Jeff Bezos is founder of Amazon.com, the world's largest online shopping retailer. Bezos is worth about $84.6 billion and on his way to shifting Bill Gates out of the wealthiest person in the world title.

On rare occasions, one must place a relationship at risk and vigorously engage a given conflict. However, in most instances, one needs to preserve the relationship, knowing fully well that one must work with the same person(s) tomorrow. One must learn when to let a conflict pass in order to preserve a relationship and how to meet a conflict while continuing the relationship.

In *Dubliners*, **James Joyce** (1914/1991) (Figure 6.1) offers a series of short stories that depicts the daily lives of those who live in Dublin, Ireland, during the turn of the 20th century. One of these stories, "Eveline," introduces a young girl faced with a dilemma: Eveline can either stay in Ireland in order to fulfill a promise to her late mother—being the caretaker for her abusive father and younger siblings—or leave for Buenos Ayres (Joyce's spelling) with a young sailor named Frank. Eveline contemplates her life in Ireland, her relationships with her family, and her courtship with Frank. She accompanies Frank to the dock after deciding to "escape"

(p. 23), but with considerable reflection on "her [relational] duty" (p. 23), Eveline grips a railing as she watches Frank fade from her vision. In the midst of a conflict, Eveline had to decide what relationships would claim extended responsibility. We can argue whether she made the correct choice, but we cannot miss the importance of making relational choices in the midst of conflict. Conflict is often a necessary test of relationships. Conflicts with persons of professional and personal importance require relational attentiveness that acknowledges the significance of others. Relationships matter—sometimes more than the conflict at hand.

FIGURE 6.1   View from the James Joyce Bridge in Dublin, Ireland.

© Artur Bogacki/Shutterstock.com

JAMES JOYCE (1882–1941) was an Irish novelist born in Dublin. His most well-known novels include *Dubliners*, published in 1914; *A Portrait of an Artist as a Young Man*, published in 1916; *Ulysses*, published in 1922; and *Finnegans Wake*, published in 1939. Joyce is known for "his experimental use of language and exploration of new literary methods," including stream of consciousness writing ("James Joyce," 2013).

INTRODUCTION

Relational maintenance in conflict engagement requires attending to two major issues. First, relational attentiveness acknowledges the importance of others. Second, conflict signals, at a basic and pragmatic level, the social nature of our lives. If affiliations with others did not matter, then conflict distress would be minimal and human action would be more brutal, lacking relational constraint. Social concern between persons can temper and restrain conflict if one seeks to have a long-term relationship. Relational attentiveness opens the door to the possibility of enduring connections between persons.

In "Relational Perception in Conflict," we explore five major sections:

1. **Web of relationships** focuses on the importance of relational connections, assuming that the depth and number of our attachments in a given relationship affect the conflict;

2. **Jealousy and envy** explores two different forms of social comparison that shift obligation for one's own lack of productivity to another;

3. **Individualism** examines the effort to stand above human history, which leaves us disconnected from social and relational constraints and restraints that shape individual identity;

4. **Relational perception and revelatory space** assumes the importance of relational discourse between persons, reminding us of our sociality and how unanticipated ideas and perceptions emerge between persons;

5. **Framing communicative leadership: Relational perception** offers an understanding and recognition of the complexity of relational conflict.

Conflict and relationship attentiveness announce the blurred and confusing dimensions inherent in living and working with others. This chapter, "Relational Perception in Conflict," counters the impulse to respond to another without initial relationship consideration; self-righteous conflict engagement too quickly dismisses the relational dimension of conflict engagement.

WEB OF RELATIONSHIPS

Julia Wood (1992) emphasizes the importance of the web of relationships that constitutes identity. Relational webs of connection function like multiple voices in a chorus, permitting one's expression to work with other declarations. A web of human interactions supports and shapes individual identity; one often senses relational possibilities as one attends to the environmental texture that composes a particular communicative dwelling. Each of us has been in situations where we sensed the uniqueness of a given environment. The differences between a welcoming place, an off-putting environment, and a dwelling of rejection may not always be easy to describe analytically, but one can sense the disparities.

An early discussion about the power of various webs of human relationships came from **Georg Simmel**, considered one of the founders of conflict theory (Turner, 1993, p. 87). Simmel (1908/1955) uses the phrase "the web of group-affiliations" (p. 125) to emphasize how webs of connections unite us. Simmel's basic assumption is that the greater the number of relational connections, the more likely one is to take into account the importance of the relationship as one participates in a conflict. Multiple relational ties can also offer greater endurance of a relationship, with numerous shared associations keeping people together.

GEORG SIMMEL (1858–1918)
was a German sociologist and philosopher. He taught at the University of Berlin from 1885 until 1914, then at the University of Strasbourg until his death in 1918. His work explores social interaction, which later led to the development of qualitative analysis in sociology ("Georg Simmel," 2013).

Relationships can span from acquaintance to friend, family member, co-worker, or member of a community or profession. Understanding the connections, the number and depth of ties in a relationship, permits one to apprehend relationships in their strength, duration, and importance. Relational connections direct how we will interpret information and experiences. Multiple connections give rise to a web of relationships, which strengthens bonds with another. Webs of relationships are akin to concentric circles that emerge from a stone tossed into the water. For example, if one considers the inner concentric circle as the family, the next concentric circle as composed of one's closest friends, and then the next concentric circle as consisting of professional friends, then one begins to conceptualize the importance of bonds and links between and among a web of relationships. Multiple relational links to family members, co-workers, and friends texture our communicative lives, providing social ground that supports all parties in a conflict.

The realm of friendship delivers multiple webs of relationships, as framed by Aristotle (trans. 1999) in *Nicomachean Ethics*. He framed three different types of relational friendship webs: (1) pleasure (centered on immediate enjoyment), (2) utility (the expectation of usefulness), and (3) **virtue** (requiring reciprocal goodwill). Each of these relational categories reminds us of the complexity of human friendship with pleasure focusing on relational immediacy, utility tied to purpose, and virtue requiring mutual support.

The relational complexity of friendship has also been addressed by William Rawlins (1992, 2009) in two important works: *Friendship Matters: Communication, Dialectics, and the Life Course* and *The Compass of Friendship: Narratives, Identities, and Dialogues*. Rawlins (1992) discussed how friendship involves dialectical tensions within relational bonds, within a larger culture, and across the life cycle. Dialectical tensions evolve and change across situations and time (p. 24). Dialectical tensions in friendships emerge from "contradictory demands" in relationships, such as "affection and instrumental assistance, judgment and acceptance, and expressiveness and protectiveness" (p. 214), "independence and dependence" (p. 144), issues of "public marginality and private morality" (p. 10), actions of "expressiveness and protectiveness" (p. 56), and engagements of "caring and utility" (p. 108). Rawlins (2009) also examines how friends use dialogue, storytelling, and narratives to create identities, cope with differences, make decisions, and establish communities. Webs of relationships, such as friendship, connect us and make our lives together important. When few relational connections are in place, a sudden intense conflict can have a disproportionate impact that may sever a relationship. Relational connections are at the heart of most conflicts; managing a relationship is a pragmatic and necessary communicative labor. Relationships that matter take time, effort, and energy.

William James, one of the founders of pragmatism, considered relational disregard an intentional malevolent action (Ayer, 1968). James (1892/2001) stated that there is "no more fiendish punishment" than to ignore another (p. 46). Disregarding and ignoring deny relational affiliation. In conflict, one endangers relational connections when the webs of relations are minimal and held in low regard. Negligible concern for the other results in intentional distancing

(Young, Kubicka, Tucker, Chávez-Appel, & Rex, 2005). Becoming quiet and denying one's negative feelings about another can invite eventual disregard, moving conflict from suppression of feelings to implosion (Canary & Lakey, 2006). Maintaining relational associations in the face of conflict is an essential feature in everyday life (Guerrero, Andersen, Jorgensen, Spitzberg, & Eloy, 1995). In addition to relational disregard, Simmel's discussion of jealousy and envy examines the shadow side of relational connections.

WILLIAM JAMES (1842–1910)
was an American philosopher and psychologist. He was the leader of pragmatism within philosophy and functionalism within psychology ("William James," 2013).

JEALOUSY AND ENVY

Simmel (1908/1955) asserted that jealousy and envy undergird social conflict. He defines **jealousy** as a form of social comparison in which the other human being has a skill set similar to one's own, with one major difference—the other person is much better at the doing, the engagement, and the use of that skill set. **Envy** is even more relationally problematic in that one demands to have a talent that one simply does not possess (p. 50). The Old Testament story about Cain and Abel (Genesis 4.1–16 [KJV]) reveals an ultimate danger, as Cain takes his brother's life out of jealousy and envy (Meeker, 2002, p. 415).

A contemporary example of jealousy and envy in action took place between two figure skaters, Tonya Harding and Nancy Kerrigan, prior to the 1994 Winter Olympics in Lillehammer, Norway. In the 1992 Olympics, held in Albertville, France, Kerrigan won the bronze medal while her U.S. competitor Tonya Harding placed just behind her in fourth. Kerrigan was a gold-medal favorite for the 1994 Winter Olympics until an assailant hired by Harding's ex-husband attacked Kerrigan after a practice at the U.S. Olympic trials, clubbing her right knee, which was her landing knee, in an effort to break her leg. With Kerrigan unable to compete, Harding was able to rise to the top of the U.S. Olympic trials winning first place and guaranteeing her a spot on the Olympic team. However, Kerrigan recovered in time to compete in the Olympics and won the silver medal for the United States while Harding placed eighth. Harding's ex-husband and bodyguard served jail time for their involvement in the crime. Harding's conviction reflected the hindering of the prosecution. She incurred a heavy fine, and was removed from the U.S. Figure Skating Association events for life (Harish, 2012). The attack on Nancy Kerrigan represents one of the ultimate acts of jealousy and unsportsmanship in competitive sports (Coughlin, 2016). Twenty years after the attack, NBC created a documentary entitled "Nancy & Tonya," which debuted before the closing ceremony of the 2014 Winter Olympics (Dowd, 2014). This story of inter-Olympian jealousy will also be portrayed in the 2018 feature film, *I, Tonya* (Hines, 2017). Jealousy opens the door to ugly actions and is, unfortunately, a common conflict generator.

Envy assumes a negative disposition against another who possesses the skill one covets (Simmel, 1908/1955, p. 53). One can think of a family member, friend, or co-worker who has a wonderful creative gift that one does not possess, generating envy. For instance, if someone has difficulty drawing recognizable figures and meets someone who is an outstanding artist, one might be tempted to feel a sense of envy toward that artist, particularly if one is unable to make accurate evaluations of one's own ability.

Jealousy and envy constitute a relational dark side (Guerrero & Andersen, 1998), announcing sociality propelled by destructive social comparison. Unproductive conflict emerges the moment we lose focus on the demanding task of devoting hours to practice and learning. Jealousy and envy are illusions in that they appear as if they are shortcuts to human recognition. One attempts to lessen one's inadequacy by stressing the limits of another—real or imagined. Envy and jealousy are negative factors in interpersonal communication because they invite inferiority and self-criticism, as well as fear, anger, loss, and rejection (Guerrero, Trost, & Yoshimura, 2005).

Being on the receiving side of jealousy and envy is difficult and inevitable as one pursues excellence, necessitating thinking dissimilar to a "herd" or "mob mentality" (Arendt, 1948/1994). We cannot control another's jealousy or envy, and we cannot ignore all people who bring the issue of jealousy and envy to relationships. We recognize a pragmatic mandate to acknowledge a diverse skill set and the importance of developing a thick skin that protects one from destructive social comparison (Fritz, 2013).

Returning to the work of Simmel (1908/1955), we unearth practical advice for addressing jealousy and envy—develop multiple relational ties. We cannot place all our relational significance at the mercy of a small band of persons. Our lives and identities need to be textured and complex. Multiple ties shape us. Complex associations can buffer the power of a small group of persons. Just as it is important to have multiple connections to one person, it is vital to have relational bonds to multiple places. The workplace cannot be the only communicative dwelling that gives one identity (Arnett, 2006); multiple relational ties provide a textured and constructively complex identity.

Social comparison that does not call us to responsible action shifts our attentiveness from responsibility to regret. Focusing on one's own practices and skill set does not guarantee success, but it does minimize the destructive power of jealousy and envy. Jealousy and envy seem to emerge with increasing clarity during the junior high/middle school experience and continue to haunt us for the remainder of our lives. Problems emerge when multiple ties do not guide us. The example *par excellence* is individualism.

INDIVIDUALISM

In *Democracy in America*, Alexis de Tocqueville (1835, 1840/1963) wrote about the emerging United States in the 1830s; he advanced a forewarning about the dangers of **"individualism"** (p. 98). Tocqueville contrasted individualism with selfishness; he contended that selfishness is actually more constructive than individualism. Individualism incorporates an assumption that it is possible to stand above human history, ignoring all social and relational ties that both propel and restrain us and additionally give us identity. Individualism acts as if the web of human associations does not matter. Individualism counters community, forgetting that social connections keep a given communicative environment healthy. Individualism is a myth that encourages us to stand above all groups and social connections, acting as if relational connections do not matter. An individualistic mythology manifests itself in public utterances such as "Pull yourself up by your bootstraps" and "If you want something done right, do it yourself."

Ian Watt (1996) offered a thorough examination of the expression of individualism played out through four literary characters well known to the development of the West. First, Watt examined the myth of *Faust*, in which **Faust** made a bargain with the devil in order to acquire great intellectual powers. Second, Watt discussed **Don Quixote's** individual refusal to admit that the world had changed and was continuing to do so (Cervantes, 1604/1993). Third, Watt

FAUST
The character of Faust first emerged in 1587 in *Faustbuch*, which was written by an unknown author. Faust has continued to appear in the works of Christopher Marlowe, Gotthold Lessing, Hector Berlioz, Charles Gounod, Adelbert von Chamisso, Christian Grabbe, Nikolaus Lenau, Heinrich Heine, Paul Valéry, Johann Wolfgang von Goethe, and Thomas Mann ("Faust," 2013).

DON QUIXOTE
Don Quixote is a character created by the Spanish poet, playwright, and novelist Miguel de Cervantes (1547–1616). *Don Quixote*, translated into over sixty languages, is a classic literary work. The title character, Don Quixote, has become a symbol of the "impractical pursuit of idealistic goals" ("Don Quixote," 2013).

reviewed the actions of **Don Juan's** behavior as an individual trickster oblivious to the concerns of others. Finally, Watt unmasked the message of **Robinson Crusoe** as a common person able to subdue nature with his individual will (Defoe, 1719/1862). In each case, the novel explicated by Watt reveals an impulse to stand above human restraints. Individualism does not attend to social ties and restraints. The communicative action of individualism is a mythic hope about the disregarding of relational constraints that is more problematic than selfishness.

DON JUAN

is a "symbol of libertinism" who has become as familiar as Don Quixote, Faust, and Shakespeare's Hamlet. Don Juan has continued to appear in works by Mozart, Molière, Prosper Mérimée, Alexandre Dumas père, Thomas Shadwell, Lord Byron, and George Bernard Shaw ("Don Juan," 2013).

ROBINSON CRUSOE

is a fictional seaman and the protagonist of Daniel Defoe's (1660–1731) *Robinson Crusoe*. The character represents "self-reliance" as he survives on his own for 28 years on an uninhabited island ("Robinson Crusoe," 2013).

Tocqueville (1835, 1840/1963) held the communicative act of selfishness in pragmatic high regard. For instance, selfishness emerges as one goes home on a Friday evening and discovers a sick relative who needs attention as one admits to oneself that helping another is not what one had hoped to do. Yet, out of selfishness, one assists a family member, knowing full well that in order to assist oneself, aid for the other is pragmatically necessary. Otherwise, one invites a horrific Saturday and Sunday. Another example of selfishness involves the common practice of volunteering to assist an organization with the rationale of gaining experience for one's resume. One recognizes that volunteer experience and work influence recommendations; volunteering gives another something to commend in a recommendation. Selfishness is not noble, but it does take into account social ties. **Selfishness** assists another and oneself in the social value of a relational exchange.

Tocqueville's notion of the American Dream, as outlined in Chapter 4, "Conflict Origins: Understanding What Matters," is a form of constructive selfishness. In *Democracy in America*, Tocqueville (1835, 1840/1961) defined the American Dream as the unity of individual success and concern for the community. If one does not take care of the community, opportunities for individual success evaporate, thereby hurting oneself. If we want individual success to work, we need to think about others and root for them, refusing narrow consideration of ourselves alone. The myth of the American Dream works only when the possibility of rags to riches is a reality for all within a community. The American Dream requires selfishness; individual success needs the success of the other—assisting and rooting for others is a pragmatic act. Individualism, on the other hand, ignores this practical social obligation.

The importance of selfishness was central to the Scottish Enlightenment; the type of selfishness described in the last paragraph embraces individual success and aids others. It is a form of tempered selfishness, termed **"enlightened self-interest"** (Ferguson, 1767/2004). The notion of capitalism, as understood by Adam Smith (1776/1925), reflects enlightened self-interest, with an objective of enhancing productivity, creativity, and individual achievement for self and others. Efforts that undercut productivity and individual achievement for those within a community reject the importance of "sympathy" that tries to understand the plight of another (Smith, 1776/1925). Smith did not equate capitalism with greed, but with advancement of an entire social group through competition that benefits all. Central to capitalism is competition, which according to Heilbroner (1999), acts as the "regulator" of capitalism—"the conflict of the self-interested actors on the marketplace. A man who permits his self-interest to run away with him will find that competitors have slipped in to take his trade away" (p. 55). Enlightened self-interest recognizes that one's own welfare is dependent on the success of others. For example, in 1997, Microsoft invested $150 million into Apple to save the struggling company (Markoff, 1997). Microsoft acted out of self-interest, realizing the importance of competition.

Today conversation is seldom about selfishness or enlightened self-interest, but about the unity of individual success and pragmatic concern for the social environment—individualism (discussed in the previous paragraphs) and social comparison (Lyubomirsky & Ross, 1997).

Social comparison can be self-enhancing if it is motivating and self-destructive if one falls into the abyss of undue jealousy and envy (Collins, 1996). Social comparison consumes time with issues as diverse as financial success and body image (Gulas & McKeage, 2000). In an organizational setting, where achieving success can be perceived as essential, social comparison can either motivate one to improve performance or encourage one to undercut another (Buunk, Carmona, Peiró, Dijkstra, & Dijkstra, 2011). Uncontrolled social comparison leads to unwillingness to welcome the stranger and the different; we gravitate toward the similar, encouraging prejudice against the unknown. Only a positive conception of the "different other" allows for multicultural settings to flourish (Berg, 2012, p. 405). Social comparison that leads to learning and does not fear difference is more akin to enlightened self-interest, seeking to achieve without forgetting the constraints of the social environment. Fundraising for nonprofit institutions counts on the enlightened self-interest of "philanthrocapitalists" (Bishop & Green, 2008). Individualism, on the other hand, ignores the fact that we are embedded creatures, situated within a complex web of social relations. The human being is best understood through connections to a web of relationships, the soil that nourishes the human condition that shapes our lives. We invite unnecessary conflict when we do not consider the sociality of communicative life. The revelatory space that emerges between persons in conversation and conflict enhances our sociality.

RELATIONAL PERCEPTION AND REVELATORY SPACE

Individualism ignores the sociality of communicative engagement with another. The web of human relationships includes multiple persons and manifold perceptions of one another. The communicative region between self and other is a revelatory space of perception that gives rise to information that would likely go unnoticed without communicative interaction with another. We perceive what would otherwise go undetected. The communicative revelatory space *between* persons is uncontrolled, giving birth to ideas and perceptions owned by neither party.

Various theorists have pointed to the perceptual space of the "between" and its revelatory qualities, such as the transactional model of communication, **coordinated management of meaning,** and **symbolic interaction**. John Stewart's (2009) transactional model of communication examines the interconnected relationships of self and other. Pearce and Cronen's (1980) coordinated management of meaning discusses the ongoing complexity of bringing diverse perspectives of meaning. **George Herbert Mead's** (1934) symbolic interaction theory examines different images of "I" and "me" (pp. 173–178) where communicative interaction becomes the main shaper of self-concept in relationship to the other.

GEORGE HERBERT MEAD (1863–1931)
was an American philosopher who was influential to social psychology and pragmatism. He studied at Oberlin College and Harvard University before teaching at the University of Michigan and the University of Chicago. Mead never published; his students published posthumously four edited volumes of his work ("George Herbert Mead," 2013).

Martin Buber outlined one of the better-known relational descriptions of multiple perceptions. He described six relational perceptions that define the perceptual meeting of two people (Arnett, 1981): (1) my image of myself; (2) my image of the other; (3) my image of the other's image of me; (4) the other's image of the other; (5) the other's image of me; and (6) the other's image of my image of the other. Buber stated that we cannot control or possess the image of self or other; each perception of self and other is negotiated in the everyday complexity of communicative life with others. Attending to multiple images of self and other reminds us of the complexity of relational perception.

Buber (1947/2002) discussed three ways in which this act of perception takes place: (1) "observing," (2) "looking on," and (3) "becoming aware" (p. 10). **Observing** attends to details about another, acknowledging the characteristics of the person. Observing is an initial reminder that one is not alone. **Looking on** involves perceiving the other in relationship within a larger context. The onlooker understands the other as part of a greater whole. The onlooker does not attend to the particular other, but does recognize the embeddedness of the other in a given place. **Becoming aware** focuses on the specific person, responding in a unique fashion to the other (Buber, 1965/1988). The perceptual act of becoming aware of the other invites the possibility of emergent and unexpected ideas that arise "between" persons (Buber, 1947/2002). The revelatory space "between" persons invites a perceptual terrain open to the unexpected. Through observing, looking on, and becoming aware, one engages in several dimensions of perceptions with the other in the terrain of everyday communicative life.

Perception via observing, looking on, and becoming aware points to the danger of conflict invited by perceptual thoughtlessness. Arendt (1963/2006) considered "thoughtlessness" as the root of great social danger. In novel form, **Sinclair Lewis** (1922), a 1930 recipient of the Nobel Prize for literature, offered such a critique of thoughtlessness in a novel about the everyday life of a common businessman. *Babbitt* is a reminder of the danger of thoughtless conformity (Lewis, 1922), which Arendt contended fueled the heart of a "banality of evil" (Arendt, 1963/2006). Dialogue and alertness to revelatory space between persons is a practical communicative counter to thoughtlessness; one must engage others and the communicative environment.

SINCLAIR LEWIS (1885–1951)
was an American novelist and social critic who, in 1930, was the first American recipient of the Nobel Prize for Literature ("Sinclair Lewis," 2013).

The key to relational perception is that it honors the uniqueness of others. The revelatory space is a constructive, relational decision-making space "between" (Buber, 1947/2002, p. 5) persons. The **space of the between** is an ontological reality that offers an opportunity for creativity of discovery in a conversational space. The "between" lives within the relationship itself. Buber's (1947/2002) notion of the between is akin to what Calvin Schrag (1986) called a "space of subjectivity" (p. 11) that takes information, context, and partners in the conversation seriously. Schrag stated that the space of subjectivity consists of the "by," "for," and "about" of communication (p. ix). Relationally, communication is by someone, for someone, and about something; this space of subjectivity is a dwelling owned by no one. Individual content shared in the communication makes the relational reality of the between possible. Each party brings something of substance to the communicative exchange. The subjective space of the between can be invited with communicative content that originates with each communicative partner. However, the revelatory insight of the "between" cannot be demanded.

We cannot mandate that the other take the relationship and the communicative environment seriously. If we do so, we seek to colonize the other—moving from an invitational realm that constitutes the "between" to a possessive act of domination (Fritz, 2013). The invitational space of the "between" is the home of dialogue and allows persons to discern insights that would remain elusive without relational connections.

The word dialogue originated from the Greek word *dialogos* (dia means "through" and logos means "the word") (Garmston & Wellman, 1998, p. 32). Words shared between persons give insight into the unexpected, thereby shaping our relational lives. Within the discipline of communication, considerable scholarship has been devoted to dialogue.[1] W. Barnett Pearce and Kimberly A. Pearce (2004) stated that dialogue finds form in the content of "concepts and traditions of practice" (p. 55). The "between" of dialogue is rich in content, generated by both parties and owned by neither.

There are multiple conceptualizations of **dialogue**, as the diverse work of Hans-Georg Gadamer, Jürgen Habermas, **Paulo Freire**, and **Mikhail Bakhtin** attest (Anderson, Baxter, & Cissna, 2004). Diverse dialogic perspectives stress "authentic human life with dialogic meeting" (Anderson et al., 2004, pp. 3–4) and the fundamental importance of attending to the other. Hans-Georg Gadamer (1976, 1982) denotes dialogue as central in engagement with the historical moment, requiring interaction of questioning and responding. Jürgen Habermas (1971, 1975, 1979, 1984, 1987) locates dialogue in the communicative discernment process in public contexts that invite discourse with differing opinions, with each requiring consideration. Paulo Freire's (1970/2000) philosophy of dialogue includes the notion of literacy and concern for the oppressed. Freire reserved dialogue for those pursuing literacy. The desire for learning opens up the possibilities for listening and engaging the other in the space of the between. Mikhail Bakhtin (1981, 1984, 1986) explored dialogue through language and the human condition, understanding the essence of life as revealed via dialogic possibilities. Dialogic approaches stress the revelatory with some conception of revelatory space, the "between" in dialogue.

PAULO FREIRE (1921–1997)
was a Brazilian educator whose most well-known work was *Pedagogy of the Oppressed* (1970). Freire displayed an innovative teaching style that empowered marginalized populations ("Paulo Freire," 2013).

MIKHAIL BAKHTIN (1895–1975)
was a Russian philosopher and literary theorist. His work focuses on cultural history, linguistics, literary theory, and aesthetics ("Mikhail Bakhtin," 2013).

---

1. Ronald C. Arnett's (1992) book *Dialogic Education: Conversations About Ideas and Between People*; Rob Anderson, Kenneth N. Cissna, and Ronald C. Arnett's (1994) edited book *The Reach of Dialogue: Confirmation, Voice and Community*; Leslie A. Baxter and Barbara M. Montgomery's (1996) book *Relating: Dialogue and Dialectics*; Rob Anderson, Leslie A. Baxter, and Kenneth N. Cissna's (2004) edited book *Dialogue: Theorizing Difference in Communication Studies*; and Arnett, Fritz and Bell's (2009) book *Communication Ethics Literacy: Dialogue and Difference* are just a few of the books that have stressed the importance of dialogue. Moreover, a special issue of *Communication Theory* (Anderson & Cissna, 2008) focused on dialogue.

Martin Buber's (1947/2002) notion of the "between" is the most well-known discussion of relational space. Genuine dialogue attends to the realm of the "between," including the communicative practices of listening to the other, trying to "experience the other side" of the relationship (Friedman, 1955, p. 87), and attending to the perspective of the other. Genuine dialogue turns toward the other with the intention of establishing a mutual relationship that has the possibility of transforming oneself and the other as one gives up the demand for possession—the space of the "between" can nourish chances to resolve conflict together.

On September 11, 2001, Greg Rodriguez died in the attacks on the World Trade Center. In November 2002, Phyllis Rodriguez, Greg's mother, had the opportunity to meet Aicha el-Wafi whose son, Zacarias Moussaoui, was tried in relation to the attacks and is currently serving a life sentence. Since that time, the two mothers have attended events together throughout Europe and the United States, telling their story of tragedy and friendship. In 2007, el-Wafi and Rodriguez received the German Quadriga Award in Berlin, an award given for humanitarianism and welfare. An unexpected and unexplainable bond nourished the relationship that grew "between" them. Each person had to recognize the other without colonizing the other's experiences. Both mothers gave up the demand for possession, leaving their individual grief and discovering a transformative relationship. Buber's notion of the "between" describes the space connecting Rodriguez and el-Wafi where genuine dialogue emerges and opens the door for healing, even from such tragic events. Their friendship is a symbol of forgiveness and genuine dialogue (Wilkinson, 2011) that emerged from the revelatory space of the "between." The space of the "between" is an ethical welcome for conversation where unexpected insight can turn conflict into opportunity for each party.

The relational nature of the "between" is both revelatory and a carrier of hope for new possibilities and insights. Courtney Waite Miller, Michael E. Roloff, and Rachel M. Reznik's (2014) essay "Hopelessness and Interpersonal Conflict: Antecedents and Consequences of Losing Hope" suggests that relational hopelessness invites hostility in argument and little relational attentiveness. Feeling immersed in hopelessness and an inability to be taken seriously by the Other enhances a decline in motivation, inviting disconfirmation of the Other and a discounting of the Other enacted in avoidance. Ongoing feelings of hopelessness bring forth irretractable conflict and changes in the relationship, moving increasingly to distance in ongoing hostility. Hopelessness requires an encounter in which both parties support and attend to relational maintenance. Such activity is akin to gardening in which one tills the soil or, in this case, attends to a relationship in hopes that new things will grow and prosper. The "between" cannot be demanded; but, without relational maintenance, the revelatory reality of new insights will not transpire.

The first practical step in the invitation of the "between," this revelatory space, is attentive listening to positions contrary to our own. To explicate the importance of a nondemanding understanding of dialogue and the "between," Arnett (2015) emphasizes monologue as the pragmatic fulcrum point for the invitation of dialogue. This perspective assumes that conflicts driven by significant points of controversy involve worldviews and opinions that are substantial and housed in conviction. To understand another, one must first comprehend the monologic point of conviction that propels another. Dialogue does not begin with the rejection of monologue, but rather with attentiveness to it with the possibility that points of conviction might later reflect revelatory new insights for both persons. Taking a monologic position of another seriously recovers the possibility for civic dialogue (Arnett, 2014). People fight, argue, and struggle for locality that matters to them. Attending ever so carefully to monologic endorsements permits one to understand what matters to another and the listening possibly invites an opening for new insights between persons to emerge.

FRAMING COMMUNICATIVE LEADERSHIP: RELATIONAL PERCEPTION

> *Conflict is not a dirty word, despite the fact that many people think it has no place in discussion. Actually, conflict is integral to effective problem solving; without it, discussion cannot be maximally effective. When conflict is properly managed it stimulates thought, increases the intensity of analysis and deliberation, and invigorates the interaction climate. (Wood, 1992, p. 226)*

The eighth chapter in *The Art of Framing: Managing the Language of Leadership* discusses the importance of mutual framing (Fairhurst & Sarr, 1996). Leadership is a relational and perceptual task. Not only are situations, visions, and people framed, but, more importantly, so are relationships. We frame our connections with one another. "Credibility" requires mutual or relational framing (Fairhurst & Sarr, 1996, p. 171). We are unable to impose the "believability" of leadership upon others (Fairhurst & Sarr, 1996, p. 171). Others bestow relational confidence upon a given leader; one does not lead by demand, but from the support of others. For leadership actions to have a lasting impact, others must confer relational credibility upon a leader.

Fairhurst and Sarr (1996) state the needed ingredients for preparation for framing:

1. **Credibility** requires doing excellent work and engaging in practices that demonstrate constructive leadership. Credibility does not emerge from the abstract or from self-proclamation. Credibility emerges from a "web of relationships" (Simmel, 1908/1955) that confirm one's ability to lead.
2. **A moral compass** is necessary as one leads. There are times one must struggle against the dark side of relationships announced all too often through "jealousy and envy" (Simmel 1908/1955). Sometimes relational connections are more painful than supportive. This reality cannot curtail the requirement to lead.
3. **Believability** rejects abstraction and individualism. A leader must engage a unique set of people in a given place.
4. **How** one frames determines whether smart ideas are going to be heard by others. The "how" of framing opens the door for dialogue that invites co-constitutive framing.

This chapter concludes with a story from one of the best-known peacemakers, who understands the power of relational framing. **Mahatma Gandhi** (Figure 6.2) was a leader in India's nationalist movement against British rule; he engaged in conflict and rebellion with a relational attentiveness. Gandhi gathered criticism for his relational maintenance with his opponents as he engaged in his nonviolent campaigning for social change. Gandhi understood the dialogic character of conflict and the necessity of being relationally attentive to all, even to those with whom he was in serious opposition (Arnett, 1980). Granted, few of us compare to the ethical commitments of Mahatma Gandhi, but serious conflicts still require relational concern for the opposition.

FIGURE 6.2   Mahatma Gandhi on a rupee note.

© SNEHIT/Shutterstock.com

MAHATMA GANDHI (1869–1948) was the leader of the Indian nationalist movement and is considered the father of India. Gandhi's nonviolent protest tactics are well known ("Mohandas Karamchand Gandhi," 2013).

REFERENCES

Anderson, R., Baxter, L. A., & Cissna, K. N. (Eds.). (2004). *Dialogue: Theorizing difference in communication studies*. Thousand Oaks, CA: Sage.

Anderson, R., & Cissna, K. N. (2008). Fresh perspectives in dialogue theory. *Communication Theory, 18*, 1–4.

Anderson, R., Cissna, K. N., Arnett, R. C. (1994). *The reach of dialogue: Confirmation, voice, and community*. Cresskill, NJ: Hampton Press.

Arendt, H. (1994). *The origins of totalitarianism*. New York, NY: Harcourt, Inc. (Original work published 1948)

—. (2006). *Eichmann in Jerusalem: A report on the banality of evil*. New York, NY: Penguin Books. (Original work published 1963)

Aristotle. (Trans. 1999). *The Nicomachean ethics* (T. Irwin, Trans.). Indianapolis, IN: Hackett Publishing.

Arnett, R. C. (1980). *Dwell in peace: Applying nonviolence to everyday relationships*. Elgin, IL: Brethren Press.

—. (1981). Toward a phenomenological dialogue. *Western Journal of Speech Communication, 45*, 201–212.

—. (1992). *Dialogic education: Conversations about ideas and between people*. Carbondale: Southern Illinois University Press.

—. (2006). Professional civility: Reclaiming organizational limits. In J. M. H. Fritz & B. L. Omdahl (Eds.), *Problematic relationships in the workplace* (pp. 233–248). New York, NY: Peter Lang.

—. (2014). Civic dialogue: Attending to locality and recovering monologue. *Journal of Dialogue Studies, 2*(2), 71–92.

—. (2015). The dialogic necessity: An acknowledging and engaging monologue. *Ohio Communication Journal, 53*, 1–10.

Arnett, R. C., Fritz, J. M. H., & Bell, L. M. (2009). *Communication ethics literacy: Dialogue & difference*. Thousand Oaks, CA: Sage.

Ayer, A. J. (1968). *The origins of pragmatism: Studies in the philosophy of Charles Sanders Peirce and William James*. San Francisco, CA: Freeman Cooper & Co.

Bakhtin, M. M. (1981). *The dialogic imagination: Four essays by M. M. Bakhtin* (M. Holquist, Ed., C. Emerson, & M. Holquist, Trans.). Austin: University of Texas Press.

—. (1984). *Problems of Dostoevsky's poetics* (C. Emerson, Ed. & Trans.). Minneapolis: University of Minnesota Press.

—. (1986). *Speech genres and other late essays* (C. Emerson & M. Holquist, Eds.; V. W. McGee, Trans.). Austin: University of Texas Press.

Baxter, L. A., & Montgomery, B. M. (1996). *Relating: Dialogue and dialectics*. New York, NY: Guilford Press.

Berg, R. (2012). The anonymity factor in making multicultural teams work: Virtual and real teams. *Business Communication Quarterly, 75*, 404–424.

Bishop, M., & Green, M. (2008). *Philanthrocapitalism: How giving can save the world*. New York, NY: Bloomsbury Press.

Buber, M. (2002). *Between man and man* (R. G. Smith, Trans.). New York, NY: Macmillan. (Original work published 1947)

—. (1988). *The knowledge of man: Selected essays* (M. S. Friedman, Ed.). Amherst, NY: Humanity Books. (Original book published 1965)

Buunk, A. P., Carmona, C., Peiró, J. M., Dijkstra, A., & Dijkstra, P. (2011). Social comparison at work: The role of culture, type of organization and gender. *Cross-Cultural Communication, 7*, 22–34.

Canary D. J., & Lakey, S. G. (2006). Managing conflict in a competent manner: A mindful look at events that matter. In J. G. Oetzel & S. Ting-Toomey (Eds.), *Sage handbook of conflict communication* (pp. 185–210). Thousand Oaks, CA: Sage.

Cervantes, M. (1993). *Don Quixote*. Hertfordshire: Wadsworth Editions Limited. (Original work published 1604)

Collins, R. L. (1996). For better or worse: The impact of upward social comparison on self-evaluations. *Psychological Bulletin, 119*, 51–69.

Coughlin, S. (2016). Why we're still not over the Tonya Harding & Nancy Kerrigan scandal. *Refinery 29*. Retrieved from http://www.refinery29.com/2016/08/120575/tonya-harding-nancy-kerrigan-attacked-olympic-ice-skaters

De Tocqueville, A. (1963). *Democracy in America* (H. Reeve, Trans.). New York, NY: Schocken Books (Original work published 1835, Vol. 1; 1840, Vol. 2)

Defoe, D. (1862). *The adventures of Robinson Crusoe*. London: S. O. Beeton. (Original work published 1719)

Don Juan. (2013). In *Encyclopaedia Britannica Online*. Retrieved from http://www.britannica .com/EBchecked/topic/168882/Don-Juan

Don Quixote. (2013). In *Encyclopaedia Britannica Online*. Retrieved from http://www.britannica .com/EBchecked/topic/1475288/Don-Quixote

Dowd, K. E. (2014, February). Nancy Kerrigan speaks out about Tonya Harding 20 years after the infamous scandal. *People*. Retrieved from http://people.com/sports/ nancy-kerrigan-speaks-out-about-tonya-harding-20-years-after-infamous-scandal/

Fairhurst, G. T., & Sarr, R. A. (1996). *The art of framing: Managing the language of leadership*. San Francisco, CA: Jossey-Bass Publishers.

Faust. (2013). In *Encyclopaedia Britannica Online*. Retrieved from http://www.britannica .com/EBchecked/topic/202814/Faust

Ferguson, A. (2004). *An essay on the history of civil society*. Kila, MT: Kessinger. (Original work published 1767)

Freire, P. (2000). *Pedagogy of the oppressed* (Special Anniversary Edition) (M. B. Ramos, Trans.). New York, NY: Continuum Press. (Original work published 1970)

Friedman, M. (1955). *Martin Buber: The life of dialogue*. New York, NY: Harper and Brothers.

Fritz, J. M. H. (2013). *Professional civility: Communicative virtue at work*. New York, NY: Peter Lang.

Gadamer, H. G. (1976). *Philosophical hermeneutics* (D. E. Linge, Ed. & Trans.). Berkeley: University of California Press.

—. (1982). *Truth and method* (2nd ed.) (G. Barden & J. Cumming, Trans.). New York, NY: Crossroad.

Garmston, R., & Wellman, B. (1998). Teacher talk that makes a difference. *Educational Leadership, 55*, 30–34.

Georg Simmel. (2013). In *Encyclopaedia Britannica Online*. Retrieved from http://www .britannica.com/EBchecked/topic/545139/Georg-Simmel

George Herbert Mead. (2013). In *Encyclopaedia Britannica Online*. Retrieved from http://www .britannica.com/EBchecked/topic/371433/George-Herbert-Mead

Guerrero, L. K., & Andersen, P. A. (1998). The dark side of jealousy and envy: Desire, delusion, desperation, and destructive communication. In B. H. Spitzberg & W. R. Cupach (Eds.), *The dark side of close relationships* (pp. 33–70). Mahwah, NJ: Erlbaum.

Guerrero, L. K., Andersen, P. A., Jorgensen, P. F., Spitzberg, B. H., & Eloy, S. V. (1995). Coping with the green-eyed monster: Conceptualizing and measuring communicative responses to romantic jealousy. *Western Journal of Communication, 59*, 270–304.

Guerrero, L. K., Trost, M. R., & Yoshimura, S. M. (2005). Romantic jealousy: Emotions and communicative responses. *Personal Relationships, 12*, 233–252.

Gulas, C. S., & McKeage, K. (2000). Extending social comparison: An examination of the unintended consequences of idealized advertising imagery. *Journal of Advertising, 29*, 17–28.

Habermas, J. (1971). *Knowledge and human interests* (J. J. Shapiro, Trans.). Boston, MA: Beacon Press.

—. (1975). *Legitimation crisis* (T. McCarthy, Trans.). Boston, MA: Beacon Press.

—. (1979). *Communication and the evolution of society* (T. McCarthy, Trans.). Boston, MA: Beacon Press.

—. (1984). *The theory of communicative action: Volume 1, Reason and the rationalization of society* (T. McCarthy, Trans.). Boston, MA: Beacon Press.

—. (1987). *The theory of communicative action: Volume 2, Life world and system: A critique of functionalist reason* (T. McCarthy, Trans.). Boston, MA: Beacon Press.

Harish, A. (2012, August 1). The attack on Nancy Kerrigan. *ABC News*. Retrieved January 30, 2013, from http://abcnews.go.com/Sports/olympics/tour-worst-olympics-scandals /story?id=16907278#1

Heilbroner, R. L. (1999). *The worldly philosophers: The lives, times, and ideas of the great economic thinkers*. New York, NY: Touchstone.

Hines, R. (2017, January). Tonya Harding movie 'I, Tonya' casts Caitlin Carver to play Nancy Kerrigan. *Today*. Retrieved from http://www.today.com/popculture/ tonya-harding-movie-i-tonya-casts-caitlin-carver-play-nancy-t107348

James, W. (2001). *Psychology: The briefer course*. Mineola, NY: Dover Publications. (Original work published 1892)

James Joyce. (2013). In *Encyclopaedia Britannica Online*. Retrieved from http://www.britannica .com/EBchecked/topic/306875/James-Joyce

Lewis, S. (1922). *Babbitt*. New York, NY: Harcourt, Brace and Company, Inc.

Lyubomirsky, S., & Ross, L. (1997). Hedonic consequences of social comparison: A contrast of happy and unhappy people. *Journal of Personality and Social Psychology, 73*, 1141–1157.

Markoff, J. (1997, August 7). Microsoft comes to aid of rival Apple. *New York Times*. Retrieved May 25, 2013, from http://partners.nytimes.com/library/cyber/week/080797apple.html

Mead, G. H. (1934). *Mind, self, and society*. Chicago, IL: University of Chicago Press.

Meeker, K. (2002). *Philosophy of religion: A reader and guide*. Edinburgh: Edinburgh University Press.

Mikhail Bakhtin. (2013). In *Encyclopaedia Britannica Online*. Retrieved from http://www .britannica.com/EBchecked/topic/49580/Mikhail-Bakhtin

Miller, C. W., Roloff, M. E., & Reznik, R. M. (2014). Hopelessness and interpersonal conflict: Antecedents and consequences of losing hope. *Western Journal of Communication, 78*(5), 563–585.

Mohandas Karamchand Gandhi. (2013). In *Encyclopaedia Britannica Online*. Retrieved from http://www.britannica.com/EBchecked/topic/225216/Mohandas-Karamchand-Gandhi

Paulo Freire. (2013). In *Encyclopaedia Britannica Online*. Retrieved from http://www .britannica.com/EBchecked/topic/218854/Paulo-Freire

Pearce, W. B., & Cronen, V. E. (1980). *Communication 'action' and meaning: The creation of social realities*. New York, NY: Praeger.

Pearce, W. B.. & Pearce, K. A. (2004). Taking a communication perspective on dialogue. In R. Anderson, L. A. Baxter, & K. N. Cissna (Eds.), *Dialogue: Theorizing difference in communication studies* (pp. 39–56). Thousand Oaks, CA: Sage.

Rawlins, W. K. (1992). *Friendship matters: Communication, dialectics, and the life course*. Hawthorne, NY: Aldine de Gruyter.

—. (2009). *The compass of friendship: Narratives, identities, and dialogues*. Thousand Oaks, CA: Sage.

Robinson Crusoe. (2013). In *Encyclopaedia Britannica Online*. Retrieved from http://www .britannica.com/EBchecked/topic/1672908/Robinson-Crusoe

Schrag, C. O. (1986). *Communication praxis and the space of subjectivity*. Bloomington: Indiana University Press.

Simmel, G. (1955). *Conflict and The web of group affiliations*. (K, H. Wolff & R, Bendix, Trans.). New York, NY: The Free Press. (Original work 1908)

Sinclair Lewis. (2013). In *Encyclopaedia Britannica Online*. Retrieved from http://www.britannica.com/EBchecked/topic/338212/Sinclair-Lewis

Smith, A. (1925). *An inquiry into the nature and causes of the wealth of nations*. London: G. Bell and Sons. (Original book published 1776)

Sontag, S. (2003). *Regarding the pain of others*. New York, NY: Penguin.

Stewart. J. D. (2009). *Bridges not walls: A book about interpersonal communication* (10th ed.). Columbus, OH: McGraw-Hill.

Turner, J. H. (1993). *Classical sociological theory: A positivist's perspective*. Chicago, IL: Nelson-Hall.

Watt, I. (1996). *Myths of modern individualism: Faust, Don Quixote, Don Juan, Robinson Crusoe*. Cambridge, UK: University of Cambridge Press.

Wilkinson, P. (2011, September 2). Mother of 9/11 conspirator: I was blind to son's extremism. *CNN*. Retrieved on March 4, 2013, from http://www.cnn.com/2011/WORLD/europe/09/01/september.11.moussaoui.mother/index.html

William James. (2013). In *Encyclopaedia Britannica Online*. Retrieved from http://www.britannica.com/EBchecked/topic/299871/William-James

Wood, J. T. (1992). *Spinning the symbolic web: Human communication as symbolic interaction*. New York, NY: Ablex.

Young, S. L., Kubicka, T. L., Tucker, C. E., Chávez-Appel, D., & Rex, J. S. (2005). Communicative responses to hurtful messages in families. *Journal of Family Communication*, 5, 123–140.

Chapter Seven

EMOTION AND CONFLICT

Our passions, when well exercised, have wisdom; they guide our thinking, our survival. But they can easily go awry, and do so all too often. As Aristotle saw, the problem is not with emotionality, but with the appropriateness of emotion and its expression. The question is, how can we bring intelligence to our emotions—and civility to our streets and caring to our communal life. (Goleman, 1995/2005, p. xxiv)

"Emotion and Conflict" recognizes emotion as a temporary motivator for engaging interpersonal conflict. Conflict and emotion are common companions in an epoch played out in interpersonal dispute, an era defined by diverse and contradictory views of the good. This chapter's *Spotlight on Leadership* features Steve Jobs, cofounder of Apple Computers. His passion and emotion created successful products and ignited conflicts throughout his career.

© Bloomicon/Shutterstock.com

Steve Jobs revolutionized modern technology, including the iPod, iPhone, and iPad. He died in 2011 after the debilitating effects of pancreatic cancer.

Emotion provides energy and motivation for engaging interpersonal conflict. An emotional response offers a "why" for contending with problematic issues. Emotions act as mandates and rationales for meeting interpersonal disputes, reminding us why something matters sufficiently to call forth conflict engagement.

Emotions provide vitality that can propel us constructively and sometimes move us in problematic directions. Research has shown that emotions have both a positive and negative influence on a student's academic journey (Blair, 2002; Raver, 2002; Valiente, Swanson, & Eisenberg, 2012). The emotions of joy, hope, and pride positively correlate with students' overall achievement in courses, academic interest, and effort put into courses (Pekrun et al., 2004). In contrast, negative emotions such as sadness and fear result in lower achievement scores and grade point averages (Gumora & Arsenio, 2002). Emotions have a lasting impact on our personal and professional lives. For example, Steven Slater, a JetBlue flight attendant who was dealing with the death of his father and his mother's cancer diagnosis, erupted in an emotional outburst that led to charges filed against him. On a flight from Pittsburgh to New York, Slater received a blow to the head from a passenger's bag, taken abruptly from an overhead compartment; the passenger refused to apologize. Slater vented his frustration at the entire plane, utilizing the public address system. He then grabbed beer from the galley and activated the evacuation slide so he could exit the plane. He later pled guilty to attempted criminal mischief and agreed to undergo counseling and substance abuse treatment. After completing the court-ordered counseling treatment program, he received a sentence of 1-year probation. Emotion and passion form a fuel that energizes, and sometimes such emotional combustion misdirects. One might surmise that Slater's emotional outburst was completely negative—yet the outcome permitted him to get counseling and reminded a public that flight attendants also have emotions. Flight attendants must undertake the "emotional labor" (Hochschild, 1983/2003; Murphy, 1998) of "managing" emotions (Omdahl, 2012). Managing emotion is demanded because of issues related to branding, the nature of service, and threats to emotional work (Omdahl, 2012, p. 24). Emotional labor requires practicing self-control and self-constraint when managing expression (Omdahl, 2012, p. 27).

INTRODUCTION

Terms such as "emotional intelligence" (Mayer & Salovey, 1997; Mikolajczak, Balon, Rousi, & Kotsou, 2012; Salovey & Mayer, 1990) and "emotional labor" (Hochschild, 1983/2003; Kruml & Geddes, 2000; Morris & Feldman, 1996; Rafaeli & Sutton, 1987) announce the importance of human feeling in our communicative lives. Emotion awakens us to the need to involve ourselves in necessary conflict action. This chapter suggests that appropriate emotion is ideally attentive and responsive to the conflict situation at hand, not misdirected by one's prior emotional state, as illustrated by the JetBlue example.

In "Emotion and Conflict," we explore three major sections:

1. **Emotional awareness: An awakening** discusses the importance of paying attention to all our senses, which generally offer insight prior to developing analytic clarity on ideas;
2. **Attending to advance notice: Emotional intelligence** examines the connection between emotion and an appropriate response to a unique situation;
3. **Framing communicative leadership: Emotional alerts** highlight the importance of leaders using emotion in the meeting and framing of conflict.

We can experience a vast number of **emotions**. Positive emotions consist of amusement, awe, compassion, contentment, gratitude, hope, interest, joy, love, and pride, whereas negative emotions include anger, contempt, guilt, disgust, embarrassment, sadness, fear, and shame (Cohn, Fredrickson, Brown, Mikels, & Conway, 2009). Positive emotions are more difficult to observe and differentiate because they occur more naturally in individuals (Ekman, 1992; Ellsworth & Smith, 1988). As we engage with other people, we can easily notice when someone is expressing negative emotions. For example, when a close friend is having a bad day you may observe sadness and anger; whereas, when a close friend is having a great day, you are not as aware of the joyful emotions. Moreover, researchers are more inclined to focus on the negative outcomes that create problems to be solved (Valiente, Swanson, & Eisenberg, 2012). The ethics of emotion teeter on the Aristotelian (trans. 1992) reminder of "excess" (too much) and "deficiency" (too little) (p. 16). The emotional standard for understanding the difference between excess and deficiency is situationally dependent. Emotions both cloud and clarify perceptions of a particular place. The functional good of emotions in conflict is that they alert us to what matters, the ethical good that one seeks to protect and promote.

EMOTIONAL AWARENESS: AN AWAKENING

Gross (2010) discusses how research on human emotions traces back to **Charles Darwin's** (1872) seminal work, *The Expression of the Emotions in Man and Animals*. Darwin's work revealed consistency in emotional expression that underscores the theory of evolution. For example, he found similarities in how the lips of a chimpanzee protrude much like the pouting lips of a child when illustrating disappointment (Figure 7.1) (Gross, 2010). The study of human emotion has roots in anthropology, sociology, history, psychology, and, of course, the hard sciences of biology and chemistry (Visser, 2008, p. 265), with communication research suggesting that emotion manifests five themes. First, emotions are a response to stimuli that may disrupt or enrich one's goals (Guerrero & La Valley, 2006, p. 70). Individuals sense the emotion of happiness as they achieve goals and witness constructive results. Second, affect is a fundamental element of one's emotional experience (Guerrero & La Valley, 2006, p. 70), generating emotions as we respond to various stimuli. A specific emotion may not be evident until one interprets and labels one's feelings about a particular setting. Third, physiological changes often accompany emotional reactions (Guerrero & La Valley, 2006, p. 70), which influence demonstrative intensity. Fourth, cognition assists with interpreting emotional responses (Guerrero & La Valley, 2006, p. 70) as one assigns blame and/or praise in conflict

FIGURE 7.1   Pouting chimpanzee

events. Fifth, different emotions produce various actions and "behavioral profiles" (Guerrero & La Valley, 2006, p. 70) tied to diverse emotions, such as anger, violence, fear, and avoidance.

Emotion has complex implications for conflict engagement, affecting interactions with family and friends, workplace colleagues, and responses to strangers. In conflict, one's communication often finds origin in emotional responses (Guerrero & La Valley, 2006). Research indicates that no one set of generally accepted rules governs emotional cues; appropriate emotional responses are contextual. As Rajah, Song, and Arvey (2011) noted, "similar events may lead to different emotions, similar emotions may be associated with different outcomes, and different emotions may be related with the same indicators" (p. 1108). For example, Kramer and Hess (2002) stated that in the organizational context, six emotional rules are central to defining the communicative setting: (1) express emotions in a professional manner, maintaining control over the feelings; (2) express emotions to improve circumstances, seeking to prevent or correct problems; (3) express emotions to the appropriate person at the appropriate time and in the appropriate manner; (4) express emotions that assist and support others; (5) express emotions appropriate to one's organizational role; and (6) curtail the impulse to express emotions for personal benefit that are detrimental to others. Outside of a professional organizational setting, we move quickly from one emotion to another. However, within a formal setting, consistency and predictability are advantageous.

Common emotions associated with conflict include anger, jealousy, hurt, and guilt (Guerrero & La Valley, 2006, p. 74). Permitted to go unchecked, such emotions can destroy relationships (Sanford, 2007a, 2007b). We examined "envy" and "jealousy" (Simmel, 1908/1955) in Chapter 6, "Relational Perception in Conflict." Anger is described by Raymond W. Novaco (2000) in the *Encyclopedia of Psychology* as emotion characterized by antagonism toward someone or something that is "wrong." Hurt entails reaction to what another says or does to one. Guilt arises from regret for treating another unjustly (Guerrero & La Valley, 2006); guilt connects behavior to a narrative of importance. One's capacity to navigate a variety of emotions in conflict situations displays "**emotional resilience**" (Sergeant & Laws-Chapman, 2012, p. 14). Emotional resilience permits one to adapt to various communicative conditions.

Emotion presents power and strength that, at times, are almost supernatural. Consider, for example, Tony Cavallo, a high school junior, who was working on a car when the jack collapsed, pinning him underneath. Angela Cavallo, Tony's mother, who was in her late 50's, lifted the 1964 Chevy Impala off of her teenage son and held it for almost five minutes until neighbors were able to pull Tony out from underneath the car (Beck, 2011; Golden, 2011). The power of human emotional impulses were central to **Dylan Thomas's** (1951/2001) contention that we must "rage, rage against the dying of the light" in his poem "Do Not Go Gentle into that Good Night," displaying emotion and passion to the last breath. Emotions remind us of what matters and is worthy of conflict.

A well-known description of emotion and passion displayed to the very end comes from **Elisabeth Kübler-Ross** (1969/1997), who recorded stages of human emotion via interviews with dying patients. In *On Death and Dying*, Kübler-Ross outlines five stages of emotional responses to the existential reality of oncoming death (Figure 7.2). The first emotional stage is "denial and isolation" (pp. 38–49), which permits the suppression of unwanted news, allowing time to process the situation. Denial then yields to the second emotional stage, "anger" (pp. 50–81), which through "partial acceptance" (p. 40) generates a response of "rage, envy, and resentment" (p. 50) that is often displaced in multiple directions such as onto family members, doctors, nurses, and God. The third emotional stage, "bargaining" (pp. 82–84), enters into a mythical agreement to postpone death (p. 83). In the fourth stage, "depression" (pp.

© *marekuliasz/Shutterstock.com*

FIGURE 7.2   Five stages of grief.

85–111), anger and rage complement a sense of loss, sadness, guilt, and shame. "Acceptance" (pp. 112–137), the final emotional stage, is not happiness, but rather a form of existential acknowledgement—life ends for each of us (p. 100). Acceptance embraces the final stand against the inevitable (Frankl, 1959/2006). Emotions have a direction, unlike what we would commonly term a "mood" (Burleson & Planalp, 2000; Frijda, 1993, 1987).

ELISABETH KÜBLER-ROSS (1926–2004)
was an American psychiatrist who was born in Switzerland. Her work focuses on the study of terminally ill patients, death, and dying. Her most well-known work, *On Death and Dying*, published in 1969, outlined the five stages of grief ("Elisabeth Kübler-Ross," 2013).

All of us experience rapid shifts in moods and emotions. A bad mood clouds one's experience in a dismal grey while a good mood lightens up one's day. Moods and emotions are constantly changing as we engage the other and the world. Emotions react to a specific stimulus or event (Frijda, 1993), whereas **moods** are more general (Frijda, 1987) and can last for longer periods of time (Frijda, 2009). Burleson and Planalp (2000) stated that moods are "global and diffuse in character, tend to be less intense states than emotions, are comparatively enduring (often lasting for many minutes, even hours), and usually are not tied to any particular provoking incident" (p. 223). Mood states affect communication (Burleson & Planalp, 2000), judgment (Sinclair & Mark, 1992), and attitude (Nichols & Schumann, 2012). Moods are more general than emotions, categorized on a continuum from an experience of a bad mood to being in a good mood (Morris, 1992), with each extreme influencing interpersonal interactions (Householder & Wong, 2011) and relationships (Morse & Volkman, 2010). Forgas (1998, 1999) found that persons in bad moods display higher levels of competitiveness and indirectness in their communication with others than people in good moods. In contrast, Carlson, Charlin, and Miller (1988) found that those in good moods generate a positive social outlook on life, experiencing a higher quality of social support than those in bad moods (Egbert, 2003).

Martin Heidegger (1962/2008) articulated that we are situated in the world and propelled by existential moods.[1] Moods come from being in the world; they not only propel us into action but also shift our understanding of existence. Moods and emotions walk hand in hand, framing our perception of conflict. Life is more than information and empirical data; both moods and emotions shape interpretive lives. Emotions and moods contour perception, giving us a powerful sense of what matters and yielding to conflict as a natural outcome when what is important to us meets challenge and/or resistance.

MARTIN HEIDEGGER (1889–1976)
was a German philosopher whose work explored ontology and metaphysics. He was a student of Edmund Husserl at the University of Freiburg, where he later taught from 1919 until 1923. Heidegger then became a professor at the University of Marburg, where he taught Hannah Arendt. Heidegger's Being and Time, published in 1927, generated world acclaim. From 1933 until 1934, Heidegger served as the elected rector of the University of Freiburg where he delivered "The Self-Assertion of the German University," his most controversial speech due to Heidegger's membership and seeming support for the Nazi Party ("Martin Heidegger," 2013).

We live with an existential fact: as emotions shift, they reframe how we understand and participate in existence. As we communicate about emotions, we alert others and ourselves to feelings that shape our lives together. We perceive relationships and conflict through the tinted glasses of emotion. For example, think of a girlfriend or boyfriend who engaged in an action that others considered an annoying habit, and while dating that person, you considered that habit endearing—in fact, wonderful. When, or if, the relationship falls apart, the response to the previously "endearing habit" shifts to disdain. One's perceptual world shifts and changes with emotions. Emotions influence our perceptions. As emotions shift, so does the "I" of perception.

Social media offer an opportunity for connection as well as disassociation. In "'I Don't Like You Any More': Facebook Unfriending by Israelis During the Israel-Gaza Conflict of 2014," Nicholas A. John and Shiva Dvir-Gvirsan (2015) examine how unfriending on Facebook offers interesting insights. The less ties one has to another, the more likely that unfriending quickly will occur. Such an insight is similar to the work of conflict theory founder, Georg Simmel (1908/1955). Unfriending can also provide an algorithm for a social media platform

1. Martin Heidegger (1962/2008) identifies the human being (the *Dasein*) in four parts: (1) concern, (2) being-toward-death, (3) existence, and (4) moods (*Stimmungen*).

to decide what information should be filtered in your direction. Unfriending has political implications for ties with other human beings and for the information made readily available to us by the controllers of social media platforms.

Unfriending in social media is one form of polarized communication as discussed by Maria Armoudian (2015) in "Constructing 'the Others' During Conflict: How Journalism's Norms and Structures Temper Extreme Portrayals." Partisan divides of us versus them and good versus evil frame discourse in a way that permits us to discount difference and otherness. Having a position encourages communication with undue commitment to a partisan position that denies the voice of the others and their opinions. The other becomes a stranger; indeed, the other becomes the discarded unimportant other.

When people use the phrase "I feel," the interaction is understood as centered on oneself (Samp, 2013, p. 90). Individuals concerned with achieving self-oriented goals employ an increased amount of self-focused messages such as "I am the person that matters here" (Samp, 2013, p. 90). At its best, an "I" statement reflects ownership of an emotion rather than enacting an accusatory response upon another (Kirchhoff, Wagner, & Strack, 2012). When using "I" statements, one explicitly personalizes the message and tries to refrain from holding others responsible for what is going on (Hess & Tucker, 1980). However, to use "I" before an emotional outburst without some prior consideration invites problems. Failure to monitor a fleeting emotive "I" can move relationships in destructive directions. The emotive "I" is but a partial presentation of the self.

Erving Goffman's (1959) classic work, *Presentation of Self in Everyday Life*, discusses how "individuals tend to treat the others present on the basis of the impression they give now about the past and the future" (p. 249). Goffman (1959) employs the analogy of theater to describe how individuals interact in face-to-face social settings. Goffman (1959) defines a performance as "all the activity of a given participant on a given occasion which serves to influence in any way any of the other participants" (p. 15). As one enacts a performance, each person presents the self to others while attempting to control and guide the impression one is making on others. Just as an actor presents a character to an audience, individuals are constantly presenting the self to others.

Impressions matter not only to others, but account for self-identity as well. Contemporary applications of Goffman's work on identity and presentation of self appear in blogging and Second Life (SL) contexts where users create avatars for participation in a virtual world (Bullingham & Vasconcelos, 2013) and in demanding communicative environments, such as drug and alcohol group therapy sessions (Becker, 2005). Emotions and moods propel us into conflict. Reflection upon emotions and moods can move us from outburst to impressions to presentations of the self in conflict that can lend confidence. In order to present an impression consistent with one's identity, one must first pay attention, taking notice of emotional reactions to issues that matter.

ATTENDING TO ADVANCE NOTICE: EMOTIONAL INTELLIGENCE

As emotions alter our participation in existence, the ground under our feet seems to shift. Emotions function as communicative alerts, offering advance notice of a change in existence. This emotional altering is a form of metacommunication that adds another layer to conversation, commenting on its significance and meaning. Ruesch and Bateson (1951/2009) defined **metacommunication** as "communication about communication" (p. 209). Their work offers a foundational contribution to the field of communication (Knapp, Daly, Albada, & Miller, 2002). In organizational communication, metacommunication is a strategy for discussing tensions associated with contradictory messages. Limiting metacommunication contributes to increased ambiguity in organizational messages that can lead to job stress or burnout (Tracy, 2004). In the field of instructional communication, metacommunication helps to make the classroom a more effective learning environment (Worley, Titsworth, Worlet, & Cornett-DeVito, 2007). Metacommunication helps students to assimilate newly acquired information into previously learned information (Ausubel, 2000). In political communication, Esser, Reinemann, and Fan (2001) describe the significance of metacommunication as journalists and public relations professionals analyze campaign speeches, which permits them to comment about the discourse resulting in multiple levels of investigation. Metacommunication is a reflective perspective on the significance of meaning that can be a warning to self and others, urging all to take notice of change that is afoot. Emotions function as metacommunication alerts, urging attention to a unique communicative context.

Different communicative milieus, intrapersonal and interpersonal, require us to navigate emotional terrain with great care or with what Hochschild (1983/2003) calls "emotional labor" (p. 7). She defines **emotional labor** as that which "requires one to induce or suppress feeling in order to sustain the outward countenance that produces the proper state of mind in others"

© Minerva Studio/Shutterstock.com

FIGURE 7.3 The "managed smile."

ers" (p. 7). Hochschild uses the term "emotional labor" to describe the nature of work in jobs where workers are expected to display certain emotions to satisfy the organization's role expectations. Hochschild stresses the difference between "surface acting" and "deep acting" to designate one's emotional connection to others in the organization (p. 33). For example, her original work looked at flight attendants in which the employee must put on the smile of surface acting.

The danger of the "managed smile" (Arnett, 1992, p. 114) emerges when an attendant breaks loose, as the JetBlue story depicted.

Emotional labor announces itself in various disciplines, including sociology, management, and communication (Fineman, 2000; Wharton, 1999) and has been studied in occupations such as restaurant servers (Leidner, 1993), flight attendants (Murphy, 1998), emergency call center workers (Shuler & Sypher, 2000), and cruise ship employees (Tracy, 2000). One understands that emotional labor brings exhaustion, but it also brings an ongoing inner conflict when verbalized frustration is not welcome. Individuals who perform this function are able to address negative conflict situations with a positive tone and outward appearance. Perhaps, the key to such emotionally draining jobs is that they generate a great deal of intrapersonal conflict.

One's emotional response to this change is consistent with Kant's (1764/2003) view of progress tied to the species; it generated "melancholy" (p. 47), disrupting emotional lives. On an everyday level, consider the following example of melancholy tied to the demand for individual progress. Let us imagine an energetic little boy who thought at an early age, "If only I could go to elementary school." Then, when he was in school, he found disenchantment and melancholy. Next, he thought perhaps the movement into junior high/middle school and then high school would bring greater happiness. But yet again, melancholy followed him. The young man's hope emerged again as he attended a good college and thought if he could find a wonderful major the world would be more enjoyable, only to have the shadows of disenchantment follow. The next step was graduate school, and he assumed that this change would cure him of melancholy, but alas, he was still disappointed. Then, the hope of marriage and children resulted in undue demands, as did the banality of work. Then came the thrill of the children leaving the nest, which should provide more time for creativity, but instead resulted in loneliness with the delight of retirement replaced by uselessness. Finally, the culmination of all this progress was death. As depressing as this scenario seems, we realize that wishing for what comes next does not always bring happiness, and indeed invites continual dissatisfaction. One must meet the world on its own terms and struggle with the demands of the moment. Such a time is before us now.

Kant's notion of progress as disconnected from the individual fits existential reality. We sit in the city of Pittsburgh, Pennsylvania, and reflect upon the closing of steel mills and the displaced families who had great jobs and then found themselves unemployed seemingly the next day. An estimated 30,000 steel worker jobs (Bednarzik & Szalanski, 2012) and 100,000 manufacturing jobs were lost in the Pittsburgh area during the 1980s (Bednarzik & Szalanski, 2012). Susan Swan (2003) writes that "families used to union wages and benefits now struggled to make ends meet with minimum wage jobs or government aid" (pp. 85–86). In Pittsburgh, the demise of manual labor union jobs called forth job growth from education, technology, and health care sectors. However, job growth in these areas did not bring about improved economic conditions for families affected by the closing of the steel mills (Swan, 2003). Unemployment was still as high at 27% in the Pittsburgh area during the 1980s (Klibanoff, 2016, para. 3). As Pittsburgh recovered from the devastating job losses, the city sought to assist the workers. The Community College of Allegheny County provided educational training free of cost. The city attempted to "reinvest and reinvent" (Klibanoff, 2016, para. 15) the city's mission and workforce.

Pittsburgh is just one example that illustrates the decline of manufacturing jobs reported by the Bureau of Labor Statistics and the U.S. Census Bureau; those who lost their jobs would not embrace the call of progress. According to the Bureau of Labor Statistics (2013), the unemployment rate in 2000 in the manufacturing industry was 3.5%, and by 2011, that percentage had risen to 9%. There were 361,000 job openings in the manufacturing industry in December 2000, compared to 218,000 in 2011. Manufacturing employees numbered 18 million in 1988 compared to 11 million in 2011 (Bureau of Labor Statistics, 2013). The emotional anger related to this change of circumstances defines a number of diverse groups challenging the circumstances that are disrupting the middle classes.

In the classic movie *Modern Times* (Chaplin, 1936), **Charlie Chaplin** plays a factory worker who is struggling to survive an organizational push toward progress. Chaplin participates in an experiment that requires workers to perform tasks while they eat. A feeding machine promises to increase assembly line productivity and efficiency, but it fails. Even if the machine had worked, it would have discouraged the workers from independent thought and time for reflection and relaxation. The push toward progress throughout the factory in other ways reveals the inefficiency of undue efficiency, as Chaplin suffers a nervous breakdown. Too much demand for the progress of efficiency can result in a major emotional alert, a breakdown.

Scholarship on the decline of the middle class (Davis & Huston, 1992; Foster & Wolfson, 2010; Kuttner, 1983) points to rising inequality (Danziger & Gottschalk, 1993) as distribution of income becomes more polarized. This trajectory encourages the rise of the affluent and the emergence of the new poor. Pressman (2007) describes four causes for the declining middle class in the United States: (1) demographic factors, (2) the loss of middle-class manufacturing jobs and the decline of labor unions, (3) unemployment resulting from the business cycle, and (4) government fiscal policy (p. 183). According to McCall and Percheski (2010), inequality in wages, earnings, and total family incomes in the United States has increased since 1980 (p. 332). Additionally, the level of inequality today, for both market income and disposable income, is greater than at any point in the past 40 years (McCall & Percheski, 2010), a trend that began in 1968 (Jones & Weinberg, 2000), and is continuing for the long term, according to the U.S. Census Bureau.

A major factor contributing to disparities in income is earnings inequality, with the gains primarily in the higher income quintiles. Executive base salary and bonus compensation tripled from 1970 to 2000 (Jensen, Murphy, & Wruck, 2004; McCall & Percheski, 2010). Today, a family has a 17% chance of its income dropping by more than half as compared to 7% in 1970 (Zuckerman, 2007, p. 72). The emotional response to this environment is clear.

Emotional alerts function as metacommunication, telling us that something is amiss. Our emotions rebel against the mantra of progress that attempts to silence emotional responses to change (Graetz & Smith, 2010). Emotional alerts call for thoughtful and reflective engagement. Of course change happens; however, one must attend to emotional alerts that call into question some forms of supposed progress. Insensitivity to emotional alerts invokes conflict.

Our emotional alerts demand a recalibration of the system (Barge, 2006) and can unmask myths that call us to remain emotionally silenced. Meeting the world with honest, creative engagement is the practical definition of **emotional intelligence**.

Although people experience varied and demanding emotional lives, we differ in the extent to which we identify, understand, regulate, and respond to our own emotions and those of others (Mikolajczak et al., 2012). Emotional intelligence unites various inquiries, viewing emotions as useful sources of information that assist in navigating the social environment (Salovey & Grewal, 2005, p. 281). For example, in marital life, emotional intelligence is an ability that helps couples traverse conflicts and contributes to positive emotional interactions (Fitness, 2001). The notion of emotional intelligence was popularized by Daniel Goleman's (1995/2005) best-selling publication, *Emotional Intelligence*, which brought the research of Salovey and Mayer (1990) to the masses. Salovey and Mayer (1990) defined emotional intelligence as "the ability to monitor one's own and others' feelings, to discriminate among them, and to use this information to guide one's thinking and action" (p. 189). Their later work on emotional intelligence included four abilities: perceiving, accessing, understanding, and regulating emotions (Mayer & Salovey, 1997, p. 10). **Perceiving** (Mayer & Salovey, 1997, p. 10) is the ability to identify emotion in oneself and others. One might recognize the shakiness in someone's voice as the person responds, "I am fine." **Accessing** feelings to facilitate thought (Mayer & Salovey, 1997, p. 12) involves generating emotions that assist in judgment. One may feel nervous the night before a presentation; however, that emotion can drive preparation for the presentation. **Understanding** (Mayer & Salovey, 1997, p. 13) involves one's ability to analyze emotions and recognize how they connect to our actions. Forgetting to tell a colleague about an important phone call might encourage that person to reciprocate with a similar action. **Regulating** emotions (Mayer & Salovey, 1997, p. 14) permits one to offer and receive criticism appropriately. Individuals who are able to incorporate their emotions appropriately have greater success in their relationships (Akerjordet & Severinsson, 2007). Emotional intelligence influences performance in countless communicative environments.

Researchers agree that people with high emotional intelligence are consistently top performers (Burgess, 2005, p. 97). Emotionally intelligent people function more efficiently on a team, have less stressed subordinates (Mikolajczak et al., 2012), possess positive attitudes, and exhibit adaptability (Akerjordet & Severinsson, 2007). Moreover, executives with emotional intelligence are more likely to achieve significant business outcomes, permitting subordinates and direct managers to recognize their effective leadership (Rosete & Ciarrochi, 2005). Emotional intelligence influences how one collaborates with others and how one interprets and responds to difference. Sensing and perceiving emotions open conflict differently, calling for varied responses to a unique situation. Emotional intelligence suggests that one explanation for how some individuals are skillful in their interactions with others rests largely with this attribute.

Emotional intelligence plays a pivotal role in human communication. Jorfi, Yacco, and Shah (2012) examined the interplay of emotional intelligence, communication effectiveness, and job satisfaction. They articulated the importance of management's designing and including emotional intelligence in organizational training with the intention of increasing communication effectiveness and job satisfaction. Sigmar, Hynes, and Hill (2012) are proponents of incorporating emotional intelligence into the communication curriculum. They believe emotional intelligence is essential for preparing students to be effective contributors to the global marketplace. Emotional intelligence is necessary for participation in a social world (Sigmar, Hynes, and Hill, 2012). One's inability to sense what is emerging in the communicative environment is often due to an inability to be attentive to emotional alerts that trigger emotional intelligence—such ability assists in the navigating of conflict between and among persons.

FRAMING COMMUNICATIVE LEADERSHIP: EMOTIONAL ALERTS

I am convinc'd that, where Men are most sure and arrogant, they are commonly the most mistaken, and have there given Reins to Passion, without that proper Deliberation and Suspen[s]e, which can alone secure them from the grossest Absurdities. (Hume, 1751/1945, p. 186)

The sixth chapter in *The Art of Framing: Managing the Language of Leadership* discusses "mixed messages" in the act of framing (Fairhurst & Sarr, 1996, p. 127). Leadership needs to listen to mixed messages and recognize that emotions matter. Leadership understands the importance of emotional expressiveness, emotional intelligence, or whatever term describes the importance of emotional thoughtfulness. A basic fact of the human condition is that much of motivation for performing at high levels of excellence emanates from emotions. Excellence does not emerge from the implementation of processes and procedures alone. In an era when creativity needs to move many companies to excellence, mere routine is insufficient. Emotions are part of work in the 21st century; the postindustrial era has given way to an information age composed of learning workers (Cohen, 2002, p. 78). In order to engage emotions creatively, one must attend to information clarity that is inclusive of emotional intelligence.

Fairhurst and Sarr (1996) provide ingredients for preparation for framing that is attentive to emotional alerts:

1. **Contradictions** are part of any communicative experience. We need to minimize contradictions, and when engaging them, do so intentionally. Sometimes life requires a "unity of contraries" (Buber, 1965/1988), in which we must be firm as a leader and speak with a gentle sense of grace. Emotional intelligence assists with contradictions, supporting the discernment of why the two responses are simultaneously necessary.
2. **Interpretation** of messages and signals requires reflection on one's initial response, which can be on target or miss the mark. Emotions require interpretation and consideration. Leaders cannot simply follow their emotions, but they still must attend to them.
3. **Mixed messages** are at the heart of daily communicative confusion. We must frame by differentiating ideas within a mixed message. Emotions are the first step in discerning

whether or not a mixed message is present. This initial reaction should begin thoughtful consideration of the complexity of the messages received.

4. **Emotional contagion** suggests that the energy of emotions grows. Just as enthusiasm is infectious, contrary emotions are, as well. Leaders need to understand emotions as a wave that can constructively undergird or overwhelm a communicative context (Fairhurst & Sarr, 1996, p. 121).

Emotional intelligence requires that we pay attention. Thoughtful consideration of emotions is a pragmatic communicative gesture. Our emotions wire us to sensatory connection with the communicative environment. Thoughtful consideration of emotional alerts assumes that the information that comes to us is important, but the information combined with emotional intelligence requires reflective and well-considered communicative action. Conflict can awaken our emotions, and thoughtful engagement can open up opportunities for communicative leadership, framing messages that can provide clarity of direction.

REFERENCES

Akerjordet, K., & Severinsson, E. (2007). Emotional intelligence: A review of the literature with specific focus on empirical and epistemological perspectives. *Journal of Clinical Nursing, 16*, 1405–1416.

Aristotle. (1992). *The eudemian ethics* (M. Woods, Trans.). Oxford: Oxford University Press.

Armoudian, M. (2015). Constructing "the others" during conflict: How journalism's norms and structures temper extreme portrayals. *The International Journal of Press/Politics, 20*, 360–381.

Arnett, R. C. (1992). *Dialogic education: Conversation about ideas and between persons.* Carbondale: Southern Illinois University Press.

Ausubel, D. P. (2000). *The acquisition and retention of knowledge: A cognitive view.* Boston, MA: Kluwer Academic Press.

Barge, K. J. (2006). Dialogue, conflict, and community. In J. G. Oetzel & S. Ting-Toomey (Eds.), *Sage handbook of conflict communication* (pp. 517–544). Thousand Oaks, CA: Sage.

Beck, J. (2011). Can a woman really lift a car off her pinned child? *Popular Science, 279*, 82.

Becker, J. A. H. (2005). A Goffmanian analysis of (in)attentiveness as involvement in group therapy sessions. *Qualitative Research Reports in Communication, 6*, 51–58.

Bednarzik, R. W., & Szlanski, J. (2012). *An examination of the work history of Pittsburgh steelworkers, who were displaced and received publicly-funded retraining in the early 1980s.* Bonn, Germany: Institute for the Study of Labor.

Blair C. (2002). School readiness: Integrating cognition and emotion in a neurobiological conceptualization of children's functioning at school entry. *American Psychologist, 57*, 111–127.

Buber, M. (1988). *The knowledge of man: Selected essays* (M. S. Friedman, Ed.). Amherst, NY: Humanity Books. (Original work published 1965)

Bullingham, L., & Vasconcelos, A. (2013). The presentation of self in the online world: Goffman and the study of online identities. *Journal of Information Science, 39*, 101–112.

Bureau of Labor Statistics. (2013). Industries at a glance: Manufacturing. Retrieved on February 8, 2013, from http://www.bls.gov/iag/tgs/iag31-33.htm#workforce

Burgess, R. C. (2005). A model for enhancing individual and organizational learning of 'emotional intelligence': The drama and winner's triangles. *Social Work Education, 24,* 97–112.

Burleson, B., & Planalp, E. (2000). Producing emotion(al) messages. *Communication Theory, 10,* 221–250.

Carlson, M., Charlin, V., & Miller, N. (1988). Positive mood and helping behavior: A test of six hypotheses. *Journal of Personality and Social Psychology, 55,* 211–229.

Chaplin, C. (Writer/Director/Producer). (1936). *Modern Times* [Motion picture]. Burbank, CA: Warner Home Video.

Cohen, E. A. (2002). Managing national security in the information age. In The Emirates Center for Strategic Studies and Research (Ed.), *Leadership and management in the information age* (pp. 65–82). Abu Dhabi, United Arab Emirates: The Emirates Center for Strategic Studies and Research.

Cohn, M. A., Fredrickson, B. L., Brown, S. L., Mikels, J. A., & Conway, A. M. (2009). Happiness unpacked: Positive emotions increase life satisfaction by building resilience. *Emotion, 9,* 361–368.

Danziger, S., & Gottschalk, P. (Eds.). (1993). *Uneven tides: Rising inequality in America.* New York, NY: Russell Sage Foundation.

Darwin, C. (1872). *The expression of the emotions in man and animals.* New York, NY: D. Appleton & Company.

Davis, J., & Huston, J. H. (1992). The shrinking middle-income class: A multivariate analysis. *Eastern Economic Journal, 18,* 277–285.

Egbert, N. (2003). Support provider mood and familiar versus unfamiliar events: An investigation of social support quality. *Communication Quarterly, 51,* 209–224.

Ekman, P. (1992). Facial expressions of emotion: New findings, new questions. *Psychological Science, 3,* 34–38.

Elisabeth Kübler-Ross. (2013). In *Encyclopaedia Britannica Online.* Retrieved from http://www .britannica.com/EBchecked/topic/324278/ Elisabeth-Kubler-Ross

Ellsworth, P. C., & Smith, C. A. (1988). Shades of joy: Patterns of appraisal differentiating pleasant emotions. *Cognition and Emotion, 2,* 301–331.

Esser, F., Reinemann, C., & Fan, D. (2001). Spin doctors in the United States, Great Britain, and Germany: Metacommunication about media manipulation. *The Harvard International Journal of Press/Politics, 6,* 16–45.

Fairhurst, G. T. (2011). *The power of framing: Creating the language of leadership.* San Francisco, CA: John Wiley & Sons.

Fairhurst, G. T., & Sarr, R. A. (1996). *The art of framing: Managing the language of leadership.* San Francisco, CA: Jossey-Bass.

Fineman, S. (2000). Commodifying the emotionally intelligent. In S. Fineman (Ed.), *Emotion in organizations* (2nd ed.). London: Sage.

Fitness, J. (2001). Emotional intelligence and intimate relationships. In J. Ciarrochi, J. P. Forgas, & J. D. Mayer (Eds.), *Emotional intelligence in everyday life* (pp. 98–112). Florence, KY: Psychology Press.

Forgas, J. P. (1998). On feeling good and getting your way: Mood effects on negotiator cognition and bargaining strategies. *Journal of Personality and Social Psychology, 74,* 565–577.

—. (1999). On feeling good and being rude: Affective influences on language use and request formulations. *Journal of Personality and Social Psychology, 76,* 928–939.

Foster, J. E., & Wolfson, M. C. (2010). Polarization and the decline of the middle class: Canada and the U.S. *Journal of Economic Inequality, 8*, 247–273.

Frankl, V. E. (2006). *Man's search for meaning.* Boston, MA: Beacon Press. (Original work published 1959)

Frijda, N. H. (1987). Emotion, cognitive structure, and action tendency. *Cognition and Emotion, 1*, 115–143.

—. (1993). Moods, emotion episodes and emotions. In M. Lewis & J. M. Haviland (Eds.), *Handbook of emotions* (pp. 381–403). New York, NY: Guilford.

—. (2009). Mood. In D. Sander & K. R. Scherer (Eds.), *The Oxford companion to emotion and the affective sciences* (pp. 258–259). New York, NY: Oxford University Press.

Goffman, E. (1959). *The presentation of self in everyday life.* New York, NY: Anchor Books.

Golden, B. (2011, October 27). Turn to yourself first for finding solutions. *The Press.* Retrieved March 5, 2013, from http://www.presspublications.com/opinionscolumns/146-dare-to-live-without-limits/7945-turn-to-yourself-first-for-finding-solutions

Goleman, D. (2005). *Emotional intelligence.* New York, NY: Bantam Dell. (Original work published 1995)

Graetz, F., & Smith, A. T. (2010). Managing organizational change: A philosophies of change approach. *Journal of Change Management, 10*, 135–154.

Gross, D. M. (2010). Defending the humanities with Charles Darwin's *The expression of the emotions in man and animals* (1872). *Critical Inquiry, 37*, 34–59.

Guerrero, L. K., & La Valley, A. G. (2006). Conflict, emotion, and communication. In J. G. Oetzel & S. Ting-Toomey (Eds.), *The Sage handbook of conflict communication* (pp. 69–96). Thousand Oaks, CA: Sage.

Gumora, G., & Arsenio, W. F. (2002). Emotionality, emotion regulation, and school performance in middle school children. *Journal of School Psychology, 40*, 395–413.

Heidegger, M. (2008). *Being and time.* New York, NY: Harper & Row. (Original work published 1962)

Hess, H. J., & Tucker, C. O. (1980). *Talking about relationships* (2nd ed.). Prospect Heights, IL: Waveland Press.

Hochschild, A. R. (2003). *The managed heart: Commercialization of human feeling.* Berkeley: University of California Press. (Original work published 1983)

Householder, B. J. & Wong, N. C. H. (2011). Mood state or relational closeness: Explaining the impacts of mood on the ability to detect deception in friends and strangers. *Communication Quarterly, 59*, 104–122.

Hume, D. (1945). *An enquiry concerning the principles of morals.* London: Millar. (Original work published 1751)

Jensen, M. C., Murphy, K. J., & Wruck, E. (2004). *Remuneration: Where we've been, how we got to here, what are the problems, and how to fix them.* Harvard NOM Working Paper No. 04-28; ECGI - Finance Working Paper No. 44/2004. Available at SSRN: http://ssrn.com/abstract=561305 or http://dx.doi.org/10.2139/ssrn.561305

John, N. A., & Dvir-Gvirsman, S. (2015). "I don't like you any more": Facebook unfriending by Israelis during the Israel-Gaza conflict of 2014. *Journal of Communication, 65*, 953–974.

Jones, A. F., & Weinberg, D. H. (2000). The changing shape of the nation's income distribution. *Current Population Reports* (pp. 60–204). Washington, DC: U.S. Census Bureau.

Jorfi, H., Yacco, H. F. B., & Shah, I. M. (2012). Role of gender in emotional intelligence: Relationship among emotional intelligence, communication effectiveness and job satisfaction. *International Journal of Management, 29*, 590–597.

Kant, I. (2003). *Observations on the feelings of the beautiful and sublime* (J. T. Goldthwait, Trans.). Berkeley: University of California Press. (Original work published 1764)

Kirchhoff, J., Wagner, U., & Strack, M. (2012). Apologies: Words of magic? The role of verbal components, anger reduction, and offence severity. *Peace and Conflict: Journal of Peace Psychology, 18*, 109–130.

Klibanoff, E. (2016). How to close a steel mill: Lessons from Pittsburgh. *Crossroads*. Retrieved from http://crossroads.newsworks.org/index.php/local/keystone-crossroads/90146-how-to-close-a-steel-mill-lessons-from-pittsburgh

Knapp, M. L., Daly, J. A., Albada, K. F., & Miller, G. R. (2002). Background and current trends in the study of interpersonal communication. In M. L. Knapp & J. Daly (Eds.), *Handbook of interpersonal communication* (3rd ed.), (pp. 3–20). Thousand Oaks, CA: Sage.

Kramer, M. W., & Hess, J. A. (2002). Communication rules for the display of emotions in organizational settings. *Management Communication Quarterly, 16*, 66–80.

Kruml, S. M., & Geddes, D. (2000). Exploring the dimensions of emotional labor: The heart of Hochschild's work. *Management Communication Quarterly, 14*, 8–49.

Kübler-Ross, E. (1969). *On death and dying.* New York, NY: MacMillan Publishing Co, Inc.

Kuttner, R. (1983). The declining middle. *The Atlantic Monthly, 252*, 60–72.

Leidner, R. (1993). *Fast food, fast talk: Service work and the routinization of everyday life.* Berkeley: University of California Press.

Martin Heidegger. (2013). In *Encyclopaedia Britannica Online.* Retrieved from http://www.britannica.com/EBchecked/topic/259513/Martin-Heidegger

Mayer, J. D., & Salovey, P. (1997). What is emotional intelligence? In P. Salovey & D. Sluyter (Eds.), *Emotional development and emotional intelligence: Educational implications* (pp. 3–31). New York, NY: Basic Books.

McCall, L., & Percheski, C. (2010). Income inequality: New trends and research directions. *Annual Review of Sociology, 36*, 329–347.

Mikolajczak, M., Balon, N., Rousi, M., & Kotsou, I. (2012). Sensitive but not sentimental: Emotionally intelligent can put their emotions aside when necessary. *Personality and Individual Differences, 52*, 537–540.

Modern Times. (2013). In *Encyclopaedia Britannica Online.* Retrieved from http://www.britannica.com/EBchecked/topic/387247/Modern-Times

Morris, J. A., & Feldman, D. C. (1996). The dimensions, antecedents, and consequences of emotional labor. *Academy of Management Review, 21*, 986–1010.

Morris, W. M. (1992). A functional analysis of the role of mood in affective systems. In M. S. Clark (Ed.), *Review of personality and social psychology* (Vol. 13, pp. 256–293). Newbury Park, CA: Sage.

Morse, C. R., & Volkman, J. E. (2010). An examination into the dyadic effects of mood in social interactions. *Communication Research Reports, 27*, 330–342.

Murphy, A. G. (1998). Hidden transcripts of flight attendant resistance. *Management Communication Quarterly, 11*, 499–535.

Nichols, B., & Schumann, D. W. (2012). Consumer preferences for assimilative versus aspirational models in marketing communications: The role of product class, individual difference, and mood state. *Journal of Marketing Theory & Practice, 20*, 359–376.

Novaco, R. W. (2000). Anger. In A. E. Kazdin (Ed.), *Encyclopedia of psychology*. Washington, DC: American Psychological Association and Oxford University Press.

Omdahl, B. L. (2012). The role of emotion in problematic relationships in the workplace. In B. L. Omdahl & J. M. H. Fritz (Eds.), *Problematic relationships in the workplace*, Vol. 2 (pp. 18–40). New York, NY: Peter Lang.

Pekrun, R., Goetz, T., Perry, R. P., Kramer, K., Hochstadt, M., & Molfenter. S. (2004). Beyond test anxiety: Development and validation of the Test Emotions Questionnaire (TEQ). *Anxiety, Stress, & Coping, 17*, 287–316.

Pressman, S. (2007). The decline of the middle class: An international perspective. *Journal of Economic Issues, 41*, 181–200.

Rafaeli, A., & Sutton, R. I. (1987). Expression of emotion as part of the work role. *Academy of Management Review, 12*, 23–37.

Rajah, R., Song, Z., & Arvey, R. D. (2011). Emotionality and leadership: Taking stock of the past decade of research. *The Leadership Quarterly, 22*, 1107–1119.

Raver, C. C. (2002). Emotions matter: Making the case for the role of young children's emotional development for early school readiness. *Social Policy Report, Society for Research in Child Development, 16*, 3–18.

Rosete, D., & Ciarrochi, J. (2005). Emotional intelligence and its relationship to workplace performance outcomes of leadership effectiveness. *Leadership & Organizational Development Journal, 26*, 388–399.

Ruesch, J., & Bateson, G. (2009). *Communication: The social matrix of psychiatry*. New Brunswick, NJ: Transaction Publishers. (Original work published 1951)

Salovey, P., & Mayer, J. (1990). Emotional intelligence. *Imagination, Cognition, and Personality, 9*, 185–211.

Salovey, P., & Grewal, D. (2005). The science of emotional intelligence. *American Psychological Society, 14*, 281–285.

Samp, J. A. (2013). Goal variability and message content during relational discussions. *Communication Studies, 64*, 86–105.

Sanford, K. (2007a). The couples emotion rating form: Psychometric properties and theoretical associations. *Psychological Assessment, 19*, 411–421.

—. (2007b). Hard and soft emotion during conflict: Investigating married couples and other relationships. *Personal Relationships, 14*, 65–90.

Sergeant, J., & Laws-Chapman, C. (2012). Creating a positive workplace culture. *Nursing Management, 18*, 14–19.

Shuler, S., & Sypher, B. D. (2000). Seeking emotional labor: When managing the heart enhances the work experience. *Management Communication Quarterly, 17*, 58–84.

Sigmar, L., Hynes, G. E., & Hill, K. L. (2012). Strategies for teaching social and emotional intelligence in business communication. *Business Communication Quarterly, 75*, 301–317.

Simmel, G. (1955). *Conflict & the web of group affiliations*. (K. H. Wolff & R. Bendix, Trans.). New York: The Free Press. (Original work published 1908)

Sinclair, R. C., & Mark, M. M. (1992). The influence of mood state on judgment and action: Effects on persuasion, categorization, social justice, person perception and judgmental accuracy. In L. L. Martin & A. Tesser (Eds.), *The construction of social judgments* (pp. 165–194). Hillsdale, NJ: Lawrence Erlbaum.

Swan, S. (2003). From urban classroom to urban community. In B. McComiskey & C. Ryan (Eds.), *City comp: Identity, spaces, practices* (pp. 85–94). Albany: State University of New York Press.

Thomas, D. (2001). Do not go gentle into that good night. In R. Reynolds & J. Stone (Eds.), *On doctoring: Stories, poems, essays* (p. 151). New York, NY: Simon & Schuster. (Original work published 1951)

Tracy, S. J. (2000). Becoming a character for commerce: Emotional labor, self subordination, and discursive construction of identity in a total institution. *Management Communication Quarterly, 14*, 90–128.

—. (2004). Dialectic, contradiction, or double bind? Analyzing and theorizing employee reactions to organizational tension. *Journal of Applied Communication Research, 32*, 119–146.

Valiente, C., Swanson, J., & Eisenberg, N. (2012). Linking students' emotions and academic achievement: When and why emotions matter. *Child Development Perspectives, 6*(2), 129–135.

Visser, M. (2008). *The gift of thanks: The roots and rituals of gratitude.* New York, NY: Houghton Mifflin Harcourt Publishing.

Wharton, A. S. (1999). The psychosocial consequences of emotional labor. *Annals of American Academy of Political and Social Science, 561*, 158–176.

Worley, D., Titsworth, S. Worley, D., & Cornett-DeVito, M. (2007). Instructional communication competence: Lessons learned from award-winning teachers. *Communication Studies, 58*, 207–222.

Zuckerman, M. (2007, June 3). Uneasy in the middle. *US News & World Report*, 72.

Chapter Eight

DIALOGUE AND INTERNAL CONFLICT

Intrapersonal communication…allows conflict to be kept alive in everyday life. (Honeycutt & McCann, 2008, p. 29)

"Dialogue and Internal Conflict" acknowledges a pragmatic necessity as we experience intrapersonal conflict. Internal conflict ignites reflection on ongoing events that take place before, during, and after an interpersonal conflict. **Internal dialogue** permits us to think before we speak to another, consider before we act, and learn from intrapersonal conflict before entering interpersonal disputes. Internal dialogue is a pragmatic caution requiring us to function thoughtfully, avoiding the communicative mistake of clueless and thoughtless speech.

Internal dialogue requires reflection, internal editing, and a contextually sensitive filter. This chapter's *Spotlight on Leadership* features Elon Musk, founder of Tesla Motors and SpaceX.

Musk thoughtfully communicates his futuristic transportation vision as he presents ideas on electric cars, space exploration, and clean energy sources.

In 2002, Elon Musk founded the Musk Foundation, which funds projects in education, pediatric health, energy, and the environment.

© Jag_cz/Shutterstock.com

The act of **silent speech** (Brown & Keller, 1979) assists in uniting word and deed; such a unity does not eliminate conflict, but decreases the chance of falling into unnecessary conflict due to heedless speech and action.

The response of Michael O'Leary, CEO of the Irish airline Ryanair, to customers who complained of unfair fees and penalties was an example of thoughtless speech. In September 2012,

O'Leary garnered criticism as he called Ryanair passengers "stupid." He referred to passengers who forget their boarding passes or fail to print their boarding passes before arriving at the airport. One family criticized the airline through social media, stating that the financial penalties were unfair. This family of five flew from Alicante, Spain to Bristol, England; they paid $380 to have their boarding passes printed at the airport. More than half a million people responded to the social media post. O'Leary defended the practice of charging passengers to print out boarding passes, supporting the airline's financial penalty. O'Leary clarified his comments. He denied calling all passengers stupid; however, he contended that passengers are stupid if they think Ryanair would change its policies or fees (Tuttle, 2012).

Another example of thoughtless speech transpired during the British Petroleum (BP) oil spill in 2010. In April of that year, BP's Deep Water Horizon well exploded, sending an estimated 4.9 million barrels of oil into the Gulf of Mexico for 87 days (Krauss, 2013). During this massive tragedy, the CEO of BP, Mr. Tony Hayward, was quoted in a television interview saying, "I'm sorry. We're sorry for the massive disruption it's caused their lives. There's no one who wants this over more than I do. I'd like my life back" (Durando, 2010, para. 2). Hayward's thoughtless comment called into question his concern for people whose lives were devastated, the lingering effects of the environmental disaster, and the multitude of jobs lost in the region. Hayward exemplified a man who cared only about disruption to his own life. This public relations sound bite hastened Tony Hayward's dismissal as CEO. His replacement, Robert Dudley, had one top priority—to assist affected people throughout the region of the event, which included large coastal areas of Louisiana, Mississippi, Texas, Alabama, and Florida. The spill was the largest oil spill in American history and has caused tremendous damage to communities, wildlife, fisheries, and natural ecosystems (Fowler, 2013). Hayward was thoughtless, void of internal dialogue capable of absorbing complexity in the act of reflection and ongoing consideration. The advantage of intrapersonal conflict is that it makes us think before, during, and after a dispute—only thoughtfulness enhances the odds of a creative resolution.

© Cheryl Casey/Shutterstock.com

FIGURE 8.1 Clean-up efforts on Pensacola Beach, Florida after the BP oil spill, June 23, 2010.

INTRODUCTION

This chapter stresses a pragmatic warning—think before you speak and act. Reflective practices frame contextually appropriate comments. Internal dialogue challenges one's own thought, functioning as the first testing ground of an idea, position, or perspective. Public scrutiny is the second, not the first, test of one's speech and actions. The initial stage of internal reflection challenges multiple positions in a dialogue within the self. This communicative process of self-questioning is the home of what Immanuel Kant (1798/1974) referred to as the first conversation, an internal dialogue.

In "Dialogue and Internal Conflict," we articulate the pragmatic necessity of reflective internal dialogue in five sections:

1. **Internal dialogue** highlights communicative engagement in a questioning conversation with oneself;
2. **Intrapersonal communication** details the study of how people process messages internally (Salwen & Stacks, 1996);
3. **Uncertainty reduction theory** describes communicative paths used to decrease the unknown;
4. **Creative engagement and conflict maps** provides a personal blueprint of the content and coordinates that configure a given conflict;
5. **Framing communicative leadership: Internal dialogue** examines the manner in which inner speech frames thoughtful action and minimizes undisciplined communicative practices in the conflict process.

Internal dialogue offers opportunity for reflection and learning, permitting us to discern and prepare for conflict; it is a necessary form of practical self-education that assists our communicative formation. Internal dialogue clarifies the goods that we consider worthy of protecting and promoting as we prepare for and learn before, during, and after a given conflict.

INTERNAL DIALOGUE

Immanuel Kant outlined the importance of internal dialogue. He, along with Hannah Arendt, emphasized the necessity of reflective thought with a focus on **"inner dialogue"** (Arnett, 2013, pp. 148, 215) with the objective of facilitating examination of multiple sides of ideas, issues, and actions. Kant's ethical system requires challenging oneself, thinking through the implications and consequences of multiple perspectives. Kant wrote in an era that championed individual autonomy and independence of thought. His era, the 18th century, known as the Age of Reason or the Enlightenment, was a moment in which many perceived danger emerging from unreflective, blind allegiance to external authority. The Enlightenment was a historical moment defined by reflective self-thought and independence of decision making.

Kant (1781/1965) sought to liberate people from the demand of blind fidelity that put them at the mercy of an external sovereign. Kant empowered the individual as a self-governing thinker, giving each person the means to think independently, regardless of social rank. Kant wanted to free people from those who seek to dominate or dictate how one should think and act. Kant's (1798/1974) stress on internal dialogue was an effort to enhance individual autonomy and independence of thought.

Kant (1797/1996) supported the Enlightenment at a time that encouraged a spirit of individual emancipation, permitting each individual person to determine for himself or herself the correct and appropriate answer and action. Kant considered the exercise of internal dialogue and individual autonomy a "**moral imperative**" (p. 31). He championed individual responsibility with an inner reflection on the complexity of issues and decisions, privileging internal editing of ideas and challenging one's own personal perspectives before acting and speaking.

The task of internal dialogue requires one to know one's own ideas and perspectives well through the examination of contrary positions and perspectives. This internal communicative education assists in understanding one's own standpoint, comprehending viewpoints contrary to one's own. Internal dialogue tempers rash action and speech by seeking internal clarity as one discerns weaknesses, loopholes, and problematic assumptions in one's own ideas before taking them to the test of the public arena. Internal dialogue is a way to "focus and organize individuals' thoughts on communication" in preparation for engaging others in conversation (Honeycutt & McCann, 2008, p. 77). Through the test of ideas in the public arena, the outcomes of one's internal dialogue find correction or confirmation (Cathcart & Gumpert, 1983). "Internal-reflective deliberation" within the individual is a necessary first step for public deliberation (Goodin, 2000, p. 84). Participation in public deliberation requires individual reflection on public policy issues prior to communicative exchanges (Marques & Maia, 2010). Internal dialogue engages private argument with oneself in order to avoid thoughtless conflict with others.

Another practical application of internal dialogue emerged from the lectures and scholarship of American pragmatist George Herbert Mead. American pragmatism can be considered a theory of inner speech (Wiley, 2006). Pragmatists **Charles Sanders Peirce**, William James, George Herbert Mead, and **John Dewey** referred to the self as an internal dialogue (Wiley, 2006, p. 5).[1] Scholarship on intrapersonal communication often cites the work of American philosopher and social theorist George Herbert Mead and Soviet psychologist **L. S. Vygotsky** (Vocate, 1994). Even though Mead and Vygotsky did not directly influence each other, they shared views on the social self, internalization, and the origins of language (Glock, 1986). Both Mead and Vygotsky emphasized the role of internal dialogue (Vygotsky, 1934/1986) or "internal conversation" (Mead, 1934, p. 151) in the creation of meaning and understanding. However, they differed somewhat in their areas of emphasis. Mead addressed theories on the social nature of the self, while Vygotsky focused on the social and cultural/historical theories that develop thought and speech (Vari-Szilagyi, 1991).

---

1. For a discussion of pragmatism and inner speech, see Norbert Wiley's (2006) "Pragmatism and the Dialogical Self" from the *International Journal for Dialogical Science*.

George Herbert Mead (1934) articulated the connection between the developments of the self through language, consisting of the "I" and the "me" (pp. 173–179). For Mead, an individual becomes aware of the self through communication. The oft-cited book *Mind, Self, and Society from the Standpoint of a Social Behaviorist* is a compilation of Mead's lectures edited by his former student, Charles Morris. Mead differentiates between the "I" and the "me," with the "I" referring to the self that gives order and expresses feelings and the "me" referring to the self that brings forth the influence of others into consciousness. Mead emphasized the development of mind and self in the process of social interaction (Bryant & Miron, 2004). One application of Mead's work is in ritual communication (Carey, 1989). Carey (1989) viewed communication as a "symbolic process whereby reality is produced, maintained, repaired, and transformed" (p. 23). This work is particularly dependent on Mead's conception of the "me," which gives us access to a larger social world. Mead stresses mind, self, and society as constituted through communication (Underwood, Brown, Sherard, Tushabe, & Adur-Rahman, 2011).

Mead's contemporary, L. S. Vygotsky, studied the linkage between linguistics and philosophy. Vygotsky (1934/1986) contended that the development of "inner speech" (p. 100) depends upon our sociocultural experiences and suggested that language has its roots in social communication. Vygotsky defined inner speech as "both a dialogue with the self and the process of a thought being realized in words" (Vocate, 1994, p. 7). Both Mead and Vygotsky understood internal dialogue as fundamental preparation for social discourse.

Internal dialogue plays a vital role in one's approach to interpersonal conflicts (Cloven & Roloff, 1993). When engaging in a conflict, internal dialogue provides a mechanism for asking and responding to one's own questions about the conflict. Internal dialogue permits one to consider multiple issues in preparation for interpersonal interactions and conflict. Engaging in the communicative practice of self-talk is often the difference between constructive meeting of a conflict situation and the clumsy igniting of unnecessary conflict that spirals out of control. More conventionally within the discipline of communication, internal self-talk and dialogue are foundational for intrapersonal communication.

INTRAPERSONAL COMMUNICATION

Immanuel Kant's (1798/1974) stress on internal dialogue contributed to insights reflected in early work in the emerging area of intrapersonal communication within the scope of interpersonal engagement. This perspective guided Charles T. Brown and Paul W. Keller's (1979) *Monologue to Dialogue: An Exploration of Interpersonal Communication*. They stressed "self-talk" (p. 172). The work of Brown and Keller reminds us of an important connection between self-talk and individual autonomy. Their work aligned with scholarship emphasizing self-talk, self-dialogue, and self-awareness in intrapersonal communication (Cloven & Roloff, 1993).

Articulation of the pragmatic necessity of intrapersonal communication has a long history. The first article to discuss the foundational role of intrapersonal communication was Barker and Wiseman's "A Model of Intrapersonal Communication," published in the *Journal of Communication* in 1966 (Macke, 2008). In this article, Barker and Wiseman (1966) defined **intrapersonal communication** as the "creating, functioning, and evaluating of symbolic processes which operate primarily within oneself" (p. 173). Intrapersonal communication differs from other forms of communication in that it centers on self-conversation, which includes thinking, listening, meditating, reflecting silently, and self-talk (Barker & Wiseman, 1966).

After the publication of Barker and Wiseman's article, the area of intrapersonal communication gained traction within the communication discipline. In 1986, the Speech Communication Association, now the National Communication Association, established a commission on intrapersonal communication processes, making it a topic of "substantial study" (Vocate, 1994, p. x). In the *Yearbook of Communication*, Cunningham (1992) reviewed the history of intrapersonal communication within the communication literature. Works such as *Intrapersonal Communication* (Barker & Edwards, 1980) and *Intrapersonal Communication Processes* (Roberts & Watson, 1989) strengthened the significance of the term in the field, while works such as *A Taxonomy of Concepts in Communication* (Blake & Haroldsen, 1975), *A Dictionary of Communication and Media Studies* (Watson & Hill, 1989), and *Key Concepts in Communication* (O'Sullivan, Hartley, Saunders, Montgomery, & Fiske, 1993) highlighted the uniqueness of intrapersonal communication as a concept.

As the study of intrapersonal communication continued, the definition evolved. Roberts, Edwards, and Barker (1987) stated that intrapersonal communication includes "all of the physiological and psychological processing of messages that happens within individuals at conscious and nonconscious levels as they attempt to understand themselves and their environment" (p. 2). Moreover, intrapersonal communication refers to the "internal or intrapsychic dialogue that is commonly referred to as 'talking to oneself'" (Berger, 1995, p. 11). Salwen and Stacks (1996) suggested that intrapersonal communication is the study of how people process messages within the self. In *Intrapersonal Communication Processes*, Aitken and Shedletsky (1997) discussed how the field of intrapersonal communication had grown to include "imagined interactions, mental verbal exchanges with oneself, voice mail to oneself, and more" (p. xii). More recent work in the area of intrapersonal communication examines intrapersonal communicative experiences as the phenomenological embodiment of social and cultural relations, framing an "intrapersonal communicology," which begins with the assumption that "the experience of a message is intersubjective and that it does not constitute independent data processed through the mechanism of mind" (Macke, 2008, p. 124). For Macke, intrapersonal communication consists of phenomenological intersubjective experiences. Honeycutt and McCann (2008) highlighted the experience of culture as central in their study of differences associated with intrapersonal communication in America, Japan, and Thailand.

One of the primary works on intrapersonal communication, *Intrapersonal Communication: Different Voices, Different Minds*, provides a theoretical foundation and a working theory of intrapersonal communication that distinguishes between self-talk and inner speech with self-talk necessary for understanding inner speech (Vocate, 1994, p. 14). The purpose of **self-talk** is "the creation of meaning for the self" (Vocate, 1994, p. 10) expressed in silent and verbal dialogue with the self (Vocate, 1994, p. 7). Honeycutt, Zagacki, and Edwards (1989) worked on "imagined interactions" (p. 166), a phenomenon that offers another example of the silent, internal process of inner speech. **Imagined interactions** occur as individuals envision conversations with significant others (Zagacki, Edwards, & Honeycutt, 1992).

Intrapersonal communication is essential for conflict preparation. The term is recognized by the National Communication Association's definition of mediation and dispute resolution, which refers to "the study of understanding, management, and resolution of conflict within intrapersonal, interpersonal, and intergroup situations" ("National Communication Association," 2011, para. 15). Conflict discovery and recognition of difference often emerge intrapersonally. Littlejohn and Domenici (2007) categorize the most common sources of intrapersonal conflict into (1) cognitive inconsistency, (2) goal conflict, and (3) value conflict (p. 39). Each source of intrapersonal communication (cognitive inconsistency, goal conflict, and value conflict) generates uncertainty that prompts us to reduce ambiguity associated with a conflict situation.

M. G. Antony (2016) in "Exploring Diversity through Dialogue: Avowed and Ascribed Identities" describes self-talk in the manner in which it is negotiated and contested. Our attributions often say more about our intrapersonal worlds than the other before us. The intrapersonal danger begins with preexisting viewpoints; our willingness to push beyond what we assume and assert opens up new understanding and a recognition that attending to otherness can facilitate a richer understanding of our intrapersonal worlds.

UNCERTAINTY REDUCTION THEORY

Internal dialogue, self-talk, and intrapersonal communication can decrease uncertainty and assist with finding direction in the midst of a large variety of options. Uncertainty reduction begins with self-talk, a thoughtful inner dialogue, which helps one to understand others, the immediate context, and the larger communicative environment. Charles R. Berger and

Richard J. Calabrese (1975) introduced **uncertainty reduction theory** to the field of communication with their examination of the role of ambiguity in relationship development between strangers. The premise of their theory was that people self-disclose in order to reduce uncertainty about self and others in relationships. Their original theory included three stages of relational development, seven axioms, and 28 theorems.

The three stages of initial uncertainty reduction theory focus on information acquired during an initial relational interaction. The "entry" stage centers on evaluation of physical characteristics that are governed by social norms (p. 99). The "personal" stage consists of sharing attitudes, beliefs, and values (p. 100). The "exit" stage includes deciding whether one should pursue future interactions or abandon pursuit of the relationship (p. 100).

The axioms currently central to uncertainty reduction theory describe cause-effect relationships between uncertainty and various communicator behaviors: (1) verbal communication reduces uncertainty, which encourages interaction with others (pp. 101–103); (2) nonverbal warmth decreases uncertainty as we attend to unspoken communicative gestures (p. 103); (3) information seeking decreases uncertainty as we acquire evidence about another (p. 103); (4) uncertainty is minimized when one becomes more comfortable with the other (pp. 103–105); (5) high levels of uncertainty prompt more reciprocal communication (pp. 105–106); (6) similarity between and among persons yields more certainty (pp. 106–107); (7) liking another reduces uncertainty (p. 107); and (8) shared communicative networks reduce uncertainty (Berger & Gudykunst, 1991, p. 27); and (9) during initial interaction, uncertainty decreases as communication satisfaction increases (Neuliep & Grohskopf, 2000, p. 75). By pairing the axioms, Berger and Calabrese generated 28 theorems that describe relationships among communication variables, predicting how one would act when reducing uncertainty. Uncertainty is low when one predictable communicative outcome is likely, whereas uncertainty is high when several outcomes are conceivable. Individuals are motivated to reduce uncertainty (Berger & Calabrese, 1975).

Berger (1979) identified three strategies to reduce uncertainty: (1) passive, (2) active, and (3) interactive (p. 134). Passive strategies focus on an "unobtrusive observation" of others for the purpose of acquiring information about them (p. 134). Active strategies rely on attaining information from a third party to reduce uncertainty about the other. Interactive strategies are instigated by questions and shared information. When individuals engage in social interaction, they encounter some form of uncertainty (Berger, 2009). Uncertainty reduction begins with our taking responsibility for knowing our own position and contrary perspectives before offering a public utterance; otherwise, we generate unnecessary conflict from thoughtlessness that continues to generate and augment uncertainty.

Three decades of research have highlighted the strengths and applications of uncertainty reduction theory (Knobloch, 2008). The following material offers a view of the scope of uncertainty reduction theory applications: (1) in intercultural engagement, marked by diverse symbol systems (Gudykunst, 1995); (2) in the field of health communication, such as with alexithymia, a personality trait characterized by one's inability to identify and describe feelings (Hesse, Rauscer,

& Wenzel, 2012); (3) in a wide assortment of interpersonal interactions (Knobloch, 2006); and (4) in job transfers (Kramer, 1993). In an article from *Harvard Business Review*, "Avoiding Decision Paralysis in the Face of Uncertainty," Johnson (2015) suggests that leaders must embrace uncertainty and the reality of not having all the answers. An example of such leadership transpired as Target CEO Brian Cornell stated that leadership requires decision making without complete certainty. He faced several challenges at Target, including the aftermath of a major security breach, the necessity to improve online and in-store shopping experiences, and the importance of addressing the failing Target Canada stores (Johnson, 2015). When Cornell was determining his strategy for Target Canada, he sought to reduce ambiguity by looking at the data indicating that Target Canada would not be profitable until 2021. Considering these future projections helped him to make the difficult decision of closing all 133 Canadian stores. Moving out of Canada permitted Cornell and his team to refocus and restore certainty in the company's U.S. brand. Closing Target Canada allowed for more attention on the U.S. brand, which minimized ambiguity and moved the company in a productive direction.

In *Managing Uncertainty in Organizational Communication*, Kramer (2004) offers the example of Tom Watson, CEO of IBM, and Lucille Burger, an IBM employee, who used security badge procedures to illustrate how organizational interactions can cause uncertainty. On one occasion, Tom Watson did not have the proper identification to enter a particular area of the complex, causing Lucille, whose role was to check identification, to experience uncertainty about how to address the situation. Lucille realized that Watson was the CEO of IBM, but he did not have the correct color badge. She struggled with the uncertainty of either letting him enter the area or following the rules and denying him access. Watson grappled with being impressed by Lucille's fortitude in following the rules and being disgruntled at the inconvenience he experienced. Watson finally assisted by retrieving his badge (pp. 192–196).

Both public and private comments result in uncertainty. We must think prior to speaking, editing internal speech before it is tested in public space. Direction is found in editing and conscientious meeting of public challenges. We must learn to test ourselves and edit our comments before sharing them. To discern a direction or action in a conflict setting requires one to practice internal dialogue, which reduces personal uncertainty. Another step in reducing uncertainty is the creation of a conflict map, which can promote constructive conflict engagement.

CREATIVE ENGAGEMENT AND CONFLICT MAPS

Uncertainty reduction is a prime motivator for the construction and use of conflict mapping. Architects and contractors understand the importance of blueprints, which provide public documentation of decisions that shape the structure of a building. A **conflict map** is a practical theory that frames the coordinates of a given conflict and offers insights for engaging that conflict. **Theory** functions as a public map that announces a perceptual frame that guides one's investigation (Arnett, Fritz, & Bell, 2009). A theory makes public the presuppositions that one takes into a setting; in the case of conflict, a theory yields a starting point for making sense of a situation. A theory, like a blueprint, can be altered, changed, or reconfigured. A conflict map (Fisher et al., 2000; Wehr, 1979) is a theory or public blueprint that assists internal dialogue and works to reduce uncertainty.

We conceptualize a conflict map as a personal theory constructed to assist the user. A conflict map reflects a personal expression of a particular way of navigating conflict between persons. The conflict map is an intrapersonal guide that reminds us of multiple coordinates that constitute a given conflict. One must discover a way to map and conceptualize conflict engagement that is particular to one's unique skills. We consider the following key coordinates in constructing a conflict map important to internal dialogue that can aid interpersonal conflict. A conflict map consists of four elements: (1) the *persons* who are included in the conflict, (2) the *context* of the conflict, (3) an understanding of the larger *background* to the conflict, and (4) the *ethical significance/importance* attached to the content of the conflict. These coordinates remind us that constructive conflict centers on a struggle over a given good or goods within a context that must be understood within a larger background and between and among the unique set of people involved in the conflict.

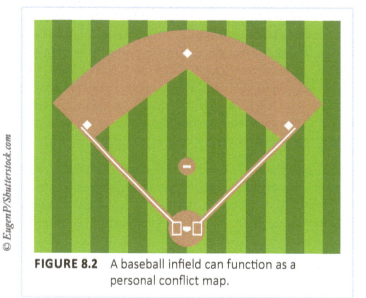

© EugenP/Shutterstock.com

FIGURE 8.2 A baseball infield can function as a personal conflict map.

There are numerous means by which one might configure a personal public map of conflict. The key to personal map-making is to frame a conflict guide with coordinates that one knows and understands. Therefore, for us, we turn to the image of a baseball infield (Figure 8.2), which has particular markers that offer ready-made coordinates: (1) first base (persons in the conflict), (2) second base (context of the conflict), (3) third base (conflict background), and (4) home plate (ethical good/content). The bases function as convenient conceptual coordinates, keeping the major issues of a given conflict consideration before us.

Consider the interaction between a college president and two students in *The Social Network*, a movie that depicts the necessity of crafting a conflict map. Twin brothers Tyler and Cameron Winklevoss approached the then-president of Harvard University, Larry Summers, to express discontent over the actions of their classmate Mark Zuckerberg, who allegedly stole their idea for a social networking site, which became Facebook. The Winkelvosses claimed that Zuckerberg stole a computer code from ConnectU, a social networking site they created that

Zuckerberg had worked on briefly (Lattman, 2012). President Summers stated that he would meet them as a favor to their father, who was an acquaintance of Summers. He proceeded to inform the brothers that they should have gone through the proper channels if they wanted to make a complaint. Summers commented on the interaction, stating, "Rarely have I encountered such swagger, and I tried to respond in kind" (FoxNews, 2011). The Winklevoss twins skipped the chain of command and ignored Harvard University conventions.

A possible conflict map for the Winklevoss twins includes: (1) the persons in conflict (Zuckerberg, Winklevoss twins, Summers), (2) conflict context (Zuckerberg allegedly stealing intellectual property from the twins), (3) conflict background (the twins' disregard for the protocol when making their complaint and bringing a sense of privilege to their conversation), and (4) a contention over ethical goods (with the twins and Zuckerberg seeking to protect and promote contrasting perspectives on the drama). A conflict map does not resolve a conflict, but it does keep one focused on the issues at hand, providing greater clarity and understanding.

In addition to our framework for conflict mapping, we find two alternative models helpful for consideration: one by Paul Wehr (1979) and one by Fisher et al. (2000). Wehr (1979) offered an embedded story of conflict and how it shapes the communicative experience. Wehr expressed conflict mapping as "a first step in intervening to manage a particular conflict. It gives both the intervener and the conflict parties a clearer understanding of the origins, nature, dynamics and possibilities for resolution of the conflict" (p. 18). In *Conflict Regulations*, Wehr discussed eight basic elements for the construction of a conflict map: (1) draft a conflict summary; (2) consider the conflict history; (3) identify the conflict context; (4) ascertain the conflict parties; (5) attend to the conflict issues that include goals and interests; (6) follow the fluidity and movement of the conflict (conflict dynamics); (7) discern alternative routes to a solution; and finally (8) attend to the conflict and its long-term impact upon the relationship (conflict resolution or regulation potential) (pp. 18–22). Wehr painted a theoretical picture of a conflict map that outlines historical differences that divide persons with the aim of clarifying all the perspectives in a conflict.

Fisher et al. (2000) viewed conflict mapping as a strategy for graphically representing the individuals and issues involved in a given conflict. They emphasized the importance of parties in the dispute who should work together to construct a conflict map. This process often uncovers each party's assumptions, priorities, and goals. Fisher et al. submit four steps for mapping a conflict situation: (1) decide what you want to map, when, and from what point of view; (2) place yourself and your organization on the map; (3) point toward action, asking "What can be done?" (p. 22); and (4) map the issues between the parties that are in conflict. For example, when mapping a family conflict, circles and various lines connecting the members depend upon the type/strength of relationships in the family. A bold line may indicate a strong relationship while two lines would indicate an alliance (Fisher, et al., 2000). By using this mapping technique, family members identify relationships and visually interpret the situation more carefully.

When a conflict map is not in place, one can easily forget coordinates that assist in addressing the conflict with thoughtful care. Once we are in conflict, it is sometimes difficult to think quickly. Our suggestion is to have a small number of major coordinates. Again, we suggest four crucial coordinates for a conflict map: (1) the *persons* who are included in the conflict; (2) the *context* of the conflict; (3) an understanding of the larger *background* to the conflict; and (4) the *ethical significance/importance* attached to the content of the conflict. A conflict map offers guidance. We do not contend that one conflict map fits all situations, but a conflict map begins an internal dialogue central to constructive conflict engagement.

Conflict maps reduce uncertainty and direct creative conflict engagement, but each conflict is unique and requires a creative response. No one set of coordinates provides all answers. Conflict maps are forever being conceptualized as we gather new insight. Stephanie Norander and Gloria Galanes (2014), in their essay, "'Bridging the Gap': Difference, Dialogue, and Community Organizing," discuss the necessity of understanding race and diversity as central conceptualizations of dialogue in action, attentive not simply to my view of the world but to difference. In otherness and difference, learning resides. In my own impression and determined action, I find repetition of what I have done and know. Networking and social events take us beyond our comfort zones that permit engagement with others and with knowledge acquired in communal living defined by difference.

Conflict requires creativity on the spot, responding thoughtfully to the unexpected. Creativity is at the heart of Immanuel Kant's (1781/1965) project to differentiate fantasy and imagination. **Fantasy** involves the abstract. **Imagination**, on the other hand, pushes off a concrete reality, something that actually exists. Conflict negotiation expert William L. Ury's (2000) highlights on "the third side" and management expert Stephen R. Covey's (2012) focus on "the third alternative" emphasize creative problem solving in hopes of identifying a third option for responding to conflict. Both concepts rely on creativity and imagination, not fantasy; to construct a unique solution moves beyond a conventional compromise between two sides. Creative imagination begins with meeting what is before us, engaging in internal dialogue assisted by a thoughtful conflict map, and knowing that we must discern creatively how to respond as we encounter the unexpected in conflict situations. One seeks to protect and promote an ethical good of thoughtfulness that remains nimble, never forgetting that it is the moment, not abstract theory, that ultimately directs conflict engagement.

FRAMING COMMUNICATIVE LEADERSHIP: INTERNAL DIALOGUE

> *Thinking is talking with ourselves...so it is also listening to ourselves inwardly (by reproductive imagination). (Kant, 1798/1974, p. 65)*

The seventh chapter in *The Art of Framing: Managing the Language of Leadership* discusses learning how to "frame spontaneously" (Fairhurst & Sarr, 1996, p. 143). Leadership needs to have thoughtful and continuous self-talk in order to be alert to moments in which important issues can and should be framed. Internal conversation that challenges one's initial impulse is the communicative "how" of leadership. The spontaneity of framing comes from thoughtful and considered practice. Leaders cannot afford to be the cause of a conflict because a phrase, a sentence, or a story was uttered without prior consideration, reflection, and self-challenge. Spontaneous comments must arise from inner dialogue that has already challenged ideas and positions prior to testing them in the public domain of leadership.

Ann Cunliffe's (2016) award-winning essay "On Becoming a Critically Reflexive Practitioner: Redux: What Does It Mean to Be Reflexive?" addresses the large number of corporate scandals, employee suicides, cover-ups, irresponsibility in decision making, and corporate damage, in which leaders refused to engage in necessary reflexivity when deciding their response. She links actions specifically to reflexivity. Considerable reflexivity in "organizational practices, policies, social structures, and knowledge bases" (p. 741) will not eliminate problems but will go a long way to at least minimize them. She points to a reflexivity that is relational and inter-subjective in that it takes into account not only one's own thoughtful considerations but also seeks the reflexive considerations of others. She offers no technique for being reflexive but considers it the heart of decision making as one engages the insights of another and one's own in the hopes of minimizing mistakes, catastrophes, and tragedies that have too often defined actions that go unquestioned once they are initially engaged. Reflexive action never ceases to question even the most assured assumptions in one's own leadership.

Fairhurst and Sarr (1996) state the ingredients for preparation for spontaneous framing:

1. **Priming** (p. 145) is the communicative act of repetitive reflection, permitting "mental readiness" to assist in framing on the spot (p. 168). The vitality of inner dialogue makes the notion of priming a communicative reality.
2. **Anticipation** recognizes that some situations are similar and permit one to practice an imaginative response. Visualizing an expected communicative situation requires one's intrapersonal communication grounded in imagination, not fantasy.
3. **Impact** in framing requires considerable practice prior to the moment in which one offers a perspective. Awareness of the coordinates of a conflict map and their connection to a given place can promote leadership.

Leaders in conflict situations lead with conversations considered in advance. They lead with previously challenged ideas. They lead with perspectives that have already been self-tempered with alternative considerations. Internal dialogue permits the appearance of spontaneity. Internal dialogue begins with a conflict map that guides leaders through the coordinates and the multi-directional trajectories of conflict. Leadership commences with internal dialogue and serious thoughtfulness, which decreases the chances that one will fuel, rather than temper, a conflict.

REFERENCES

Aitken, J. E., & Shedletsky, L. (1997). *Intrapersonal communication processes*. Annandale, VA: National Communication Association.

Antony, M. G. (2016). Exploring diversity through dialogue: Avowed and ascribed identities. *Communication Teacher, 30*(3), 125–130.

Arnett, R. C. (2013). *Communication ethics in dark times: Hannah Arendt's rhetoric of warning and hope*. Carbondale: Southern Illinois University Press.

Arnett, R. C., Fritz, J. H., & Bell, L. M. (2006). *Communication ethics literacy: Dialogue and difference*. Thousand Oaks, CA: Sage.

Barker, L. L., & Edwards, R. (1980). *Intrapersonal communication*. Dubuque, IA: Gorsuch Scarisbrick.

Barker, L. L., & Wiseman, G. (1966). A model of intrapersonal communication. *Journal of Communication, 16*, 172–179.

Berger, A. A. (1995). *Essentials of mass communication theory*. Thousand Oaks, CA: Sage.

Berger, C. R. (1979). Beyond initial interaction: Uncertainty, understanding and the development of interpersonal relationships. In H. Giles & R. St. Clair (Eds.), *Language and social psychology* (pp. 122–144). Oxford: Blackwell.

—. (2009). Interpersonal communication. In D. W. Stacks & M. B. Salwen (Eds.), *An integrated approach to communication theory and research* (pp. 260–279). New York, NY: Routledge.

Berger, C. R. & Calabrese, R. J. (1975). Some exploration in initial interaction and beyond toward a developmental theory of interpersonal communication. *Human Communication Research, 1*, 99–112.

Berger, C. R., & Gudykunst, W. B. (1991). Uncertainty and communication. In. B. Dervin & M. J. Voight (Eds.), *Progress in communication sciences*, (Vol. 10, pp. 21–66). Norwood, NJ: Ablex.

Blake, R. H., & Haroldsen, E. O. (1975). *A taxonomy of concepts in communication*. New York, NY: Hastings House.

Brown, C. T., & Keller, P. W. (1979). *Monologue to dialogue: An exploration of interpersonal communication*. Upper Saddle River, NJ: Prentice-Hall.

Bryant, J., & Miron, D. (2004). Theory and research in mass communication. *Journal of Communication, 54*, 662–704.

Carey, J. (1989). *Communication as culture: Essays on media and society*. New York, NY: Routledge.

Cathcart, R., & Gumpert, G. (1983). Mediated interpersonal communication: Toward a new typology. *Quarterly Journal of Speech, 69*, 267–277.

Charles Sanders Peirce. (2013). In *Encyclopaedia Britannica Online*. Retrieved from http://www.britannica.com/EBchecked/topic/448884/Charles-Sanders-Peirce

Cloven, D., & Roloff, M. E. (1993). Sense-making activities and interpersonal conflict, II: The effects of communicative intentions on internal dialogue. *Western Journal of Communication, 57*, 309–329.

Covey, S. R. (2012). *The 3rd alternative: Solving life's most difficult problems*. New York, NY: First Free Press.

Cunliffe, A. L. (2016). "On becoming a critically reflexive practitioner" redux: What does it mean to be reflexive? *Journal of Management Education, 40*, 740–746.

Cunningham, S. B. (1992). Intrapersonal communication: A review and critique. *Communication Yearbook, 15*, 597–620.

Durando, J. (2010, June 1). BP's Tony Hayward: 'I'd like my life back.' *USA Today*. Retrieved on February 11, 2013, from http://content.usatoday.com/communities/greenhouse/post/2010/06/bp-tony-hayward-apology/1#.URmoTfJ41X8

Fairhurst, G. T., & Sarr, R. A. (1996). *The art of framing: Managing the language of leadership.* San Francisco, CA: Jossey-Bass Publishers.

Fisher, S., Abdi, D.I., Ludin, J., Smith, R., Williams, S., & Williams, S. (2000). *Working with conflict: Skills and strategies for action.* New York, NY: St. Martin's Press.

Fowler, T. (2013, February 25). Accusations fly as trial over gulf oil spill begins. *Wall Street Journal.* Retrieved March 8, 2013, from http://online.wsj.com/article/SB1000142412788732 38843045783261935756632754.html

Fox News. (2011, July 20). Former Harvard president Larry Summers slams Winklevoss twins. *Fox News.* Retrieved on February 11, 2013, from http://www.foxnews.com/tech/2011/07/20/former-harvard-president-larry-summers-slams-winklevoss-twins/#ixzz26TxSORCh

Glock, H. J. (1986). Vygotsky and Mead on the self, meaning and internalisation. *Studies in Soviet Thought, 31,* 131–148.

Goodin, R. E. (2000). Democratic deliberation within. *Philosophy & Public Affairs, 29,* 81–109.

Gudykunst, W. B. (1995). Anxiety/uncertainty management (AUM) theory: Current status. In R. L. Wiseman (Ed.), *Intercultural communication theory* (pp. 8–58). Thousand Oaks, CA: Sage.

Hesse, C., Rauscher, E. A., & Wenzel, K. A. (2012). Alexithymia and uncertainty management. *Communication Research Reports, 29,* 343–352.

Honeycutt, J. M., & McCann, R. M. (2008). Predicting intrapersonal communication satisfaction on the basis of imagined interactions in the Pacific Rim. *Journal of Intercultural Communication Research, 37,* 25–42.

Honeycutt, J. M., Zagacki, K. S., & Edwards, R. (1989). Intrapersonal communication, social cognition and imagined interactions. In C. V. Roberts, & K. W. Watson (Eds.), *Intrapersonal communication processes: Original essays* (pp. 166–184). New Orleans, LA: Spectra.

John Dewey. (2013). In *Encyclopaedia Britannica Online.* Retrieved from http://www.britannica.com/EBchecked/topic/160445/John-Dewey

Johnston, P. (2015). Avoiding decision paralysis in the face of uncertainty. *Harvard Business Review.* Retrieved from https://hbr.org/2015/03/avoiding-decision-paralysis-in-the-face-of-uncertainty

Kant, I. (1965). *Critique of pure reason* (P. Guyer & A. W. Wood, Eds.). New York, NY: Cambridge University Press. (Original work published 1781)

—. (1974). *Anthropology from a pragmatic point of view* (M. J. Gregor, Trans.). Netherlands: Martinus Nijhoff. (Original work published 1798)

—. (1996). *The metaphysics of morals* (M. Gregor, Ed.). New York, NY: Cambridge University Press. (Original work published 1797)

Knobloch, L. K. (2006). Relational uncertainty and message production within courtship: Features and appraisals of date request messages. *Human Communication Research, 32,* 244–273.

—. (2008). Uncertainty reduction theory: Communicating under conditions of ambiguity. In L. A. Baxter & D. O. Braithwaite (Eds.), *Engaging theories in interpersonal communication: Multiple perspectives* (pp. 133–144). Thousand Oaks, CA: Sage.

Kramer, M. W. (1993). Communication and uncertainty reduction during job transfers: Leaving and joining processes. *Communication Monographs, 60,* 178–198.

—. (2004). *Managing uncertainty in organizational communication.* Mahwah, NJ: Erlbaum.

Krauss, C. (2013, February 19). Battle lines drawn for BP's day in court. *New York Times.* Retrieved March 8, 2013, from http://www.nytimes.com/2013/02/20/business/battle-lines-drawn-for-bps-day-in-court.html?pagewanted=all&_r=0

Lattman, P. (2012, November 13). Winklevoss twins lead investment in start-upshopping site. *The New York Times*. Retrieved on March 10, 2013, from http://dealbook.nytimes.com/2012/11/13/winklevoss-twins-lead-investment-in-start-up-shopping-site/

Littlejohn, S. W., & Domenici, K. (2007). *Communication, conflict, and the management of difference*. Long Grove, IL: Waveland Press.

Macke, F. (2008). Intrapersonal communicology: Reflection, reflexivity, and relational consciousness in embodied subjectivity. *Atlantic Journal of Communication, 16*, 122–148.

Marques, A. C. S., & Maia, R. C. M. (2010). Everyday conversation in the deliberative process: An analysis of communicative exchanges in discussion groups and their contributions to civic and political socialization. *Journal of Communication, 60*, 611–635.

Mead, G. H. (1934). *Mind, self, and society from the standpoint of a social behaviorist* (C. W. Morris, Ed.). Chicago, IL: University of Chicago Press.

National Communication Association. (2011). The discipline of communication. Retrieved on February 11, 2013, from http://www.natcom.org/Tertiary.aspx?id=236

Neuliep, J. W., & Grohskopf, E. L. (2000). Uncertainty reduction and communication satisfaction during initial interaction: An initial test and replication of a new axiom. *Communication Reports, 13*, 67–77.

Norander, S., & Galanes, G. (2014). "Bridging the gap": Difference, dialogue, and community organizing. *Journal of Applied Communication Research, 42*(4), 345–365.

O'Sullivan, T., Hartley, J., Saunders, D., Montgomery, M., & Fiske, J. (1993). *Key concepts in communication*. London: Methuen.

Roberts, C. V, Edwards, R., & Barker, L. L. (1987). *Intrapersonal communication processes*. Scottsdale, AZ: Gorsuch Scarisbrick Publishers.

Roberts, C. V., & Watson, K. W. (Eds.). (1989). *Intrapersonal communication processes: Original essays*. New Orleans, LA: Spectra.

Salwen, M. B., & Stacks, D. (1996). *An integrated approach to communication theory and research*. Mahwah, NJ: Lawrence Erlbaum Associates.

Tuttle, B. (2012). That's some quirky marketing strategy: CEO calls his customers 'idiots.' *Time*. Retrieved from http://business.time.com/2012/09/11/thats-some-quirky-marketing-strategy-ceo-calls-his-customers-idiots/

Underwood, C., Brown, J., Sherard, D., Tushabe, B., & Adur-Rahman, A. (2011). Reconstructing gender norms through ritual communication: A study of African transformation. *Journal of Communication, 61*, 197–218.

Ury, W. L. (2000). *The third side: Why we fight and how we can stop*. New York, NY: Penguin Books.

Vari-Szilagyi, I. (1991). G. H. Mead and L. S. Vygotsky on action. *Studies in Soviet Thought, 42*, 93–121.

Vocate, D. R. (1994). *Intrapersonal communication: Different voices, different minds*. Hillsdale, NJ: Lawrence Erlbaum Associates, Inc.

Vygotsky, L. S. (1986). *Thought and language* (A. Kozulin, Ed.). Cambridge, MA: MIT Press. (Original work published 1934)

Watson, J., & Hill, A. (1989). *A dictionary of communication and media studies* (2nd ed.). London: Edward Arnold.

Wehr, P. E. (1979). *Conflict regulation*. Boulder, CO: Westview Press.

Wiley, N. (2006). Pragmatism and the dialogical self. *International Journal for Dialogical Science, 1*, 5–21.

Zagacki, K. S., Edwards, R., & Honeycutt, J. M. (1992). The role of mental imagery and emotion in imagined interaction. *Communication Quarterly, 40*, 56–68.

Chapter Nine

ATTENDING TO OPINIONS IN CONFLICT

A democracy is based on the premise that public opinion should matter in deciding the course of society. Yet what counts as such an opinion, how we learn its content, and how it gets represented are anything but certain. (Hauser, 1999, p. 1)

"Attending to Opinions in Conflict" acknowledges the value of thoughtful opinions and simultaneously recognizes that opinions are not of equal utility in discerning action in a conflict. "Data driven" is a frequently used phrase to describe a particular form of organizational decision making (Miller, 2001). After gathering data, a group, a committee, and/or a given leader must ultimately assess the meaning of the information and its implications for a given company or unit. The data must be interpreted to discern its meaningful significance. Information is seldom the instigator of conflict; issues arise with contending opinions about the meaning

© *Krista Kennell/Shutterstock.com*

of the data. This chapter's *Spotlight on Leadership* features Warren Buffet, one of the world's most successful investors. He is able to analyze data to make informed investment decisions.

Buffet is a renowned philanthropist, pledging to give 99% of his entire fortune to charitable causes. His donation to the Bill & Melinda Gates Foundation was the largest charitable gift in U.S. history.

The reality of conflict lives within the realm of opinion; one must learn to navigate contrary judgments about what information means.

Later, in Chapter 14, we will conclude this work, *Conflict between Persons: The Origins of Leadership*, with an examination of **Homer's** (trans. 1967/1991) *Odyssey* with specific focus on the leadership of Odysseus (Figure 9.1). In the final chapter, we allude to a poignant dispute of opinions in the public domain of what we term the Western world. Roman author **Virgil** (trans. 1909) (Figure 9.2) turned to Homer's Greek epic, *Odyssey*, when writing his own epic, *Aeneid*.

FIGURE 9.1 Homer, author of the *Odyssey*.

FIGURE 9.2 Virgil, author of the *Aeneid*. (Statue on the Los Angeles public library building.)

Aeneas, the *Aeneid's* protagonist, is "a superior Odysseus" (Cairns, 1989, p. 193). From a Greek perspective, Odysseus was clever and cunning, a man of leadership. This Homeric conception of Odysseus is in contrast to Virgil's Roman *Aeneid*, which interprets Odysseus as deceitful, cruel, the antithesis of constructive leadership (Cairns, 1989, p. 193). Interestingly, both opinions dwell within the historical heritage of the West shaped by both Greek and Roman cultures.

HOMER
was an Ancient Greek poet who lived during the 8th or 9th century BCE and was the author of the epic poems, the *Iliad* and the *Odyssey* ("Homer," 2013).

VIRGIL (70 BCE–19 BCE)
was an Ancient Roman poet and author of the epic poem the *Aeneid*, which is partially based on Homer's epics ("Virgil," 2013).

INTRODUCTION

In everyday life, trustworthy opinions are worth their weight in gold. If we find a person willing to attend to our concern and uniqueness during a conflict situation, we have discovered a helpful advisor—one who pays attention to us and the unique setting, refusing to relate everything back to his or her own life. Opinions grounded in the abstract or in the life of another generally miss the mark of helpfulness. This chapter emphasizes the importance of evidence-driven opinions.

In "Attending to Opinion in Conflict," we lend weight to the pragmatic importance of learning from and sorting through different opinions in four major sections:

1. **Emotivism as individualistic decision making** addresses the problematic role of personal preference (MacIntyre, 1981, p. 11) as a conflict guide;
2. **Attribution theory** describes the meaning-seeking behavior of human beings;
3. **Evidence and public opinion** discusses the importance of public proof;
4. **Framing communicative leadership: Beginning with opinion** discusses the interplay of opinion and evidence as a practical foundation for learning in the act of leadership.

Multiplicity of opinion begins the moment we seek to protect and promote goods that are different from those of another. When opinions clash, conflict occurs as we witness ethical goods in collision. Moments of conflict permit us to learn, reminding us that we live in a world that does not always conform to our opinions. Our beliefs form in response to diversity of perspectives and assessments in the public sphere. Within this chapter, we examine ways in which opinions both assist and problematize the process of conflict.

EMOTIVISM AS INDIVIDUALISTIC DECISION MAKING

Emotivism, as coined by Alasdair MacIntyre (1981), stresses decision making by personal preference (p. 11). It is essential to differentiate opinion that is evidence-supported from the notion of emotivism. Thoughtful, **evidence-based opinions** are unique perspectives that emerge between one's knowledge and a particular situation; attending to all viewpoints (those of our own and others) is an essential communicative characteristic of thoughtful opinion. Emotivism is problematic because it is opinion based solely on personal inclinations; it connects to a narrow, private world marked by inability or unwillingness to understand that diversity of positions requires presentation of **public evidence**. Without learning from contrary orientations, we then adhere to our own private emotive assertions. Personal opinion inattentive to public evidence, the other, and the communicative environment ignores opportunities for collaboration with social connections.

Emotivism is decision making based upon one's immediate needs (Arnett, 2011, p. 41). Taylor and Hawes (2010) suggest that emotivism ignores "external accountability" (p. 106) and focuses on personal preferences. Emotivism is a failure to recognize situatedness within a narrative, relying solely upon oneself. Socially, emotivism is more problematic than selfishness. As stated in Chapter 6, "Relational Perception in Conflict," selfishness takes into account communal constraints, acknowledging the reality of the social nature of human life. Emotivism, however, is the decision-making arm of individualism, ignoring social restraints and limitations. Emotivism encapsulates a person within a narrow decision-making bubble, oblivious to social ties.

An example of emotivism at work is the deceitful acts of Wells Fargo, a banking and financial services company. In September 2016, reports surfaced that Wells Fargo employees created millions of unauthorized bank and credit card accounts without the consent of customers. These practices allowed the bank to earn fees and increase individual employee sales figures. Employees were motivated to create fake accounts because of the bonuses they would receive for exceeding sales targets. The bank paid $185 million in fines and $5 million in customer refunds. Wells Fargo also fired 5,300 employees (Egan, 2016). The credit card accounts scandal hurt the financial performance of Wells Fargo, forcing the company to close at least 400 branches by the end of 2018 (Wieczner, 2017). Another example of emotivism is financier Bernie Madoff, who was responsible for the world's largest Ponzi scheme[1]; he used new investor money to pay dividends[2] owed to older investors. The deceit lasted for several decades and began to unravel in 2008 as the recession motivated numerous investors to withdraw money faster than Madoff was able to acquire new funds. The size of his scheme's fraud was approximately $64.8 billion and affected more than 4,800 of Madoff's clients, including foreign banks, hedge funds,[3] celebrities, and charities (Henriques, 2009, para. 3–4). Madoff received a 150-year prison term, was ordered to make restitution, and was required to forfeit proceeds from the scheme. Emotivism played a role in Bernie Madoff's Ponzi business; he counted on decision making by personal opinion oblivious of the need for public evidence (Lenzner, 2008, para. 4). Personal opinion void of necessary research actually legitimized his company.

Emotivism is decision making based upon one's immediate impulses; it is unresponsive to the particular historical, social, and cultural contexts that give texture and meaning to decisions. In Aristotelian terms, one might propose that emotivism, which ignores the particular demands of a communicative context, is akin to pursuing pleasure void of concern for others. Aristotle outlined public virtues central to an Athenian *polis*; these practices later formed the heart of Western philosophy in action. Pleasure is not one of the foundational public virtues. In the *Nicomachean Ethics*, Book VII, Aristotle (trans., 1999) describes pleasure as "an unimpeded

---

1. A Ponzi scheme is a get-rich-quick tactic that begins with an initial large investment whose dividends are paid from the shares purchased from secondary shareholders. The second group of investors is then paid from the financial ventures of a third group and so on, until the scheme collapses. The scheme is named after Carlo Ponzi, an Italian immigrant who cheated New Englanders out of millions of dollars from 1919 to 1920 ("Ponzi Scheme," 2013).
2. Dividends are regularly paid to shareholders from the profits earned from investments.
3. Hedge funds are partnerships of investors using high-risk investment methods for capital gains.

activity of the natural state" (Warne, 2006, p. 106). Aristotle (trans., 1999) suggests that those who devote themselves to pleasure choose the life of grazing animals because they devote themselves to ceaseless physical gratification (p. 4). For Aristotle, a life of relentless gratification seeks pleasure, which at its best is a vulgar good, particularly when sought in excess. Pleasure is vulgar because it is void of consideration of the context and all its implications (Aristotle, trans. 1999). Aristotle stated that the most vulgar of virtues is pleasure; it only masquerades as a good. Emotivism is a decision-making expression of pleasure that focuses on *my* preferences, ignoring the particular moment and uniqueness of the communicative environment.

In November 2014, United Technologies Corporation CEO Louis Chenevert abruptly announced his retirement—surprising employees, investors, and stock analysts. United Technologies Corporation, maker of Pratt & Whitney jet engines, Sikorsky helicopters, Otis elevators, and Carrier air conditioning units, operates in the commercial aerospace, defense, and building industries. Shortly before this announcement, he reportedly made a side trip to Taiwan to check on the construction of his 110-foot yacht. Following this trip, Chenevert met with the board of directors who questioned his commitment to business priorities. Directors and senior managers believed his private interests distracted him from company operations. Chenevert's exit package was worth more than $195 million (Huddleston, 2015).

Another example is the overspending of the U.S. General Services Administration (GSA) that was documented by the Office of the Inspector General and made public in April 2012. The GSA is responsible for purchasing and managing goods and services for the U.S. government. The GSA employs approximately 13,000 people across the country (Bash & Walsh, 2012, para. 30). The reports of lavish spending upwards of $823,000 at the 2010 conference held in Las Vegas prompted a GSA deputy administrator to initiate an investigation about questionable spending at the event (Bash & Walsh, 2012, para. 29). The Office of the Inspector General report stated that the GSA portrayed certain events as award ceremonies in order to validate food and beverage costs typically not paid for by government funds. Additional examples of excessive behavior included more than $6,000 for commemorative coins for conference attendees; $75,000 for a team-building exercise; the hiring of a mind reader as entertainment; and the use of funds for an outside scouting agency that helped with conference planning and "scouting visits" (excuses for multiple preliminary trips to Las Vegas) (Cohen, 2012, para. 30). The fallout from the 2010 conference spending included resignations of Jeff Neely, the GSA official who organized the conference, and Martha Johnson, a GSA administrator. Two of Johnson's deputies also lost their jobs. The conference was an exemplar of emotivism, decision making based upon personal preference, pleasure, and excess.

Emotivism centers opinion on one's own personal experience. One practical way to counter this impulse is to attend to diversity of viewpoints, which is, at its best, the goal of opinion polling. The goal of public opinion polls is to offer a snapshot of what the entire population is thinking regarding a particular issue. The earliest forms of public opinion polls date back to the political campaigns of Franklin D. Roosevelt during the 1932 and 1936 presidential election years (Clark, 2005). The public opinion polling process remains intimately linked to political campaigns. According to Clark (2005), knowing the public's opinion is imperative for the creation of public policy and understanding marketing and research in a variety of fields. Public opinion reveals trends and patterns that shape the decision-making process. Public opinion content offers a glimpse of diversity in the public domain.

A constraint to public polling rests in the effort to limit the notion of the public to the majority (Mortensen, 2010, p. 360). This perspective is commonly associated with public opinion polling—for example, the Gallup Poll reveals a diversity of perspectives on issues ranging from foreign policy to the experiences of CEOs and physicians. The Gallup Poll has existed for 75 years and gathers information and data from individuals living in 160 countries. While the results of opinion polls claim to be truth, research suggests that sampling error and selection bias are two specific challenges associated with this process (Converse & Traugott, 1986). For example, errors in the results of the polls occur when a sample relies on contacting individuals through a home phone landline. This poll remains skewed toward an older population of adults who rely on a landline rather than a cellular phone as a primary source of communication. Polls also become less accurate depending upon the types of questions asked—slight modification in wording results in differing outcomes (Perrin & McFarland, 2011). The difficulty of discerning opinion results in the reality of multiple opinions, which is central in constructing a view of the public consistent with the orientation of this chapter. Failure to attend to diversity of opinion yields emotivism, once again.

All too often, another person makes an emotivistic judgment without any concern for the particular details that might alter or texture a decision. Someone may arrive at work in an unpleasant mood after a morning traffic rush. The response to the immediate demands of the moment, such as a co-worker in crisis or a boss demanding input on an important annual report, too easily finds influence through negative energy. Some people are absorbed in emotivistic abstraction, focusing only on themselves. People who make decisions by emotivism may occasionally be correct, just like a broken clock. Emotivism attends more to personal preference than to the uniqueness of circumstances. Emotivism protects the good of personal convenience, putting at risk one's connection with others and opening the door to conflict that is inattentive to interactions with others. Another way to examine decision making is through the application of attribution theory, where individuals assign meaning based upon ascriptions made on the basis of others' actions.

ATTRIBUTION THEORY

In the everyday vernacular, we witness attribution theory at work. This perspective seeks to explain how we assign causes to other persons' behaviors; what we believe causes people to behave a certain way, attributing meaning to their actions (Heider, 1958). In **attribution theory**, "individuals are motivated to evaluate a situation in order to understand why an outcome/event occurred" (Karakowsky & Siegel, 1995, p. 293). Heider (1958) believed that people continually analyze others' behaviors and attribute their actions to a "disposition," such as someone's personality, or to environmental effects that influence a particular context or person (p. 146). Narula (2006) connects attribution theory to the field of communication, linking Heider's attribution theory to a relational theory of interpersonal communication by proposing three assumptions about the assigning of communicative attributions: (1) the cause of specific communication behavior, (2) the responsibility for specific communication behavior, and (3) the meaning attributed to specific communicative behavior (p. 110). Relationships, formed and preserved, also find attribution of meaning of a given action not just through interpersonal communication behaviors, but also through attribution of meaning in action.

Understanding attributions in relationship to communication behaviors provides a productive framework for working with others (Manusov, 2006, p. 193). In organizations, stakeholder attributions influence how a company attempts to recover from a crisis. Coombs (2007) uses attribution theory to describe how people assign responsibility and blame others during an organizational crisis. Responding effectively to a calamity requires that organizational leaders identify the attributions made about the situation (p. 136). In interpersonal relationships, Young (2004) states, attribution theory explains why the "said" is often less important than the assumed "why" for a statement (p. 345). One's interpretation of the "why" shapes communicative responses and outcomes in a particular interaction. For example, if one sees a friend in the library and says "Hi," but the friend keeps walking, one might assume that the friend is angry; as a result, one might commence an unnecessary conflict simply because one did not hear the friend's greeting. In such a case, each of us might be tempted to attribute a reason to a friend's actions, such as anger, haste, or preoccupation. Good attributions require knowledge of the particular context and persons.

Researchers suggest that when people ask about the reasons for their behavior, individuals are often caught off guard, admitting that they are generally unaware of the underlying causes (Bargh & Chartrand, 2000). In order to compensate for lack of knowledge about rationales for behavior, people often generate whatever explanation seems plausible at the time, even if the answer is not remotely accurate (Bar-Anan, Wilson, & Hassin, 2010). The **fundamental attribution error** occurs when one has a tendency to overemphasize the internal and underestimate the external causes of another's behavior (Ross, 1977, p. 184). **Internal causes of behavior** refer to the character flaws of a given individual. **External causes** relate to particular circumstances beyond the control of the individual (Nisbett & Ross, 1980, p. 201). By formulating assumptions about internal motivation, one attempts to make generalizations about the other that are without evidence and that are too reliant upon personal opinion.

Communication scholars recognize attribution theory as a description of everyday sense making between persons. Of course, without careful consideration and evidence, such communicative behavior can languish in naïve psychology in which people attempt to connect observable behaviors to unobservable causes (Littlejohn, 1983, p. 132). Problematic attributions emerge with too little information and can lead to unintended negative consequences that are unanticipated and generate adverse side effects. Cavalier attributions often give rise to unexpected conflict. Attribution theory describes normative communicative behavior. The theory describes; it does not control or seek to persuade the manner or meaning of particular attributions. Such a task is part of our everyday responsibility to and with one another. Manusov and Spitzberg (2008) suggest that humans are naturally inquisitive and wonder why and how things occur. However, our assumptions can have serious consequences if they are wrong. Attributions about a partner's motive for behavior during a conflict can shape the event in problematic ways (Bippus, 2003; Sillars, 1980, 1981). A misplaced focus of attention can lead to missing the entire communicative activity. Imagine watching a classical concert and wondering about a world-class violinist's source of motivation for engaging in hours and hours of practice. If one sits through the concert wondering *why* a person would spend a lifetime practicing a musical craft, one misses the entire performance. We need to engage questions of attribution with caution and care. Constructive attributions derive from observation and evidence. Recognizing repetitive behaviors offers clarity within the conflict situation. Gathering **public evidence** keeps our focus of attention on constructing the best possible explanation as we make decisions, discern communicative direction, and meet conflict constructively.

EVIDENCE AND PUBLIC OPINION

Climate change is one of the most significant public issues in the current historical moment. Many different perspectives on climate change exist due to differing viewpoints on the causes of global warming and the appropriate response strategies. One perspective is that climate change results from human activity and requires stricter plant emission limits. Other perspectives suggest that climate change follows natural patterns in the Earth's environment. An additional perspective argues that there is no solid evidence that the Earth is getting warmer (Funk & Rainie, 2015). Climate change is a global concern with stakeholders representing the scientific community, private industry, public sector entities, and the general population. As the conflict continues, additional evidence appears that seems to reinforce each of the opposing sides.

Evidence refers to the material that supports a particular claim (Carlson, 1994). Recall the discussion from Chapter 3, "Human Sentiment: From Argument to Conflict," that illustrates Toulmin's (1958/2003) description of evidence as "the facts we appeal to as the foundation for the claim" (p. 97). Argumentation is also central to the scholarship of David Zarefsky (1990, 1986/2005, 2013). He suggested that evidence is a fundamental part of a public argument. "The role of evidence is to provide the justification for claims that solutions will be effective or that courses of action should be taken" (Baughman, Dorsey, & Zarefsky, 2011, p. 62). Evidence acts as support for decisions and communicative practices in personal and professional life.

Evidence tested in the public sphere was central to the work of Scottish Enlightenment philosopher George Campbell (1719–1796). Campbell's (1776/1990) *The Philosophy of Rhetoric* offered insights on different sources of verification. Some contend that George Campbell authored the most important work in rhetorical theory during the Enlightenment (Walzer, 2003, p. 1). In *The Philosophy of Rhetoric*, Campbell classified evidence into two broad categories: "intuitive" (p. 755) and "deductive" (p. 760). **Intuitive evidence** comes from three sources: (1) "intellection" (p. 755), (2) "consciousness" (p. 756), and (3) "common sense" (p. 757). **Intellection** relies on mathematical axioms, for example, 2 + 2 = 4. **Consciousness** is evidence based on judgments that arise from internal senses, sensations, and passions—for example, from seeing or feeling. Campbell defined **common sense** as "an original source of knowledge common to all mankind" (p. 757), which cannot be arrived at through reason alone. For example, the belief that the sun will set, even if not observed, relies upon common sense. The second broad category, **deductive evidence**, is either "demonstrative" or "moral" (p. 760). **Demonstrative evidence** transpires through intellection and scientific reasoning. Mathematical calculations such as velocity and weight are demonstrative evidence. For example, throwing a rock into a lake and watching it sink provides repeatable evidence for the same outcome with various-sized rocks. **Moral evidence** refers to "experience" (p. 764), "analogy" (p. 766), "testimony" (p. 766), and "calculations of chances" (p. 768). Both intuitive and deductive evidence find collaboration or denial in the public sphere.

To persuade in the public sphere requires evidence supportive of one's argument (Ottesen, 2008). Carlson (1994) offers three criteria for judging evidence in the public sphere: (1) relevance to a publicly stated perspective (p. 21); (2) role in advancing the argument (pp. 21–22); and (3) credibility of the source (p. 22). Claims tested in the public sphere become socially accepted when they shape opinions with public evidence. The use of public evidence to shape decisions propelled by public opinion is contrary to the act of emotivism.

The relationship between public evidence and public opinion surfaces in the debate between fact and interpretation. In "Communicology and the Worldview of Antidepressant Medicine," Isaac Catt (2012) addresses the reality of this debate between fact and interpretation—evidence and opinion—during a time described as the "depression era" (Moreira, 2007, p. 194). Catt problematizes the massive movement within the United States toward antidepressant medical treatments. Catt argues that while we live in a precarious historical moment, "there is plenty to be depressed about" (p. 84). The public and medical evidence to support antidepressant medication is lacking. Catt writes:

> *If it could be established that depression is a disease of the body, say like diabetes where evidence for treatment is based in urine and blood evidence, then medical practices should logically proceed with treatment of the brain organ. However, such evidence has never been found.* (p. 82, emphasis in original)

Rather than a disease verified in biological malfunction, Catt labels depression as an illness, "a conscious experience" (p. 95)—an "interpretation of signs" (p. 89). Catt addresses the common association of depression, antidepressants, and brain chemicals (pp. 93–94) and outlines ten considerations to frame a case "against blaming the brain" (p. 93). A sample of these considerations include the following points: (1) the reality that drugs producing similar effects in regard to brain chemicals do not alleviate depression; (2) the biological causes of depression are unknown; (3) alternative sources for "good" brain chemicals represent approximately half of the chemical production; (4) there are indecisive correlations between chemical imbalances and depression—that is, many people who experience chemical imbalances do not experience depression; and (5) depression's diagnosis is grounded in interpretation rather than tested evidence such as blood tests or brain scans (pp. 93–94). His argument adds a considered scholarly opinion to the public domain, one that counters conventional commercial thought.

Thoughtful opinions require public evidence, examination of the context, and reflection upon potentially unintended consequences. Problematic opinions emerge from unreflective emotivistic venting. If you know someone who consistently offers quips, cavalier comments that are penetratingly caustic and lack thoughtful reflection, you might discover someone driven more by an immediate mood than long-term thoughtfulness. The possibility for participation in the public sphere with a given public opinion requires thoughtfulness. Arendt's (1977) conception of opinion in the public domain is in contrast to unreflective and thoughtless assertions. Arendt's (2005) conception of the "promise of politics" rests with the vitality of a public domain that consists of multiple opinions shaped by inner conversation tested in open discussion. Arendt contended that Plato rejected the importance of *doxa* or "opinion" (p. 7) because he drew the incorrect conclusion from Socrates. She asserted that Socrates did not seek to eradicate opinion; his mission was to challenge untextured and thoughtless opinion. "Socrates brought the notion of *doxa* to the self—one must question one's own opinions. Living with others simply begins by living with oneself. It is for this reason that 'solitude' is important in conversation with oneself" (Arnett, 2013, p. 186). Opinions supported by evidence include thoughtfully considered ideas that provide conceptual ground from which to argue, which permits new positions to emerge as we attend to differing insights posed by others.

Constructive public opinion requires the mindful use of evidence and thoughtful attentiveness to the immediate situation. Too often, past failures and successes color and obscure one's ability to meet the immediate moment. One must learn to shape one's own opinions with a combination of public evidence and responsiveness to the particular setting. The notion of best practices must be adapted to the specific and unique demands of a given organization. Best practices address the needs of a unique moment and particular organization. Arendt (1977), as a political critic, offers a textured and attentive perspective on the role of opinion in the public sphere. She quotes James Madison's assertion that we cannot learn when surrounded by those who "have entertained the same opinions" (p. 235). One needs to consult opinions outside the province of one's daily discourse. Public and textured evidence needs to inform opinions. The public domain gathers strength from a diversity of thoughtful opinions, not from a single pristine truth that takes on a "despotic character" offered by a ruler with absolute power (p. 241). One must be wary of assertions about a given pristine truth that is contemptuous of all other opinions. "A 'revolution of contempt' is not sufficient long-term for the governing of a nation or a people" (Arnett, 2013, p. 87). Arendt's conception of the public domain includes multiple opinions and assumes the danger of derision for contrasting opinions. Diversity of opinion in the public domain decreases the chance of domination by a single power. In *Communication*

Ethics in Dark Times: Hannah Arendt's Rhetoric of Warning and Hope, Arnett (2013) articulated Arendt's position:

> *Arendt emphasizes that an individualistic conscience seeks to hold one's own opinion. In the political sphere, it is not "I alone" but persons holding a given opinion that make a difference. Public opinion does not rest in the pristine confidence of individualistic assurance but in standards external to the self. (p. 137)*

For Arendt, public opinion is the interactive link among experience, tradition, authority, and autonomous judgment—opinion is the connecting hub that brings all forms of evidence together in the act of decision making. Diversity of public opinion is a check and balance on singular perspectives that a small number of persons can impose upon others.

Rather than taking the perspective that locates public opinion with consensus (Perrin & McFarland, 2011; Sturgis & Smith, 2010), Arendt (1958/1998) contends that the public domain is composed of multiple perspectives/opinions. After the work of Arendt, this perspective continues with Jürgen Habermas, who provided the most thorough discussion of the philosophical roots of public opinion. Habermas (1962/1991) repeatedly stressed the importance of "public" (p. 6), public evidence, and "public opinion" (p. xii). He described the public sphere as "the private people, gathered to constitute a public" (p. 127) that shapes the needs of a society functioning within the state.

Numerous writers in the discipline of communication examine scholarship tied to the public domain (e.g., Arnett, 2001, 2012; Rawlins, 1998). One of the central communication figures writing about the public domain is Gerard Hauser (1999), who contends that the public domain is essential for civic conversation and must include many voices. Hauser points to difficulties in defining the term public—what counts as public opinion, its formation and detection. Hauser, in *Vernacular Voices: The Rhetoric of Publics and Public Spheres*, refers to the public sphere as "the undifferentiated public domain in which civic conversation, in general, occurs" (p. 40). Hauser assumes that political choice is not always rational or constituted by high-quality public argument, but these voices nevertheless constitute public evidence that must constitute acknowledged public evidence. Hauser understands the power of vernacular voices as a vital part of the public domain. He contends that the public sphere is somewhat informal and loosely tied to institutional norms; it finds shape through participation that involves compromise rather than rational consensus. Differences in the public sphere promote multiple ideas and practices and form a public based on collaboration and compromise (Hauser, 2008). The public acts as a voice of diversity of opinion that needs serious consideration. The public is an opinion terrain that requires learning from contrasting perspectives. Inclusion in the public sphere is a shared activity based on social norms, cultural relations, and values that conflict with one another. The public aims at self-regulation in an effort to reconcile different opinions with the intention of producing civil discourse (Hauser, 2004), which promotes discussion within the public sphere. Hauser stresses the importance of making a public space for opinions that compose a collective public sphere, containing a multiplicity of positions to shape the decision-making process for leaders.

The communicative life of a university president requires contending with opinions from students, faculty groups, board members, parents, and the local community. When considering a policy change, a president must consider the reality of diversity of opinions in the public domain. This process invites conflict as leaders attempt to discern between trustworthy and untrustworthy opinions and contrary perspectives. The public space of a university is larger than one person or perspective. Susan Resneck Pierce (2012), in her book *On Being Presidential: A Guide for College and University Presidents*, discusses that an effective president needs to understand and appreciate the various perspectives of faculty, staff, and students (p. 101). When a president is able to understand the opinions of multiple constituents connected with an institution, a more effective decision is likely. Pierce understands that the practical role of a president requires thoughtful consideration of both evidence-based opinion and sentiments propelled by less well-considered positions.

Now more than ever, leaders are perceived through various social media platforms such as Facebook, Twitter, LinkedIn, Foursquare, and Instagram, which offer outlets for proclamations of opinion without evidence. According to the National Labor Relations Board, the frequency of incidents involving employees who are terminated from their jobs as a result of inappropriate use of social media is increasing dramatically (Singletary, 2011). Top business leaders are not immune to social media gaffes. Gene Morphis, former Chief Financial Officer of Francesca's, a clothing retailer with 300 stores, tweeted "Board meeting. Good numbers=Happy Board." He lost his job for "improperly communicating company information through social media" because the official earnings had not been released to all investors (Holmes, 2012, para. 4). Morphis also had a history of posting work-related activities on his Facebook page including "Earnings released," "Conference call completed," "How do you like me now Mr. Shorty?" and "[Investor] roadshow completed. Sold $275 million of secondary shares. Earned my pay this week" (Silverman, 2012, para. 7). Opinions matter, and when shared in a cavalier manner, unexpected personal and professional consequences appear.

Multiple opinions in the public domain serve the hope of good decision making. One must attend to opinions without evidence with the hope that evidence will trump. As one gathers evidence, it is, additionally, important to avoid falling prey to an imperial effort of imposing one's opinion on another. As stated earlier, Arendt (1977) stressed diversity of opinion in the public domain. This position is further textured by Elisabeth Noelle-Neumann (1974, 1977, 1984, 1991), who reminds us of the dark side of a singular understanding of the public domain, where only the "right" opinion counts.

The reality of opinion complexity is at the heart of Noelle-Neumann's (1974, 1977, 1984, 1991) **spiral of silence** theory, outlined in the *Journal of Communication* and in *Communication Yearbook*. Noelle-Neumann, founder and director of the Allensbach Institute for Public Opinion Research Center in Allensbach, Germany, developed the spiral of silence theory to explain the growth and development of personal opinion and its relationship to public opinion. Noelle-Neumann linked the spiral of silence theory to increased pressure on people to conceal their personal opinions when they are in the minority. Noelle-Neumann (1984) defines public opinion as "opinions on controversial issues that one can express in public without isolating oneself" (pp. 62–63). Noelle-Neumann's theory assumes that fear of isolation results in a reluctance to express an opinion that counters prevailing public sentiment. Fear is the consequence of anticipated negative social sanctions, embarrassment, and social shunning. People conform to problematic opinions in order to identify with an in-crowd; few of us want to be shunned because of upholding an opposing point of view.

Noelle-Neumann (1984) believes humans discern the climate of public opinion and test their personal opinions via five bodily receptors: (1) eye/sight, (2) ear/sound, (3) tongue/taste, (4) nose/smell, and (5) skin/touch. Noelle-Neumann believes in a sixth sense or a "quasistatistical sense organ" (p. 115), an intuitive response to assist in discerning the general direction of public opinion. Noelle-Neumann (1974, 1977, 1984, 1991) predicts that people who recognize that their own personal opinions are taken seriously and restated by others are more likely to voice future opinions with self confidence in public, whereas those whose personal opinions are in dissonance with a given public become more reserved about sharing their estimations.

The work of Arendt (1977) and Noelle-Neumann (1974, 1977, 1984, 1991) points in a similar direction—beware of one imposed voice. Arendt demands that we protect opinions other than our own, and Noelle-Neumann reminds us of the practically closed nature of a public domain that tends toward exclusion. They both offer pragmatic wariness about the danger of one opinion alone and our ethical responsibility to keep the public domain vibrant with ideas other than our own. Both Arendt's diversity of opinion in the public domain and Noelle-Neumann's understanding of the practical relationship between personal and public opinion require us to protect the good of thoughtfulness that fosters opinion shaped by evidence, multiple perspectives, and reflective response to experiences. Public opinion, whether gathered through a public poll or discussed through the theoretical insights of Arendt, Habermas, Hauser or Noelle-Neumann, requires thoughtfulness as one gathers evidence and applies it to a unique setting. Understanding the public domain as a dwelling for diversity of ideas and perspectives is an ethical commitment that makes conflict inevitable in the short run and creative ideas available that can assist resourceful innovation in the long run.

More recent literature examines the importance of public opinion research. Gordon R. Mitchell (2015), in "Public Opinion, Thinly Sliced and Served Hot," aligns the limits of continuous response measurement (CRM), particularly tied to public debate and actions centered on political candidates. CRM is not a new phenomenon. The essay takes us to connections to CRM and radio in the late 1930s and early 1940s. Research by a Frankfurt School theorist, Theodor Adorno, argued against snap judgments and the herd effect of such insights. Making judgments too quickly is often uncritical of larger conceptual questions and issues, attempting to render a judgment of a thin slice of perception and data.

James N. Druckman (2014) uses the term *pathologies* in reference to studying public opinion. Leadership must respond to the citizens' preferences without simply imitating them. Public opinion research that yields an isomorphic connection between opinion and necessary action misses the reality of democratic responsiveness. The essay asserts that perhaps the last 50 years of public opinion has yielded little; indeed, the question about motivation and larger conceptual issues in response to public opinion need further and additional attention and study. The 2016 presidential election is an exemplar: The public assumption that Hillary Clinton would win revealed a conceptual polling error when Donald J. Trump became the 45th president of the United States.

In "Elite Polarization and Public Opinion: How Polarization Is Communicated and Its Effects" by Joshua Robison and Kevin J. Mullinix (2016), we discover the problematic nature of consistent framing of polarization. Framing polarized positions reifies them, instead of reporting separation and difference, which might invite a larger series of possibilities of response. The emphasis on polarization invites a two-sided world of limited partisanship.

Thomas Hanitzsch, Folker Hanusch, and Corinna Lauerer (2016) examine questions of public opinion and the standpoint of the gathering of information and gatekeepers in the soliciting of information on public opinion. The questions are not socially and culturally neutral but announce a perspective and an orientation that implicitly or explicitly renders a direction. The task of leadership requires recognizing the perspective and standpoint from which data gathering and presenting from a given orientation renders particularity of insight.

FRAMING COMMUNICATIVE LEADERSHIP: BEGINNING WITH OPINION

> *Opinions are formed in a process of open discussion and public debate, and where no opportunity for the forming of opinions exists, there may be moods—moods of the masses and moods of individuals, the latter no less fickle and unreliable than the former—but no opinion. (Arendt, 1963/1990, pp. 268–269)*

The first chapter in *The Power of Framing: Creating the Language of Leadership* discusses "the reality of framing" (Fairhurst, 2011, p. 1). Opinion does not emerge from a vacuum. Leadership does not confuse opinion with emotivism. Decision making by personal preference is an insufficient foundation for leadership. The only way in which imposed emotivistic opinion can function is through fear, a form of totalitarian proclamation. Leadership is also wary of mindless attributions, which take one's focus off the real issue, attending to the consequences rather than the purity of individual engagement in or motivation for a given activity. Leadership looks for coordinating common places in which public conflict will occur and attends to public evidence, knowing full well that public evidence is not pristine or pure. Public evidence is colored by public opinion. The evidence structures opinion, and opinion shapes evidence. Leadership understands that evidence-based opinion is significantly dissimilar to emotivism. Unreflective attribution connects to a narrow perceptive stance and misses the implications of practices, getting lost in the motivations. Leadership attentive to evidence requires an attentive examination of the situation and content. Fairhurst stresses that framing begins with the world before us, not with our own personal preferences.

Fairhurst (2011) offers ingredients for preparation for framing that is sensitive to multiple factors:

1. **Situation and context** (pp. 2–5) scaffold how a leader will frame. The conversation begins with the immediately demanded. Responsiveness to situation and context initiates the first step toward communicative leadership not driven by emotivism;
2. **Uncertainty** (pp. 7–8) is part of all contexts and situations. Leaders need to interpret the meaning of communicative events. One must learn to reduce uncertainty without missing an opportunity for creative innovation.
3. **Responsiveness** (pp. 8–9) is crucial to framing; it unites the context with public evidence. People need to witness common sense framing of "opinions" that have both public and contextual roots.

Emotivism privatizes evidence. Thoughtless attributions presuppose knowledge of the motivations of another, but opinion situated within public evidence provides coordinates for a conversation involving multiple persons. Leadership cannot rely upon decisions from the "I," whether right or not, because imposed opinion is emotivistic. Leadership cannot trust attribution of motives for another's actions and behavior, whether accurate or not. Leaders need to provide public evidence that keeps the conversation attentive to contextual coordinates in a conflict. Communicative leadership works with opinions that make public sense in a particular place at a given time. Conflict is more likely to bear good fruit if evidence-based opinions of multiple constituents shape the public domain.

REFERENCES

Arendt, H. (1977). *Between past and future: Eight exercises in political thought*. New York, NY: Penguin Books.

—. (1990). *On revolution*. New York, NY: Penguin Books. (Original work published 1963)

—. (1998). *The human condition*. Chicago, IL: University of Chicago Press. (Original work published 1958)

—. (2005). *The promise of politics* (J. Kohn, Ed.). New York, NY: Schocken Books.

Aristotle. (Trans., 1999). *Nicomachean ethics* (2nd ed.) (T. Irwin, Trans.). Indianapolis, IN: Hackett Publishing Company.

Arnett, R. C. (2001). Dialogic civility as pragmatic ethical praxis: An interpersonal metaphor for the public domain. *Communication Theory, 11*, 315–338.

—. (2011). Existential civility: Leaning forward into the rapids. *Spiritan Horizons, 6*, 39–48.

—. (2012). Biopolitics: An Arendtian communication ethic in the public domain. *Communication & Critical/Cultural Studies, 9*, 225–233.

—. *Communication in dark times: Hannah Arendt's warning of rhetoric and hope*. Carbondale: Southern Illinois University Press.

Bargh, J. A., & Chartrand, T. (2000). Studying the mind in the middle: A practical guide to priming and automaticity research. In H. Reis & C. Judd (Eds.), *Handbook of research methods in social psychology* (pp. 253–285). New York, NY: Cambridge University Press.

Bar-Anan, Y., Wilson, T. D., & Hassin, R. R. (2010). Post-priming confabulation causes erroneous self-knowledge. *Journal of Experimental Social Psychology, 46,* 884–894.

Bash, D., & Walsh, D. (2012, April 6). Deeper investigation of GSA spending needed, lawmaker says. *CNN.* Retrieved on March 16, 2013, from http://www.cnn.com/2012/04/06/politics/gsa-fallout/index.html?iref=allsearch

Baughman, W. A., Dorsey, D. W., & Zarefsky, D. (2011). Putting evidence in its place: A means not an end. *Industrial and Organizational Psychology, 4,* 62–64.

Bippus, A. M. (2003). Humor motives, qualities, and reactions in recalled conflict episodes. *Western Journal of Communication, 67,* 413–426.

Cairns, F. (1989). *Virgil's Augustan epic.* Cambridge: University of Cambridge Press.

Campbell, G. (1990). *The philosophy of rhetoric: Book I.* In P. Bizzell and B. Herzberg (Eds.), *The rhetorical tradition: Readings from classical times to the present* (pp. 749–795). Boston, MA: Bedford Books. (Original work published 1776)

Carlson, A. C. (1994). How one uses evidence determines its value. *Western Journal of Communication, 58,* 20–24.

Catt, I. (2012). Communicology and the worldview of antidepressant medicine. *The American Journal of Semiotics, 28,* 81–103.

Clark, D. A. T. (2005). Indigenous voice and vision as commodity in a mass-consumption society: The colonial politics of public opinion polling. *American Indian Quarterly, 29,* 228–238.

Cohen, T. (2012, April 17). Who's on first? Hearing shows GSA's dysfunction. *CNN.* Retrieved March 16, 2013, from http://www.cnn.com/2012/04/17/politics/gsa-hearing/index.html?iref=allsearch

Converse, P. E., & Traugott, M. W. (1986). Assessing the accuracy of polls and surveys. *Science, 234,* 1094–1098.

Coombs, W. T. (2007). Attribution theory as a guide for post-crisis communication research. *Public Relations Review, 33,* 135–139.

Druckman, J. N. (2014). Pathologies of studying public opinion, political communication, and democratic responsiveness. *Political Communication, 31,* 467–492.

Egan, M. (2016). 5,300 Wells Fargo employees fired over 2 million phony accounts. *CNN Money.* Retrieved from http://money.cnn.com/2016/09/08/investing/wells-fargo-created-phony-accounts-bank-fees/

Fairhurst, G. T. (2011). *The power of framing: Creating the language of leadership.* San Francisco, CA: Jossey-Bass.

Funk, C., & Rainie, L. (2015). Americans, politics, and science issues. *Pew Research Center.* Retrieved from http://www.pewinternet.org/2015/07/01/chapter-2-climate-change-and-energy-issues/

Grynbaum, M. M. (2013, March 11). Judge blocks New York City's limits on big sugary drinks. *The New York Times.* Retrieved March 17, 2013, from http://www.nytimes.com/2013/03/12/nyregion/judge-invalidates-bloombergs-soda-ban.html?pagewanted=all&_r=0

Habermas, J. (1991). *The structural transformation of the public sphere: An inquiry into a category of Bourgeois society* (T. Burger & F. Lawrence, Trans.). Cambridge, MA: MIT Press. (Original work published 1962)

Hanitzsch, T., Hanusch, F., & Lauerer, C. (2016). Setting the agenda, influencing public opinion, and advocating for social change: Determinants of journalistic interventionism in 21 countries. *Journalism Studies, 17*, 1–20.

Hauser, G. A. (1999). *Vernacular voices: The rhetoric of publics and public spheres*. Columbia: University of South Carolina Press.

—. (2004). Rhetorical democracy and civic engagement. In G. Hauser & A. Grim (Eds.), *Rhetorical democracy: Discursive practices of civic engagement* (pp. 1–14). Mahwah, NJ: Erlbaum.

—. (2008). Rethinking deliberative democracy: Rhetoric, power and civil society. In T. F. McDorman & D. M. Timmerman (Eds.), *Rhetoric and democracy* (pp. 225–264). East Lansing: Michigan State University Press.

Heider, F. (1958). *The psychology of interpersonal relations*. Hillsdale, NH: Lawrence Erlbaum Associates, Inc.

Henriques, D. (2009, March 10). Madoff will plead guilty; faces life for vast swindle. *The New York Times*. Retrieved March 17, 2013, from http://www.nytimes.com/2009/03/11/business/11madoff.html?pagewanted=all

Holmes, R. (2012, August 23). Social media compliance isn't fun, but it's necessary. *HBR Blog Network*. Retrieved on February 14, 2013, from http://blogs.hbr.org/cs/2012/08/social_media_compliance_isnt.html

Homer. (2013). In *Encyclopaedia Britannica Online*. Retrieved from http://www.britannica.com/EBchecked/topic/270219/Homer

Homer. (Trans. 1991). *Odyssey* (R. Lattimore, Trans.). New York, NY: HarperCollins Publishers, Inc. (Original translation published 1967

Huddleston, T. (2015). Former CEO of United Technologies left with $195 million. *Fortune*. Retrieved from http://fortune.com/2015/02/06/united-technologies-exit-pay/

Karakowsky, L. & Siegel, J. P. (1995). The effects of demographic diversity on causal attributions of work group success and failure: A framework for research. In M. J. Martinko (Ed.), *Attribution theory: An organizational perspective* (pp. 289–314). Delray Beach, FL: St. Lucie Press.

Lenzner, R. (2008, December 12). Bernie Madoff's $50 billion Ponzi scheme. *Forbes*. Retrieved February 11, 2013, from http://www.forbes.com/2008/12/12/madoff-ponzi-hedge-pf-ii-in_rl_1212croesus_inl.html

Littlejohn, S. W. (1983). *Theories of human communication*. Belmont, CA: Wadsworth.

MacIntyre, A. (1981). *After virtue: A study in moral theory*. Notre Dame, IN: University of Notre Dame Press.

Manusov, V. L. (2006). Attribution theories: Assessing causal and responsibility judgments in families. In L. A. Baxter & D. O. Braithwaite (Eds.), *Engaging theories in family communication: Multiple perspectives* (pp. 181–196). Thousand Oaks, CA: Sage.

Manusov, V. L., & Spitzberg, B. (2008). Attribution theory. In L. A. Baxter & D. O. Braithwaite (Eds.), *Engaging theories in interpersonal communication: Multiple perspectives* (pp. 37–49). Thousand Oaks, CA: Sage.

Miller, K. I. (2001). Quantitative research methods. In F. M. Jablin & L. L. Putnam (Eds.), *The new handbook of organizational communication: Advances in theory, research, and methods* (pp. 137–160). Thousand Oaks, CA: Sage.

Mitchell, G. R. (2015). Public opinion, thinly sliced and served hot. *International Journal of Communication, 9*, 21–45.

Moreira, V. (2007). Critical phenomenology of depression in Brazil, Chile, and the United States. *Latin-American Journal of Fundamental Psychopathology, 4*, 193–218.

Mortensen, P. B. (2010). Political attention and public policy: A study of how agenda setting matters. *Scandinavian Political Studies, 33*, 356–380.

Narula, U. (2006). *Dynamics of mass communication theory and practice.* New Delhi: Atlantic.

Nisbett, R. E., & Ross, L. D. (1980). *Human inference: Strategies and shortcomings of social judgment.* Englewood Cliffs, NJ: Prentice-Hall.

Noelle-Neumann, E. (1974). The spiral of silence: A theory of public opinion. *Journal of Communication, 24*, 43–51.

—. (1977). Turbulences in the climate of opinion: Methodological application of the spiral of silence theory. *Public Opinion Quarterly, 41*, 143–158.

—. (1984). *The spiral of silence: Public opinion—Our social skin.* Chicago, IL: University of Chicago Press.

—. (1991). The theory of public opinion: The concept of the spiral of silence. In J. A. Anderson (Ed.), *Communication Yearbook 14* (pp. 256–287). Newbury Park, CA: Sage.

Ottesen, J. L. (2008). Put some punch in your pen. *AACE International Transactions*, 1–9.

Perrin, A. K., & McFarland, K. (2011). Social theory and public opinion. *Annual Review of Sociology, 37*, 87–107.

Pierce, S. R. (2012). *On being presidential: A guide for college and university presidents.* San Francisco, CA: John Wiley & Sons.

Ponzi scheme. (2013). In *Encyclopaedia Britannica Online.* Retrieved from http://www.britannica .com/EBchecked/topic/1568561/Ponzi-scheme.

Rawlins, W. K. (1998). Theorizing public and private domains and practices of communication: Introductory concerns. *Communication Theory, 8*, 369–380.

Robinson, J., & Mullinix, K. J. (2016). Elite polarization and public opinion: How polarization is communicated and its effects. *Political Communication, 33*(2), 261–282.

Ross, L. (1977). The intuitive scientist and his shortcoming. In L. Berkowitz (Ed.), *Advances in experimental social psychology* (Vol. 10, pp. 174–220). New York, NY: Academic Press.

Sillars, A. L. (1980). Attributions and communication in roommate conflicts. *Communication Monographs, 47*, 180–201.

—. (1981). The sequential and distributional structure of conflict interactions as a function of attributions concerning locus of responsibility and stability of conflicts. In D. Nimmo (Ed.), *Communication Yearbook 4* (pp. 218–235). New Brunswick, NJ: Transaction.

Silverman, R. E, (2012, May 14). Facebook and Twitter postings cost CFO his job. *The Wall Street Journal.* Retrieved on February 11, 2013, from http://online.wsj.com/article/SB100014 24052702303505504577404542168061590.html

Singletary, M. (2011, September 14). Can Facebook get you fired? Watch what you say about your employer on social media. *The Washington Post.* Retrieved on February 14, 2013, from http://articles.washingtonpost.com/2011-09-14/ business/35275285_1_social-media-postings-facebook-conversation

Sturgis, P., & Smith, P. (2010). Fictitious issues revisited: Political interest, knowledge, and the generation of nonattitudes. *Political Studies, 58*, 66–84.

Taylor, B. C., & Hawes, L. C. (2010). What are we, then? Postmodernism, globalization, and the meta-ethics of contemporary communication. In G. Cheney, S. May, & D. Munshi (Eds.), *The handbook of communication ethics* (pp. 99–118). New York, NY: Routledge.

Toulmin, S. E. (2003). *The uses of argument*. Cambridge, UK: Cambridge University Press. (Original work published 1958)

Virgil. (2013). In *Encyclopaedia Britannica Online*. Retrieved from http://www.britannica.com/EBchecked/topic/629832/Virgil

Virgil (Trans., 1909). *Virgil's Aeneid: Part 13 Harvard Classics* (J. Dryden, Trans.). New York, NY: P. F. Collier & Sons.

Walzer, A. E. (2003). *George Campbell: Rhetoric in the age of enlightenment*. Albany: State University of New York Press.

Warne, C. (2006). *Aristotle's 'Nicomachean Ethics': A reader's guide*. New York, NY: Continuum International Publishing Group.

Wieczner, J. (2017). Here's how much Wells Fargo's fake accounts scandal is hurting the bank. *Fortune*. Retrieved from http://fortune.com/2017/01/13/wells-fargo-fake-accounts-scandal-closing-branches-earnings/

Young, S. L. (2004). What the ---- is the problem? Attribution theory and perceived reasons for profanity usage during conflict. *Communication Research Reports*, *21*, 338–347.

Zamost, S., & Griffin, D. (2012, August 24). Kansas City GSA employee works from home—in Hawaii. *CNN*. Retrieved March 16, 2013, from http://www.cnn.com/2012/08/23/politics/gsa-hawaii-teleworking/index.html?iref=allsearch

Zarefsky, D. (1990). *Lincoln, Douglas, and slavery: In the crucible of public debate*. Chicago, IL: University of Chicago Press.

—. (2005). *President Johnson's war on poverty: Rhetoric and history*. Tuscaloosa: University of Alabama Press. (Original work published 1986)

—. (2013). *Public speaking: Strategies for success* (7th ed.). Boston, MA: Allyn and Bacon.

Chapter Ten

CONFLICT STYLES: THE DANGERS OF UNTHINKING FAMILIARITY

There are three ways of dealing with difference: domination, compromise, and integration. By domination only one side gets what it wants; by compromise neither side gets what it wants; by integration we find a way by which both sides may get what they wish. (Follett, 1942, p. 200)

"Conflict Styles: The Dangers of Unthinking Familiarity" investigates conventional styles of conflict engagement, stressing the importance of a diversity of conflict options. Engaging a contextually inappropriate conflict style can enflame and augment conflict between persons. A minimalist objective in a communicative struggle should be to enact a style of conflict that assists, or, at the very least, does not make the situation worse. The key is to learn from conflict and, if possible, to assist both parties in the dispute. This chapter's *Spotlight on Leadership* features Ken Chenault, one of the first African Americans to serve as CEO of a Fortune 500 firm, American Express, and is the longest-serving top executive at a major U.S. financial services firm. Chenault guided the company during the devastating September 11, 2001, attacks. Most recently, he responded to the challenges of changing digital technologies.

© lev radin/Shutterstock.com

Ken Chenault assisted numerous organizations, including the National September 11 Memorial & Museum at the World Trade Center Foundation and the NYU Langone Medical Center. Chenault also serves as a director of International Business Machines Corporation (IBM) and The Procter & Gamble Company. In 2010, he received the Third Lantern Award for his leadership and dedication to public service. This award recognizes the highest commitment to public service.

Diversity of people, contexts, and differing ethical goods in a conflict underscore the importance of multiple conflict styles. Constructive conflict requires an organic connection between conflict style and the specific quarrel between persons.

Extraordinary examples of constructive conflict and healthy competition have occurred on the track at the 2016 Summer Olympics in Rio de Janeiro and during a senior day softball game between Central Washington and Western Oregon. In the first example, American runner Abbey D'Agostino and New Zealand runner Nikki Hamblin collided about 3,000 meters into their 5,000-meter race when Hamblin stumbled into D'Agostino. They both fell to the ground. Although D'Agostino was able to convince Hamblin to get back up, D'Agostino was badly injured. Together, they managed to encourage each other to finish the race. Doctors later determined that D'Agostino had torn her ACL and had a strained MCL in her knee. The two women received the Pierre de Coubertin medal for their display of sportsmanship during the competition (Bruner, 2016).

In the second example, Central Washington was one game behind Western Oregon in the Great Northwest Athletic Conference. Central needed to win the second game of a double header in order to secure a berth in the National Collegiate Athletic Association's (NCAA) Division II playoffs. As Western Oregon's right fielder, Sara Tucholsky, approached the plate, it was the second inning with two runners on base. Then the unexpected struck: Tucholsky, with a .153 batting average, hit the first home run of her career (Prince, 2008, para. 8). As Tucholsky watched the ball pass over the fence, she missed first base (Prince, 2008, para. 9). When she turned quickly to touch first, she collapsed with an injured right knee (Prince, 2008, para. 9). She could not make it around the bases on her own. The umpires ruled that a substitute runner could enter in her place, but the homerun would be voided, replaced by a single with 2 RBIs (Runs Batted In) (Prince, 2008, para. 12). The substitute seemed to be Western Oregon's only option since NCAA rules did not allow Tucholsky's teammates to help her round the bases. Then all witnessed competition at its best. Mallory Holtman, Central Washington's first baseman and the conference's all-time home run leader, offered to help carry Tucholsky home, pausing for her to touch each base. Holtman and another Central Washington teammate Liz Wallace carried their opponent, Tucholsky, to home plate and to victory. Central Washington displayed an elite sense of competition, caring more for the game than for victory at any price. The decision to assist resulted in Central Washington's losing any hope for a playoff bid. Western Oregon won the game 4–2 with those in the stands having watched victory more fundamental than that on the scoreboard. The conflict style one uses can sometimes turn a destructive moment into a creative opportunity for both parties.

INTRODUCTION

This chapter encourages one to reflect before, during, and after conflict, avoiding old, repetitious acts of unthinking familiarity. One's routine conflict style is often unreflectively manifested when one is exhausted, a little frazzled, and with seemingly no time to think. Our thoughtless use of a conflict style can hinder constructive conflict enactment. We must examine the conflict situation and not unthinkingly follow a comfortable style. The context, not our preferences, needs to guide our selection of a conflict style. The conflict milieu and the particular clash of goods need to inform our conflict style.

In "Conflict Styles: The Dangers of Unthinking Familiarity," we explore four major issues:

1. **The danger of unreflective routine** reminds us not to fuel an additional conflict via our style of dealing with a dispute;
2. **Conflict styles** explores five conventional ways people address conflict—avoiding, accommodating, competing, compromising, and collaborating;
3. **Existential trust and communicative environment** underscores the necessity of having confidence in the communicative environment;
4. **Framing communicative leadership: Existential trust** examines how leaders frame a conflict mode appropriate in a particular conflict context.

Engaging multiple conflict modes in relation to a given conflict situation provides a communicative education, if we read the contextual signs that emerge before, during, and after a dispute. Differing styles of conflict assist persons as contexts and conflicting ethical goods shape contentious moments. In conflict, the pragmatic communication ethics issue is to keep our focus of attention on the question at hand, not to exacerbate the problem by a problematic conflict style. We must counter the impulse to use a familiar conflict style that fits us but is inappropriate for a given conflict setting; our minimal goal is to avoid turning one conflict into two, with the second conflict being propelled by the use of a problematic conflict style.

THE DANGER OF UNREFLECTIVE ROUTINE

In order to utilize a variety of conflict styles, one must begin with knowledge of one's favorite conflict approach, held in reserve unless called for by the context. The context drives appropriate selection among conflict styles. We all know people with outstanding abilities who are unable to convince others of their plans due to a problematic communication and conflict style. Early on in the academic career of one of the authors, the search for talent included one criterion—looking for the person with the greatest talent, finding the smartest candidate. However, all too often, the brilliant person can make the organization less productive if that person does not connect the appropriate conflict style to a specific dispute situation. One of the criteria for organizational success is finding people who make those around them smarter by the creative manner in which they meet conflict. Such people make organizations sharper, more inventive, and bigger. The misuse of conflict style decreases productive opportunities within an organization.

Immanuel Kant (1724–1804) and Hannah Arendt (1906–1975) stressed the importance of going beyond one's own provincial visceral impulses and attending to a larger environment (Arendt, 1968, p. 79; Kant, 1792/2006). Our contention is that one's conflict style should assist in enlarging the communicative space. Take, for example, Tammy Tibbetts, cofounder of She's the First, an organization and movement committed to girls' education in low-income countries. While working at Hearst Publications, Tibbetts thought of an idea for a social media–driven campaign that would inspire millennial women to fundraise for girls' education in low-income countries ("Founding Story," 2017). With the goal of creating first-generation graduates, the She's the First movement has sponsored more than 1,200 years of girls' education. Although She's the First began as a grassroots movement in 2009, as of July 2016, the organization assisted more than 750 scholars and their families. There are approximately 4,000 chapter members across almost 200 university campuses. Our contention is that communicative space grows with the presence of persons who engage conflict with thoughtful use of style that matches the location.

People who help a communicative space to feel greater give us energy and invoke an infectious desire to learn while assisting others. Such people build communicative dwellings that encourage the movement from "good to great" (Collins, 2001; Collins & Hansen, 2011). Such institutions nourish places that put wind beneath the wings of others, allowing people to prosper beyond expectation. Those who make communicative environments feel grander offer counter-examples to those who seem to make communicative environments smaller and increasingly more provincial. People who assist with amplifying the sense of a communicative environment recognize the necessity of multiple conflict styles; we must pay attention to the local soil out of which a conflict emerges.

Limiting oneself to a single conflict style is a sure recipe for making places feel smaller. The assumption that there is only one correct viewpoint is a "**two-valued orientation**" (Hayakawa & Hayakawa, 1991, p. 13). Hayakawa and Hayakawa (1991) suggest that in conflict, the two-valued orientation is ever present and almost unavoidable (p. 128). The more invested a person is in a particular idea, the more likely that person is to adopt a two-valued orientation. A "**multi-valued orientation**" offers an alternative to a two-valued perspective (p. 126). When adopting a multi-valued orientation, one explores a variety of options for addressing the conflict situation. Knapp, Putnam, and Davis (1988) argue that there are limitations to embracing one particular style in organizational conflict—provinciality leads to forfeiture of the bigger picture. Individual and context-specific issues must be evaluated with an awareness of a "**systems perspective**" that understands the whole as greater than the sum of the parts and comprehends the uniqueness of each component (p. 429).

Two communication scholars who focus on baseball are Gary Gumpert and Susan Drucker (2002); they offer an analysis of the communication that occurs within the sport and between the game and society at large. For example, if one plays on a major league baseball team and is intent on winning every game, disappointment will reign. It is impossible to win every game; the season is simply too long to go undefeated. Major league baseball statistics reveal that the team winning the World Series every year did not always have the best record in baseball. From 1995 to 2012, the team with the best record during the regular season won the World Series only three times. Over the last 25 years, 20 different teams have finished the regular season with over 100 victories, and of those teams, only two won the World Series (Berri, 2012). The message is clear—keep a larger perspective than an individual win.

One's focus of attention must include short and long term perspectives, outlined in the work of D'Aveni and MacMillan (1990). Their research compares the written communication of managers within failing and surviving firms. Their goal was to identify the specific environmental aspects that maintained the focus of attention of each group of managers. D'Aveni and MacMillan found that managers of surviving firms pay equal notice to both the short-term and long-term aspects of the company. D'Aveni and MacMillan suggest that failing firms avoid focusing on long-term problems because of short-term constraints. The leaders' focus of responsiveness determines the success or failure of the firms. A **focus of attention** includes thoughtful concentration on the needs and demands of a particular context in a given moment (Greve, 2008). Careful consideration requires a "set of processes that allow us to process certain information to the (relative) exclusion of other information" (Racer & Dishion, 2012, p. 32). Attention assists us in differentiating between pertinent information and irrelevant content and permits one to discern "**communicative meaning**" (Arnett & Arneson, 1999, p. 145), which offers temporal clarity. Arnett and Holba (2012) stress communicative meaning as central to philosophy of communication, which emerges in the performance of the "doing" of philosophy of communication. They write:

> It is in the doing, the praxis of philosophy of communication, that one understands a unique and meaningful communicative texture, turning a two-dimensional understanding of a given event into a three-dimensional meaningful understanding that cannot be totally possessed. (p. 9)

One offers temporal clarity for finding direction in the midst of conflict. It is important to connect the right conflict style to a given situation, keeping one's focus of attention on the right issues. Awareness of a larger picture requires one to ignore provincial impulses. The term coined by Kant (1792/2006) was cosmopolitan (p. 694).

Multiplicity shapes communicative environments and systems. Learning a multiplicity of conflict styles moves us from a single conflict orientation, a mindless technique, to thoughtful and unique responses. Such conflict wisdom does not ensure a constructive outcome, but it does make it more likely. Working with others in varied contexts requires thoughtful consideration. Before we enter a conflict, we need to ask ourselves what conflict style is called for in a given situation.

CONFLICT STYLES

The effectiveness of a given conflict style is context dependent. Discerning which conflict style to use in a particular context requires one to learn to read the setting as a first guidance for direction. Manning (1992) states that "communication is context dependent and draws on many social sources of meaning other than the content of a given message or series of messages" (p. 17). "Context dependent" suggests that we do not impose upon a situation or upon others; we must respond to it and them. Thomas and Kilmann (1974) framed what is now the conventional understanding of a multiplicity of conflict styles. Their work is a benchmark, highlighting five different approaches: avoiding, accommodating, competing, compromising, and collaborating (p. 5). Their understanding of conflict style continues to dominate conflict literature in the field of communication (Konovsky, Jaster, & McDonald, 1989; Mitchell & Boster, 1998; Nicotera, 1993; Ross & DeWine 1988; Shockley-Zalabak, 1988; Thomas, Thomas, & Schaubhut, 2008; Wilson & Waltman, 1998; Womack, 1988).

The first style, **conflict avoidance**, occurs when individuals intentionally remove themselves from the dispute situation. There are numerous reasons why people avoid conflict; some are constructive and others problematic. For example, one must decide if a conflict is worth the time, effort, and energy that will be required. Avoiding conflict may indicate that a particular issue is simply not of sufficient importance to engage. However, avoiding conflict can be detrimental to a relationship if one continually pretends that an issue does not exist, permitting the conflict to gather further momentum.

Within the communication literature, conflict avoidance is generally a negative behavior used for relational maintenance that contributes to later explosions between persons (Ayers, 1983; Dainton & Gross, 2008). Conflict avoidance behaviors can be dysfunctional when they escalate existing conflicts and create additional ones (Roloff & Wright, 2009). Failing to address important conflict issues can result in an avalanche of complaints thrown at the other.

An **accommodating** conflict style may be appropriate when it is important and/or necessary to concur with another's position. There are numerous instances when it is prudent to coexist with the sentiments of the group or of another person. However, continually agreeing with the viewpoints of others without consideration of the context leads to "appealing acts" (Rausch, Barry, Hertel, & Swain, 1974, p. 115) where one engages a prolonged focus on the other's motives.

Appropriate use of a **competing** style of conflict requires one to discern whether a struggle is worth the engagement. In competition, we can easily forget about the other and the issue at hand, moving our focus toward winning alone. If one has ever thought, "I must have the last word" or "I am not losing this argument," one has engaged in the shadow side of competition, which insists on being right at any relational cost. A competitive spirit that cares more about the best idea or task is an alternative to the view of competition above. According to Georg Simmel (1908/1955), "genuine competition" resists what would "prevent the full application of [a person's] strength in the competitive struggle" (p. 59). Healthy competition keeps the focus on excellence, with winning as a by-product or, in some cases, simply irrelevant, as the "home run with assistance" epitomized.

The art of **compromise** requires giving up a little while gaining some. Compromise obliges a give and take with another. Compromising in conflict promotes a situation perceived as fair by both parties, but neither party is fully satisfied. Compromise, however, requires tradeoffs or making one "split the difference," which does not always result in a fair resolution (Folger, Poole, & Stutman, 1993, p. 43).

Collaboration is more textured than compromise, requiring one to participate directly with another in identifying creative alternatives. Foss and Griffin (1995) state that collaboration is a form of invitational rhetoric that permits both parties to reach a resolution that offers a win/win situation. Both parties exit the conflict feeling mutually satisfied. Collaboration results in better decision making because there is a high level of concern for the interplay of self, other, context, issue, and relationship (Kuhn & Poole, 2000; Sillars, 1980; Tutzauer & Roloff,

1988). Collaboration provides a constructive response to a conflict situation (Rusbult, Johnson, & Morrow, 1984) by maximizing the gains for both parties (Canary & Cupach, 1988). Collaboration, however, takes a great deal of time, energy, and effort. It is the most privileged conflict style and the most difficult to implement (Canary & Cupach, 1988). Collaboration requires discovering solutions that do not focus solely on individuals or their ideas (Kuhn & Poole, 2000). Collaboration necessitates envisioning a bigger picture, offering opportunities to generate creative and constructive possibilities for both parties. Collaboration as a conflict style was popularized by Roger Fisher and William L. Ury (1981) in *Getting to Yes: Negotiating Agreement Without Giving In*. Collaboration allows us to work actively with another on a project of importance, opening up creative options that yield previously unseen insights.

In the aftermath of the Flint, Michigan, water crisis, we witness each of these conflict styles in action. This water crisis is "one of the largest public health crises in Michigan history" (Egan, 2016, para 3). Flint is located 70 miles north of Detroit and is 56.6% African American. According to the U.S. Census Bureau, 41.6% of residents live below the poverty line and the median household income is $24,679. Flint's water crisis began in 2014 when the

city began relying on the local Flint River as its main water source. At that time, the city was under the control of a state-appointed emergency manager. Since Flint's water was not properly treated, lead and other toxins entered the water supply. Conflict *avoidance* resulted in an estimated 8,000 children exposed to lead and other toxins (Sanburn, 2016). Children exposed to lead can experience severe neurological problems, impaired cognition, and behavioral problems. In pregnant women, lead reduces fetal growth. Conflict *accommodation,* almost 2 years later, required many Flint residents to use bottled water for drinking, cooking, and bathing. Conflict *competition* results in scarce resources. As of December 2016, 13 individuals are under investigation for the Flint water crisis and an outbreak of Legionnaires' disease, including former emergency managers, Flint city employees, current or former state employees, and a Flint water plant employee (Egan & Anderson, 2016). In January 2017, a $722 million class action lawsuit was filed against the EPA on behalf of more than 1,700 residents impacted by the water crisis (Carmody, 2017). Those protesting the unsafe conditions in Flint engaged conflict *collaboration* as an essential tool for correcting the abuse of their water supply. This crisis displays the limits of conflict *compromise* in the pursuit of public safety.

Each style of conflict engagement (avoiding, accommodating, competing, compromising, and collaborating) is a responsive option driven by the context. Different conflict styles appropriately answer the uniqueness of a situation. In workplace and everyday conflict, people must select from different conflict approaches, depending upon individual preferences and responsiveness to the uniqueness of the conflict at hand. Inviting the appropriate communicative environment frames conflict within trust.

EXISTENTIAL TRUST AND COMMUNICATIVE ENVIRONMENT

Trust conventionally rests within the realm of personal relationships. Our understanding of trust is contrary to this person-centered convention. Having trust in coworkers and in an organization has positive influences on productivity. Conventional communication scholarship focuses on person-centered approaches that consider **trust** as "people's abstract positive expectations that they can count on partners to care for them and be responsive to their needs now and in the future" (Holmes & Rempel, 1989, p. 188). The way that one communicates is associated with having trust or lacking trust in the relationship (Pearce, 1974, p. 236). Research suggests that trust has positive effects on individuals, groups, and organizational settings. Person-centered trust connects to one's positive performance within various situations (Earley, 1986; Rich, 1997; Robinson, 1996), one's overall job satisfaction (Driscoll, 1978; Ellis & Shockley-Zalabak, 2001; Muchinsky, 1977; Rich, 1997), organizational citizenship (Konovsky & Pugh, 1994; McAllister, 1995), problem solving (Zand, 1972), and cooperation (Axelrod, 1984).

If, however, one senses the opposite of trust, one becomes more interested in self-protection than in creative productivity. Therefore, we connect trust to a larger communicative environment. It is as if the ground (trusting or otherwise) that composes a given communicative environment moves one toward excellence or toward increasing acts of self-protection. Martin Buber (1967), in his description of the danger of "existential mistrust" (p. 309), contended that it is a serious problem when there is "destruction of confidence in existence, in general" (p. 309); one loses trust in the communicative environment itself. Arnett (1986) explained **existential mistrust** as a communicative "atmosphere of suspicion and judgment" (p. 49). When one cannot trust existence, the ground upon which the interlocutors stand, the communicative environment, ceases to invite a sense of confidence between persons. Without a communicative environment of trust, individual members turn to acts of self-protection. Our communicative action can either enhance or minimize existential mistrust. Communicative actions such as gossip, deceit, and lying decrease trust in a communicative environment.

Existential trust, in contrast, is "trust in existence or the ground on which one stands" (Arnett, 2001, p. 326). Maurice Friedman (1972) believed that existential trust is at the heart of Buber's work—trust undergirds an authentic communicative environment (Czubaroff & Friedman, 2000, p. 246). A model of existential trust promotes "courage, hope, and faith so as to help us lessen the threat of our differences" in various situations (Morris & Rodriguez, 2005, p. 101). Existential trust moves beyond reciprocity and undergirds the communicative environment

(Morris & Rodriguez, 2005, p. 95). Existential trust is necessary in all interactions of knowing and being in the world, offering a ground that supports the communicators (Kalman, 1999).

James Carville, a prominent figure in the Democratic Party, was the lead strategist for Bill Clinton's presidential campaign. His wife, Mary Matalin, has served as political consultant for the Republican Party, campaign director for George H. W. Bush, and assistant to George W. Bush (Matalin, Carville, & Knobler, 1994). Many people wonder how two individuals with opposite views on politics can remain in a relationship during an election year. The answer is simple—understanding the other side of an argument helps each person grow; they make each other stronger (Matalin, Carville, & Knobler, 1994). They focus on ideas that enrich their relationship, constructing a communicative home together. In conflict situations, trusting the communicative dwelling is essential. Conflict situated within a trust-laden communicative dwelling provides assurance in the process of conflict. A communicative dwelling constituted by existential trust does not fear mistakes, disagreement, or disruptions of routine. The fundamental objective is to meet each unexpected challenge with the hope of becoming more insightful as one assists a communicative dwelling to become a place of existential trust.

We offer four pragmatic suggestions for inviting a communicative environment of existential trust: (1) forgiving; (2) acknowledging the reality of "**broken covenants**" (Bellah, 1975, p. xxii) that call for responsibility; (3) differentiating optimism and hope; and (4) knowing when to conclude involvement in a given communicative environment. First, **forgiving** is an essential conflict skill, particularly when you are going to work and/or live with your disputants for a long time. Forgiveness reduces impulses for psychological aggression and allows one to move forward (Paleari, Regalia, & Fincham, 2010), permitting relationships to accrue depth and maturity (Kelley, 1998). When one does not forgive, the relationship can deteriorate quickly (Morse & Metts, 2011, p. 240). Holding on to relational pain, grief, and hurt is psychologically unhealthy. Refusal to forgive fosters a long-term hurt that disturbs not only the self but one's friends, family, and coworkers as well. Forgiveness puts one at ease with one's life and others (McCullough, Sandage, & Worthington, 1997, p. 15). Mary Johnson exhibited an act of forgiveness as she made peace with Oshea Israel, the man convicted of murdering her 20-year-old son, Laramiun, in 1993 after an argument at a party. Laramiun was her only child, and Mary realized that she desired to forgive Israel. During Israel's years in prison, Johnson frequently visited her son's killer. Shortly before Israel's release, Johnson recommended him to her landlord. Israel now lives next door to Johnson where they share a front porch. Johnson and Israel tell their story of forgiveness as they visit prisons and churches together (Hartman, 2011).

In addition, the photojournalism project, "Portraits of Reconciliation," is part of a national effort toward reconciliation and forgiveness. In 2014, photographer Pieter Hugo travelled to southern Rwanda and photographed pairs of Hutu perpetrators and Tutsi survivors. In many cases, the perpetrators killed family members or looted the property of the Tutsi villages. The individuals who agreed to be photographed worked closely with a nonprofit organization, Association Modeste et Innocent (AMI), to prepare for the meetings and to help the Hutus with the formal request for forgiveness. These photos were on display in various locations including The Hague and Rwandan memorials and churches (Dominus, 2014).

Forgiveness is pragmatic, permitting one to get on with living. Kelley and Waldron (2005) state that individuals are able to forgive easier when offending partners explicitly acknowledge the situation. The pragmatic importance of forgiveness offers existential trust in a place where excellence can be pursued, while a neurotic obsession with continual blaming of another makes a place "rotten with perfection" (Burke, 1966, p. 16).

The second pragmatic suggestion centers on **Robert Bellah's** (1975) "broken covenant" (p. xxii), which acknowledges that all organizations and relationships are flawed. Few "covenants" between people are perfect, and if they are, they are short lived. Perhaps the definition of an adult might be the ability to recognize the flawed nature of a given covenant of a group while continuing to assist the group in its quest to live up to its ideal aspirations. Sometimes we must roll up our sleeves and get to work, keeping the focus of attention on building a communicative environment of existential trust. When existential trust is lost, "we lose the ability to distinguish genuine problems from manufactured problems, the genuine friend from a disingenuous sales-person, and genuine hope from a lost cause" (Arnett & Arneson, 1999, p. 16). Existential trust must prevail in spite of broken covenants that we will undoubtedly continue to encounter.

ROBERT BELLAH (1927–2013)
was an American sociologist. Bellah studied at Harvard University, receiving his B.A. in 1950 and his Ph.D. in 1955. Bellah's works seek to "reconcil[e] traditional religious societies with social change" ("Robert Neely Bellah," 2013).

The third pragmatic suggestion differentiates optimism and hope. Christopher Lasch (1991) differentiated optimism from tenacious hope, with the former placing us in the realm of consumption and demand and the latter positioning us as active participants in the shaping of our conversational environments. Optimism turns us into consumers of "disillusionment" (p. 373), who attempt to wish the world into compliance with our needs and demands. Unfortunately, when the world moves contrary to our wishes, we complain and moan about all that fails to abide by our expectations. **Optimism** disregards "the natural limits on human power and freedom, and it cannot survive for very long in a world in which an awareness of those limits has become inescapable" (p. 530). **Hope,** on the other hand, meets what is before us and makes the best of both the good and the bad, demanding justice rather than a naïve belief in progress (p. 80). Hope is vigorous (p. 530), tenacious, and not easily discouraged.

CHRISTOPHER LASCH (1931–1994)
was an American academic and social critic. He is the author of a 1979 best seller, *The Culture of Narcissism*. Lasch received his M.A. in 1955 and his Ph.D. in 1961, both from Harvard University. He taught at the University of Iowa, Northwestern University, and the University of Rochester ("Christopher Lasch," 2013).

The fourth and final pragmatic effort is that one must know when to leave a communicative environment. The common assertion that we can talk everything out is not always true. As management scholar Stephen R. Covey (2004) states, "you can't talk your way out of problems you behave yourself into" (p. 186). Talking everything out is not an effective approach if the accompanying actions are contrary to the message. Constructive response to disputes requires participants discerning a new direction. Sometimes it is important to learn how to plant one's heel, pivot, and leave—getting on with a life and leaving a given communicative environment behind may be the best option in certain cases. Some places are so toxic that leaving is the only prudent act, calling us first to uninvest in one place and reinvest in another (Rings, Stinson, & Johnson, 1979; Tracy, 2004).

An exit strategy should not be the first, second, or even third impulse. But, at some juncture, one may have to check out in order not to damage one's own health. One's own well being is at risk, and one must find a way to leave, physically or psychologically. If one decides to stay in an organization that is toxic, constructive communication can serve to suppress the tensions experienced by employees and reduce levels of employee stress. The work of Rings, Stinson, and Johnson (1979) suggests that communicative behavior relates to aspects of role stress and satisfaction with one's place of employment. Rings et al. found that employees who perceived that their supervisors were engaging in communicative behaviors of receptiveness and responsiveness were more satisfied with their place of employment and less likely to leave the job. Sarah J. Tracy (2004) suggests that for those who decide to leave, discussing organizational tensions with employees allows them to respond in healthy rather than negative ways as they leave the organization.

If one does leave, one must consciously decide not to take learned toxic practices into another place. It is possible to run from one organizational "home" to another, creating similar problems, becoming what Omdahl and Fritz (2012) termed "a problematic Other" (p. x). The typology of problematic others offered by Fritz (2002, 2006) provides a way to recognize problematic workplace behaviors and avoid taking these behaviors to a new place of employment. For this work, the vital message is that when one leaves, one works to enhance another communicative environment and not bring problematic behavior to another place.

Of the four pragmatic communicative responses discussed above, only one of the options involves walking away from a particular communicative environment. Our ethical obligation in conflict is to struggle for communicative environments that put ground under the feet of all the communicators, offering a sense of existential trust. If one chooses to leave a particular communicative dwelling, one cannot resort to becoming a consumer and demanding that a new place take care of all one's needs. On the contrary, leaving requires that we bring communicative health to a new location, ever wary of bringing toxic communicative practices to a different location (Arnett, 1992; Lasch, 1991). One's goal is to add communicative health via the nourishing of existential trust. If a communicative environment displays existential trust, not all parties will agree on specific conflicts, but will, one hopes, concur on the importance of nurturing the ground of a given place.

The communicative environment offers clues from the first day of entrance into a given group, either placing ground under our feet that makes the move toward excellence possible or offering a constant reminder to be self-protective. We contend that it is not people but acts of performative trust and impersonal fairness that offer existential trust. Kant considered good will fundamental to human happiness.

Kant (1785/2008) stressed the necessity of good will. He stated: "Nothing in the world—indeed nothing even beyond the world—can possibly be conceived which could be called good without qualification except a *good will*" (pp. 392–393). Good will is essential if environments are to accumulate growth and health. **Good will** is "a condition of the value of happiness" (p. 12) and is defined through the categorical imperative (pp. 32–33). Kant's notion of good will stresses an existential fact—we do not work solely with people; the communicative environment can place existential trust under the feet of the participants.

Our categorical imperative is to add trust to the ground on which all communicate and work; if we cannot trust that which permits us to walk upright, then we move to modes of self-protection. Coworkers who work within an environment of communicative trust nourish generosity that assists the trustworthiness of ground that unites us. Existential trust becomes the ground that offers a **standpoint** from which we can meet and constructively encounter conflict. Sandra Harding (2006) articulates that "a standpoint is an achieved and collective position, not an ascribed position or individual opinion" (p. 85). For example, a log sticking out of the water might appear bent to an observer at one end of the lake and look straight to an observer at the opposite end of the lake (Harding, 1991). Where one stands matters and influences the assumptions one makes (Harding 2006). Julia Wood (1997) provides a communication perspective on **standpoint theory**. She writes, "The social groups within which we are located powerfully shape what we experience and know as well as how we understand and communicate with ourselves, others, and the world" (p. 250). Standpoint theory shapes one's understanding and being in the world. Our contention is that conflict within a dwelling composed of trust will not necessarily ensure a wonderful outcome, but it does make the possibility of good outcomes more likely. We argue for a standpoint that cultivates existential trust.

Communication literature addresses various forms of conflict styles. In "An Exploration of Topics, Conflict Styles, and Rumination in Romantic Nonserial and Serial Arguments," Jennifer L. Bevan, Veronica Hefner, and Amanda Love (2014) remind us of the difference between serial and unserial arguments tied to a practical reality: Serial arguments or repetitive/routine arguments invite "undue rumination" about the conflict (p. 356). One of the reasons to curtail serial arguments is to lessen internal noise in one's own reflective considerations that can spiral a conflict increasingly out of control. One way to lesson rumination/internal noise is to engage conflict from the "solution-oriented" stance. Paula Hopeck, Nathalie Desrayaud, Tyler R. Harrison, and Kristen Hatten (2014) in "Deciding to Use Organizational Grievance Processes: Does Conflict Style Matter?" provide insight into the value of this orientation that seeks to close a chapter on disputes between and among persons. To lessen internal noise frequently requires closure, conclusion of the conflict, not repetitive serial engagement. On the other hand, instead of directly engaging conflict, avoidance contextually has a place in one's repertoire of conflict styles (Han & Cai, 2015). Sometimes avoidance assists relational maintenance, the recognition that we will and must continue to work with another. In addition, conflict avoidance is appropriate in organizational settings when one must protect one's own self-interest. Even the notion of compromise, which has a questionable reputation in the West, has a place in engaging conflict. Few issues are black or white, good or bad. Most, instead, permit a gray area where compromise will bring multiple facets together. Learning this skill assists "social harmony" and a communicative practice of creatively engaging "contradicting opinions" (Kim & Kim, 2017, p. 139).

FRAMING COMMUNICATIVE LEADERSHIP: EXISTENTIAL TRUST

Mankind must evolve for all human conflict a method which rejects revenge, aggression, and retaliation. The foundation of such a method is love. (King, 1964)

The sixth chapter in *The Power of Framing: Creating the Language of Leadership* discusses the importance of ethics (Fairhurst, 2011). We contend that existential trust is a first principle in inviting an ethical communicative environment in conflict engagement. Trusting the reality of a level playing field makes constructive conflict between and among persons possible. The first and foremost conflict issue is the organic connection between conflict style and context, constituting the communicative environment. Leaders learn quickly that they cannot impose their will upon the environment; rather, they must work to invite a particular type of communicative environment. The environment is an initial conflict style, and the style we use in meeting conflict will either augment or attenuate existential trust. The ground leaders nourish is the first step toward an enactment of ethics.

Fairhurst (2011) offers the ingredients for preparation for framing when depending on context to guide conflict style:

1. **"Ethical codes"** (p. 136) within an organization inform leadership of necessary and important discourse practices. Public codes of conduct assist with predictability in a communicative environment. Codes can aid existential trust.
2. **Ethical judgment** comes from watching exemplars of such practices and engaging in them. Connecting the right conflict style with a given context or situation contributes trust and confidence in future leadership actions.
3. **"Moral positioning"** frames what matters (p. 145). We suggest that assuming a perspective larger than one's own vision is an essential leadership characteristic. Cosmopolitan perceptions are crucial to leadership.
4. **Framing through design logics** articulates that messages come to us organized with their own inherent logic (O'Keefe, 1988). For instance, message design that is expressive is dependent upon face-to-face interaction and editing in those exchanges. Message design logic that is conventional adheres to social rules, roles, and forms. Rhetorical message design logic seeks to redefine the contexts and negotiate situations between and among social selves. The manner in which leaders organize a message carries with it design logic that frames leadership in action.

Without a cosmopolitan perspective, a leader becomes a complainer, similar to T. E. Frazier, the main character of **B. F. Skinner's** (1948) *Walden Two*. Frazier got so angry at his research subjects when they did not act as he demanded that he called out, "Behave, damn you! Behave as you ought!" (p. 271). Human beings seldom behave as we demand of them. Yelling at people to do something is comparable to the behavior of a two-year-old who is frustrated because others cannot understand self-perceived obvious demands. Conflict styles require flexibility of application because the context, the people, the environment, and the moment are unique, requiring us to be led by the communicative circumstances.

B. F. SKINNER (1904–1990)
was an American psychologist who studied behaviorism. Skinner is the author of *Walden Two*, published in 1948, which offers an alternative utopia to Henry David Thoreau's *Walden* ("B. F. Skinner," 2013).

REFERENCES

Arendt, H. (1968). *Men in dark times*. New York, NY: Harcourt Brace & Co.

Arnett, R. C. (1986). *Communication and community: Implications of Martin Buber's dialogue*. Carbondale: Southern Illinois University Press.

—. (1992). *Dialogic education: Conversations about ideas and between people*. Carbondale: Southern Illinois University Press.

—. (2001). Dialogic civility as pragmatic ethical praxis: An interpersonal metaphor for the public domain. *Communication Theory, 11*, 315–338.

Arnett, R. C., & Arneson, P. (1999). *Dialogic civility in a cynical age: Community, hope, and interpersonal relationships*. Albany: State University of New York Press.

Arnett, R. C., & Holba, A. M. (2012). *An overture to philosophy of communication: The carrier of meaning*. New York, NY: Peter Lang.

Axelrod, R. (1984). *The evolution of cooperation*. New York, NY: Basic Books.

Ayers, J. (1983). Strategies to maintain relationship: Their identification and perceived usage. *Communication Quarterly, 31*, 62–67.

B. F. Skinner. (2013). In *Encyclopaedia Britannica Online*. Retrieved from http://www.britannica.com/EBchecked/topic/547663/BF-Skinner

Bellah, R. N. (1975). *The broken covenant: American civil religion in time of trial*. Chicago, IL: The University of Chicago Press.

Berri, D. (2012, November 9). Does the 'best' team win the World Series? *The Huffington Post*. Retrieved February 15, 2013, from http://www.huffingtonpost.com/david-berri/world-series-winners_b_2101859.html

Bevan, J. L., Hefner, V., & Love, A. (2014). An exploration of topics, conflict styles, and rumination in romantic nonserial and serial arguments. *Southern Communication Journal, 79*(4), 347–360.

Bruner, R. (2016). Olympic runners who helped each other after falling down just won a major honor. *Time*. Retrieved from http://time.com/4461464/olympic-runners-pierre-de-coubertin-medal/

Buber, M. (1967). Hope for this hour. In F. W. Matson & A. Montagu (Eds.), *The human dialogue: Perspectives on communication* (pp. 306–312). New York, NY: Free Press.

Buckley, C. (2012, October 28). Panicked evacuations mix with nonchalance in Hurricane Sandy's path. *New York Times*. Retrieved March 15, 2013, from http://www.nytimes.com/2012/10/29/nyregion/panicked-evacuations-mix-with-nonchalance-in-hurricane-sandys-path.html?pagewanted=all&_r=0

Burke, K. (1966). *Language as symbolic action: Essays on life, literature, and method*. Berkeley: University of California Press.

Canary, D. J., & Cupach, W. R. (1988). Relational and episodic characteristics associated with conflict tactics. *Journal of Social Science and Personal Relationships, 5,* 305–322.

Christopher Lasch. (2013). In *Encyclopaedia Britannica Online*. Retrieved from http://www.britannica.com/EBchecked/topic/330872/Christopher-Lasch

Collins, J. (2001). *Good to great: Why some companies make the leap—and others don't*. New York, NY: HarperCollins Publishers.

Collins, J., & Hansen, M. T. (2011). *Great by choice: Uncertainty, chaos, and luck—Why some thrive despite them all*. New York, NY: HarperCollins.

Covey, S. R. (2004). *The seven habits of highly effective people: Powerful lessons in personal change*. New York, NY: Free Press.

Czubaroff, J., & Friedman, M. (2000). A conversation with Maurice Friedman. *Southern Communication Journal, 65,* 243–254.

D'Aveni, R. A., & MacMillan, I. C. (1990). Crisis and the content of managerial communications: A study of the focus of attention of top managers in surviving and failing firms. *Administrative Science Quarterly, 35,* 634–657.

Dainton, M., & Gross, J. (2008). The use of negative behaviors to maintain relationships. *Communication Research Reports, 25,* 179–191.

Dermansky, J. (2013). Superstorm's aftermath. *Progressive, 17,* 22–25.

Dominus, S. (2014). Portraits of reconciliation. *New York Times Magazine*. Retrieved from https://www.nytimes.com/interactive/2014/04/06/magazine/06-pieter-hugo-rwanda-portraits.html?ref=magazine&_r=1

Driscoll, J. W. (1978). Trust and participation in organizational decision making as predictors of satisfaction. *Academy of Management Journal, 21,* 44–56.

Earley, P. C. (1986). Trust, perceived importance of praise and criticism and work performance: An examination of feedback in the United States and England. *Journal of Management, 12,* 457–473.

Egan, P. (2016). Flint report: Fix law on emergency managers. *Detroit Free Press*. Retrieved from http://www.freep.com/story/news/local/michigan/flint-water-crisis/2016/10/19/flint-water-committee-sweeping-changes/92405150/

Egan, P., & Anderson, E. (2016). Emergency managers, city officials charged in Flint water crisis. *Detroit Free Press*. Retrieved from http://www.freep.com/story/news/local/michigan/flint-water-crisis/2016/12/20/schuette-flint-water-charges/95644964/

Ellis, K., & Shockley-Zalabak, P. (2001). Trust in top management and immediate supervisor: The relationship to satisfaction, perceived organizational effectiveness, and information receiving. *Communication Quarterly, 49,* 383–398.

Fairhurst, G. T. (2011). *The power of framing: Creating the language of leadership*. San Francisco, CA: Jossey-Bass.

Fisher, R., & Ury, W. L. (1981). *Getting to yes: Negotiating agreement without giving in*. Boston, MA: Houghton Mifflin Company.

Folger, J. P., Poole, M. S., & Stutman, R. K. (1993). *Working through conflict: A communication perspective*. Glenview, IL: Scott, Foreman & Company.

Follett, M. P. (1942). *Dynamic administration: The collected papers of Mary Parker Follett* (H. C. Metcalf & L. Urwick, Eds.). New York, NY: Harper and Brothers Publishers.

Foss, S., & Griffin, C. L. (1995). Beyond persuasion: A proposal for an invitational rhetoric. *Communication Monographs, 62*, 2–18.

Friedman, M. S. (1972). *Touchstones of reality: Existential trust and the community of peace*. New York, NY: Dutton.

Fritz, J. M. H. (2002). How do I dislike thee? Let me count the ways: Constructing impressions of troublesome others at work. *Management Communication Quarterly, 15*, 410–438.

—. (2006). Typology of troublesome others at work: A follow-up investigation. In J. M. H. Fritz & B. L. Omdahl (Eds.), *Problematic relationships in the workplace* (pp. 21–46). New York, NY: Peter Lang.

Greve, H. R. (2008). A behavioral theory of firm growth: Sequential attention to size and performance goals. *Academy of Management Journal, 51*, 476–494.

Gumpert, G., & Drucker, S. (Eds.). (2002). *Take me out to the ballgame: Communicating baseball*. New York, NY: Hampton Press.

Han, B., & Cai, D. A. (2015). A cross-cultural analysis of avoidance: Behind-the-scenes strategies in interpersonal conflicts. *Intercultural Communication Studies, 24*(2), 84–122.

Harding, S. (1991). *Whose science? Whose knowledge?: Thinking from women's lives*. Cornell, NY: Cornell University Press.

—. (2006). *Science and social inequality: Feminist and postcolonial issues*. Champaign: University of Illinois Press.

Hartman, S. (2011, June 7). Love thy neighbor: Son's killer moves next door. Retrieved on March 15, 2013, from http://www.cbsnews.com/8301-18563_162-20069849.html

Hayakawa, S. I., & Hayakawa, A. R. (1991). *Language in thought and action* (5th ed.). Orlando, FL: Harcourt.

Holmes, J. G., & Rempel, J. K. (1989). Trust in close relationships. In C. Hendrick (Ed.), *Close relationships* (pp. 187–220). Newbury Park, CA: Sage.

Hopeck, P., Desrayaud, N., Harrison, T. R., & Hatten, K. (2014). Deciding to use organizational grievance processes: Does conflict style matter? *Management Communication Quarterly, 28*(4), 561–584.

Kalman, H. (1999). *The structure of knowing: Existential trust as an epistemological category*. Stockholm: Swedish Science Press.

Kant, I. (2006). *Critique of the power of judgment* (P. Guyer, Ed. & Trans.). New York, NY: Cambridge University Press. (Original work published 1792)

—. (2008). *Groundwork of the metaphysic of morals* (T. K. Abbott, Trans.). Radford, VA: Wilder Publications. (Original work published 1785)

Kelley, D. (1998). The communication of forgiveness. *Communication Studies, 49*, 255–271.

Kelley, D. L., & Waldron, V. R. (2005). An investigation of forgiveness-seeking communication and relational outcomes. *Communication Quarterly, 53*, 339–358.

Kim, J-H., & Kim, J. (2017). The dynamics of polarization and compromise in conflict situations: The interaction between cultural traits and majority-minority influence. *Communication Monographs, 84*(1), 128–141.

King, M. L. (1964, December 10). Nobel Prize Acceptance Speech.

Knapp, M. L., Putnam, L. L., & Davis, L. J. (1988). Measuring interpersonal conflict in organizations: Where do we go from here? *Management Communication Quarterly, 1*, 414–429.

Konovsky, M. A., Jaster, R., & McDonald, M. A. (1989). Using parametric statistics to explore the construct validity of the Thomas-Kilmann conflict MODE survey. *Management Communication Quarterly, 3*, 268–290.

Konovsky, M. A., & Pugh, S. D. (1994). Citizenship behavior and social exchange. *Academy of Management Journal, 37*, 656–670.

Kuhn, T., & Poole, M. S. (2000). Do conflict management styles affect group decision making? Evidence from a longitudinal study. *Human Communication Research, 26*, 558–591.

Lasch, C. (1991). *The true and only heaven: Progress and its critics.* New York, NY: W. W. Norton & Company.

Manning, P. K. (1992). *Organizational communication.* Hawthorne, NY: Aldine De Gruyter.

Matalin, M., Carville, J., & Knobler, P. (1994). *All's fair: Love, war, and running for president.* New York, NY: Random House.

McAllister, D. J. (1995). Affect- and cognition-based trust as foundations for interpersonal cooperation in organizations. *Academy of Management Journal, 38*, 24–59.

McCullough, M. E., Sandage, S. J., & Worthington, E. L. (1997). *To forgive is human: How to put the past in the past.* Downers Grove, IL: InterVarsity Press.

Mitchell, M. M., & Boster, F. J. (1998). Conflict management satisfaction and relational and sexual satisfaction. *Communication Research Reports, 15*, 388–396.

Morris, C., & Rodriguez, A. (2005). Toward an existential model of trust. *Peace Review, 17*, 95–102.

Morse, C. R., & Metts, S. (2011). Situational and communicative predictors of forgiveness following a relational transgression. *Western Journal of Communication, 75*, 239–258.

Muchinsky, P. M. (1977). Organizational communication: Relationships to organizational climate and job satisfaction. *Academy of Management Journal, 20*, 592–607.

Nicotera, A. M. (1993). Beyond two dimensions: A grounded theory model of conflict handling behavior. *Management Communication Quarterly, 6*, 282–306.

O'Keefe, B. J. (1988). The logic of message design: Individual differences in reasoning about communication. *Communication Monographs, 55*, 80–103.

Omdahl, B. L., & Fritz, J. M. H. (Eds.) (2012). *Problematic relationships in the workplace* (Vol. 2). New York, NY: Peter Lang Publishing.

One for One. (2013). *TOMS.* Retrieved March 19, 2013, from http://www.toms.com/our-movement/movement-one-for-one

Our Founding Story. (2017). Retrieved from https://shesthefirst.org/about-us/

Paleari, F., Regalia, C., & Fincham, F. D. (2010). Forgiveness and conflict resolution in close relationships: Within and cross partner effects. *Universitas Psychologica, 9*, 35–56.

Pareles, J. (2012, December 13). Wave after wave of the right tunes. *New York Times.* Retrieved March 19, 2013, from http://www.nytimes.com/2012/12/14/arts/music/at-concert-for-sandy-relief-big-names-find-the-right-tone.html?_r=0

Pearce, W. B. (1974). Trust in interpersonal communication. *Speech Monographs, 41*, 236–244.

Prince, S. (2008, April 29). Softball opponents offer unique display of sportsmanship. *The Oregonian.* Retrieved February 17, 2013, from http://blog.oregonlive.com/breakingnews/2008/04/the_best_tale_of_sportsmanship.html

Racer, K. H., & Dishion, T. J. (2012). Disordered attention: Implications for understanding and treating internalizing and externalizing disorders in childhood. *Cognitive and Behavioral Practice, 19*, 31–40.

Rausch, H. L., Barry, W. A., Hertel, R. K., & Swain, M. A. (1974). *Communication, conflict, and marriage*. San Francisco, CA: Jossey-Bass.

Rich, G. A. (1997). The sales manager as a role model: Effects on trust, job satisfaction and performance of salespeople. *Academy of Marketing Science, 25*, 319–328.

Rings, R. L., Stinson, J. E., & Johnson, T. W. (1979). Communicative behaviors associated with role stress and satisfaction variables. *Journal of Applied Communication Research, 7*, 15–22.

Robert Neelly Bellah. (2013). In *Encyclopaedia Britannica Online*. Retrieved from http://www.britannica.com/EBchecked/topic/59735/Robert-Neelly-Bellah

Robinson, S. (1996). Trust and breach of the psychological contract. *Administrative Science Quarterly, 41*, 574–599.

Roloff, M. E., & Wright, C. N. (2009). Conflict avoidance: A functional analysis. In T. Afifi & W. Afifi (Eds.), *Uncertainty, information management, and its disclosure decisions: Theories and applications* (pp. 320–340). New York, NY: Routledge.

Ross R. G., & DeWine, S. (1988). Assessing the Ross-DeWine conflict management message style. *Management Communication Quarterly, 1*, 389–413.

Rusbult, C. E. Johnson, D. J., & Morrow, G. D. (1984). Impact of couple patterns of problem solving on distress and nondistress in dating relationships. *Journal of Personality and Social Psychology, 50*, 744–753.

Sanburn, J. (2016). Flint water crisis may cost the City $400 million in long-term social costs. *Time*. Retrieved from http://time.com/4441471/flint-water-lead-poisoning-costs/

Shockley-Zalabak, P. (1988). Assessing the Hall conflict management survey. *Management Communication Quarterly, 1*, 302–320.

Sillars, A. L. (1980). Attributions and communication in roommate conflicts. *Communication Monographs, 47*, 180–200.

Simmel, G. (1955). *Conflict & the web of group affiliations*. (K. H. Wolff & R. Bendix, Trans.). New York, NY: The Free Press. (Original work published 1908)

Skinner, B. F. (1948). *Walden Two*. Indianapolis, IN: Hackett Publishing Company, Inc.

Superstorm Sandy. (2013). In *Encyclopaedia Britannica Online*. Retrieved from http://www.britannica.com/EBchecked/topic/1890569/Superstorm-Sandy

Thomas, K. W., & Kilmann, R. H. (1974). *Thomas-Kilmann conflict mode instrument*. Tuxedo, NY: Xicom, Inc.

Thomas, K. W., Thomas, G. F., & Schaubhut, N. (2008). Conflict styles of men and women at six organization levels. *International Journal of Conflict Management, 19*, 148–166.

Tracy, S. J. (2004). Dialectic, contradiction, or double bind? Analyzing and theorizing employee reactions to organizational tension. *Journal of Applied Communication Research, 32*, 119–146.

Tutzauer, F., & Roloff, M. E. (1988). Communication processes leading to integrative agreements: Three paths to joint benefits. *Communication Research, 15*, 360–380.

Wilson, S. R., & Waltman, M. S. (1998). Assessing the Putnam-Wilson Organizational Communication Conflict Instrument (OCCI). *Management Communication Quarterly, 1*, 367–388.

Womack, D. F. (1988). Assessing the Thomas-Kilmann conflict mode survey. *Management Communication Quarterly, 1*, 321–349.

Wood, J. (1997). *Communication theories in action: An introduction*. Belmont, CA: Wadsworth Thomson Learning.

Zand, D. E. (1972). Trust and managerial problem solving. *Administration Science Quarterly, 17*, 229–239.

Chapter Eleven

CONFLICT ROUTINE: ANACHRONISTIC RESPONSES

...there is nothing more difficult to execute, nor more dubious of success, nor more dangerous to administer, than to introduce political orders. (Machiavelli, 1513/2005, p. 22)

"Conflict Routine: Anachronistic Responses" emphasizes the importance of attentiveness to the historical moment when confronting conflict situations. An anachronism suggests that something is out of place and out of time; it is an idea or action still utilized that no longer addresses the needs of the current moment. Ideas, actions, theories, products, and behaviors of people become anachronistic when they are no longer applicable. This chapter's *Spotlight on Leadership* features Mary Barra, the first female CEO of one of the largest American automakers—General Motors—since 2014.

© Steve Lagreca/Shutterstock.com

Time magazine, *Forbes,* and *Fortune* acknowledge Mary Barra's accomplishments with Fortune naming her number 1 on its list of the "50 Most Powerful Women in Business."

It is important to attend to the temporally needed rather than force the use of old ideas and actions into novel and unrelated situations. One can witness an anachronism in action when a parent demands that a college student listen and obey with the ears of a twelve-year-old. A person functioning anachronistically disregards "existential messages" (Smith, 1992, p. 68) that announce the necessity of responsiveness to changes in a given moment. If one cannot attend to an "existential demand" (Arnett, 2013, e.g. pp. 3, 50, 61, 62, 103, 104, 117) for an original response, one becomes an anachronism, out of place and out of time.

Ian I. Mitroff (2003) suggests that companies falter when they fail to respond to the demands before them. In his 2003 work, *Crisis Leadership: Planning for the Unthinkable,* Mitroff cites General Motors (Figure 11.1) as an example of leadership responding to current challenges with strategies tied to an earlier historical moment. General Motors faced the following challenges: (1) a volatile economy, (2) loss of control of its inventory, (3) lack of accurate sales data, and (4) an inability/refusal of the various car divisions to share their revenues with the central corporation (p. 17). The company addressed these challenges by designing an operating structure that placed the finance committee at the very top of the corporation. According to Mitroff, "this design was the direct response to the particular set of crises that GM faced in the 1920's; *today's organizations are largely the result of the response to the crises of 80 years ago!*" (p. 17). Twenty-first century organizations, unfortunately, still follow this antiquated model. As a result, many organizations today attempt to implement anachronistic approaches that fail to adapt to a new historical era. Twenty-first century challenges for GM included the subprime-lending crisis, a decrease in sales, and diminution in demand for SUVs as a result of escalating gasoline prices. In 2008, the Big Three Detroit automakers (GM, Chrysler, and Ford) sought government assistance that would enable the companies to move out of bankruptcy (Brunel & Hufbauer, 2009, p. 1). Since the $6 billion bailout from the Troubled Assets Relief Program (TARP), GM has hired 2,000 American workers and accumulated $16 billion in profits (Krisher & Crutsinger, 2012, para. 4).

FIGURE 11.1   General Motors Headquarters in downtown Detroit, Michigan.

Additionally, GM countered anachronistic response and created innovation centers to explore new technologies that enhance their competitiveness in today's global market (Ringle, 2013, para. 4). To remain competitive, businesses need to continually respond to the current demands and challenges of the marketplace. Samsung is an example of a company that failed to recognize the demands before it.

In August 2016, Samsung launched its Galaxy Note 7 smartphone. A month later, consumers reported that their phones were overheating while charging and, in some cases, exploding. In September 2016, the U.S. Consumer Product Safety Commission urged consumers to power down their devices and stop using them (Kang, 2016). After 35 reported incidents of overheating smartphones worldwide, Samsung decided to recall every Galaxy Note 7 smartphone. Samsung Electronics reportedly lost approximately $6.2 billion in operating profits because of the smartphone recall (Mozur, 2017, para. 19). Initially, the company attributed the cause to the ion battery pack that contains a highly flammable liquid. Five months later, Samsung claimed full responsibility for the product-safety issue. Samsung director of mobile communications Koh Dong-jin stated: "We are taking responsibility for our failure to identify the issues arising out of the battery design and manufacturing process prior to the launch of the Note 7" (Mozur, 2017, para. 4). Although Samsung recalled the Galaxy Note 7 smartphones and assured the public it had fixed the problem, reports surfaced that replacement phones were also catching fire. Samsung had misdiagnosed the problem when issuing the first recall by blaming the battery suppliers. Its initial response failed to consider the design flaws and manufacturing problems in addition to the broader management concerns that this controversy exposed. By defining the wrong problem, Samsung proposed a solution that did not meet the expectations of key stakeholder groups including consumers, suppliers, and the U.S. Consumer Product Safety Commission. Because of Samsung's unwillingness to move away from routine design and manufacturing processes, the company lost billions of dollars and damaged its reputation.

Anachronistic lament comes from an unwillingness or inability to reconsider routine, even when previous actions no longer contribute to success. One continues to use past behaviors out of unreflective inertia. Shifting historical contexts require the adoption and adaptation of innovative practices and learning of creative skills responsive to the needs of today. Our contention is that the refusal to attend to existential demands for change generates conflict as one anachronistically forces the use of ideas and behaviors that are no longer applicable.

INTRODUCTION

This chapter examines the communicative missteps of anachronistic behavior that give rise to conflict when one acts like a Don Quixote figure,[1] fighting fictional windmills and engaging in imaginary battles with adversaries (Cervantes, 1604/1993). In an environment of necessary change, one must fight the impulse to use taken-for-granted assumptions and actions that have passed their life span of applicability. No theory or communicative action will last forever (Kaplan, 1964; Kuhn, 1970; Purdy, 2011). When actions and ideas no longer address the current place and time, conflict emerges as people inappropriately continue to use that which is no longer applicable. Anachronistic communicative actions inappropriately impose the familiar upon changing historical contexts.

In "Conflict Routine: Anachronistic Responses," we explore the changing nature of conflict contexts through five major sections:

1. **Responding to existence** reminds us that we must be attentive to the communicative environment;
2. **Attentive hearing and responsive listening** differentiates between a passive and active attending to others and the context;

---

1. Don Quixote is the protagonist of Miguel de Cervantes's (1604/1993) *Don Quixote*, set in central Spain during the early seventeenth century. Don Quixote perceives the world through his own reality, failing to recognize the actuality of his surroundings.

3. **Roles and responsibilities: Perspectives on conflict** offers insight into how contextual identity shapes information;
4. **Conflict confederates: Displaced conflicts** focuses on the reality of unintended consequences when we direct conflict toward the wrong person or group; and
5. **Framing communicative leadership: Innovative responsiveness** connects Gail T. Fairhurst's (2011) discussion of how leaders must avoid anachronistic imposition of ideas and actions and listen to the uniqueness of a given situation.

Responding to, listening to, and learning from the needs of a given moment offers a unique context that involves a communication ethic of existential attentiveness (Arnett, 2013). When one is more interested in ideas and actions that are familiar than in implementing what is contextually appropriate, one ignores the moment and enforces what is existentially inappropriate. One must understand the uniqueness of a given communicative environment before commanding the use of routine solutions. A responsive communication ethic requires us to understand the demands of a given context; we must give weight and importance to the uniqueness of a given moment, curtailing the desire to foist solutions driven by thoughtless routine upon a communicative setting.

RESPONDING TO EXISTENCE

Kenneth Burke (1935/1984) and **Eric Voegelin** (1952/1999) reminded us that the demands of existence cannot be ignored; they stressed this reality of "the recalcitrance of existence" (Burke, 1973, p. 131). We must meet and respond to existence on its terms. The first step in meeting a moment of conflict requires honest recognition of existence. Attending to existence carefully is often a wake-up call that demands that we notice the distinctiveness of the communicative environment. This existential wake-up call emerges from changing coordinates and dynamics in the communicative environment, which often provide unexpected insights. By attending to existence, we learn from the communication environment and attend to both the welcomed and the unwelcomed.

KENNETH BURKE (1897–1993)
was an American literary critic and rhetorician known for his theory of dramatism, where "language and human agency combine" ("Kenneth Burke," 2013).

Each transformation in a communicative environment is important; however, it generally takes a series of changes before people recognize a fundamental shift in a given place. One small difference after another can accumulate into a substantial transformative gestalt. Too often, we notice change only at the moment of substantial transformative gestalt. Only at the moment of fundamental change does one look back on a number of missed existential wake-up calls. Alteration often happens slowly until a sudden variation has a person utter in despair: this is simply not the same place.

Anachronistic behaviors are contrary to **interactional communication theory** (Haley, 1963; Louhiala-Salminen & Kankaanranta, 2011; Watzlawick, Beavin, & Jackson, 1967; Watzlawick & Weakland, 1976) where meaning is continually changing, evolving, and adapting to the context. Interactional communication focuses on symmetrical and complementary relationships that exist between participants, where all actions are potentially communicative. The context is the essential component for determining meaning within human interactions (Watzlawick & Beavin, & Jackson, 1967).

Organizations are a particularly common context where one can examine shifts in meaning. For example, an organization becomes anachronistic when there is a refusal to evolve. Continual growth within an organization requires managing adjustments rather than letting the organizational life cycle simply carry on until the organization atrophies (More, 1998). More (1998) states, "Successful organizations are those that initiate change, respond to change, plan change, and implement change as an ongoing way of life" (p. 30).

Challenges are inherent in the process of change (Van de Ven & Poole, 1995). As an organization evolves, small changes result in increased workloads, new work tasks, and different strategic goals (Pollard, 2001). Battilana and Casciaro (2012) discuss how particular organizational members known as "change agents" (p. 381) can influence others within the organization. Change agents are responsive to the immediate needs of a given communicative environment. They do what is necessary to avoid the temptation to fall prey to the routine and the familial.

Organizational culture shapes the background of a specific communicative environment (Eisenberg & Riley, 2001). Culture provides a communicative environment with guidance through signs that acknowledge values, heroes, rites, and rituals (Deal & Kennedy, 1982). The value-laden coordinates of a culture become very clear in moments of uncertainty and in times of seemingly unmanageable change; culture works as a communicative background that stabilizes a place to gather one's footing, push off, and generate creative initiatives. When a culture and daily communicative practices are at odds, conflict is likely (Pepper & Larson, 2006). As the values, rites, and rituals that shape an organization alter, individuals must adapt to an emerging culture (Risberg, 1999). Such moments generate disruptions that demand close consideration of the communicative environment.

One often misses how "scripted" (Abelson, 1981, 1982; Gioia & Poole, 1984; Honeycutt, 2011; Lord & Kernan, 1987; Putnam & Fairhurst, 2001) our day-to-day lives are until we meet a disruption. One follows a number of scripts throughout the day. **Scripts** offer mental representations of conversational events; for example, the manner in which we order a meal in a restaurant or conduct a job interview are types of scripts (Gioia & Poole, 1984). Abelson (1982) defines scripts as "an organized bundle of expectations about an event sequence" (p. 134). Scripts serve a dual purpose of assisting in the interpretation of the behavior of others and guiding our own actions (Abelson, 1981, 1982). Honeycutt (2011) states, "Individuals have scripts based on memory and experiences that create expectations about what is likely to occur during the course of their lives in different types of relationships" (p. 14). Putnam and Fairhurst (2001) contend that organizational scripts include such daily fare as performing familiar work tasks, interacting with employees during the lunch hour, and weekly meetings. Scripts involve a substantial amount of agreement regarding the processes that compose routine tasks (Lord & Kernan, 1987). With challenged routine scripts, one senses internal conflict, a lament that the familiar is no longer guiding communicative interaction.

Viktor Frankl reminds us that excessive use of lament seldom moves us forward. Our responses to both wanted and unwanted moments define us; meaning emerges in our stand against the inevitable. We are significantly fashioned by disruptions that we did not want or desire (Frankl, 1967). One must find novel direction while fighting undue obsession with misfortune. Moving from lament to action addresses moments of unwanted change, which require understanding the difference between hearing and listening to existence as one discerns an appropriate response.

VIKTOR FRANKL (1905–1997)
was an Austrian psychiatrist who developed the "'third school' of Viennese psychotherapy," after Sigmund Freud (first school) and Alfred Adler (second school). The search for meaning was central to Frankl's theory ("Viktor Frankl," 2013).

ATTENTIVE HEARING AND RESPONSIVE LISTENING

Our ability to respond to conflict involves both hearing and listening in a communicative environment. **Listening** includes a process of attending to, interpreting, and in some way responding to a message (Wolvin & Coakley, 1996). Communication scholars note the importance of listening in all contexts (Bodie, 2011; Bodie, Worthington, & Fitch-Hauser, 2011; Brownell, 2009; Flowerdew, 1995; Floyd, 1984; Purdy, 1991; Wolvin, 2010). Bodie (2011) notes, "listening is typically conceived of as a cognitive process involving steps such as sensing, processing, and responding but also as a perceived behavior" (p. 279). The major difference between hearing and listening assumes that the former is an act of perceiving sound with the ear while the latter involves consciously choosing to attend with deliberation (Lipari, 2012). Listening is participatory. **Hearing** is more akin to experiencing background music; the information does not call forth a responsive participation and engagement (Lipari, 2012); "hearing without listening is response without responsibility; it is a form of pseudodialogue without ethics" (Lipari, 2012, p. 236). Both hearing and listening, however, are necessary for understanding a communication message. Lisbeth Lipari (2014) expands this work in her book, *Listening, Thinking, Being: Toward an Ethics of Attunement*, which situates listening as a central aspect of communication and ethics, moving beyond the West's focus on speech, sight, and spatial communication. Lipari's work on listening emphasizes the phenomenological aspect of communication and human interaction.

In response to Lipari's work, Graham D. Bodie and Nathan Crick (2014) share Lipari's phenomenological engagement with listening while examining the work of Charles Sanders Peirce. Bodie and Crick want to lift listening from a slumber, connecting resistance that invokes an understanding of otherness. Peirce's phenomenology links listening with an effort to understand others through communication and the mediating relationships among and between "things, events, feelings cognitions, and actions" (p. 119). Listening implicates mediation, putting relations in touch; the authors understand listening in accordance with Peirce's work as "a dwelling place" (p. 120) from which connections to otherness inform and enrich our lives. These authors suggest that the mediating factors that encourage listening are interpersonal and intrapersonal, such as trust, social attraction, and emotional well-being. Whether one understandings listening itself as the mediating factor or the reality of other mediating factors encouraging listening, there is a common presupposition: Listening involves connection to others.

Roth (2012) describes hearing as a means of understanding that is more expansive than the auditory process of "I hear you" (p. 61). For Roth, hearing is attentive to sounds while comprehending or understanding what is producing the sound. For example, if one hears the sound of a high-pitched siren, one will understand that a fire truck is near. Listening, on the other hand, denotes the act of attentively orienting toward something or someone in order to figure out the precise meaning. Hearing benefits a global response, permitting us to learn from the ambiguous background messages (Froemming & Penington, 2011). The inability to hear affects listening and creates difficulty in understanding the communication message.

Hearing happens with or without consent. Hearing attends to sudden sounds and gentle background sounds, such as the hum of florescent lighting in a classroom. Hearing gets our notice; it involves sound waves transmitted to the ear and into the brain that function as background information from which listening occurs as responsive and involving our participation. To understand what is around us requires "**attentive hearing**" (Ting-Toomey, 2010, p. 170), which alerts us of disruptions in general, but not in specific detail. Attentive hearing is a pivot point that launches engaged listening.

"**Active listening**" occurs when one attempts to understand the other's message (Weger, Castle, & Emmett, 2010, p. 35), focusing on the content of the message, not a particular judgment about the message. Wolvin and Coakley (1996) identify five different types of listening: (1) discriminative, (2) appreciative, (3) empathic, (4) comprehensive, and (5) critical. **Discriminative listening** distinguishes between sounds. This form of listening permits one to segregate words and noises. **Appreciative listening** occurs for pleasure or enjoyment. An evening at the symphony offers opportunity for appreciative listening. **Empathic listening** provides emotional support for the person offering information. Such listening requires us to concentrate carefully, listening for the meaning tied to the worldview of the other. **Comprehensive listening** allows us to understand the complexity of the message of a speaker. Listening to a TED (Technology, Entertainment, Design) talk that focuses on innovative thinking and ideas requires comprehensive listening. **Critical listening** evaluates a message for purposes of accepting or rejecting an argument. Critical listening is foundational for a court jury that must evaluate conflicts, arguments, and evidence. In each of these conceptions of listening, responsiveness connects to our ability to interpret a given situation. Listening is vital to finding constructive resolutions for both parties involved in a conflict. Listening breaks the cycle of destructive conflict patterns and provides tools to explore constructive resolutions (Van Slyke, 1999). Conflict arises as individuals fail to hear (being alert in an environment) and to listen (actively focusing on a given issue or event).

As communicators listen for ethical positions that collide with their own, conflict often follows. Ting-Toomey and Kurogi (1998) suggest that there is a shift from listening to hearing when there is a lack of trust between or among individuals in conflict. Individuals may hear the words, but they are not listening (Ting-Toomey & Kurogi, 1998). When we are able to unite hearing and listening in constructive interplay, we are attentive to our roles and responsibilities in a given communicative setting. Hearing and listening do not emerge in the abstract; they are communicative responses to a context that includes roles and responsibilities.

In "Building Trust and Feeling Well: Examining Intraindividual and Interpersonal Outcomes and Underlying Mechanisms of Listening," Karina J. Lloyd, Diana Boer, Avraham N. Kluger, and Sven C. Voelpel (2015) remind us that listening is at the heart of all healthy relationships, that it contributes to personal and relational "emotional wellbeing," and that the ability to listen invites interpersonal trust. Listening not only provides us with new data and insights, but it also augments the relational, personal, and emotional dimensions and depth of a quality of life. Molly M. Stoltz, Karen P. Sodowsky, and Carl M. Cates (2017) in their work *Listening Across Lives* discuss the various aspects of listening tied to context, close relationships, culture, religious commitment, leadership, organizational involvement, technological engagement, health, and education. They address listening as a communicative activity that attends to role and responsibility, connecting persons and perspectives.

ROLES AND RESPONSIBILITIES: PERSPECTIVES ON CONFLICT

The **role** one takes in a conflict influences what one hears and that to which one listens. The roles of a friend, sibling, teacher, or parent do not lend themselves to the same responsibilities. Each inimitable role requires hearing and listening that begins from a special standpoint. One's "role identity" shapes one's sense of meaning (Stets, 2010, p. 648). A person's role identity guides behavior in conflict. As one relates with others, one's role becomes verified or denied by communicative interactions (Jung & Hect, 2004, p. 266). Roles become perceptual dwellings that situate the heard; they frame a responsible space from which one listens. Roles shape what we consider important, altering our perception of a given conflict.

The concept of role allows for meaningful analysis of human communication within structured settings (Sussman, 1975). Roles act as the "building blocks of social systems" (Sussman, 1975, p. 193) and help determine responsibilities. Individual roles form by expectations of self, other, relationships (Belz, Talbott, & Starck, 1989), and social and cultural norms (Rose et al., 2012). A person's roles aid the development of a social identity tied to given contexts (Biddle, 1986) and grant public dignity to those who occupy them (Fritz, 2013).

As one attempts to balance professional and personal roles, conflict can emerge (Kirby, Wieland, & McBride, 2006, p. 327). Moreover, conflict is understood differently from the vantage points of differing communicative roles (Caughlin & Vangelisti, 2006, p. 148). As individuals progress from infanthood to adulthood, the dynamics of their relationships change, requiring different roles. Role conflict and role ambiguity are likely to invite unnecessary conflict. Role conflict (Vijaya & Hemamalini, 2012, p. 575) occurs when two or more role responsibilities clash (Hardy & Conway, 1978). For example, a person engaged in the roles of being a mother, a student, and an employee experiences role conflict when the responsibilities of caring for a sick child, studying for an upcoming exam, and finding time to work 40 hours a week are in opposition with one another. Conflict emerges when roles collide (Koerner & Fitzpatrick, 2006, pp. 172–174). Role ambiguity (Vijaya & Hemamalini, 2012, p. 575) occurs when there is uncertainty about responsibilities associated with a particular function (Hardy & Conway, 1978). Chick-fil-A president Dan Cathy faced backlash from LGBTQ groups after commenting that he believed in the traditional, biblical definition of marriage. Chick-fil-A is a company founded on particularly narrow religious principles. The restaurants are closed on Sundays to allow employees to honor a day of rest with friends and family. These remarks were made on a radio show and later confirmed by the *Baptist Press*. The anti-gay marriage stance prompted boycotts and sit-ins across many of its restaurants (O'Connor, 2014). Cathy's role as a leader of a private, family-owned business clashed with his role as a public figure and needing to attract customers to its business. In this situation, there was conflict over Cathy's private role and his public role in response to the topic of gay marriage rights.

Monroe, DiSalvo, Lewis, and Borzi (2009) discuss how specific behaviors of difficult people emerge from their roles. In an organizational setting, a supervisor has the role of giving negative feedback when things are going wrong and, as a result, can be perceived as a difficult boss (p. 15). Duck, Foley, and Kirkpatrick (2006) discuss the "person-role duality" that creates difficult role stress within the workplace (p. 11). They note three classifications: (1) **person-role incompatibility**, where role requirements do not align with the person's style; (2) **person-person incompatibility**, which occurs when the personal styles of two employees conflict; (3) **role-role incompatibility**, which arises when organizational roles of two or more persons clash or collide—for example, a hospital administrator seeking to reduce expenses comes into conflict with a physician who seeks to treat an indigent patient who cannot pay for services (p. 11). In this latter case, we see that roles offer direction and also create conflict.

Roles shape what we hear and the details we listen to, which give uniqueness and character to our responses. Within official and contextually bestowed roles, we hear calls for responsibility.

Carrying out a role with its inherent set of responsibilities begins, however, with the interplay between role and the unique context of a conflict. Failure to enact one's role in a given environment can invite displaced conflict as one takes out frustrations on the wrong person. Displaced conflict happens when we are no longer paying attention to the actual conflict issue before us.

CONFLICT CONFEDERATES: DISPLACED CONFLICT

Displaced conflict occurs when we direct conflict toward the wrong person or group of people rather than confronting the appropriate persons. As we avoid people with whom we are actually in a conflict, we may misdirect irritation. Within the communication literature, the idea of "displaced dissent" (Kassing, 1997, 1998; Kassing & DiCioccio, 2004) describes employees who focus their irritation and frustration on persons not responsible for the conflict generation for the dispute.

Expressed discontent often targets people or a group who pose less of a risk. Displacing negative feelings in a conflict results in venting frustration on innocent targets (Denson, Miller, & Pederson, 2006). Displaced conflict is often over tangential issues rather than focused on the primary issue driving the actual conflict (Deutsch, 1977; Rahim, 2010). For example, Rahim (2010) discusses how displaced conflict can occur over "social entities" or "secondary issues" that have limited relation to the main battle (p. 22). Deutsch (1977) believes that in displaced conflict, parties are "arguing about the wrong thing" (p. 13). The conflict shifted from the main concern to a different issue that is less painful and easier to discuss (p. 372).

Displacing conflict moves a potential conflict discussion to another topic, causing us to miss the opportunity to address the real issue that divides us. Conflict is displaced when participants work with different assumptions about what is actually the subject matter under dispute (Cupach & Canary, 1997, p. 12). In relationships, couples may create conflict over small issues when the actual problem is about their commitment to one another (Cupach & Canary, 1997, pp. 13–14). In Chapter 6, "Relational Perception in Conflict," we discussed jealousy and envy as forms of displaced conflict. One becomes angry with another due to one's lack of a particular skill set in comparison to another. Displaced conflict shifts attention away from what truly matters.

For example, the concept of **"taking conflict personally"** (TCP) illustrates the shifting of attention from the conflict to the self (Hample & Dallinger, 1995, p. 297; Wallenfelsz & Hample, 2010, p. 471). In TCP, one focuses on the self and one's own personal reactions, rather than the main issue at hand. Hample and Dallinger (1995) define TCP as "a feeling of being personally engaged in a punishing life event. [The person] feels threatened, anxious, damaged, devalued, [and] insulted" (p. 306). TCP often results in a problematic handling of the conflict situation (Wallenfelsz & Hample, 2010, p. 476).

Displaced conflict can be understood as a "customer orientation" (Blocker, Flint, Myers, & Slater, 2011, p. 216) that blames the other while a producer orientation puts responsibility on oneself, refusing to displace the conflict onto the wrong topic or person. A customer orientation expects the producer automatically to know and respond to their needs (Blocker et al., pp. 216–217). Taken to an extreme, a customer orientation displaces responsibility in a conflict.

Instead of targeting a person or substituting a deceptive conflict, it is possible to resist the temptation of displaced conflict by leaning into the difficulty and facing the struggle head-on. Managing a conflict results in an increasing satisfaction with the interpersonal relationship (Cahn 1992, p. 97). If one manages rather than avoids the conflict, a resolution occurs that allows one to move on constructively in a relationship (Cahn, 1992, p. 24). One can envision this creative movement as akin to leaning into a problem.

The following tale comes from a friend of one of the authors who takes young people to the Youghiogheny River for rafting (Figure 11.2). This river has multiple rapids that differ in degree of difficulty, ranging from Class I to Class V+. Class I rapids are small waves with no obstacles (Figure 11.3), while Class V rapids include constant strong waves with impediments, whirlpools, fast currents, and some waterfalls (Figure 11.4). According to the American Whitewater Accident Database (2013), there were 10 reported fatalities on the Youghiogheny River between 1982 and 2011. The river too often claims lives as people fail to "lean into the rapids" (Arnett, 2011). In an effort to stabilize, people instinctively lean backwards, which permits the rapids to get under the raft, which then pushes the raft skyward, leading it to capsize and eject the occupants into

FIGURE 11.2 The Youghiogheny River in Pennsylvania.

© Steve Heap/Shutterstock.com

FIGURE 11.3 Kayakers in Class I rapids.

© i4toc2/Shutterstock.com

the river. The best defense comes from learning a counter-intuitive act—lean into the rapids. Leaning toward the problem permits people on the raft to stay atop the rapids, resisting powerful waves that would overturn the raft (Arnett, 2011).

Leaning into a conflict resists the impulse to permit displaced conflict to capsize relationships. Addressing conflict requires us to lean forward into the issue at hand. Constructive meeting of a conflict entails addressing a conflict on its own terms. Leaning into conflict suggests that one should generally meet, not displace, a genuine conflict. To walk away from all conflict puts at risk the possibility for constructive learning. Failure to lean into conflicts removes us from argumentative discussions necessary to clarify commitments and direction (Afifi, 2003; Afifi, McManus, Steuber, & Coho, 2009; Dalisay, 2012; Gottman, 1993; Roloff & Cloven, 1990; Roloff & Ifert, 2000; Schrodt, 2009; Stafford, 2010). Leaning into the rapids of conflict requires a final caveat of caution—sometimes it is prudent simply to steer around the rapids. One must learn when to go through a set of rapids and when one to steer around a problematic location. Rafting for leisure makes each challenge interesting. Rafting for transportation compels more thoughtful decisions.

FIGURE 11.4 A kayaker in a Class 5 rapid.

© Ron Hilton/Shutterstock.com

Conflicts situate social reality to such an extent that their roots and origins are inarticulate. Sometimes only tenacious patience can assist one in figuring out dividing issues. We can learn to choose between immediacy of response and a tempered, patient tenacity that discerns when to lean into conflict rapids and when to steer around them. Sometimes the best we can do is to try to keep a relational raft from capsizing as we hold on and lean forward into one contentious meeting after another, each time looking for ways to assist self and others. A considered ethical commitment requires meeting the conflict, not displacing one's anger on another or shifting to a different topic. Resisting the impulse to displace conflict requires honesty with oneself in a manner consistent with **Jean-Paul Sartre's** (1943/1992) warning to avoid "bad faith" (p. 86), or lying to oneself.

JEAN-PAUL SARTRE (1905–1980)

was a French writer and existentialist philosopher. He was the author of both novels and plays. Sartre received the Nobel Prize for Literature in 1964, but declined the award. His work centered on questions of human freedom ("Jean-Paul Sartre," 2013).

If we lean into life, taking one event, one conflict, at a time, we recognize that it is simply not possible to fix everything. Leaders seldom orchestrate significant moments of change. Outstanding leaders know they cannot force existence to abide by their demands; instead, such leaders are responsive. Additionally, one's role and responsibilities work together to create a structure in a given environment—a workplace, a classroom, a courtroom. Particular roles bring forth a given set of responsibilities. Leaders recognize that each role has a place in maintaining and sustaining the health of the environment. A leader has the obligation to determine what roles and responsibilities are appropriate in a specific conflict situation. When conflicts go awry, leaders who understand their responsibilities are able to guide others through the conflict moment with competence and grace.

FRAMING COMMUNICATIVE LEADERSHIP: INNOVATIVE RESPONSIVENESS

> *Organizations seek to make sense of crises, at least initially, by comparing them to previous events. Since crises are typically unexpected, novel, and surprising events, this dependence often results in organizations tenaciously justifying standard actions even when they fail to account for the exceptional nature of the crisis.* (Sellnow, Seeger, & Ulmer, 2002, p. 271)

The fourth chapter in *The Power of Framing: Creating the Language of Leadership* discusses the importance of "the art of framing" (Fairhurst, 2011, p. 89). The fundamentals of framing require responsiveness to a context, yielding a creative outcome that opens novel possibilities. Such responsiveness begins with hearing and listening and the ability to differentiate between them. Leaders who acknowledge the difference between hearing and listening and promote healthy attentive habits in their environment are in an enhanced position to meet conflicts before them—not because they will always have the answers, but because they are full participants in the situation.

Fairhurst (2011) suggests ingredients for preparation for framing with innovative responsiveness:

1. **Metaphorical language** opens up the imagination and avoids the dangers of taking words too literally (p. 94). Our stress on "leaning into the rapids" offers one example of understanding a response to a novel insight. Leaders must meet conflict on its own contextual terms.
2. **Simplified frames** keep the conversation close to the context and permit clarity of implications (p. 102). Leaders must frame in a manner that responds directly to existence before them, not to their wishful fantasies about the task.
3. **Believable frames** respond to a communicative context in a fashion that others deem appropriate (p. 106). Leaders unable to hear and listen often fall short of this basic objective.

4. **Stories** frame conflict constructively when leaders respond to the demands of the conflict context and avoid the temptation of displaced conflict.

Responding to others and the communicative environment requires that leaders not only hear, but also listen. When leaders merely hear another's words without actually listening, they miss the actual message and invite misunderstandings and negative feelings, losing opportunities for creative engagement. Listening plays a major role in determining what is the appropriate course of action. What leaders must apprehend is clarity of a communicative "why" that can propel their actions and decisions, providing a public framing of a unique direction needed in a given historical moment.

REFERENCES

Abelson, R. P. (1981). Psychological status of the script concept. *American Psychologist, 36,* 715–729.

—. (1982). Three modes of attitude-behavior consistency. In M. P. Zanna, E. T. Higgins, & C. P. Herman (Eds.), *Consistency in social behavior: The Ontario symposium* (Vol. 2, pp. 131–146). Hillsdale, NJ: Lawrence Erlbaum Associates.

Afifi, T. D. (2003). "Feeling caught" in stepfamilies: Managing boundary turbulence through appropriate privacy coordination rules. *Journal of Social and Personal Relationships, 20,* 729–756.

Afifi, T. D., McManus, T., Steuber, K., & Coho, A. (2009). Verbal avoidance and dissatisfaction in intimate conflict situations. *Human Communication Research, 35,* 357–383.

American Whitewater Accident Database. (2013). Retrieved May 15, 2013, from http://www.americanwhitewater.org/content/River/detail/id/708/

Arnett, R. C. (2011). Existential civility: Leaning forward into the rapids. *Spiritan Horizons, 6,* 39–48.

—. (2013). *Communication ethics in dark times: Hannah Arendt's rhetoric of warning and hope.* Carbondale: Southern Illinois University Press.

Battilana, J., & Casciaro, T. (2012). Change agents, networks, and institutions: A contingency theory of organizational change. *Academy Of Management Journal, 55,* 381–398.

Belz, A., Talbott, A. D., & Starck, K. (1989). Using role theory to study cross perceptions of journalists and public relations practitioners. *Public Relations Research Annual, 1,* 125–139.

Biddle, B. J. (1986). Recent developments in role theory. *Annual Review of Sociology, 12,* 67–92.

Blocker, C. P., Flint, D. J., Myers, M. B., & Slater, S. F. (2011). Proactive customer orientation and its role for creating customer value in global markets. *Journal of the Academy of Marketing Science, 39,* 216–217.

Bodie, G. D. (2011). The Active-Empathic Listening Scale (AELS): Conceptualization and evidence of validity within the interpersonal domain. *Communication Quarterly, 59,* 277–295.

Bodie, G. D., & Crick, N. (2014). Listening, hearing, sensing: Three modes of being and the phenomenology of Charles Sanders Peirce. *Communication Theory, 24,* 105–123.

Bodie, G. D., Worthington, D., & Fitch-Hauser, M. (2011). A comparison of four measurement models for the Watson-Barker Listening Test (WBLT)-Form C. *Communication Research Reports, 28,* 32–42.

Brownell, J. (2009). *Listening: Attitudes, principles, and skills*. Boston, MA: Pearson.

Brunel, C., & Hufbauer, G. C. (2009). *Money for the auto industry: Consistent with WTO rules*. Peterson Institute for International Economics. Number PB09-4.

Burke, K. (1973). *The philosophy of literary form: Studies in symbolic action*. Berkeley: University of California Press.

—. (1984). *Permanence and change: An anatomy of purpose* (3rd ed.). Berkeley: University of California Press. (Original work published 1935)

Cahn, D. (1992). *Conflict in intimate relationships*. New York, NY: Guilford Press.

Caughlin, J. P., & Vangelisti, A. L. (2006). Conflict in dating and marital relationships. In J. G. Oetzel & S. Ting-Toomey (Eds.), *Sage handbook of conflict communication* (pp. 129–157). Thousand Oaks, CA: Sage.

Cervantes, M. (1993). *Don Quixote*. Hertfordshire: Wadsworth Editions Limited. (Original work published 1604)

Cupach, W. R., & Canary, D. J. (1997). *Competence in interpersonal conflict*. Prospect Heights, IL: Waveland.

Dalisay, F. S. (2012). The spiral of silence and conflict avoidance: Examining antecedents of opinion expression concerning the US military buildup in the Pacific island of Guam. *Communication Quarterly, 60*, 481–503.

Deal, T., & Kennedy, A (1982). *Corporate cultures: The rites and rituals of corporate life*. Reading, MA: Addison-Wesley.

Denson, T. F., Miller, N., & Pederson, W. C. (2006). The displaced aggression questionnaire. *Journal of Personality and Social Psychology, 90*, 1032–1051.

Deutsch, M. (1977). *The resolution of conflict: Constructive and destructive processes*. New Haven, CT: Yale University Press.

Duck, S. Foley, M. K., & Kirkpatrick, D. C. (2006). Uncovering the complex roles behind the "difficult" co-worker. In J. M. H. Fritz and B. L. Omdahl (Eds.), *Problematic relationships in the workplace* (pp. 3–19). New York, NY: Peter Lang.

Eisenberg, E. M., & Riley, P. (2001). Organizational culture. In F. M. Jablin & L. L. Putnam (Eds.), *The new handbook of organizational communication: Advances in theory, research, and methods* (pp. 291–322). Thousand Oaks, CA: Sage.

Fairhurst, G. T. (2011). *The power of framing: Creating the language of leadership*. San Francisco, CA: Jossey-Bass.

Flowerdew, J. (Ed.). (1995). *Academic listening: Research perspectives*. Cambridge, UK: Cambridge University Press.

Floyd, J. (1984). *Listening: A practical approach*. Glenview, IL: Scott Foresman & Co.

Frankl, V. (1967). *Psychotherapy and existentialism: Selected papers on logotherapy*. New York, NY: Simon and Schuster.

Fritz, J. M. H. (2013). *Professional civility: Communicative virtue at work*. New York, NY: Peter Lang.

Froemming, K. J., & Penington, B. A. (2011). Emotional triggers: Listening barriers to effective interactions in senior populations. *International Journal of Listening, 25*, 113–131.

Gioia, D. A., & Poole, P. A. (1984). Scripts in organizational behavior. *Academy of Management Review, 9*, 449–459.

Gottman, J. M. (1993). The roles of conflict engagement, escalation, and avoidance in marital interaction: A longitudinal view of five types of couples. *Journal of Consulting and Clinical Psychology, 61*, 6–15.

Haley, J. (1963). *Strategies of psychotherapy*. New York, NY: Grune & Stratton.

Hample, D., & Dallinger, J. M. (1995). A Lewinian perspective on taking conflict personally: Revision, refinement, and validation of the instrument. *Communication Quarterly, 43*, 297–319.

Hardy, M. E., & Conway, M. E. (1978). *Role theory: Perspectives for health professionals*. New York, NY: Appleton-Century-Crofts.

Honeycutt, J. M. (2011). *Scripts and communication for relationships*. New York, NY: Peter Lang.

Jean-Paul Sartre. (2013). In *Encyclopaedia Britannica Online*. Retrieved from http://www.britannica.com/EBchecked/topic/524547/Jean-Paul-Sartre

Jung, E., & Hecht, M. L. (2004). Elaborating the communication theory of identity: Identity gaps and communication outcomes. *Communication Quarterly, 52*, 265–283.

Kang, C. (2016). Galaxy Note 7 owners are urged to stop using their phones. *New York Times*. Retrieved from https://www.nytimes.com/2016/09/10/technology/samsung-galaxy-consumer-product-safety.html

Kaplan, A. (1964). *The conduct of inquiry*. San Francisco, CA: Chandler.

Kassing, J. W. (1997). Articulating, antagonizing, and displacing: A model of employee dissent. *Communication Studies, 48*, 311–332.

—. (1998). Development and validation of organizational dissent scale. *Management Communication Quarterly, 12*, 183–229.

Kassing, J. W., & DiCioccio, R. L. (2004). Testing a workplace experience explanation of displaced dissent. *Communication Reports, 17*, 113–120.

Kenneth Burke. (2013). In *Encyclopaedia Britannica Online*. Retrieved from http://www.britannica.com/EBchecked/topic/85395/Kenneth-Burke

Kirby, E. L., Wieland, S. M., & McBride, M. C. (2006). Work/life conflict. In J. G. Oetzel & S. Ting-Toomey (Eds.), *Sage handbook of conflict communication* (pp. 327–357). Thousand Oaks, CA: Sage.

Koerner, A. F., & Fitzpatrick, M. A. (2006). Family conflict communication. In J. G. Oetzel, & S. Ting-Toomey (Eds.), *Sage handbook of conflict communication* (pp. 159–183). Thousand Oaks, CA: Sage.

Krisher, T., & Crutsinger, M. (2012, December 19). General Motors creates plan to be government-free within 15 months. *CNN*. Retrieved March 24, 2013, from http://www.huffingtonpost.com/2012/12/19/general-motors-buyback-stock-buys -back_n_2329279.html

Kuhn, T. S. (1970). *The structure of scientific revolutions*. Chicago, IL: University of Chicago Press.

Lipari, L. (2012). Rhetoric's other: Levinas, listening, and ethical response. *Philosophy & Rhetoric, 45*, 227–245.

Lipari, L. (2014). *Listening, thinking, being: Toward an ethics of attunement*. University Park: The Pennsylvania State University Press.

Lloyd, K. J., Boer, D., Kluger, A. N., & Voelpel, S. C. (2015). Building trust and feeling well: Examining intraindividual and interpersonal outcomes and underlying mechanisms of listening. *The International Journal of Listening, 29*, 12–29.

Lord, R. G., & Kernan, M. C. (1987). Scripts as determinants of purposeful behavior in organizations. *Academy of Management Review, 12*, 265–277.

Louhiala-Salminen, L., & Kankaanranta, A. (2011). Professional communication in a global business context: The notion of global communicative competence. *IEEE Transactions on Professional Communication, 54*, 244–262.

Machiavelli, N. (2005). *The prince* (P. Bondanella, Trans.). Oxford: Oxford University Press. (Original work published 1513)

Mitroff, I. I. (2003). *Crisis leadership: Planning for the unthinkable.* Hoboken, NJ: Wiley.

Monroe, C., DiSalvo, V. S., Lewis, J. J., & Borzi, M. G. (2009). Conflict behaviors of difficult subordinates: Interactive effects of gender. *Southern Communication Journal, 56,* 12–23.

More, E. (1998). *Managing change: Exploring state of the art.* Greenwich, CT: JAI Press.

Mozur, P. (2017). Galaxy Note 7 fires caused by battery and design flaws, Samsung says. *The New York Times.* Retrieved from https://www.nytimes.com/2017/01/22/business/samsung-galaxy-note-7-battery-fires-report.html?_r=0

O'Connor, C. (2014). Chick-fil-A CEO Cathy: Gay marriage still wrong, but I'll shut up about it and sell chicken. *Forbes.* Retrieved from http://www.forbes.com/sites/clareoconnor/2014/03/19/chick-fil-a-ceo-cathy-gay-marriage-still-wrong-but-ill-shut-up-about-it-and-sell-chicken/#7e0fa80a1a4f

Pepper, G. L., & Larson, G. S. (2006). Cultural identity tensions in a post-acquisition organization. *Journal of Applied Communication Research, 34,* 49–71.

Pollard, T. M. (2001). Changes in mental well-being, blood pressure, and total cholesterol levels during work-place reorganization: The impact of uncertainty. *Work and Stress, 15,* 14–28.

Purdy, M. (1991). Listening and community: The role of listening in community formation. *International Journal of Listening, 5,* 51–67.

Purdy, M. (2011). Grounding listening: The limitations of theory. *International Journal of Listening, 25,* 132–138.

Putnam, L. L., & Fairhurst, G. T. (2001). Discourse analysis in organizations: Issues and concerns. In F. M. Jablin and L. L. Putnam. (Eds.), *The new handbook of organizational communication: Advances in theory, research, and methods* (pp. 78–136). Newbury Park, CA: Sage.

Rahim, M. A. (2010). *Managing conflict in organizations.* Edison, NJ: Transaction Publishers.

Ringle, R. (2013, March 6). GM to hire 1,000 for high-tech Chandler innovation center. *The Phoenix Business Journal.* Retrieved March 24, 2013, from http://www .bizjournals.com/phoenix/news/2013/03/06/gm-to-hire-1000-for-high-tech.html

Risberg, A. (1999). *Ambiguities thereafter.* Lund, Sweden: Lund University Press.

Roloff, M. E., & Cloven, D. H. (1990). The chilling effect in interpersonal relationships: The reluctance to speak one's mind. In D. H. Cahn (Ed.), *Intimates in conflict: A communication perspective* (pp. 49–76). Hillsdale, NJ: Lawrence Erlbaum.

Roloff, M. E., & Ifert, D. E. (2000). Conflict management through avoidance: Withholding complaints, suppressing arguments, and declaring topics taboo. In S. Petronio (Ed.), *Balancing the secrets of private disclosures* (pp. 151–179). Mahwah, NJ: Lawrence Erlbaum.

Rose, J., Mackey-Kallis, S., Shyles, L., Barry, K., Biagini, D., Hart, C., & Jack, L. (2012). Face it: The impact of gender on social media images. *Communication Quarterly, 60,* 588–607.

Roth, W. M. (2012). *First-person methods: Toward an empirical phenomenology of experience.* New York, NY: Sense Publisher.

Sartre, J. P. (1992). *Being and nothingness: The principal text of modern existentialism.* New York, NY: Washington Square Press. (Original work published 1943)

Schrodt, P. (2009). Family strength and satisfaction as functions of family communication environments. *Communication Quarterly, 57,* 171–186.

Sellnow, T. L., Seeger, M. W., & Ulmer, R. R. (2002). Chaos theory, informational needs, and natural disasters. *Journal of Applied Communication Research, 30,* 269–292.

Smith, C. R. (1992). Roman decorum as a new praxis for existential communication. *Western Journal of Communication, 56*, 68–89.

Stafford, L. (2010). Geographic distance and communication during courtship. *Communication Research, 37*, 275–297.

Stets, J. E. (2010). Role identity. In R. L. Jackson, II (Ed.), *Encyclopaedia of identity* (pp. 648–650). Thousand Oaks, CA: Sage.

Stoltz, M. M., Sodowsky, K. P., & Cates, C. M. (2017). *Listening across lives*. Dubuque, IA: Kendall Hunt.

Sussman, L. (1975). Communication in organization hierarchies: The fallacy of perceptual congruence. *Western Journal of Communication, 39*, 191–199.

Ting-Toomey, S. (2010). Applying dimensional values in understanding intercultural communication, *Communication Monographs, 77*, 169–180.

Ting-Toomey, S., & Kurogi, A. (1998). Facework competence in intercultural conflict: An updated face negotiation theory. *International Journal of Intercultural Relations, 22*, 187–225.

Van de Ven, A. H., & Poole, M. S. (1995). Explaining development and change in organizations. *Academy of Management Review, 20*, 510–540.

Van Slyke, E. J. (1999). *Listening to conflict: Finding constructive solutions to workplace disputes.* New York, NY: AMACOM.

Vijaya, T. G., & Hemamalini, R. R. (2012). Role ambiguity, role conflict and work role balance: Influence on organizational commitment and turnover intention of faculty. *European Journal of Social Science, 30*, 574–585.

Viktor Frankl. (2013). In *Encyclopaedia Britannica Online*. Retrieved from http://www.britannica.com/EBchecked/topic/217306/Viktor-Frankl

Voegelin, E. (1999). *Order and history: Volume III, Plato and Aristotle*. Columbia: University of Missouri. (Original work published 1952)

Wallenfelsz, K. P., & Hample, D. (2010). The role of taking conflict personally in imagined interactions about conflict. *Southern Communication Journal, 75*, 471–487.

Watzlawick, P., Beavin, J. B., & Jackson, D. D. (1967). *Pragmatics of human communication*. New York, NY: Norton.

Watzlawick, P., & Weakland, J. H. (Eds.). (1976). *The interactional view*. New York, NY: Norton.

Weger, H., Castle, G., & Emmett, M. (2010). Active listening in peer interviews: The influence of message paraphrasing on perceptions of listening skill. *International Journal of Listening, 24*, 34–49.

Wolvin, A. D. (Ed.). (2010). *Listening and human communication in the 21st century*. Malden, MA: Blackwell.

Wolvin, A. D., & Coakley, C. G. (1996). *Listening* (5th ed.). Columbus, OH: McGraw-Hill.

Chapter Twelve

THRESHOLDS OF SENSITIVITY IN CONFLICT

Tell me to what you pay attention and I will tell you who you are. (Ortega y Gasset, 1962, p. 94)

"Thresholds of Sensitivity in Conflict" calls for rhetorical sensitivity to lessen unnecessary conflict by taking the presence of others and context seriously. This chapter's *Spotlight on Leadership* features Gabrielle Giffords, elected to U.S. Congress in 2005, as only the third Arizona woman to hold this office. Although no longer an elected official, she continues to be responsive to significant societal issues that contribute to public policy debates.

© Krista Kennell/Shutterstock.com

On January 8, 2011, while attending a community event at a grocery store in Tucson, Giffords was shot. She suffered a severe, life-threatening wound to the head; her recovery has been courageous and miraculous. She now leads Americans for Responsible Solutions, an organization that seeks to reduce gun violence.

A classic communication essay that explicates the importance of relational nuances is Roderick Hart and Don M. Burks's (1972) "Rhetorical Sensitivity and Social Interaction," in which a "reified" (inflexibly constant) understanding of the self and an "imperial self" unresponsive to a given context are critiqued (p. 78). Hart and Burks announced the importance of "rhetorical sensitivity"; their argument was consistent with that of Philip Rieff (1966) and Richard Sennett (2008), who rejected relational language tied to a sovereign self. Hart and Burks use the word "rhetoric" to stress audience and context, accentuating a self that is relationally sensitive to the context and to the uniqueness of others. Communicative inattentiveness to the environment invites a "culture of talking about the inconsequential," misses the uniqueness of the moment, and languishes in self-satisfying preoccupation (Darby, Egyed, & Jones, 1989, p. 114). Hart and Burks (1972), Eadie and Paulson (1984), Darby, Egyed, and Jones (1989), and Dilbeck and McCroskey (2009) emphasize concern for context and the other, not just oneself.

The nonprofit organization Alex's Lemonade Stand Foundation (ALSF) was founded by a four-year-old child, Alexandra Scott (1996–2004), with the help of her family in order to raise money for children with cancer. Diagnosed with a neuroblastoma before her first birthday, Alex turned her focus to encouraging other children to become involved with the effort to cure cancer. Alex passed away, in 2004, at the age of eight. At the time of her death, Alex's initiative on her behalf raised more than one million dollars toward a cure for cancer. As of 2017, the nonprofit organization has funded 690 research projects and has raised more than 140 million dollars for pediatric cancer research ("Our Mission & History," 2017, para. 6). Alex's ingenuity demonstrated rhetorical sensitivity in the midst of a tragic diagnosis (context) through a profitable fundraising for cancer (attentiveness to others).

INTRODUCTION

Constructive conflict engagement assumes the importance of sensitivity to persons, context, and the larger communicative environment. "Thresholds of Sensitivity in Conflict" suggests, in Aristotelian (trans. 1999) terms, that relational sensitivity rests between "interpersonal colonization" (Arnett, Fritz, & Holba, 2007, p. 124) (excess) and ignoring the Other (deficiency). Conflict is enflamed by those seeking such relational hegemony. Each of us knows individuals who ignore people, contexts, and communicative environments or try to possess them. Their threshold of sensitivity is minimal. Additionally, we have met people attentive and sensitive to so many complex issues that they are unable to make a decision (Darnell & Bockriede, 1976; Kelley & Kelley, 2011, p. 29). People who are hyper-responsive to the complexity of a context, uniqueness of persons, and the variability in the larger communicative environment can become virtually paralyzed, unable to make decisions; such people conceptualize events with so much texture and difference that a sensitive decision that is good, but not perfect, is outside of their reach. Rhetorical sensitivity requires **attentiveness** without losing perspective on a basic existential fact—we are communicative participants; we are not in control of each person or communicative setting.

In "Thresholds of Sensitivity in Conflict," we examine the centrality of communicative sensitivity through four major sections:

1. **Interactive sensitivity** understands oneself as embedded within a social history and within a particular communicative context composed of a unique set of persons;
2. **Impersonal responsibility** stresses another aspect of relational sensitivity in which concern for another does not revolve around reciprocity;
3. **Performative trust** discusses the confidence that is cultivated in a conflict situation via communicative action;
4. **Framing communicative leadership: Sensitivity in conflict** examines Gail T. Fairhurst's insights on sensitivity toward others and the context in a conflict setting.

Relational sensitivity requires discerning what another, in a given context, considers important enough to protect and promote. Rather than communicative inattentiveness that refuses to acknowledge the value of differing persons and contexts, we stress sensitivity to context, persons, and the larger communicative environment. To impose oneself without regard for the other and the communication situation has many names, such as bully (Fritz, 2002, 2006; Lutgen-Sandvik, Namie, & Namie, 2009; Namie & Namie, 2000), problematic or troublesome other (Fritz, 2002, 2006), and, at its extreme, dictator (Kecskemeti, 1950). In everyday life, long-term acts of imposition eventually invite conflict and resistance (Kimura, 2003; Lutgen-Sandvik, 2003).

INTERACTIVE SENSITIVITY

As one engages conflict, one must understand how attentiveness to context, others, and the larger communicative environment can enlarge one's self-conception with the inclusion of others and communicative context. Conflict is inevitable when negligence of context, others, and the larger communicative environment results in the multiplication of clashes.

Sensitivity requires paying attention to experiences within social groups and the larger world (Collins, 1990, p. 252) of social standing, race, gender, and economic status (Allen, 1998); such communicative interplay textures our perception. Appropriate relational sensitivity recognizes that cultural biases curtail understanding another's perspective (Craig, 2007, pp. 256–257). It is not possible to abandon our own perceptions, but we must seek to reach beyond our own provincial limits.

Rhetorically sensitive persons seek to understand the communicative environment in which they must live and learn (Eadie & Paulson, 1984, p. 390). Hart, Carlson, and Eadie (1980) suggested five elements of **rhetorical sensitivity**: (1) accept role-taking as part of the human condition; (2) avoid stylized verbal behavior; (3) undertake the strain of adaptation; (4) distinguish between information that is acceptable and unacceptable for communicating to others; and (5) understand that conversation can open and terminate possibilities (p. 1). Additionally, Darnell and Brockriede (1976) provided a range of interpersonal styles that situated rhetorical sensitivity in the middle of the continuum of communicative options. They described two opposing orientations, the "noble self" and the "reflector" (p. 180). The **noble self** is insensitive to others and context and is obsessed with personal goals. **Rhetorical reflection** requires a constant altering of one's own personal goals in order to adapt to another person. Situated at the middle of these two extremes is rhetorical sensitivity, which creates a balance between one's personal integrity and one's proclivity to adapt to others and contexts.

Rhetorical sensitivity describes how effective interpersonal communicators analyze a situation (Dilbeck & McCroskey, 2009). Knutson, Komolsevin, Chatiketu, and Smith (2003) suggest that rhetorical sensitivity requires people to consider their own positions, their partners' perspectives, and the various constraints present within the situation and context. Those who engage in rhetorical sensitivity avoid rigid communication patterns, finding a balance among self, other, and context.

Rhetorical sensitivity is central to **communication competence** (Dilbeck & McCroskey, 2009, p. 256). Persons who demonstrate communication competence accomplish personal goals while maintaining relational goals (Wiemann, 1977). Competent communicators flexibly adapt their communication styles depending on the needs of the other and a given location (Martin & Rubin, 1994; Spitzberg, Canary, & Cupach, 1994). Communication competence requires an "ability to manage interpersonal relationships in communication settings" (Martin & Rubin, 1994, p. 33). Competent communicators consider responses that are appropriate to a context, others, and the larger communicative environment (Spitzberg & Cupach, 2002). When both parties are communicatively competent, their relational satisfaction and commitment increase (Arroyo & Segrin, 2011, p. 558).

The necessity to adapt while navigating complex situations and environments is central to relational engagement that does not create undue conflict between and among persons. In times of conflict, lack of confidence in the other and in the environment is often high (O'Connell & Mills, 2003), making communicative competence a pragmatic necessity. One needs sensitivity to learn from all that is contrary to routine expectations. We contend that one must determine to do two relational acts simultaneously, which together yield a **"unity of contraries"** (Buber, 1948, p. 17): becoming increasingly sensitive to persons and contexts and simultaneously developing a thicker social skin. Rhetorical sensitivity and communicative competency point to the importance of interactional sensitivity, particularly in times of conflict.

Interactive sensitivity is at the heart of symbolic interactionism, which examines the way in which individuals interpret their environment and respond to particular contexts (Hewit, 2003, p. 307). **Symbolic interactionism**[1] is a theory that examines the exchange and interpretation of communication between people. Hewit (2003) stated, "Symbolic interactionism proposes that human beings employ symbols, carve out and act toward objects rather than merely respond to stimuli, and act on the basis of interpreted and not only fixed meanings" (p. 307). Symbolic interactionists view communication not as a transfer of information, but as content that influences others (p. 308).

Symbolic interactionism commenced with the work of George Herbert Mead (1863–1931) and John Dewey (1859–1952). In 1894, Mead and Dewey accepted positions at the University of Chicago where they worked with prominent scholars on pragmatism (Reynolds, 2003, p. 67). For 38 years, Mead lectured on and developed ideas that were later compiled and edited by his students into a series of four books: *The Philosophy of the Present* (Mead, 1932/2002); *Mind, Self, and Society from the Standpoint of a Social Behaviorist* (Mead, 1932); *Movements of Thought in the Nineteenth Century* (Mead, 1935/1972a); and *The Philosophy of the Act* (Mead, 1938/1972b) (Reynolds, 2003, p. 68). Mead is considered to be the founder of interactionism (Reynolds, 2003). His *Mind, Self, and Society* (Mead, 1932) continues to serve as the

---

1. Scholars of symbolic interactionism include George Herbert Mead, Charles Horton Cooley, John Dewey, and Herbert Blumer.

foundation for symbolic interaction theory. Martindale (1981) stated that Mead transformed the "inner structure of the theory of symbolic interactionism, moving it to a higher level of theoretical sophistication" (p. 329). Mead contended that human beings actively create the world in which we live; we base our knowledge of the world on social experiences. Humans derive meaning from social interactions; as a result, one's view of the world changes and evolves as one interacts with others and gains new experiences (Blumer, 1969).

Mead (1932) uses the term "**generalized other**" (p. 90) to describe the collective thoughts, ideas, or attitudes of a group, community, or society that guide how individuals behave in various contexts. He explains:

> *The very universality and impersonality of thought and reason is from the behaviorist standpoint the result of the given individual taking the attitudes of others toward himself and of his family crystallizing all of these particular attitudes into a single attitude or standpoint which may be called that of the 'generalized other.'* (Mead, 1932, p. 90)

Interacting with the generalized other requires attentiveness to self and other as well as the environment or context. Symbolic interactionism offers a distinctive approach to the study of human life and conduct (Blumer, 1969) and is particularly relevant to communication because of its emphasis on communicative interaction (Littlejohn, 1977).

Symbolic interactionism provides a framework for communication theory and a broad overview of the vital role of communication in society (Littlejohn, 1977, p. 91). Pearson and Van-Horn (2004) use symbolic interaction as the framework for perceiving gender identity, noting that symbolic interactionism describes how people create an identity through communicative interfaces with others (p. 285). Honeycutt, Choi, and DeBerry (2009) employ a symbolic interactionist framework to explore how persons conceptualize possible relational outcomes through imagined interactions. Edwards (1990) applies symbolic interactionism to explain sensitivity in the act of receiving and accepting feedback from others. She suggests, "Individuals who receive more feedback should develop more complex 'selves'" (p. 103).

Julia Wood (2011) discusses how the generalized other shapes the reality of our lives and develops our sense of self. Through the generalized other, we internalize views that enhance our awareness of our surroundings. Wood also referenced Seyla Benhabib's (1987) emphasis on the importance of communicative movement from the general to the "particular." Benhabib emphasized the importance of the particular other when people become a significant part of our lives. The term used by Benhabib for emphasizing the particular other is the "concrete other." The **concrete other** comprehends "the [unique] needs of the other, his or her motives, what he or she searches for and desires" (p. 167). The concrete or particular other and the "generalized other" define relationships between the self and other (Benhabib, 1987). The generalized other assumes we are born into a human communication with assumptions that frame our interactions, and the particular other continues to socialize us to innovative insights.

Anytime the other is central, the notion of reciprocity emerges as relevant. Unfortunately, conflict can be invited when one begins to demand reciprocity in relationships. Of course, reciprocity is a natural desire, but what happens when such a demand gets in the way of responsibility as a friend, leader, teacher, or spouse? Emmanuel Levinas, one of the premier ethicists of the 20th century (Arneson, 2007; Arnett, 2003; Cheney, May, & Munshi, 2010; Christians & Traber, 1997; Cook & Holba, 2008), offers us a controversial alternative—an "impersonal" call to responsibility (Levinas, 1982/1994, p. 69). At first glance, the term "impersonal" strikes one as out of character, particularly after we have paid so much attention to relational sensitivity. However, Aristotle (trans. 1992) was correct—errors dwell in "excess" and "deficiency"—too much and too little (p. 16). Therefore, we stress the "unity of contraries" (Buber, 1948, p. 17) of relational sensitivity and the impersonal as necessary companions in conflict engagement.

Debbie Ging and James O'Higgins Norman (2016), in "Cyberbullying, Conflict Management or Just Messing? Teenage Girls' Understandings and Experiences of Gender, Friendship, and Conflict on Facebook in an Irish Second-Level School," describe teenage girls as reluctant to label particular statements and actions as forms of cyberbullying. Reluctance to identify cyberbullying rests primarily in a manic desire to be popular and accepted. One of the critical elements of cyberliteracy, perhaps, is a more complex and textured understanding of friendship and belonging. The findings of the authors align with insights of Hannah Arendt (1958/2000), who state that the hyper-desire to belong is often destructive and curtails genuine friendship.

The study by Yuping Mao and Claudia L. Hale (2015) indicates the hypersensitivity linked to an unwillingness to acknowledge cyberbullying. Interpersonal, intercultural sensitivity, and communicative tendencies vary from person to person and more substantially from culture to culture. Mao studies the communicative sensitivity in Chinese employees, noticing that it did not vary when the subject was in China and another subject was abroad. What triumphs in this analysis is that the culture is so powerful that the Chinese employee carries such sensitivity with him or her locally and abroad. How one understands the world and responds to it emerges from our cultural background; the stronger the culture, the greater the reach of the sensitivity beyond a local place.

IMPERSONAL RESPONSIBILITY

Before we outline the importance of the impersonal, we need to frame how we are using the term differently than Emmanuel Levinas (1982/1994, p. 69). Levinas equates ethical conduct with responding uniquely to the Other, regardless of the Other's personal characteristics and what that person can do for us. For Levinas (1982/1985), "the best way of encountering the Other is not even to notice the color of his eyes!" (p. 85). Levinas emphasized the impersonal as an alternative to limiting ethics and caring to those who meet one's relational approval.

We suggest that in a conflict when we have major responsibilities, we need to attend to the expectations others have of us. Take, for instance, a teacher who has a student who is not likeable; such knowledge does not lessen the teacher's responsibility for the student. The responsibility emerges from an impersonal engagement that demands that we assist all, not just those whom we find relationally favorable. The same is true in a business; one must work with those whom one does not like to fulfill one's responsibility (Fritz, 2013). Rhetorical sensitivity must include, at times, an impersonal responsibility that does seek reciprocity but rather responds appropriately to another.

Emmanuel Levinas discusses the importance of **impersonal engagement**. The term "impersonal" is jarring, yet it does not suggest ignoring others. On the contrary, it attends both to those who are and to those who are not part of our relational connections. In an era of emotivism (decision making by personal preference; MacIntyre, 1981), individualism (attempting to stand above the historical moment and social constraints; de Tocqueville, 1835, 1840/1963), and optimism (demanding that the world satisfy our needs and demands; Lasch, 1991), it is appropriate to revisit impersonal responsibility. Therefore, we ironically situate the impersonal within a repertoire of communicative possibilities as a key element of rhetorical sensitivity; sometimes the people and the context call for impersonal responsibility in order to keep the focus on what is before us, not on ourselves alone.

Wayne Booth (1974) suggests that "irony is usually seen as something that undermines clarities, opens up vistas of chaos, and either liberates by destroying all dogma or destroys by revealing the inescapable canker of negation at the heart of every affirmation" (p. ix). Booth suggests a series of steps for assessing meaning from the ironical: (1) literal meaning must be rejected due to a degree of incongruity—either within the statement or between the statement and general experience (p. 10); (2) potential alternative explanations to the "traditional definition" are considered (p. 11); (3) consideration of the "author's knowledge and beliefs" indicates a decision as to whether a statement was intended to be ironic (p. 11); and (4) "reconstructed meaning" emerges that will be "in harmony" with the readers' "unspoken beliefs" (p. 12). Booth closely links irony and context. Ironically, only relational sensitivity can offer insight into when impersonal engagement is essential.

Sensitivity requires paying attention to everything around us without the self-absorbed sensitivity that misses the particularities of context and the concrete other. Genuine relational sensitivity requires attentiveness to what is before us and a rejection of the impulse to demand repeatedly that the world conform to our wishes. Too much sensitivity to the self misses the other, and too much doting on the other may drive a manic desire for the other's approval, which opens the door to a false guise of concern for the other. There are times when one cannot afford a conflict of interests. During such intervals, an impersonal obligation puts one at a distance from persons and context. Such distance permits space between persons, reducing the impulse to dominate or possess another. Impersonal responsibility contrasts with the action of **Gollum** in *Lord of the Rings* (Figure 12.1), who wants to possess the ring personally—he keeps stating, "My precious, my precious" (Tolkien, 1965, p. 224). Too much personal involvement takes one into a realm of possession. The impersonal guided Levinas's (1969) ethics project, which rejected the impulse to control, possess, dominate, and colonize the Other. The notion of the impersonal invites respect for that which we do not possess; we must meet existence and not seek to dominate the other, even with a smile (Arnett, 1992, p. 114).

J. R. R. TOLKIEN (1892–1973) was an English writer and author of the *Lord of the Rings* series and *The Hobbit*. The character Gollum appears in both, and in each, he is obsessed with maintaining possession of the ring, the central symbol in the novels ("J. R. R. Tolkien," 2013).

© Neftali/Shutterstock.com

FIGURE 12.1   Gollum from *The Lord of the Rings* trilogy (stamp from New Zealand).

Music and friendship are two avenues for understanding the interplay of sensitivity and an impersonal sense of distance. One must be sensitive to a musical performance, but if one is too close to an orchestra, one fails to hear all the instruments (Martens, 1919/2006). Additionally, friendship requires us to be sensitive and simultaneously separate; friends have the right to live their own lives. Those who depend upon us in a conflict situation need to trust our ability to enact the contradictory actions of sensitivity and ability to recognize the importance of an appropriate use of impersonal distance.

Emmanuel Levinas (1967) goes so far as to articulate the danger of communication based upon reciprocity (pp. 140–141). We concur, particularly when a given responsibility requires responsiveness to others and for a given communicative context. In pragmatic terms, we cannot control the actions of another, but we can govern our own actions. Impersonal communication channels are one-way communication outlets such as newspapers, magazines, and television news (Wei, Frankwick, Gao, & Zhou, 2011); these channels are needed as persons reduce uncertainty upon receipt of new information. Studies have revealed the importance and effectiveness of one-way impersonal communication channels (McPheters, 1991; Rubinson, 2009) that do not demand a particular response from the other. In interpersonal contexts, impersonal communication restrains one from overstepping boundaries in relationships. For example, we become uncomfortable when inappropriate personal information is self-disclosed to us (McBride & Bergen, 2008). Impersonal communication allows one to draw the lines between public and private settings (Arendt, 1958/1998) and eludes a relational quicksand that drags one into compromised positions.

Without some support for impersonal exchanges, there is an overemphasis on relational exchanges manifested by those with a "**managed smile**" (Arnett, 1992, p. 114). The managed smile has two related sides: (1) those seeking to dominate others with a smile, and (2) those subjugated to the demand to appear constantly upbeat. The managed smile reminds us that domination comes in many forms; it originates in communicative assumptions potentially cloaked in a smile (Arnett, 1992). Sometimes the impersonal liberates a given communicator from relational colonization. When the option of the impersonal is not in place, we find good ol' boy, good ol' girl, and good ol' friend networks driving decision making and marginalizing and ostracizing (Sias, 2012) others. The presence of relationally dominated networks can result in employee turnover (Krishnan, 2009), intimidation by colleagues (Wentling & Thomas, 2009), and unequal access to resources, including information, influence, and status (McDonald, 2011). If one is not part of an accepted in-group, those relational ties exclude one. Such was the reason that Hannah Arendt (1975/2003) stressed the danger of a manic need to belong (p. 5). Without some possibility of movement from the personal to the impersonal, we can feel as if we are in a contemporary version of a medieval world of fiefdoms and serfs. It was this relational form of domination that was at the heart of Adam Ferguson's (1767/2004) call for a civil society based upon criteria broader than local relational connections of kinship and proximity. The unity of contraries of relational sensitivity and the impersonal played out in **performative trust** form contextual rhetorical sensitivity that tells us what matters. In conflict settings, it is the doing, not the saying, that ultimately permits one to trust—one witnesses trust in action.

ADAM FERGUSON (1723–1816)
was a philosopher of the Scottish Enlightenment, whose work focused on civil society and explored "common sense" philosophy ("Adam Ferguson," 2013).

PERFORMATIVE TRUST

Our construct of performative trust has roots in the insights of Judith Butler (1988, 1997, 2006). She describes the notion of identity in performative terms. Performative identity, constructed through specific performative acts, are socially shared and historically situated. Identity emerges in the performance of "language, gesture, and all manner of symbolic social sign" (Butler, 1988, p. 519). Performative acts begin to constitute an identity shift; performance matters in the shaping of human identity. Butler (1997) connects identity to process (p. 153). There is no point in which clarity of identity completely maturates; identity changes during the course of a life through performative acts. Butler accentuates the dialectic of the individual and the context or environment, with each influencing performative acts. This conception of identity rejects individualism, which we detailed as ignoring of all social constraints (Tocqueville, 1835, 1840/1963), and the autocratic nature of a reified conception of the communicative environment. Performative acts frame identity via response to the context, giving shape and importance to the person.

Sara Salih's (2002) conception of Butler's view of identity as a "subject-in-process" (p. 30) announces identity as ongoing and reconfigured by performative acts. Salih frames performative doing, suggesting that we do not live in static photos, or pastoral paintings, or as actors in a well-edited cinematic production. What we do and what we perform shapes personal identity. We perform acts in response to contexts of joy and disappointment, hope and failure. The performative nature of identity suggests for us the notion of performative trust that moves from a focus on the individual alone to an individual responsively engaging a communicative environment. One can witness performative acts through communicative practices that offer a public declaration of direction. When observing others, one witnesses performative acts that announce the identity of a person, pointing toward performative trust that is materially publicized through communicative practices. Trust shifts from the individual alone to the factuality of performative acts/communicative practices.

Performative trust does not happen abstractly in a person or organization but lives in practiced action. Our contention is that conflict engaged with persons and in a place of "performative trust" offers a constructive hope of justice, where both the parties in the dispute and those not present are taken into consideration (Levinas, 1988/1994, p. 174). When one does what seems right and appropriate for persons and context, regardless of another's reciprocal response, one displays a "performative trust" that others can witness—announcing a conflict process guided by fairness and justice, not dependent upon relational ties alone. People watch communicative actions and discern the existence or lack of performative trust. Those who demonstrate acts of performative trust require witnesses who offer testimony about given actions. The interaction of spectators and actors (Kant, 1793/2006, p. 61) permits the reality of performative trust to matter.

Freedom of action generates lives enacted in an unscripted drama with our movements evaluated by those around us—spectators and critics observe and watch our performative actions, just as we attend to theirs. Kant stated that spectators lend meaning to events; in this case, they affirm acts of performative trust. Again, we discover that a single communication agent is not in control of meaning discerned by others; one has control of actions, not perception (Arendt, 1989, p. 61). Frosh and Pinchevsky (2009) define media witnessing as "the systematic and ongoing reporting of the experiences and realities of distant others to mass audiences" (p. 1). Media witnessing is an experience "shared ... by both viewers and those depicted" (Frosh

& Pinchevsky, 2009, p. 10). Observations and evaluations of whether or not we contribute to performative trust in a given place are largely dependent upon spectators/witnesses who disclose the story. The interplay of the communicative actor engaging in performative trust and witnesses telling the story provide an ambiance of confidence for those in a conflict situation. The "social practice" of trust is central to the work of Flores and Solomon (1998, p. 206). They refer to a type of trust grounded in one's actions, one's choices, and one's speech acts (p. 206). Flores and Solomon turn to J. L. Austin's (1962) notion of "performatives," which depend on language, context, and circumstances (Flores & Solomon, 1998, p. 221). Performative trust is particularly important in conflict when crucial decisions occur. Outstanding performances under pressure reveal the reality or its lack of performative trust in a given place.

In a classic organizational crisis example, we witness performative trust in action. The response of Johnson & Johnson following the Tylenol poisoning in 1982 illustrates a company that demonstrates performativity of their mission statement. A source outside of the Johnson & Johnson Company injected the Tylenol capsules. After the tampering with the product became public, sales of Tylenol capsules, the company's most profitable product, declined dramatically. In response, Johnson & Johnson withdrew the entire Tylenol stock from stores, and then responded within six months by creating triple-safety-seal packaging that included a plastic covering surrounding the neck of the bottle and foil covering the bottle opening. By implementing all of these protections, Tylenol became an exemplar of performative trust (Berge, 1990). In 1990, James Burke, former CEO of Johnson & Johnson, was inducted into *Fortune*'s National Business Hall of Fame, with the accolade that "he managed the crisis so well that he not only restored Tylenol, his company's single most important profitmaker, to preeminence, but he also enhanced the company's fine reputation in the process" (Moore, 2012, para. 2). The Tylenol crisis, featured in *Fortune* as a case with historical importance (Moore, 2012), finds concurrence with and from communication scholars (Dilenschneider, 2007; Fearn-Banks, 2001; Foster, 2002; Mitroff, 2004; Murray & Shohen, 1992; Seeger, Sellnow, & Ulmer, 2003; Ulmer, Sellnow, & Seeger, 2007). Scholars who cite the actions of Burke at Tylenol as classic provide spectator affirmation of the importance of performative trust in action.

Conflict is invited when one imposes the power of an official role without a track record of performative trust, demanding compliance by authority alone. Research by Ellis and Shockley-Zalabak (2001) examines trust in organizational roles of top management and immediate supervisors. A major finding of their work is that the amount of information received by workers regarding employment and organizational issues influences the extent to which employees recognize trust in the communicative environment. We contend that the ongoing distribution of information invites a form of performative trust. The potential for performative trust rests in everyday communicative actions. The work of Fritz, O'Neil, Popp, Williams, and Arnett (2013) has verified the importance of leaders walking the walk and talking the talk (p. 260), rather than simply talking about trust; such word/deed alignment leads to decreased cynicism and increased employee commitment. Performative trust starts on the ground, not in abstract policies and rules. Furthermore, the nature of communication matters, as Thomas, Zolin, and Hartman (2009) note in their study of communication and trust among coworkers, supervisors, and top management. Specifically, the quality and quantity of information indicates the extent to which individuals perceive organizational openness and their own commitment to organizational goals (Thomas, Zolin, & Hartman, 2009). In their study, trust originated in meaningful communicative practices of coworkers, supervisors, and top management, announcing performative trust.

Conflict opens the door to the witnessing of performative trust in action. Spectators are important and vital to performative trust. One cannot assert one's trustworthiness to others. The validation of trust emerges via a witness, announcing the performative characteristics of trust. Performative trust in conflict emerges from an oxymoronic origin, the interplay of the impersonal and relational sensitivity played out in our communicative practices. We are social creatures; we act, watch, testify with our performances, and witness to interactions that announce performative trust.

FRAMING COMMUNICATIVE LEADERSHIP: SENSITIVITY IN CONFLICT

> *Act in such a way that you treat humanity, whether in your own person or in the person of any other, never merely as a means to an end, but always at the same time as an end. (Kant, 1785/1959, p. 30)*

The second chapter in *The Power of Framing: Creating the Language of Leadership* (Fairhurst, 2011) emphasizes the importance of sensitivity to the particular during times of conflict. Successful leaders understand that performative trust comes from acting in accordance with mission and vision, particularly in moments of conflict. Performative trust is the perceived result of the enactment of a specific mission statement in the midst of conflict. Performative trust matters most in critical situations where one's communication action has significant consequences.

Fairhurst (2011) states the ingredients for preparation for framing with relational sensitivity:

1. **"Core framing tasks"** assume that one of the central elements of leadership is the instilling of trust (p. 50). We have outlined the importance of performative trust, which assumes paying attention to protected and promoted communicative actions of a leader. The importance of this concept is the connection of framing to work, events, or projects coordinated under the word *task*. The goal of framing is to assist productivity and clarity about the importance of the task in the workplace.
2. **Cultural Discourses** suggest that each communicative environment has its own unique possibilities. In order to navigate the individuality of the communicative environment, rhetorical sensitivity is pragmatically important.
3. **Framing coordination** suggests that leaders cannot always secure complete agreement; however, working with others in a manner that continues to coordinate a given initiative

is essential. At times, impersonal requests for support trump any relational efforts. If the initiative is successful, one is likely to accrue greater support for later ventures, framing performative trust.

Conflict moments often mandate impersonal responsibility, lessening the demand to like another. In conflict, differing strengths may open up creative possibilities. Engaging impersonal responsibility allows for creativity and multiplicity of perspectives. The goal is to engage conflict constructively, requiring one to attend to ideas, persons, contexts, and a larger communicative environment.

REFERENCES

Adam Ferguson. (2013). In *Encyclopaedia Britannica Online*. Retrieved from http:// www.britannica.com/EBchecked/topic/204623/Adam-Ferguson

Allen, B. J. (1998). Black womanhood and feminist standpoints. *Management Communication Quarterly, 11*, 575–586.

Arendt, H. (2000). *Rahel Varnhagen: The life of a Jewess.* Baltimore, MD: Johns Hopkins University Press. (Original work published 1958)

Arendt, H. (1989). *Hannah Arendt: Lectures on Kant's political philosophy* (R. Beiner, Ed.). Chicago, IL: University of Chicago Press.

—. (1998). *The human condition.* Chicago, IL: University of Chicago Press. (Original work published 1958)

—. (2003). Prologue. In J. Kohn (Ed.), *Responsibility and judgment* (pp. 3–14). New York, NY: Schocken Books. (Original work published 1975)

Aristotle. (1992, Trans.). *The Eudemian ethics* (M. Woods, Trans.). Oxford: Oxford University Press.

—. (1999, Trans.). *Nicomachean ethics* (2nd Ed., T. Irwin, Trans). Indianapolis, IN: Hackett Publishing Company.

Arneson, P. (Ed.). (2007). *Exploring communication ethics: Interviews with influential scholars in the field.* New York, NY: Peter Lang.

Arnett, R. C. (1992). *Dialogic education: Conversation about ideas and between persons.* Carbondale: Southern Illinois University Press.

—. (2003). The responsive 'I': Levinas's derivative argument. *Argumentation and Advocacy, 40,* 39–50.

Arnett, R. C., Fritz, J. M. H., & Holba, A. (2007). The rhetorical turn to otherness: Otherwise than humanism. *Cosmos and History: The Journal of Natural and Social Philosophy, 3,* 115–133.

Arroyo, A., & Segrin C. (2011). The relationship between self- and other-perceptions of communication competence and friendship quality. *Communication Studies, 62,* 547–562.

Austin, J. L. (1962). *How to do things with words.* Oxford: Clarendon Press.

Benhabib, S. (1987). The generalized and the concrete other: The Kohlberg-Gilligan controversy and moral theory. In E. F. Kittay & D. T. Meyers (Eds.), *Women and moral theory.* Lanham, MD: Rowman and Littlefield.

Berge, D. (1990). *The first 24 hours.* Cambridge, MA: Basil Blackwell, Inc.

Blumer, H. (1969). *Symbolic interactionism: Perspective and method.* Berkeley: University of California Press.

Booth, W. C. (1974). *A rhetoric of irony.* Chicago, IL: University of Chicago Press.

Buber, M. (1948). *Israel and the world.* New York, NY: Schocken.

Butler, J. (1988). Performative acts and gender constitution: An essay in phenomenology and feminist theory. *Theatre Journal, 40,* 519–531.

—. (1997). *Excitable speech: A politics of the performative.* New York, NY: Routledge.

—. (2006). *Gender trouble: Feminism and the subversion of identity.* New York, NY: Routledge Classics.

Cheney, G. May, S., & Debashish, M. (Eds.). (2010). *The handbook of communication ethics.* New York, NY: Routledge.

Christians, C. G., & Traber, M. (Eds.) (1997). *Communication ethics and universal values.* Thousand Oaks, CA: Sage.

Collins, P. H. (1990). *Black feminist thought: Knowledge, consciousness, and the politics of empowerment.* Boston, MA: Unwin Hyman.

Cook, M. A., & Holba, A. M. (Eds.). (2008). *Philosophies of communication: Implications for everyday experience.* New York, NY: Peter Lang.

Craig, R. T. (2007). Issue forum introduction: Cultural bias in communication theory. *Communication Monographs, 74,* 256–258.

Darby, T., Egyed, B., & Jones, B. (Eds.). (1989). *Nietzsche and the rhetoric of nihilism: Essays on interpretation, language, and politics.* Montreal: McGill-Queens University Press.

Darnell, D., & Brockriede, W. (1976). *Persons communicating.* Englewood Cliffs, NJ: Prentice Hall.

de Tocqueville, A. (1963). *Democracy in America* (H. Reeve, Trans.). New York, NY: Schocken Books (Original work published 1835, Vol. 1; 1840, Vol. 2)

Dilbeck, K. E., & McCroskey, J. C. (2009). Socio-communicative orientation, communication competence, and rhetorical sensitivity. *Human Communication, 12,* 255–266.

Dilenschneider, R. (2007). 25 years after Tylenol: What have we learned? *Directorship, 33,* 42.

Eadie, W. F., & Paulson, J. W. (1984). Communicator attitudes, communicator style, and communication competence. *Western Journal of Speech Communication, 48,* 390–407.

Edwards, R. (1990). Sensitivity to feedback and the development of self. *Communication Quarterly, 38,* 101–111.

Ellis, K., & Shockley-Zalabak, P. (2001). Trust in top management and immediate supervisor: The relationship to satisfaction, perceived organizational effectiveness, and information receiving. *Communication Quarterly, 49,* 382–398.

Fairhurst, G. T. (2011). *The power of framing: Creating the language of leadership.* San Francisco, CA: Jossey-Bass.

Fearn-Banks, K. (2001). Crisis communication: A review of some best practices. In R. L. Heath (Ed.), *Handbook of public relations* (pp. 479–485). Thousand Oaks, CA: Sage.

Ferguson, A. (2004). *An essay on the history of civil society.* Kila, MT: Kessinger. (Original work published 1767)

Flores, F., & Solomon, R. C. (1998). Creating trust. *Business Ethics Quarterly, 8,* 205–232.

Foster, L. G. (2002). Tylenol 20 years later. *Public Relations Strategist, 8,* 16¬–20.

Fritz, J. M. H. (2002). How do I dislike thee? Let me count the ways: Constructing impressions of troublesome others at work. *Management Communication Quarterly, 15,* 410–438.

—. (2006). Typology of troublesome others at work: A follow-up investigation. In J. M. H. Fritz & B. L. Omdahl (Eds.), *Problematic relationships in the workplace* (pp. 21–46). New York, NY: Peter Lang.

—. (2013). *Professional civility: Communicative virtue at work.* New York, NY: Peter Lang.

Fritz, J. M. H., O'Neil, N. B., Popp, A. M., Williams, C., & Arnett, R. C. (2013). The influence of supervisory behavioral integrity on intent to comply with organizational ethical standards and organizational commitment. *Journal of Business Ethics, 114,* 251–263.

Frosh, P., & Pinchevsky, A. (2009). Why media witnessing? Why now? In P. Frosh & A. Pinchevsky (Eds.), *Media witnessing: Testimony in the age of mass communication* (pp. 1–19). Houndmills, Basingstoke, UK: Palgrave Macmillan.

Ging, D., & O'Higgins Norman, J. (2016). Cyberbulling, conflict management or just messing? Teenage girls' understandings and experiences of gender, friendship, and conflict on Facebook in an Irish second-level school. *Feminist Media Studies, 16*(5), 805–821.

Hart, R. P., & Burks, D. M. (1972). Rhetorical sensitivity and social interaction. *Speech Monographs, 39,* 75–91.

Hart, R. P., Carlson, R., & Eadie, W. (1980). Attitudes toward communication and the assessment of rhetorical sensitivity. *Communication Monographs, 47,* 1–22.

Hewit, J. P. (2003). Symbols, objects and meanings. In L. T. Reynolds & N. J. Herman-Kinney (Eds.), *Handbook of symbolic interactionism* (pp. 307–325). Walnut Creek, CA: AltaMira.

Honeycutt, J. M., Choi, C. W., & DeBerry, J. R. (2009). Communication apprehension and imagined interactions. *Communication Research Reports, 26,* 228–236.

J. R. R. Tolkien. (2013). In *Encyclopaedia Britannica Online.* Retrieved from http:// www.britannica.com/EBchecked/topic/598643/JRR-Tolkien

Judith Butler. (2013). In *Encyclopaedia Britannica Online.* Retrieved from http:// www.britannica.com/EBchecked/topic/1564989/Judith-Butler

Kant, I. (1959). *Foundations of the metaphysics of morals* (L.W. Beck, Trans.). Indianapolis, IN: Bobbs-Merrill. (Original work published 1785)

—. (2006). On the common saying: That may be right in theory but does not work in practice. In P. Kleingeld (Ed.), *'Toward perpetual peace' and other writings on politics, peace, and history* (D. L. Colclasure, Trans.). New Haven, CT: Yale University Press. (Original work published 1793)

Kecskemeti, P. (1950). Totalitarian communications as a means of control. *Public Opinion Quarterly, 14,* 224–234.

Kelley, B., & Kelley, S. (2011). *Undecided: How to ditch the endless quest for perfect and find the career—and life—that's right for you.* Berkeley, CA: Seal Press.

Kimura, H. (2003). Overcome toxic management. *Nursing Management, 34,* 26–29.

Knutson, T. J., Komolsevin, R., Chatiketu, P., & Smith, V. R. (2003). A cross-cultural comparison of Thai and US American rhetorical sensitivity: Implications for intercultural communication effectiveness. *International Journal of Intercultural Relations, 27,* 63–78.

Krishnan, H. A. (2009). What causes turnover among women on top management teams? *Journal of Business Research, 62,* 1181–1186.

Lasch, C. (1991). *The true and only heaven: Progress and its critics.* New York, NY: W. W. Norton & Company.

Levinas, E. (1967). Martin Buber and the theory of knowledge. In P. A. Schilpp & M. Friedman (Eds.), *The philosophy of Martin Buber* (pp. 133–150). La Salle, IL: Open Court.

—. (1969). *Totality and infinity: An essay on exteriority*. Pittsburgh, PA: Duquesne University Press.

—. (1985). *Ethics and infinity* (R. A. Cohen, Trans.). Pittsburgh, PA: Duquesne University Press. (Original work published 1982)

—. (1994). *Beyond the verse: Talmudic readings and lectures* (G. D. Mole, Trans.). London: Athlone Press. (Original work published 1982)

—. (1994). *In the time of the nations* (M. B. Smith, Trans.). London, Athlone Press. (Original work published 1988)

Littlejohn, S. W. (1977). Symbolic interactionism as an approach to the study of human communication. *Quarterly Journal of Speech, 63*, 84–91.

Lutgen-Sandvik, P. (2003). The communicative cycle of employee emotional abuse. *Management Communication Quarterly, 14*, 471–501.

Lutgen-Sandvik, P., Namie, G., & Namie, R. (2009). Workplace bullying: Causes, consequences, and corrections. In P. Lutgen-Sandvik & B. Davenport Sypher (Eds.), *Destructive organizational communication: Processes, consequences, and constructive ways of organizing* (pp. 27–52). New York, NY: Routledge/Taylor & Francis.

MacIntyre, A. (1981). *After virtue: A study in moral theory*. Notre Dame, IN: University of Notre Dame Press.

Mao, Y., & Hale, C. L. (2015). Relating intercultural communication sensitivity to conflict management styles, technology use, and organizational communication satisfaction in multinational organizations in China. *Journal of Intercultural Communication Research, 44*(2), 132–150.

Martens, F. H. (Ed.). (2006). *Violin mastery: Interviews with Heifetz, Auer, Kreisler, and others*. Mineola, NY: Dover Publications, Inc. (Original work published 1919)

Martin, M. M., & Rubin, R. B. (1994). Development of a communication flexibility measure. *Southern Communication Journal, 59*, 171–178.

Martindale, D. (1981). *The nature and types of sociological theory*. Boston, MA: Houghton Mifflin.

McBride, M., & Bergen, K. (2008). Communication research: Becoming a reluctant confidant: Communication privacy management in close friendships. *Texas Speech Communication Journal, 33*, 50–61.

McDonald, S. (2011). What's in the 'old boys' network? Accessing social capital in gendered and racialized networks. *Social Networks, 33*, 317–330.

McPheters, R. (1991). The effectiveness of print advertising. *Journal of Advertising Research, 31*, 5–12.

Mead, G. H. (1932). *Mind, self, and society from the standpoint of a social behaviorist*. (C. W. Morris, Ed.). Chicago, IL: University of Chicago Press.

—. (1972a). *Movements of thought in the nineteenth century*. (C. W. Morris, Ed.). Chicago, IL: University of Chicago Press. (Original work published 1935)

—. (1972b). *The philosophy of the act*. (C. W. Morris, Ed.). Chicago, IL: University of Chicago Press. (Original work published 1938)

—. (2002). *The philosophy of the present*. (C. W. Morris, Ed.). New York, NY: Prometheus Books. (Original work published 1932)

Mitroff, I. I. (2004). *Crisis leadership: Planning for the unthinkable*. Hoboken, NJ: John Wiley & Sons.

Moore, T. (2012, October 7). The fight to save Tylenol (Fortune, 1982). *Fortune*. Retrieved March 25, 2013, from http://features.blogs.fortune.cnn.com/2012/10/07/the-fight-to-save-tylenol-james-burke/

Murray, E., & Shohen, S. (1992). Lessons from the Tylenol tragedy on surviving a corporate crisis. *Medical Marketing & Media, 27,* 4–19.

Namie, G., & Namie, R. (2000). *The bully at work: What you can do to stop the hurt and reclaim your dignity on the job.* Naperville, IL: Sourcebooks.

O'Connell, C. J., & Mills, A. J. (2003). Making sense of bad news: The media, sensemaking, and organizational crisis. *Canadian Journal of Communication, 28,* 323–339.

Ortega y Gasset, J. (1962). *Man and crisis.* New York, NY: W. W. Norton & Company.

Our Mission & History. (2017). Retrieved from https://www.alexslemonade.org/about/our-mission-history

Pearson, J. C., & VanHorn, S. B. (2004). Communication and gender identity: A retrospective analysis. *Communication Quarterly, 52,* 284–299.

Reynolds, L. T. (2003). Early representatives. In L. T. Reynolds & N. J. Herman-Kinney (Eds.), *Handbook of symbolic interactionism* (pp. 59–81). Walnut Creek, CA: AltaMira.

Rieff, P. (1966). *The triumph of the therapeutic.* New York, NY: Harper Torchbooks.

Rubinson, J. (2009). Empirical evidence of television advertising effectiveness. *Journal of Advertising Research, 49,* 220–226.

Salih, S. (2002). *Judith Butler.* New York, NY: Routledge.

Seeger, M. W., Sellnow, T. L., & Ulmer, R. R. (2003). *Communication and organizational crisis.* Westport, CT: Praeger.

Sennett R. (2008). *The craftsman.* New Haven, CT: Yale University Press.

Sias, P. (2012). Exclusive or exclusory: Workplace relationships, ostracism, and isolation. In B. L. Omdahl & J. M. H. Fritz (Eds.), *Problematic relationships in the workplace* (Vol. 2) (pp. 105–121). New York, NY: Peter Lang.

Spitzberg, B. H., Canary, D. J., & Cupach, W. R. (1994). A competence-based approach to conflict. In D. D. Cahn (Ed.), *Conflict in interpersonal relationships.* Hillsdale, NJ: Lawrence Erlbaum Associates.

Spitzberg, B. H., & Cupach, W. R. (2002). Interpersonal skills. In M. L. Knapp & J. A. Daly (Eds.), *Handbook of interpersonal communication* (pp. 564–611). Thousand Oaks, CA: Sage.

Thomas, G. F., Zolin, R., & Hartman, J. L. (2009). The central role of communication in developing trust and its effects on employee involvement. *Journal of Business Communication, 46,* 287–310.

Tolkien, J. R. R. (1965). *The return of the king (The lord of the rings, 3).* Boston, MA: Houghton Mifflin.

Ulmer, R. R., Sellnow, T. L., & Seeger, M. W. (2007). *Effective crisis communication: Moving from crisis to opportunity.* Thousand Oaks, CA: Sage.

Wei, Y., Frankwick, G. L., Gao, T., & Zhou, N. (2011). Consumer adoption intentions toward the internet in China: The effects of impersonal and interpersonal communication channels. *Journal of Advertising Research, 51,* 594–607.

Wentling, R. M., & Thomas, S. (2009). Workplace culture that hinders and assists the career development of women in information technology. *Information Technology, Learning, and Performance Journal, 25,* 25–43.

Wiemann, J. M. (1977). Explication and test of a model of communication competence. *Human Communication Research, 3,* 195–213.

Wood, J. (2011). *Mosaics: An introduction to the field of communication.* Boston, MA: Wadsworth.

Chapter Thirteen

DESTRUCTIVE CONFLICT: DO NOT DO THIS TO ME AND TO US

Better understanding employees' emotions about workplace bullying is an important part of attending to its negative effects on personal and organizational awareness. (Tracy, Lutgen-Sandvik, & Alberts, 2006, pp. 149–150)

"Destructive Conflict: Do Not Do This to Me and to Us" begins with a basic communication and conflict reminder: Be careful as you communicate with others—relationships matter. This chapter's *Spotlight on Leadership* features Malala Yousafzai, an advocate for education rights who questioned the Taliban at the age of 11. Despite receiving death threats for their education advocacy work, Malala and her father continued to fight for education for women.

© JStone/Shutterstock.com

In 2011, Malala Yousafzai received Pakistan's first National Youth Peace Prize and received a nomination for the International Children's Peace Prize. In October 2012, on the way home from school, Malala was shot with a single bullet that went through her head, neck, and shoulder. Malala miraculously survived and later cofounded The Malala Fund in 2013, which promotes awareness of girls' education.

Conflict reminds us of a basic human reality—life is social and involves working with a wide range of people, including those we like and those we do not like. This chapter examines the impact on the individual and the community when destructive conflict guides our communicative lives together.

"Stand for the Silent," an antibullying effort, was started in 2010 by a group of students from the Oklahoma State University–Oklahoma City Upward Bound Chapter. At the forefront of this effort were Kirk and Laura Smalley, who lost their son after he committed suicide as a result of bullying. Representatives from "Stand for the Silent" visit over 200 schools and community groups each year. Since May 2010, Kirk and Laura Smalley have traveled to 1,000 schools and spoken with 1 million school children ("About our Organization," 2017, para. 2).

By educating others about the importance of standing up and responding if one witnesses bullying, "Stand for the Silent" hopes to change the prevalence of this type of destructive conflict in our schools and communities. Bullies are the antithesis of our basic message—relationships matter.

INTRODUCTION

We all have been guilty of letting anger get the best of us, propelling us to say things that we later regret. Apologies, unfortunately, do not quickly erase destructive words and actions from consciousness; our emotional and mental storage keeps problematic issues alive. One may apologize multiple times and then say, "I should never have said that;" only to find that the unreflective use of words continues to haunt us. Words have an impact; they can hurt, leaving a negative impression long after their delivery.

In "Destructive Conflict: Do Not Do This to Me and to Us," we explore three major sections:

1. **Divisive conflict** undermines the credibility of persons not present, those unable to defend themselves and/or speak on their own behalf;
2. **Resistance to the problematic** presents a public roadmap, detailing how to work constructively with another;
3. **Framing communicative leadership: Attending to the problematic** describes Gail T. Fairhurst's work on how leaders discern whether a particular conflict is a functional necessity or a dysfunctional action within an organization.

This chapter illuminates the danger of destructive conflict that emerges from petty and, at times, mean-spirited words and actions. Word choice has a positive and negative impact on relationships (Afifi, McManus, Hutchinson, & Baker, 2007; Bisel, Messersmith, & Kelley, 2012; Park, Lee, Lee, & Truex, 2012). For example, the quantity and nature of information that parents choose to self-disclose to children during a divorce affects their future relationships (Afifi et al., 2007). In an organizational setting, like in a demanding family crisis, choosing words wisely is important in supervisor-subordinate relationships (Bisel et al., 2012) and in building trust with clients and colleagues (Park et al., 2012). Our words and actions carry ethical importance; we generate and perpetuate challenging relationships when we refuse to recognize that relationships matter.

DIVISIVE CONFLICT

Divisive conflict unnecessarily separates persons through problematic conversations that lessen the credibility and influence of another (Burrell, Buzzanell, & McMillan, 1992, p. 142). Advantageous conditions arise when one speaks directly with another, opening multiple and divergent vantage points of consideration within a conflict (Collins, 2009, p. 2). Divisive conflict foments unnecessary struggles at another's expense.

Divisive conflict generation is in sharp contrast to communicative practices that invite friendship. A pragmatic view of friendship routinely offers support and protects a friend's back while providing honest and direct discourse. Such communication is quite contrary to divisive conflict generation. William Rawlins (1992/2008) believes friendships inherently involve various "dialectical tensions" (p. 2). As one engages dialectical tensions, friendships either evolve or disintegrate. Friendships require working out shared expectations for the relationship (Rawlins, 2009, p. ix). As Rawlins (1992/2008) notes, "Friendships cannot be imposed on people; it is an ongoing human association voluntarily developed and privately negotiated" (p. 9). Relationally appropriate communicative actions uphold a friendship.

Julia Wood (2006/2012) contends that friendship trust takes time, effort, and energy to cultivate. If one does not understand the investment needed to build a friendship, then there is a lack of trust, limited support for the other, an absence of communication, and an ongoing neglect of the relationship. Such practices signal a friendship on its way to a conclusion. Few friendships last forever. Friendships do not endure the constant reality of divisive communication. Such comments undercut productivity and activity; they give us tangible reasons not to trust another.

Divisive conflict undermines the credibility of another, leading to unproductive communicative actions (Clegg & van Iterson, 2009, p. 227). The research of Golish and Caughlin (2002) concluded that adolescents avoid conversations with stepparents in order to undermine their credibility, giving rise to distancing conflict and dissatisfaction in the relationship. Multiple metaphors illustrate the diversity of communicative acts that constitute divisive conflict. In the remainder of this section, we highlight three problematic communicative

FIGURE 13.1 Gossip, bullying, and harassment all involve a power differential where the victim in the relationship has less power.

behaviors: gossip, bullying, and harassment. **Gossip** can be associated with a form of incivility where the intent to harm is often ambiguous (Metts, Cupach, & Lippert, 2006, pp. 251–252). **Bullying** is a more severe form of incivility characterized by "intense and typically repeated" actions with a more direct intent to harm (Metts, Cupach, & Lippert, 2006, p. 252), and **harassment** becomes abuse when "embedded with a pattern of mistreatment" (Metts, Cupach, & Lippert, 2006, p. 253). What unites these terms is that they require a power differential between persons; in each case, someone has less power (Figure 13.1).

Gossip

Gossip pilfers power from the person talked about as one engages in a conversation in which another cannot respond (Clegg & Iterson, 2009, p. 286). One seeks power over the other by "spreading news about the…[activities] of another" without the victim's knowledge of the information (Rosnow & Fine, 1976, p. 87). Generally, the impulse for gossip emerges out of peripheral issues that undercut another's contribution to a community (Luna, Garcia, Chou, & Jackson, 2013). Some **problematic others** are skilled at being stealth-like; they generate hearsay behind the scenes, initiating conflict that pulls others apart. In such a communicative environment, one is blindsided by unanticipated information and news. In a work situation, gossip can be a communicative form of throwing sand into the gears in hopes of lessening another's productivity (Smith, Houmanfar, & Denny, 2012). Gossip calls into question a person's credibility with another by "idle talk or rumor, especially about personal or private affairs of others" (Hafen, 2004, p. 224). Gossip twists and distorts the importance of another's accomplishments and hard work.

Gossip generates conflict between and among others. A number of communication researchers examined this problematic communicative action (Hafen, 2004; Suls, 1977; Tovares, 2006; Turner, Mazur, Wendel, & Winslow, 2003; Yoo, 2009). Gossip is evaluative talk about a person who is not present (Eder & Enke, 1991); it is a form of verbal abuse (Johnson & Indvik, 2006). Gossip can be a form of resistance to a closed social power structure within the workplace (Mumby, 2005) or used as a vehicle for persons to exert control over others (Farley, Timme, & Hart, 2010). Gossip attributes negative behavior and/or motives to another, contributing to interpersonal conflict when one discovers the deeds (McDonald, Putallaz, Grimes, Kupersmidt, & Coie, 2007). Gossip creates power differentials within the workplace, influencing relationships (Kurland & Pelled, 2000). Talking about a person who is not present limits that person's power and influence.

A national study conducted by The Creative Group, a recruiting firm that places skilled employees into the fields of design, marketing, advertising, and public relations, revealed that 84% of advertising and marketing executives reported that office gossip is a common workplace behavior (The Creative Group, 2008). In that same study, 63% of respondents reported that gossip had a negative effect on the workplace (The Creative Group, 2008). An analysis of gossip within an elementary school conducted by Hallet, Harger, and Eder (2009) involved videotaping occurrences of gossip in formal school meetings. The research concluded that gossip is a part of everyday educational life. Gossip is a realistic reality; however, one must manage gossip by keeping people on task. Hallet, one of the authors of the elementary school study, shared with the *New York Times* a helpful verbal retort for when gossip gets out of hand—"Don't we have some work to do here" (Tierney, 2009, para. 28). Gossip is a distraction from doing one's work. Gossip damages the reputations of the speaker, the listener, and the target; it is essential to understand the implications of one's words and actions (Tierney, 2009, para. 24).

Perhaps the first time one meets the reality of gossip in the workplace, one professionally awakens to its danger and the necessity to be ever alert (Hafen, 2004; Turner et al., 2003). One must counter gossip that undercuts people and practices of work and productivity, which damages morale. Sometimes it seems that the only control one has in an environment propelled by gossip is to keep one's head down and do one's work. There is a scene in an old Kevin Costner movie, *For Love of the Game*, where Costner's character stands on the pitcher's mound and says to himself, "Clear the mechanism" (Abraham, 1999). At that moment, there are only two people in the stadium, the pitcher and the catcher—no other distractions. This intense focus on practices is necessary in order to contend with gossip that can generate internal noise and discontent (Narula, 2006). An even more intense form of destructive confrontation emerges from bullying.

Bullying

Bullying involves attacks upon those with fewer resources and power; it is difficult for those bullied to marshal protection. Bullying is an organized process that focuses on unequally matched participants who are vulnerable to negative, aggressive, and unjust behavior (Einarsen, 2000; Hazler & Miller, 2001; Pörhölä, Karhunen, & Rainivaara, 2006). Bullying is a toxic activity, defined as aggressive behavior that attempts to inflict harm or discomfort on another.

The National Communication Association, a professional organization composed of scholars, teachers, and practitioners, developed an antibullying project under the direction of 2016 President Christina S. Beck. This presidential initiative, "Enhancing Opportunities," "strives to foster collaborations between Communication scholars and other stakeholders (such as policy makers, educators, the media, and the general public) in anti–social aggression efforts" (NCA Anti-Bullying, 2017, para. 1). This initiative recognizes the contributions of communication scholars to bullying research and prevention strategies. NCA has created an anti-bullying digital repository of topic-related resources on general bullying, workplace bullying, bystanders, cyberbullying, social aggression, harassment, and stalking.

Within the communication discipline, the terms *workplace bullying* and *generalized nonsexual harassment* often coexist (Namie & Lutgen-Sandvik, 2010). In bullying, however, destructive acts repeat over time (Olweus, 1997, p. 496). Bullying in the workplace is an extension of what many experienced as children in elementary school and as teenagers. Bullying occurs when one person intimidates another with actions that include hostile quips, the misplacing of one's work and/or tools, and other forms of personal disruption to daily routine. There are those who walk into work each day feeling as though they have a knot in their stomach, fearful of a bully. This anxiety comes not from the task of doing the job but from engaging others who make life difficult and miserable in an organization. Bullies require countering and if necessary curtailing destructive action in the workplace.

Often, the target of a bully needs someone else to assist with stopping the actions of a bully. Defense often emerges through a coalition of people working to stop such behavior by detailing and documenting the actions in the workplace (Buchli & Pearce, 1975). Coworkers who form coalitions have a shared vision, which ultimately affects the larger structure, creating a precedent for how things should be done (Broom & Avanzino, 2010); a partnership of concerned persons is more likely than a single individual to stop a bully.

The aggressive behavior associated with bullying is repetitive and has vicious intent (Smorti, Menesini, & Smith, 2003) that includes personal attacks, social ostracism, and a multitude of painful verbal and nonverbal messages and/or interactions (Lutgen-Sandvik, 2006). Bullying fosters a negative ambiance within a group that disrupts communication, cohesion, and performance. Bullying creates a hostile environment that includes apprehension, distrust, anger, and suspicion of others (Frost, 2003). Bullying is a communicative activity that seeks to embarrass and hurt others (Kowalski, 2007). Pörhölä et al. (2006) suggest that social penetration theory (Altman & Taylor, 1973) and uncertainty reduction theory (Berger, 1987) describe why and how bullies emerge. Bullies use both verbal (Greene & Burleson, 2003) and nonverbal communication (Burgoon & Hale, 1988) within interpersonal relationships (Cupach & Spitzberg, 2002; Hess, 2003), small groups (Anderson, Riddle, & Martin, 1999; Bormann, 1996), organizations (Leets & Giles, 1999), and cultural contexts (Meares, Oetzel, Torres, Dekacs, & Ginossar, 2004). Bullies use divisive communication skills to exert inappropriate power over others.

Bullying transpires in a variety of locations, such as the playground (Mills & Carwile, 2009), the workplace (Bandow & Hunter, 2008), and social media sites (Festl & Quandt, 2013). The following example demonstrates how many rallied around a bus monitor bullied by her students. On Monday, June 18, 2012, a student posted a 10-minute cell phone video to Facebook, which revealed four middle school students from Greece Athena Middle School near Rochester, New York, bullying their 68-year-old bus monitor, Karen Klein. On Tuesday, the video was moved from Facebook to YouTube, and by Wednesday the video had gone viral with 1.5 million views by Thursday morning (Freile & McDermott, 2012, para. 6) and 4.2 million views by Friday (Dobbin, 2012, para. 20). The video shows "a vile chorus includ[ing] profanity, taunts, insults, jeers, physical ridicule, and outright threats to Klein's person and home" (Freile & McDermott, 2012, para. 8). The bus monitor tried to ignore the acts of bullying, but, as she fought back the urge to cry, the attacks continued.

Within the week, the video garnered nationwide news attention. When a 25-year-old man from Toronto saw the video, he started a fund to raise $5,000 to send Klein on a vacation (Miller, 2012, para. 6). In less than 24 hours, the fund reached $305,000 (Freile & McDermott, 2012, para. 2) and then rose to $605,000 as of June 23, 2012 (Miller, 2012, para. 2), with over 29,000 contributors (Petri, 2012, para. 8). Klein was overwhelmed with letters, emails, and Facebook messages that demonstrated outrage and support from individuals she did not even know. The four boys suffered suspension for 1 year with a requirement to attend a reengagement center that provides their coursework, allowing them to stay on track for graduation. The boys were prohibited from using school transportation, required to volunteer 50 hours with a senior center, and mandated to complete a program in bullying prevention, respect, and responsibility (Preston, 2012, para. 7–8). This was a very public case of bullying; unfortunately, there are many cases that go unreported and do not end on a constructive note.

As Mahboub Hashem (2015) argues in "Bullying and Labelling as Communication Tools of Control and Domination," bullying is an international phenomenon. Hashem cites that in Middle Eastern educational systems, 20% of those interviewed ages 16 to 23 indicated that bullying and labeling continued even after their high school experience. Subjects have endured frequent acts of bullying, offering specific percentages from Arab countries that vary from 20% at the low end to 44.2% at the high end (p. 139). Interestingly, the majority of bullying acts arise from same-gender exchanges. One of the most negative by-products of bullying is that it encourages defensive discourse that moves people into forms of internal protection, seeking a safe space from communication that is malicious and generates ongoing acts of suspicion (p. 141).

Alan K. Goodboy, Matthew M. Martin, and Christine E. Rittenour (2016), in "Bullying as a Display of Social Dominance Orientation," connect acts of bullying to social dominance, utilizing social dominance theory. They outline communication that bullies invite bigotry and propel abusive communication traits with principal objectives to victimize another and to construct clarity of dominance between and among persons.

Alan K. Goodboy, Matthew M. Martin, and Elizabeth Brown (2016), in "Bullying on the School Bus: Deleterious Effects on Public School Bus Drivers," extend this theme to international, not simply local, roots. They emphasize such behavior not only in the classroom but also outside school grounds, specifically examining bullying behavior on school buses. The authors recommend that when bullying occurs on school buses, intervention is at times necessary and active support from administration is required. Unfortunately, training for bus drivers is necessary and needs to go beyond mechanical responses into creative efforts to lesson victimization. When students bully the bus drivers themselves, active response from administrators must follow. Students require an authority figure. When it is challenged, the safety of the entire environment is put at risk. The next stage or level of divisive conflict is harassment.

Harassment

Workplace harassment includes "repeated activities with the aim of bringing mental (but sometimes physical) pain and directed toward one or more individuals who for some reason or another are not able to defend themselves" (Björkqvist, Osterman, & Hjelt-Back, 1994, p. 173). Harassment in the workplace occurs when one tries to use one's power to belittle another by monopolizing, offending, or controlling behavior in the interaction (Fiske, 2010, p. 964). Typically, a harassment victim is in a position of lower socio-cultural power (Gruber & Bjorn, 1986).

Harassment is against the law; it creates an intimidating, hostile, and offensive work environment that interferes with an employee's work performance. According to the U.S. Department of State (2008):

> *Discriminatory harassment is verbal or physical conduct that denigrates or shows hostility toward an individual because of his or her race, color, gender, national origin, religion, age (40 or over), physical or mental disability, sexual orientation, or because of his or her opposition to discrimination or his or her participation in the discrimination complaint process. (para. 4)*

Racial harassment (Allen, 2009) and sexual harassment receive significant research attention because communication both enables and counters these specific types of harassment. Brian K. Richardson and Juandalynn Taylor (2009), in "Sexual Harassment at the Intersection of Race and Gender: A Theoretical Model of the Sexual Harassment Experiences of Women of Color," explicate the problem of sexual harassment. They articulate the compounded nature of this abuse when tied to racial discrimination. Racial discrimination and sexual harassment can occur simultaneously. Bullying shares with acts of racial discrimination a desire to marginalize and limit workplace influence. A communicative approach to managing sexual harassment in the workplace draws upon various approaches—assertiveness, nonassertiveness, and aggressiveness, depending on the circumstance of the situation (Bingham, 1991). For example, if one's main goal is to get the harasser to leave one alone, one might use an aggressive style that makes the offender realize that the practices are unwanted and inappropriate. If the harasser is a supervisor, one may be more inclined to be nonassertive. If one wants to address the issue without causing serious harm to relationships, one may engage in an assertive communication style. Managing sexual harassment in the workplace is a complex issue because each incident of sexual harassment remains contextually embedded within particular circumstances (Bingham, 1991). Researchers disagree on the role of power in sexual harassment; some research indicates that harassers hold a higher status than the harassed, while other research indicates that a harasser's behavior is often driven by lack of status (Lafontaine & Tredeau, 1986).

By identifying specific behaviors, one can counter potential sexual harassment within the workplace. Buzza (1983) discusses sexual harassment within a three-fold approach to responsibility: (1) thoughtfully communicating about sexual harassment that considers the intricacies of the issue (p. 83); (2) directly indicating that harassing activity is unwanted (pp. 83–84); and (3) engaging in reflective consideration on how particular actions will be received as professionally improper (p. 84). Hickson, Grierson, and Linder (1991) discuss a six-step process for assessing sexual harassment: (1) "aesthetic appreciation" (p. 113), (2) "active mental groping" (p. 113), (3) "social touching" (pp. 113–114), (4) "foreplay harassment" (p. 114), (5) "sexual abuse" (p. 115), and (6) "ultimate threat" (p. 115). In the **aesthetic appreciation** stage, the harasser begins by complimenting the victim on his or her physical appearance. **Active mental groping** involves the harasser's imagination that seems projected upon the communicative environment. Sometimes, but not always, the harasser's behavior can be observed by others. **Social touching** includes behaviors where the harasser arranges to be close to the victim, permitting opportunities to touch the victim. **Foreplay harassment** moves beyond touching with the harasser attempting to initiate more involved activities. **Sexual abuse** includes the type of touch such as "strokes, brushes, and squeezes" (p. 115) and the location of touch on the body. There are also verbal behaviors that constitute sexual harassment. Ultimate threat refers to a *quid pro quo* type of harassment that makes the victim believe that not obliging the harasser will result in serious consequences (Hickson, Grierson, & Linder, 1991).

In July 2016, Gretchen Carlson claimed that when she refused the sexual advances of Fox News Channel chairman and CEO Roger Ailes, he retaliated by decreasing her air time and eventually firing her. After hosting Fox's morning show, "Fox and Friends," from 2006 to

2013, Carlson was moved to an afternoon show "The Real Time with Gretchen Carlson," a move she viewed as a demotion. Ailes fired her on June 23, 2016, after 11 years with the network (Castillo, 2016). As Carlson's story became public, more women came forward describing similar experiences with Ailes. Ailes then resigned from his role as chairman and CEO of Fox News Channel and Fox Business Network, and his role as chairman of Fox Television Stations (Balakrishnan & Castillo, 2016). In September 2016, 21ˢᵗ Century Fox reached a $20 million settlement with Carlson accompanied by an apology (Stelter, 2016, para. 1).

Today, sexual harassment training is a common human resource[1] activity within companies as they seek to protect employees' right to work in a harassment-free environment (Perry, Kulik, & Field, 2009). Corporations spend hundreds of millions of dollars a year on sexual harassment training programs and management workshops (Green, 2011). According to a 2010 survey of 460 companies conducted by the Society for Human Resource Management, 82% required sexual harassment training for their employees (Green, 2011). Sexual harassment prevention training is crucial for organizational socialization.

Gossip, bullying, and harassment are common communicative tools of problematic and destructive communicators (Fritz & Omdahl, 2006; Omdahl & Fritz, 2012). These problematic communicative behaviors require communicative remedies (Fritz, 2009), all of which can be encouraged and fostered within the organizational setting. Organizational socialization, professional civility, and principles of critical theory offer communicative means of resistance to these destructive communicative behaviors.

RESISTANCE TO THE PROBLEMATIC

Resistance to problematic others is largely dependent on socialization within a large company. Organizational socialization is an inherently communicative process (Kramer, 2010). **Socialization** begins before organizational entry with the anticipatory phase and proceeds through the encounter and metamorphosis phases (Van Maanen, 1975). These phases do not necessarily happen in sequence, but they do occur somewhere in the larger socialization process. **Anticipatory socialization** begins with the application, the interview, and preparation for engaging a new social setting (Van Maanen, 1975). The **encounter** phase occurs when one initially enters an organization and tries to make sense of that place (Van Maanen, 1975, p. 222). **Metamorphosis** arises when one moves from being a novice to a more seasoned participant in an organization (Van Maanen, 1975, p. 223), giving one the ability to predict events and institutional direction with greater accuracy.

Socialization processes announce a communicative public roadmap of how we should work constructively with one another. Socialization begins before the moment of employment, beginning with the application, the interview, and initial encounters with potential colleagues.

---

1. The human resources office is commonly a place where people go to discuss issues or policies regarding fair practices in the workplace (Louw-Potgieter, 2012).

Socialization is not reified in time; it requires learning a story of an organization that will augment one's participation. The socialization process is marked by "turning points" that allow individuals to become further connected to the organization (Bullis & Bach, 1989). From the first time one walks into a given place, implicit socialization conveys whether or not gossip, bullying, and harassment will be tolerated. Socialization, at its best, forewarns and announces the necessity of commentary on sexual harassment and to whom one must report.

Fritz and Omdahl (2006; Omdahl & Fritz, 2012) explore problematic work relationships, the effects of those relationships, and ways of addressing them. Professional civility (Fritz, 2013; Arnett & Fritz, 2003; Arnett, 2006) offers one way to address problematic relationships. Fritz (2013) defines **professional civility** as a communicative virtue that protects and promotes productivity, one's place of employment, and persons with whom we carry out tasks in the workplace (p. 17). Fritz's virtue ethics framework requires professional civility to frame social-ization as individuals learn standards of behavior and practices that manifest communicative virtue in a specific place of work (Fritz, 2013, p. 27). Fritz (2013) writes, "Socialization to a particular organization requires attentiveness to local norms in the development of embedded or localized professional competence" (p. 28). Professional civility acts as a form of communi-cative resistance by privileging rules and norms that guide acceptable workplace behavior and minimizing problematic narratives. When constructive socialization is not in place, one must learn to address "problematic others" (Fritz, 2006) with creative competence. However, a more pervasive problem in the organizational settings may reside at the level of the organization itself. Critical theory offers resistance to problematic narratives within an organization.

The study and practice of critical theory gives insight into the importance of countering an entire narrative structure. **Critical theory** assists in uncovering discrepancies between what an organization proclaims and what it does, unmasking problematic and inadequate narra-tives. Critical theory is concerned with "transformative processes" (Eastland, 1994, p. 162) for individuals and society with the goal of emancipating people, meanings, and values (McK-innon, 2009). Critical theory emerged in 1937 with the publication of Max Horkheimer's (1937/1976) "Traditional and Critical Theory." Horkheimer differentiated between traditional and critical theory by suggesting that the former supports the status quo, while the latter aims to critique and change society. Farrell and Aune explicated the significance of this work for the communication discipline in a 1979 literature review published in the *Quarterly Journal of Speech*. From a communication perspective, "the task of Critical Theory is to locate the poten-tial or existing failures in the process of social communication" (Hardt, 1993, p. 58).

Communication scholars draw on critical theory in two distinct ways. First, they apply prin-ciples and concepts of critical theory—power, domination, social transformation, aesthetics, authenticity, and alienation—to specific areas of communication, including rhetoric (McK-errow, 1989), intercultural communication (Halualani, Mendoza, & Drzewiecka, 2009), health communication (Airhihenbuwa & Obregon, 2000), and organizational communica-tion (Mumby, 1993; Trethewey, 2001). Second, communication scholars rely on critical theo-rists such as Jürgen Habermas (b. 1929), a student of Max Horkheimer, to offer theoretical frameworks for their research (Alvesson & Deetz, 2006; Burleson & Kline, 1979; Fusfield, 1997; Deetz, 1999). Habermas (1971, 1973, 1983/1990, 2012) is concerned with discourse ethics as central in challenging unreflective assumptions and normative claims.

Communication scholars Alvesson and Deetz (2006) describe the importance of critical theory for organizational communication, advocating congruence of story and practices that ensure equal opportunity for individuals and freedom from ideological domination. Mumby (2004) connects critical theory to organizational discourse by examining the relationships among power, resistance, and social practices. Critical theory seeks to emancipate workers from communicative environments that deny participation and active engagement in decision making. Principles and concepts of critical theory relevant to communication scholars include issues of power, structures of domination, social transformation, aesthetics, authenticity, and alienation.

Questions about power emerge as one investigates existing hierarchical structures within a society that give privilege to certain groups of people (Ting-Toomey, 2010). Persons who hold positions of power influence communication systems in ways that reflect their own experiences. The work of Hardt (1993) addresses the role of communication in examining "authenticity" (p. 49) and "alienation" (p. 49) in relation to critical theory. Critical theory propounds a theoretical frame for describing the difficulty of achieving authentic discourse within social, political, and cultural constraints. The lack of authentic discourse often leads to alienation as individuals drift out of touch with themselves as a result of problematic constraints within a communicative environment (Hardt, 1993).

Critical theory reminds us that there are sometimes very good reasons for narrative contention. Critical theory calls into question the discrepancy between a stated position of a given communicative environment and its communicative practices, opening up conversation that reveals incongruences and, at times, acts of hypocrisy. Critical theory unmasks conflict that has been dormant and permits it to become more visible. Critical theory unmasks problematic issues manifested in the discordance between speech and action, between the telling and the doing. Critical theory reveals what is already present, opening up opportunities for examination and growth. Critical theory presupposes that problematic communicative environments are not the work of individuals alone, but by a potentially destructive narrative.

FRAMING COMMUNICATIVE LEADERSHIP: ATTENDING TO THE PROBLEMATIC

If a man lets it have the mastery, the continually growing world of It overruns him and robs him of the reality of his own I. (Buber, 1937/2000, p. 23)

The seventh chapter in *The Power of Framing: Creating the Language of Leadership* discusses the importance of leadership (Fairhurst, 2011). We contend that a central test of leadership is dealing with problematic persons and conflict contexts. Leaders need to meet, utilize, and understand all forms of conflict with creative competence. In addition, leaders need to manage and minimize conflict that takes us nowhere. Disingenuous conflict activity works to move leadership into marginalized positions within a community. Problematic colleagues require our attention, as does a problematic larger communicative environment. Critical theory demands that leaders recognize the inevitability of conflict in response to disparities between what leaders say and what they do and to the increasing negation of autonomy and freedom. Critical theory reminds us that there is a reason for conflict. People seek acknowledgement and recognition for their work, productivity, and accomplishments—narratives that embrace incongruences between speech and action invite conflict. Leadership must discern between functional and dysfunctional conflict in order to assist a given communicative environment.

Fairhurst (2011) suggests the following ingredients for preparation for framing when managing destructive conflict:

1. **Clarity** about communicative coordinates of "who, what, when, where, and why" (p. 158). In order to lead, one must understand the communicative terrain and the communicative context.
2. **Clarity of task** must determine a leader's direction. Conflict emerges when one spends too much time on wrong or inappropriate tasks. A leader must begin with clarity of commission.
3. **The engagement of resources** must be responsive to the particularlity of a given situation. Leaders recognize that conflict emerges when resources are not present and one attempts to lead by personality alone, which is ultimately insufficient.
4. **Attributes of leadership** keep before us a basic reality—when leadership fails to garner support, conflict emerges. One must understand the persons with whom one works in order to lead. Fairhurst (2016) reminds us, however, that "conflict often emerges even in the presence of leadership, especially given the prominence of tensions, contradictions and paradoxes in today's organizations" (personal correspondence).
5. **The role of framing** in everyday leadership guides one to frame according to the availability of resources and the audience, both of which help constitute one's power.

The basic communicative rule for leadership is to be attentive to the environment, engaging all communicative coordinates and constituents. Leadership must pay attention. For a leader, the most wretched communicative act is to ignore the task, context, and all those affected by the labor. Attentiveness matters; otherwise, leaders join the ranks of problematic others (Arnett, 2012).

REFERENCES

About Our Organization. (2017). Retrieved from http://www.standforthesilent.org/who-we-are.html#aboutus

Abraham, M. (Executive Producer). Raimi, S. (Director). (1999). *For love of the game* [Motion picture]. United States: Universal Studios.

Afifi, T. D., McManus, T., Hutchinson, S., & Baker, B. (2007). Inappropriate parental divorce disclosures, the factors that prompt them, and their impact on parents' and adolescents' well-being. *Communication Monographs, 74,* 78–102.

Airhihenbuwa, C. O., & Obregon, R. (2000). A critical assessment of theories/models used in health communication for HIV/AIDS. *Journal of Health Communication, 5,* 5–15.

Allen, B. J. (2009). Racial harassment in the workplace. In P. Lutgen-Sandvik & B. Davenport Sypher (Eds.), *The destructive side of organizational communication: Processes, consequences and constructive ways of organizing* (pp. 164–183). New York, NY: Routledge.

Altman, I., & Taylor, D. (1973). *Social penetration: The development of interpersonal relationships.* New York, NY: Holt.

Alvesson, M., & Deetz, S. A. (2006). Critical theory and postmodern approaches to organization. In S. R. Clegg, C. Hardy, T. B. Lawrence, & W. R. Nord (Eds.), *The Sage handbook of organization studies* (pp. 255–282). Thousand Oaks, CA: Sage.

Anderson, C. M., Riddle, B. L., & Martin, M. M. (1999). Socialization processes in groups. In L. R. Frey, S. S. Gouran, & M. S. Pool (Eds.), *The handbook of group communication theory and research* (pp. 139–166). Thousand Oaks, CA: Sage.

Arnett, R. C. (2006). Professional civility: Reclaiming organizational limits. In J. M. H. Fritz & B. L. Omdahl (Eds.), *Problematic relationships in the workplace* (Vol. 1, pp. 233–248). New York, NY: Peter Lang.

—. (2012). The bureaucrat as problematic other: Arendt's warning. In B. L. Omdahl & J. M. H. Fritz (Eds.), *Problematic relationships in the workplace* (Vol. 2, pp. 145–163). New York, NY: Peter Lang.

Arnett, R. C., & Fritz, J. M. H. (2003). Sustaining institutional ethics and integrity: Management in a postmodern moment. In A. S. Iltis (Ed.), *Institutional integrity in health care* (pp. 41–71). Dordrecht: Kluwer.

Balakrishnan, A., & Castillo, M. (2016). Roger Ailes resigns as CEO of Fox News. *CNBC.* Retrieved from http://www.cnbc.com/2016/07/21/fox-news-confirms-that-roger-ailes-is-leaving-company.html

Bandow, D., & Hunter, D. (2008). Developing policies about workplace behavior. *Business Communication Quarterly, 71,* 103–106.

Berger, C. R. (1987). Communicating under uncertainty. In M. Roloff & G. Miller (Eds.), *Interpersonal processes: New directions in communication research* (pp. 39–62). Newbury Park, CA: Sage.

Bingham, S. (1991). Communication strategies for managing sexual harassment in organizations: Understanding message options and their effects. *Journal of Applied Communication Research, 19,* 88–115.

Bisel, R. S., Messersmith, A. S., & Kelley, K. M. (2012). Supervisor-subordinate communication: Hierarchical mum effect meets organizational learning. *Journal of Business Communication, 49,* 128–147.

Björkqvist, K., Osterman, K., & Hjelt-Back, M. (1994). Aggression among university employees. *Aggressive Behavior, 20,* 173–184.

Bormann, E. G. (1996). Symbolic convergence theory and communication in group decision making. In R. Y. Hirokawa & M.S. Poole (Eds.), *Communication and group decision making* (2nd ed., pp. 81–113). Thousand Oaks, CA: Sage.

Broom, C., & Avanzino, S. (2010). The communication of community collaboration: When rhetorical visions collide. *Communication Quarterly, 58,* 480–501.

Buber, M. (2000). *I and Thou* (R. G. Smith, Trans.). New York, NY: Scribner. (Original work published 1937)

Buchli, R. D., & Pearce, W. B. (1975). Coalition and communication. *Human Communication Research, 1*, 213–221.

Bullis, C., & Bach, B. W. (1989). Socialization turning points: An examination of change in organizational identification. *Western Journal of Speech Communication, 53*, 273–293.

Burgoon, J. K., & Hale, J. (1988). Nonverbal expectancy violations: Model elaboration and application to immediacy behaviors. *Communication Monographs, 55*, 58–79.

Burleson, B. R., & Kline, S. L. (1979). Habermas's theory of communication: A critical explication. *Quarterly Journal of Speech, 65*, 412–428.

Burrell, N. A., Buzzanell, P. A., & McMillan, J. J. (1992). Feminine tensions in conflict situations as revealed by metaphoric analysis. *Management Communication Quarterly, 6*, 115–149.

Buzza, B. W. (1983). Three communication responsibilities concerning sexual harassment. *Association for Communication Administration Bulletin, 46*, 82–85.

Castillo, M. (2016). Fox News host Gretchen Carlson sues Roger Ailes for sexual harassment. *CNBC.* Retrieved from http://www.cnbc.com/2016/07/06/fox-news-host-carlson-sues-roger-ailes-for-sexual-harassment.html

Clegg, S. R., & van Iterson, A. (2009). Dishing the dirt: Gossip in organizations. *Culture and Organization, 15*, 275–289.

Collins, S. D. (2009). *Managing conflict and workplace relationships.* Mason, OH: South-Western. The Creative Group. (2008). Steer clear of the company rumor mill. Retrieved February 24, 2013, from http://creativegroup.mediaroom.com/index.php?s=43&item=9

Cupach, W. R., & Spitzberg, B. H. (2002). Interpersonal skills. In M. L. Knapp & J. A. Daly (Eds.), *Handbook of interpersonal communication* (3rd ed., pp. 564–612). Thousand Oaks, CA: Sage.

Deetz, S. A. (1999). Multiple stakeholders in social responsibility in the international business context: A critical perspective. In P. Salem (Ed.), *Organization, communication, and change: Challenges in the next century* (pp. 289–319). Cresskill, NJ: Hampton Press.

Dobbin, D. (2012, June 24). What made the Karen Klein story go viral? *Rochester Democrat and Chronicle.* Retrieved January 8, 2013, from http://www.democratandchronicle.com/article/20120624/NEWS01/306240023/school-bus-monitor-Karen-Klein-Emily-Good-Justin-McElwain?odyssey=tab[topnews[text[Local%20News&nclick_check=1

Eastland, L. S. (1994). Habermas, emancipation, and relationship change: An exploration of recovery processes as a model for social transformation. *Journal of Applied Communication Research, 22*, 162–176.

Eder, D., & Enke, J. L. (1991). The structure of gossip: Opportunities and constraints on collective expression among adolescents. *American Sociological Review, 56*, 494–508.

Einarsen, S. (2000). Harassment and bullying at work: A review of the Scandinavian approach. *Aggression and Violent Behavior, 5*, 397–401.

Fairhurst, G. T. (2011). *The power of framing: Creating the language of leadership.* San Francisco, CA: Jossey-Bass.

Farrell, T., & Aune, J. (1979). Critical theory and communication: A selected literature review. *Quarterly Journal of Speech, 65*, 93–107.

Farley, S., Timme, D., & Hart, J. (2010). On coffee talk and break-room chatter: Perceptions of women who gossip in the workplace. *The Journal of Social Psychology, 150*, 361–368.

Festl, R., & Quandt, T. (2013). Social relations and cyberbullying: The influence of individual and structural attributes on victimization and perpetration via the Internet. *Human Communication Research, 39,* 101–126.

Fiske, S. T. (2010). Interpersonal stratification: Status, power, and subordination. In S. T. Fiske, D. T. Gilbert, & G. Lindzey (Eds.), *Handbook of social psychology* (5ᵗʰ ed., Vol. 2) (pp. 941–982). Hoboken, NJ: John Wiley & Sons, Inc.

Freile, V. E., & McDermott, M. (2012, June 22). Bus monitor bullied. *Rochester Democrat and Chronicle.* Retrieved June 29, 2012, from http://www.wgrz.com/news/article/172031/1/Rochester-Area-School-Investigating-Making-Bus-Monitor-Cry-Video

Fritz, J. M. H. (2006). Typology of troublesome others at work: A follow-up investigation. In J. M. H. Fritz & B. L. Omdahl (Eds.), *Problematic relationships in the workplace* (Vol. 1, pp. 21–46). New York, NY: Peter Lang.

—. (2009). Rudeness and incivility in the workplace. In Wright, S., & Morrison, R. (Eds.), *Friends and enemies in organizations: A work psychology perspective* (pp. 168–194). Hampshire, England: Palgrave Macmillan.

—. (2013). *Professional civility: Communicative virtue at work.* New York, NY: Peter Lang.

Fritz, J. M. H., & Omdahl, B. L. (Eds.). (2006). *Problematic relationships in the workplace* (Vol. 1). New York, NY: Peter Lang.

Frost, P. J. (2003). *Toxic emotions at work: How compassionate managers handle pain and conflict.* Boston, MA: Harvard Business School Press.

Fusfield, W. (1997). Communication without constellation? Habermas's argumentative turn in (and away from) critical theory. *Communication Theory, 7,* 301–320.

Goodboy, A. K., Martin, M. M., & Brown, E. (2016). Bullying on the school bus: Deleterious effects on public school bus drivers. *Journal of Applied Communication Research, 44*(4), 434–452.

Goodboy, A. K., Martin, M. M., & Rittenour, C. E. (2016). Bullying as a display of social dominance orientation. *Communication Research Reports, 33*(2), 159–165.

Golish, T., & Caughlin, J. (2002). "I'd rather not talk about it:" Adolescents' and young adults' use of topic avoidance in stepfamilies. *Journal of Applied Research, 30,* 78–106.

Green, J. (2011, November 17). The silencing of sexual harassment. *Businessweek.* Retrieved February 24, 2013, from http://www.businessweek.com/magazine/the-silencing-of-sexual-harassment-11172011.html

Greene, J. O., & Burleson, B. R. (Eds.). (2003). *Handbook of communication and social interaction skills.* Mahwah, NJ: Lawrence Erlbaum Associates.

Gruber, J., & Bjorn, L. (1986). Women's responses to sexual harassment: An analysis of sociocultural, organizational, and personal resources models. *Social Science Quarterly, 67,* 814–826.

Habermas, J. (1971). *Knowledge and human interests.* Boston, MA: Beacon Press.

—. (1973). *Legitimation crisis.* (T. McCarthy, Trans.). Boston, MA: Beacon Press.

—. (1990). *Moral consciousness and communicative action.* (C. Lenhardt & S. W. Nicholsen, Trans.). Cambridge: Massachusetts Institute of Technology. (Original work published 1983)

—. (2012). *The crisis of the European Union: A response* (C. Cronin, Trans.). Malden, MA: Polity.

Hafen, S. (2004). Organizational gossip: A revolving door of regulation and resistance. *Southern Communication Journal, 69,* 223–240.

Hallet, T., Harger, B., & Eder, D. (2009). Gossip at work: Unsanctioned evaluative talk in formal school meetings. *Journal of Contemporary Ethnography, 38,* 584–618.

Halualani, R. T., Mendoza, S. L., & Drzewiecka, J. A. (2009). Critical junctures in intercultural communication studies: A review. *The Review of Communication Journal, 9,* 17–35.

Hardt, H. (1993). Authenticity, communication, and critical theory. *Critical Studies in Mass Communication, 10,* 49–69.

Hashem, M. (2015). Bullying and labeling as communication tools of control and domination. *Journal of Arab & Muslim Media Research, 8*(2), 117–146.

Hazler, R. J., & Miller, D. L. (2001). Adult recognition of school bullying situations. *Educational Research, 43,* 133–146.

Hess, J. A. (2003). Maintaining undesired relationships. In D. J. Canary & M. Dainton (Eds.), *Maintaining relationships through communication: Relational, contextual, and cultural variations* (pp. 103–126). Mahwah, NJ: Lawrence Erlbaum Associates.

Hickson, M., Grierson, R. D., & Linder, B. C. (1991). A communication perspective on sexual harassment: Affiliative nonverbal behaviors in asynchronous relationships. *Communication Quarterly, 39,* 111–118.

Horkheimer, M. (1976). Traditional and critical theory. In P. Connerton (Ed.), *Critical sociology: Selected readings* (pp. 206–224). Great Britain: Penguin. (Original work published 1937)

Johnson, P. R., & Indvik, J. (2006). Sticks and stones: Verbal abuse in the workplace. *Journal of Organizational Culture, Communication and Conflict, 10,* 121–126.

Kowalski, R. M. (2007). Teasing and bullying. In B. H. Spitzberg & W. R. Cupach (Eds.), *The dark side of interpersonal communication* (2nd ed., pp. 169–197). Hillsdale, NJ: Erlbaum.

Kramer, M. (2010). *Organizational socialization: Joining and leaving organizations.* Malden, MA: Polity.

Kurland, N. B., & Pelled, L. H. (2000). Passing the word: Toward a model of gossip and power in the workplace. *The Academy of Management Review, 25,* 428–438.

Lafontaine, E., & Tredeau, L. (1986). The frequency, sources and correlates of sexual harassment among women in traditional male occupations. *Sex Roles, 21,* 433–442.

Leets, L., & Giles, H. (1999). Harmful speech in intergroup encounters: An organizational framework for communication research. In M. E. Roloff (Ed.), *Communication Yearbook* (Vol. 22, pp. 91–138). Thousand Oaks, CA: Sage.

Louw-Potgieter, J. (2012). Evaluating human resource interventions. *South African Journal of Human Resource Management, 10,* 1–6.

Luna, A. L., Garcia, D. C., Chou, S. Y., & Jackson, S. (2013). Can "tight" groups at work be detrimental? A theoretical view of gossip from the network tie strength and density perspective. *Global Journal of Business Research, 7,* 91–100.

Lutgen-Sandvik, P. (2006). Take this job and…: Quitting and other forms of resistance to workplace bullying. *Communication Monographs, 73,* 406–433.

McDonald, K. L., Putallaz, M., Grimes, C. L., Kupersmidt, J. B., & Coie, J. D. (2007). Girl talk: Gossip, friendship, and sociometric status. *Merrill-Palmer Quarterly, 53,* 381–411.

McKerrow, R. (1989). Critical rhetoric: Theory and praxis. *Communication Monographs, 56,* 91–111.

McKinnon, S. (2009). Critical theory. In S. W. Littlejohn & K. A. Foss (Eds.), *Encyclopedia of communication theory* (pp. 237–243). Thousand Oaks, CA: Sage.

Meares, M. M., Oetzel, J. G., Torres, A., Derkacs, D., & Ginossar, T. (2004). Employee mistreatment and muted voices in the culturally diverse workplace. *Journal of Applied Communication Research, 32,* 4–27.

Metts, S., Cupach, W., & Lippert, L. (2006). Forgiveness in the workplace. In J. M. H. Fritz, & B. L. Omdahl (Eds.), *Problematic relationships in the workplace* (pp. 249–274). New York, NY: Peter Lang.

Miller, J. R. (2012, June 22). Donations for bullied New York bus monitor surpass $600G. *Fox News*. Retrieved June 29, 2012, from http://www.foxnews.com/us/2012/06/22/donations-for-bullied-new-york-bus-monitor-approach-450000/?test=latestnews

Mills, C. B., & Carwile, A. M. (2009). The good, the bad, and the borderline: Separating teasing from bullying. *Communication Education, 58,* 276–301.

Mumby, D. K. (1993). Critical organizational communication studies: The next ten years. *Communication Monographs, 60,* 18–25.

—. (2004). Discourse, power and ideology: Unpacking the critical approach. In D. Grant, C. Hardy, C. Oswick, & L. Putnam (Eds.), *The Sage handbook of organizational discourse* (pp. 237–258). London: Sage.

—. (2005). Theorizing resistance in organization studies. *Management Communication Quarterly, 19,* 19–44.

Namie, G., & Lutgen-Sandvik, P. (2010). Active and passive accomplices: The communal character of workplace bullying. *International Journal of Communication, 4,* 343–373.

Narula, U. (2006). *Handbook of communication: Models, perspectives, strategies.* New Delhi: Atlantic.

National Communication Association Anti-Bullying Resource Bank. (2017). Retrieved from http://natcom.org/stopbullying/

Olweus, D. (1997). Bully/victim problems in school: Facts and intervention. *European Journal of Psychology of Education, 12,* 495–510.

Omdahl, B. L., & Fritz, J. M. H. (Eds.). (2012). *Problematic relationships in the workplace* (Vol. 2). New York, NY: Peter Lang.

Park, J., Lee, J., Lee, H., & Truex, D. (2012). Exploring the impact of communication effectiveness on service quality, trust and relationship commitment in IT services. *International Journal of Information Management, 32,* 459–468.

Perry, E. L., Kulik, C. T., & Field, M. P. (2009). Sexual harassment training: Recommendations to address gaps between the practitioner and research literatures. *Human Resource Management, 48,* 817–837.

Petri, A. (2012, June 25). Karen Klein the bus monitor and the noisy handful. *Washington Post.* Retrieved January 3, 2013, from http://www.washingtonpost.com/blogs/compost/post/karen-klein-the-bus-monitor-and-the-noisy-handful/2012/06/25/gJQAuMU12V_blog.html

Pörhölä, M., Karhunen, S., & Rainivaara, S. (2006). Bullying at school and in the workplace: A challenge for communication research. *Communication Yearbook, 30,* 249–301.

Preston, J. (2012, June 29). Students are suspended for verbally abusing school bus monitor. *New York Times.* Retrieved December 30, 2012, from http://thelede.blogs.nytimes.com/2012/06/29/students-suspended-for-verbally-abusing-school-bus-monitor/

Rawlins, W. K. (2008). *Friendship matters: Communication, dialectics, and the life course.* Hawthorne, NY: Aldine de Gruyter. (Original work published 1992)

—. (2009). *The compass of friendship: Narratives, identities and dialogues.* Thousand Oaks, CA: Sage.

Richardson, B. K., & Taylor, J. (2009). Sexual harassment at the intersection of race and gender: A theoretical model of the sexual harassment experiences of women of color. *Western Journal of Communication, 73*(3), 248–272.

Rosnow, R. L., & Fine, G. A. (1976). *Rumor and gossip: The social psychology of hearsay*. New York, NY: Elsevier.

Smith, G., Houmanfar, R., & Denny, M. (2012). Impact of rule accuracy on productivity and rumor in an organizational analog. *Journal of Organizational Behavior Management, 32*, 3–25.

Smorti, A., Menesini, E., & Smith, P. K. (2003). Parents' definitions of children's bullying in a five-country comparison. *Journal of Cross-Cultural Psychology, 34*, 417–432.

Stelter, B. (2016). Fox News settles with Gretchen Carlson and "handful" of other women. *CNN*. Retrieved from http://money.cnn.com/2016/09/06/media/gretchen-carlson-fox-news-lawsuit-settled/

Suls, J. M. (1977). Gossip as social comparison. *Journal of Communication, 27*, 164–168.

Tierney, J. (2009, November 2). Can you believe how mean office gossip can be? *New York Times*. Retrieved January 3, 2013, from http://www.nytimes.com/2009/11/03/science/03tier.html?_r=1&

Ting-Toomey, S. (2010). Applying dimensional values in understanding intercultural communication. *Communication Monographs, 77*, 169–180.

Tovares, A. V. (2006). Public medium, private talk: Gossip about a TV show as "quotidian hermeneutics." *Text and Talk, 26*, 463–492.

Tracy, S. J., Lutgen-Sandvik, P., & Alberts, J. K. (2006). Nightmares, demons, and slaves: Exploring the painful metaphors of workplace bullying. *Management Communication Quarterly, 20*, 148–185.

Trethewey, A. (2001). Reproducing and resisting the master narrative of decline: Midlife professional women's experiences of aging. *Management Communication Quarterly, 15*, 183–226.

Turner, M. M., Mazur, M. A., Wendel, N., & Winslow, R. (2003). Relational ruin or social glue? The joint effect of relationship type and gossip valence on liking, trust, and credibility. *Communication Monographs, 70*, 129–141.

U.S. Department of State. (2008). *Discriminatory harassment policy*. Retrieved April 2, 2013, from http://www.state.gov/s/ocr/c24959.htm

Van Maanen, J. (1975). Police socialization: A longitudinal examination of job attitudes in an urban police department. *Administrative Science Quarterly, 20*, 207–228.

Wood, J. T. (2012). *Communication in our lives* (6th Ed.). Boston, MA: Wadsworth Cengage Learning. (Original work published 2006)

Yoo, J. H. (2009). The power of sharing negative information in a dyadic context. *Communication Reports, 22*, 29–40.

Chapter Fourteen

A CONFLICT ODYSSEY: STORY-CENTERED LEADERSHIP

An important application of the constitutive power of communication in organizational settings that makes the point well is available in Fairhurst's work (2011) on framing as a meaning-making task of leadership. Communicative framing by organizational leaders has the potential to shape multiple arenas of organizational life; such framing carries ethical implication emerging from the responsibility of organizational leaders, whether in formal positions of power or in less visible contexts, to protect and promote institutions (Fritz, 2011). (Fritz, 2013, p. 116)

"A Conflict Odyssey: Story-Centered Leadership" follows the lead of Hannah Arendt (1958/1998). Arendt contended that behavior resides within a story before it is understood as meaningful action. In an era of increased virtue and narrative contention, the story that frames the conflict is paramount. This work, *Conflict between Persons: The Origins of Leadership*, emphasizes creative and constructive reactions to conflict responsiveness in three basic coordinates: (1) *learn* before, during, and after a conflict, (2) *understand* what matters to you and others, and (3) *acknowledge* that conflict engagement involves alertness to, and understanding of, what matters in the interplay of self and others and the immediate and larger communicative environment. Engaging conflict in a historical moment of narrative and virtue contention unites discernment about ethics (what is protected and promoted) with learning from the uniqueness of a conflict situation. To exemplify leadership in response to ethics in dispute within a changing communicative environment, we turn to the story of the *Odyssey* (Homer, trans. 1967/1991) as a classic example of **story-centered leadership**. The *Odyssey* has been termed one of the most important books about leadership within the West (Forster et al., 1999; Gibson, Tesone, & Buchalski, 2000; Latemore, & Callan, 1999; Nelson, 2008); the number of books and articles written on the *Odyssey* is vast.[1] Leadership frames the larger significance of behavior, announcing what matters and turning isolated conduct into meaningful action situated within a story.

---

1. Lattimore's translation, *The Odyssey of Homer*, is cited by more than 115 books and articles.

INTRODUCTION

The *Odyssey* functions as an exemplar of story-centered leadership. As we emphasized throughout this project, we consider story fundamental to the human condition. We stressed the insights of Walter Fisher (1989) and his reference to the human person as *homo narrans* and the scholarship of W. Barnett Pearce (Pearce, 1989; Pearce & Cronen, 1980; Pearce & Littlejohn 1997) as reminders of the importance of story. The central player in our emphasis on story was Hannah Arendt, as outlined in *Communication Ethics in Dark Times: Hannah Arendt's Rhetoric of Warning and Hope* (Arnett, 2013). Arendt articulated that story has multiple political functions. First, there is a difference between a behavior and action in that the latter is story-informed. Behavior is akin to a tree falling in a forest with no one present to hear it collapse. Action includes the telling about the tumbling of the tree understood within a story that frames the action. Second, story has an organizing function; it preserves "great deeds" (Arendt, 1954/1993, p. 47) that would be forgotten if left as isolated events. Deeds remembered within a story generate a "community of memory" (Bellah, Madsen, Sullivan, Swidler, & Tipton, 1985). Third, the story-centered nature of action unites a communicator and a spectator; it is the latter who moves behavior to action by framing action within a story (Kant, 1793/2006).

In this chapter, "A Conflict Odyssey: Story-Centered Leadership," we turn to Odysseus's struggles throughout the *Odyssey* to exemplify conflict that is vetted in story form in two major sections:

1. **Engaging the particular: Leadership as loss, betrayal, and cunning** reviews the *Odyssey*, touching on significant elements of the drama;
2. **From behavior to action** connects a central theme from each of the individual chapters in *Conflict between Persons: The Origins of Leadership* to the story of the *Odyssey*, concluding with an emphasis on the interplay of ethics and conflict that calls forth moral height in a conflict response.

Responsiveness to conflict in an era without clarity about normative rules, goods, and agreed-upon external standards results in sole reliance upon the self. This argument is at the center of Lasch's (1984) *Minimal Self: Psychic Survival in Troubled Times* and MacIntyre's (1981/2007) *After Virtue: A Study in Moral Theory*. Their descriptive predictors are now normative indicators of the world in which we live. A pragmatic counter to the loss of confidence in external standards and the subsequent danger of individualistic responses necessitates communicative engagement via story. We need to frame the meaning of behavior. Music is a form of story-centered action, no longer understood as mere behavior or individual notes. Story makes isolated events meaningful. This final chapter exemplifies a story-framed understanding of communication and conflict that underscores the interplay of ethics and conflict in communicative leadership.

ENGAGING THE PARTICULAR: LEADERSHIP AS LOSS, BETRAYAL, AND CUNNING

In the classical world, Plato's student Aristotle (trans. 2011) stressed the importance of the particular within the *polis*. Aristotle understood the importance of living an ethical life in response to the particular; ethics in action does not rest in abstract ideals. Aristotle used stories within the *Iliad* and the *Odyssey* as the chief guide and reference in the construction of his famous work, *Nicomachean Ethics*.[2] We now turn to the story of the *Odyssey* (Homer, trans. 1967/1991), which has inspired ethical thinking in moments of conflict out of which leadership is forged.

This chapter relies upon a translation of *The Odyssey of Homer* by **Richmond Lattimore** (1967/1991). We attend to this translation for three reasons. First, it is one of the finest English versions of the *Odyssey*. Second, Lattimore was an exceptional classical scholar. Third, Lattimore's life announced the reality of conflicting goods during the **McCarthy Era** in the United States. Richmond Lattimore, born in Paotingfu, China in 1906, and his brother, Owen, born in Washington, DC in 1900, both faced conflict during the McCarthy Era. **Owen Lattimore** was a Sinologist;[3] he studied classical Chinese language and literature from a philological perspective.[4] Owen's association with China resulted in blacklisting him in the United States during the McCarthy years. Owen suffered personally and professionally for nearly two years until the charges ceased in 1955. Loss of a homeland is central to the *Odyssey* and was a real measure of life within the journey of the Lattimore family.

RICHMOND LATTIMORE (1906–1984) received a B.A. from Dartmouth in 1926, a B.A. from Oxford in 1932, and a Ph.D. from the University of Illinois in 1934. Lattimore worked as a faculty member teaching Greek Studies at Byrn Mawr College and as a visiting professor at the University of Chicago (1947), Columbia (1948/1950), Johns Hopkins (1958), the University of Toronto (1966), and the University of California at Los Angeles (1974). Lattimore was a recipient of both the Rockefeller Post-War Fellowship and the Fulbright Research Fellowship for study in Greece. In 1984, the Academy of American Poets elected Lattimore as a Fellow. Apart from his translation of Homer's Odyssey, his works include translations of *The Complete Greek Tragedies, Homer's Iliad,* and *The Poetry of Greek Tragedies* (Bryn Mawr College, 2013).

---

2. Aristotle (trans., 2011) references the *Odyssey* in six instances throughout *Nicomachean Ethics*.

3. Sinology is the study of Chinese language and customs.

4. Philology is the study of language, including "the historical study of literary texts" ("Philology," 2013). Comparative philology places emphasis on "the comparison of the historical states of different languages" ("Philology," 2013). The philological tradition includes exhaustive textual analysis and is related to literary history ("Philology," 2013).

Lattimore broadly outlines the *Odyssey* in four different struggles:

1. The Telemachy or Adventures of Telemachos, books 1 through 4
2. The Homecoming of Odysseus, books 5 through 8 and the beginning of book 13
3. The Great Wanderings, books 9 through 12
4. Odysseus on Ithaka, the latter part of book 13 and books 14 through 24

The story of the *Odyssey* is an explication of Greek leadership in action. One witnesses acts of courage, honor,
friendship, and justice (Isle, 2006, p. 16) lived out as
virtues that defined the role of leadership in Greek
culture. The *Odyssey* is the sequel to the *Iliad*, which
depicted the Battle of Troy during the Trojan War
(Figure 14.1). Odysseus, the *Odyssey's* protagonist, left
behind his infant son Telemachos and wife Penelope
in order to fight in the Trojan War. The *Odyssey* begins
with Odysseus imprisoned after ten years of fighting. Odysseus takes another ten years to return home,
engaging one dangerous adventure after another. The
assumption of many back in Ithaka, Odysseus's homeland, is that he had been killed in battle. Suitors quickly
come and surround his kingdom, paying respects to
and courting Penelope.

© Willierossin/Shutterstock.com

FIGURE 14.1 The Battle of Troy.

The Adventures of Telemachos

The narrator begins the story of the *Odyssey* by stating that all heroes who survived the Battle
of Troy made their way home quickly with the exception of Odysseus, leading to the assumption of his death. The goddess Athene visits Ithaka in the image of one of Odysseus's old
friends, Mentor, and informs his son, Telemachos, that Odysseus is still alive. Athene instructs
Telemachos to dispatch the suitors and to begin a journey to find his father. Telemachos
then prepares an excursion to two cities: Pylos, on the southwest coast of Greece, and Sparta,
located in southeastern Laconia on the bank of the Eurotas River. Meanwhile, the suitors
refuse to disband; they convey to Telemachos that Penelope is confusing them—telling the

suitors that she will marry one of them after she finishes weaving a burial shroud for Laertes, her old father-in-law. Essentially, however, she never completes the task—what she knits during the day, she tears asunder at night. "Therefore in the daytime she would weave at her great loom, but in the night she would have torches set by, and undo it" (Homer, trans., 1967/1991, p. 42). Telemachos chastises his mother as he begins to lead the expedition to find his father; he does not comprehend her actions as bold and **cunning**.

When Telemachos arrives in Pylos with Athene, who remains disguised as Mentor, he asks Nestor, the King of Pylos, about Odysseus. Nestor explains that he has heard nothing of Odysseus since the end of the Trojan War and the falling out of the two brothers of Greece, Agamemnon and Menelaos. After the quarrel between Agamemnon and Menelaos, Nestor left Troy with Menelaos; Odysseus stayed with Agamemnon in Troy. Agamemnon was then murdered by a man he found with his wife. Then, Agamemnon's son, Orestes, took revenge on his father's murderers in order to preserve his father's kingdom. Nestor tells Telemachos that he knows nothing of the men who stayed with Agamemnon, but he encourages Telemachos to visit Menelaos is order to ask about his father. After offering Athene and Telemachos a place to reside for the night, Peisistratos, the son of Menelaos, joins Telemachos as he departs for Sparta.

AGAMEMNON
was the leader of the expedition against Troy, and Menelaos was the hero of the *Iliad*. Athene sparked a conflict between the two sons of Atreus over the placement of the Achaian people.

The king and queen of Sparta, Menelaos and Helen, are pleased to meet Telemachos when he arrives. They divulge numerous tales of his father's bravery and cunning during the war of Troy—telling the story of Odysseus's role in the devising and use of the Trojan horse:

> In my time I [Menelaos] have studied the wit and counsel of many men who were heroes, and I have been over much of the world, yet nowhere have I seen with my own eyes anyone like him, nor known an inward heart like the heart of enduring Odysseus. (Homer, trans., 1967/1991, p. 72)

Menelaus then informs Telemachos that Odysseus is alive and a prisoner at the hands of Kalypso, a goddess nymph. Telemachos and Peisistratos, Nestor's son, prepare to return to Pylos and then arrive in Ithaka. Before they return to Ithaka, the suitors uncover the fact that they are to arrive home. The suitors construct a plan to murder Telemachos when he reaches Ithaka.

The Great Wanderings

The story then shifts from Telemachos to Odysseus. The gods meet with Athene, who argues that Kalypso should release Odysseus. This argument takes place at a meeting of the gods when Poseidon (Figure 14.2) is not present. The gods decide to free Odysseus and give him a ship after Kalypso loses an argument with Zeus about Odysseus. Poseidon, who is not part of the decision to release Odysseus, recognizes Odysseus's ship and out of anger over the decision to grant Odysseus his freedom—without his consent—directs a storm to destroy the craft.

POSEIDON
is the lord of the sea. He is an enemy of Odysseus, the brother of Zeus, and the father of Polyphemos

Odysseus is saved by the goddess Ino, who bequeaths him a protective covering that keeps him alive during the destruction of the ship. As the ship wrecks, Odysseus awakes in a forest on the island of the Phaiakians.[5] Athene once again assists Odysseus, encouraging a young Phaiakian princess to go to the river and find Odysseus; she finds him, and Odysseus keeps his identity to himself. Odysseus then prays thanks to Athene and meets the Queen of the Phaiakians, Arete, who asks him, "Stranger and friend, I myself first have a question to ask you. What man are you, and whence?" (Homer, trans., 1967/1991, p. 117). Odysseus's response provides details about the shipwreck, but he does not disclose his identity. Odysseus has a similar exchange with the King of the Phaiakians, Alkinoös, again not revealing his identity.

Odysseus falls asleep, and when he wakes up, he finds the Phaiakians at a feast held in his honor for the purpose of discovering his identity. During the feast, Demodokos, a blind Phaiakian singer, sings of Odysseus at Troy; Odysseus begins to cry at Demodokos's performance. Alkinoös quickly shifts from feasting to another activity, competitive

FIGURE 14.2 The Greek god Poseidon.

INO
also called Leukothea, is a once-human sea goddess. She is the daughter of Kadmos, the founder of the Egyptian city, Thebes.

5. The Phaiakians are the people of Phaeacia

games, in order to console Odysseus. Odysseus argues that he does not want to participate in the games, but finds himself increasingly annoyed by one of participants, Euryalos.[6] Odysseus then joins the discus competition and wins easily. His competitive spirit continues as he begins to argue with others. Again, there is a shift in the venue—this time from competitive games to another feast.

Demodokos walks to the center of the feast to entertain the guests with his singing and dancing. Demodokos strikes his lyre and sings the story of Ares and Aphrodite. Odysseus, pleased with the singing of Demodokos, asks the blind singer to sing about the story of Trojan horse.

Demodokos accepts, and as he sings about the attack on Troy and of Odysseus's great fight at the house of Deïphobos,[7] Odysseus begins to weep. No one notices Odysseus weeping except for Alkinoös, who is sitting next to Odysseus. Alkinoös asks Demodokos to stop singing and calls upon Odysseus to identify himself and tell of his life: "Tell me the name by which your mother and father called you in that place, and how the rest who live in the city about you call you. No one among all the peoples, neither base man nor noble, is altogether nameless" (Homer, trans., 1967/1991, p. 135). Odysseus, in response to Alkinoös, reveals himself and recounts to the Phaiakians his journey, beginning with his departure from Troy.

FIGURE 14.3 Greek helmet.

Odysseus begins his tale with him and his men happy to have escaped death at the Battle of Troy. He continues by telling of the many obstacles the men encountered. Odysseus and his men found themselves on an island of Cyclopes, one being Polyphemos, who is the son of Poseidon, who eats two of Odysseus's men and places Odysseus in prison. Odysseus is able to get Polyphemos intoxicated as Odysseus continues to retain information about his identity, referring to himself as *nobody*—"Nobody is my name. My father and mother call me Nobody, as do all the others who are my companions" (Homer, trans., 1967/1991, p. 146). Odysseus then stabs Polyphemos in his only eye, giving him and his men a chance to escape (Figure 14.3). When they arrive back on the ship, Odysseus engages in imprudent behavior that is in contrast to his usual sense of cunning. Odysseus

6. Laodamas, son of Alkinoös, urges Odysseus to play in the competitive games. Euryalos, a young Phaiakian, speaks rudely to Odysseus, and Odysseus tells Euryalos that he is not well-spoken.

7. Demodokos sings the story of the Trojan horse and overthrowing the city of Troy. He tells that while inside the city, Odysseus, alongside Menelaos, goes to the house of Deïphobos, Helen's husband. While there, Odysseus endures "the grimmest fighting that ever he had, but won it there too, with the great-hearted Athene aiding" (Homer, trans., 1967/1991, p. 134).

boasts to Polyphemos about his real identity, which results in Polyphemos asking his father, Poseidon, to enact revenge upon Odysseus. Polyphemos curses:

> Hear me, Poseidon who circles the earth, dark-haired. If truly I am your son, and you acknowledge yourself as my father, grant that Odysseus, sacker of cities, son of Laertes, who makes his home in Ithaka, may never reach that home; but if it is decided that he shall see his own people, and come home to his strong-founded house and to his own country, let him come late, in bad case, with the loss of all his companions, in someone else's ship, and find troubles in his household. *(Homer, trans., 1967/1991, pp. 150–151).*

This episode is a witness to hubris that eclipses Odysseus's general sense of cunning, which ensures difficulties for his journey home.

Odysseus and his men arrive next at Aiolian Island. Aiolos, controller of the winds and beloved by the immortal gods, sends Odysseus on his way back to his homeland with everything he needs for the trip, including gold and silver. Shortly after their departure from Aiolian Island, a great storm confronts Odysseus's ship. Reluctantly, they returned to Aiolian Island. Due to their return, Aiolos thinks Odysseus is now at odds with the gods and terminates the winds necessary for the movement of the ship. Odysseus's men must then row, making their way toward the island of giants, Lamos. The Laistrygones,[8] the people of Lamos, throw rocks and sink all vessels with the exception of Odysseus's ship. He sails on to Aiaia, where the goddess Circe[9] turns Odysseus's men into pigs. Hermes, the son and messenger of Zeus, advises Odysseus to eat an herb and seize Circe when she threatens him. Odysseus does so; he lives with Circe for a year as her lover. Finally, Odysseus asks for Circe's help in getting back to Ithaka. Circe informs him that he must sail through the house of Hades[10] and meet with the spirit of a blind prophet, Teiresias, in order to discern how to get home to Ithaka. When Odysseus arrives in Hades, he talks to Teiresias, who pronounces what will happen when he arrives home as long as he, Odysseus, abides by one warning:

> If you can contain your own desire, and contain your companions', at that time when you first put in your well-made vessel at the island Thrinakia, escaping the sea's blue water, and there discover pasturing the cattle and fat sheep of Helios, who sees all things, and listens to all things. Then, if you keep your mind on homecoming, and leave these unharmed, you might all make your way to Ithaka, after much suffering; but if you do harm them, then I testify to the destruction of your ship and your companions. *(Homer, trans., 1967/2011, p. 171)*

---

8. The Laistrygones are a cannibal people in the city of Lamos.
9. Circe is the goddess of her land, Aiaia.
10. The house of Hades is the home of the lord of the dead. No one prior to Odysseus had successfully traveled there.

HERMES,
also referred to as Argeïphontes, is Zeus's messenger, the son of Zeus and Maira. He picks Odysseus a moly herb—an herb used by the gods to give power and withstand other drugs.

TEIRESIAS
is the blind Theban seer whose ability to prophesy is carried into the underworld, where Odysseus seeks his counsel.

The seer, Teiresias, warns Odysseus to keep his focus of attention on one objective—getting home. Before he leaves Hades, he meets his mother, who died mourning over his supposed demise; Odysseus takes time to talk with her and other famous figures in Hades, including Sisyphos and Tantalos. This period in Hades reminds the reader of ongoing demands that go unfulfilled. Finally, Odysseus and his men hurry back to the ship. However, Odysseus and his crew must first take the body of one their men, Elpenor, who had fallen from the roof of Circe's palace, back to Aiaia. The ghost of Elpenor speaks to Odysseus, stating, "Remember me, and do not go and leave me behind, unwept, unburied, when you leave, for fear I might become the gods' curse upon you" (Homer, trans., 1967/2011, p. 170). Odysseus promises to fulfill his companion's request to burn his body and bury the remains at the beach of the gray sea. Odysseus then encounters other ghosts from his past. The story interludes with Alkinoös and the Phaiakians who remain "stricken to silence" during Odysseus's storytelling. Alkinoös asked the Phaiakians to keep Odysseus as their guest for another day while gifts and resources are collected to support Odysseus on his voyage to Ithaka. Odysseus, thankful to Alkinoös, agrees to stay and resumes his storytelling.

SISYPHOS,
the condemned hero, is tormented in the land of the dead to roll a stone uphill continually.

TANTALOS,
also tormented in the land of the dead, sits in a pool of water while suffering from never-ending thirst. Each time Tantalos bends to take a sip of water, the water dissipates.

Circe gives Odysseus and his men advice—do not listen to the Sirens during the journey home. Odysseus furnishes his men beeswax for their ears, and he is himself bound, hand and foot, to the ship in order to enjoy the song of the sirens without falling victim to them. The men and Odysseus avoid the seductive sound of the Sirens, but they must navigate between Skylla, a six-headed monster who eats ships, and the Charybdis, a whirlpool. Odysseus successfully traverses between the dangers, but he still loses some men to Skylla. Finally, Odysseus enters the island of the sun, Thrinakia, about which Teiresias and Circe have given him forewarning. On the island, Odysseus's men steal sheep, promoting the sun god, Helios Hyperion, to ask Zeus to punish them. The result is the destruction of their ship in a storm with the loss of both ship and crew. Fortunately, Odysseus reaches the safety of Kalypso's island as he holds onto a piece of the ship. This event told by Odysseus to the Phaiakians ends Odysseus's tale. From here, the *Odyssey* shifts to tell of Odysseus's voyage home from Alkinoös's kingdom.

Onward to Ithaka

Alkinoös prepares for Odysseus's departure. Odysseus and Alkinoös bid their farewells, and Alkinoös's herald leads Odysseus to a ship and a crew waiting to aid Odysseus on his voyage. The Phaiakians' ship arrives at Ithaka, and Odysseus is asleep; the Phaiakians carry him ashore and promptly turn around and leave. Poseidon is angry with the Phaiakians for assisting Odysseus and sinks their boat in their attempted return voyage. When Odysseus awakens, he does not know where he is; Athene has made his homeland, Ithaka, appear strange. Odysseus is initially angry with the Phaiakians for leaving him in a strange land. Odysseus then meets Athene, who is dressed as a beggar. Both Odysseus and Athene engage in cunning, refusing to disclose their true identities. Odysseus reveals his identity only after Athene announces her distinctiveness. Athene then divulges to him that he must take revenge on the suitors. She then helps Odysseus take on the manner of a shepherd as she informs Odysseus that his son, Telemachos, who has searched for him, is now safe. Athene answers: "Let him not be too much on your mind. It was I myself who saw him along on that journey, so he would win reputation by going there" (Homer, trans., 1967/1991, p. 209). Odysseus then meets his loyal swineherd, Eumaios, who does not recognize him. When asked about his origins, Odysseus states that he is from Crete, fought in the Trojan War, and knows that Odysseus is alive.

The storyline moves back to Athene, who returns to Sparta to find Telemachos and Peisistratos and informs Telemachos about an impending ambush from the suitors. Odysseus, whose real identity is unknown, continues to stay in the small house of Eumaios—protected from the suitors. When Telemachos arrives in Ithaka, he goes to Eumaios and speaks with Odysseus without recognizing him. Eumaios then informs Odysseus's wife, Penelope, of Telemachos's safe arrival. When Eumaios leaves, Athene returns Odysseus to his past glory.

After the shock of meeting his father again, Telemachos devises a plan with Odysseus to contend with the suitors:

If truly you are my own son, and born of our own blood, then let nobody hear that Odysseus is in the palace; let not Laertes hear of it, neither let the swineherd; let no one in the household know, not even Penelope herself; you and I alone will judge the faith of the women, and, besides these, we can make trial of the serving men, to see whether any of them is true to us and full of humility, or whether one cares nothing for you, and denies your greatness. (Homer, trans., 1967/1991, p. 248)

Telemachos answers his father, "Father, I think you will learn what my spirit is like, when the time comes" (Homer, trans., 1967/1991, p. 248). Telemachos goes to his father's palace and informs his mother that Odysseus is alive. Telemachos recounts information that he learned from Pylos and Sparta, leaving out firsthand information about Odysseus's arrival. Odysseus meets the suitors; they treat him poorly. He remains in disguise, and one of the leading suitors, Antinoös,[11] dismissively hits him on the head with a small chair. When Penelope hears of this act, she asks to meet the beggar, Odysseus, in masquerade. Before this encounter occurs, another man, this time a real beggar, challenges Odysseus to a fight, and Odysseus wins handily. After his victory, a suitor, Amphinomos, congratulates Odysseus. In gratitude, a still disguised Odysseus quietly warns Amphinomos that he should leave because Odysseus is returning. Unfortunately, Amphinomos foolishly remains.

Penelope then enters the scene; she informs the suitors that they need to bring gifts for her, instead of consuming her food and resources. The suitors oblige by bringing gifts, as they continue to heap verbal and physical abuse on Odysseus. As Odysseus becomes increasingly angry, Telemachos enters the room. When all are asleep, the father and son hide weapons that they can later locate during battle. Additionally, Penelope wants to talk to this man who knew Odysseus (actually Odysseus himself). Odysseus communicates to her the story of Troy again, framing Odysseus as a classic Greek hero. Penelope, emotionally moved, cries. Odysseus, still withholding his true identity, ends the conversation with assurance that Odysseus will return.

Odysseus stays the night and sleeps on the floor, refusing an offer of a bed by Penelope. He does, however, permit Eurynome, one of Penelope's housekeepers, to wash his feet. Eurynome discovers a scar on his foot that he received when he was young and hunting boar. She immediately recognizes Odysseus, which then prompts him to demand that she remain quiet about his identity. That night Odysseus has difficulty finding sleep. He cannot fathom how he and his son, Telemachos, can defeat the suitors. Then Odysseus scolds himself, putting fear aside: "Bear up, my heart" (Homer, trans., 1967/1991, p. 298). The next day the suitors continue to annoy and anger Odysseus; Athene makes sure he is ready for battle all day. She also dramatically shifts the tone of the room by covering faces and the room in blood. Finally, the suitors begin to understand the potential gravity of the situation with the conclusion of the day foretold.

The suitors gather around, along with Penelope, Odysseus, and Telemachos. Penelope proceeds to entertain an earlier promise of marrying someone who is capable of using Odysseus's bow to shoot an arrow through twelve axes. All the suitors fail the task. Telemachos then

---

11. Antinoös is the son of Eupeithes, who was killed by Odysseus's father, and one of the two leading suitors.

demands that Odysseus (still in disguise) receive a chance to display his skill; he succeeds without difficulty. Odysseus then turns and uses the arrows on the suitors, whose forewarning did little to curtail their extreme shock and astonishment. In the battle, Telemachos and Odysseus receive support from Athene. All the suitors die, Melanthios last of all. Telemachos executes the disloyal servants. He hangs them in the courtyard. During this entire bloody event, Penelope sleeps. When she awakes, she immediately recognizes Odysseus. Her initial action toward him is distant; she is afraid that a god is mocking her. When he utters information about their home unknown by all others, she is convinced he is really Odysseus.

The final scene has Hermes taking the suitors' souls into Hades. There is also a brief interlude during which Agamemnon and Achilleus, a former soldier of Agamemnon's army and a leader of the expedition against Troy, argue over which of them had the more noble and courageous death. Then the reader returns to Ithaka, where we discover Odysseus meeting his father, Laertes. Odysseus barely recognizes Laertes because his father has aged from worry about the fate of his son. Then the parents of the dead suitors prepare to attack Odysseus, but Athene stops the violence, returning the kingdom to peace. The story ends abruptly with this intervention of Athene. Peace reigns once again in Odysseus's kingdom and family at a great cost of time and lives.

FROM BEHAVIOR TO ACTION

This final section connects major themes of the first thirteen chapters with the events of the *Odyssey*. This classic story offers a unique view of leadership in action. We briefly revisit what we consider the principal idea of each chapter and connect it to ethics, leadership, and conflict considerations. We limit the concluding sections to selected macro themes that emphasize the central outline of this book, *Conflict between Persons: The Origins of Leadership*.

1. The Interplay of Ethics and Conflict.

> Ethics, leadership, and conflict are announced in The Odyssey, driven by diversity of standpoint, the interplay of background and foreground, and a basic human fact: People engage conflict and, at times, are even willing to die over competing understandings of the good.

We meet a tale of conflict over contrary goods; it is a sequel within the Homeric tradition. Homer's first book, the *Iliad*, records the Battle of Troy begun by Paris of Troy as he took Helen from her husband, the king of Sparta, Menelaos. This classic work of Greek mythology takes us to basic issues of competing goods, a covetousness toward another that results in a tragic conflict. The *Odyssey* is an exemplar of an ethical dispute that begins with the epic Battle of Troy and concludes with another in Ithaka.

Having survived the war and then imprisonment for another ten years, Odysseus begins his struggle home. He encounters numerous conflicts defined by competing goods, concluding in the battle with the suitors. We are invited into a tale of conflict over contrary goods. Odysseus, as a king of Ithaka, begins and ends his test of leadership in the interplay of ethics and conflict.

a. *Ethics.* Standpoint matters; it is not just behavior, but as Arendt insisted, it is the story within which specific behavior is understood that shapes interpretive meaning of action. Such is the first principle of ethics in an era of narrative and virtue contention—we cannot assume that our understanding of ethics is a normative assumption for all. Ethical meaning dwells within behavior vetted by story.

b. *Leadership.* The task of leadership is not neutral; leaders turn acts and behavior into story-laden accountability. There is no abstract view of leadership; its evaluation rests within stories told by others. Perceptions find shape through standpoint, which is story-informed.

c. *Conflict.* The *Odyssey* reveals disputes over goods that should be protected and promoted. A good matters, but its significance is story-bound. Conflict arises not only in actions, but also from the collision of interpretations. The task of leadership in conflict is to frame interpretations that are meaningfully connected to the demands before us, giving actions public validity.

2. Framing.

Ethics, leadership, and conflict require framing a direction that is contextually attentive. Together, context and appropriate framing offer a vision that people can understand and follow. Odysseus offered such a vision.

The story of the *Odyssey* centers on Odysseus. He is a hero, correct? Or is it possible that there is yet another perspective on his character and actions? Interestingly, a classical Greek perspective praises Odysseus for his cunning and ability to withhold important information while he searches for weaknesses in others that can aid his cause. Yet in the eyes of some, his actions resemble deceit and lying, not heroic leadership. The Romans did not concur with the Greek appraisal of Odysseus's actions. The Roman perspective did not suggest anything close to praise. The Romans viewed Odysseus as a falsifier of speech. Virgil (trans., 1909) referred to Odysseus by an alternate name, Ulysses—as "fallacious Ulysses" (p. 106), "sly Ulysses" (p. 109), and "false Ulysses" (p. 317). Ulysses, according to Virgil, acted as a sly, dishonorable fraud. Odysseus's actions did not adhere to the Roman conception of honor.

Tricks and cunning were appropriate arsenals within the war chest of any Greek hero; in contrast, these same acts were despicable fraud, according to a Roman conception of the hero (Cairns, 1989, p. 193). The Greek and Roman cultures read the *Odyssey* quite contrarily. The same behavior exists, but the meaning transpired from antagonistic perspectives. The different story-frames in which an audience or a reader comprehends Odysseus's actions lend credence to incompatible conceptions of his leadership. Our contention is that both Greek and Roman views are now part of the opinion structure within the public domain of the Western world. Secrecy and forthrightness are both options, dependent upon the context and the vision that shapes action.

a. *Ethics.* If one has always considered Odysseus a hero, then one is surprised to learn that juxtaposing perspectives are possible. The Greeks and Romans witnessed the same behavior and then testified to contrasting ethical perspectives regarding the actions of Odysseus.

b. *Leadership.* The actions of a leader require understanding via context and standpoint, which are story-framed. Leadership is not a behavior alone, but a public story-informed account of action. The ability to lead hinges on interpretation and the framing of the behavior.

c. *Conflict.* Only in considering the interplay of context and vision is it possible to ascertain whether one is witnessing a leader engaged in cunning or a demagogue engaged in fraud. The context assists in framing the answer; leaders do not impose their demands, but frame from interplay of story and the needs of a particular context. The major task of leadership in conflict rests in how we frame a context and how our standpoint structures the goods and behaviors within a story we seek to protect and promote.

3. Human Sentiment.

Ethics, leadership, and conflict involve sentiment that can propel argument and eventuate conflict. The Odyssey offers one example after another in which this movement of argument to conflict reflects contrasting sentiments and concerns.

Throughout the *Odyssey*, we watch Odysseus rely upon his senses. He must traverse unknown and difficult terrain, making decisions when he is unsure of the context due to lack of familiarity, finding himself in one place of trial after another. Each location challenges his safety—from the Battle of Troy to his arduous return to his home in Ithaka to his eventual struggle with the suitors. Odysseus must trust his sentiment in order to discern the correct course of action as he navigates strange lands and customs; his cognitive knowledge of places is inadequate. Odysseus must depend upon his senses. The Greek love of cunning hinges upon a creative blend of past experience and an attentive sensing of the demands of a unique environment.

Additionally, the story orbits around the power of human sentiment that begins with a battle over love, involves a son and his determined courage, witnesses the creative actions of Penelope that fended off the suitors during Odysseus's long absence from home, and ends with a battle that commences with Odysseus greatly outnumbered. The emotive engine that drives Odysseus is human sentiment—courage, honor, friendship, and justice are vital guides as he fights for that which matters—family and Ithaka, home. Human sentiment provides an emotive sense of "why" some goods are more important than others.

a. *Ethics.* Human sentiment, understood as embodied forms of attentiveness, is important and requires protection and promotion. Ethical inclinations embodied in human sentiment propel us. They are not always cognitive, but rather exist in practices that shape and reflect sentiments that matter.

b. *Leadership.* Perhaps one of the major sources of leadership is the habituation of human sentiment that assists with decision making. One cannot always make analytic decisions that have emerged after weighing all options. Sentiment is a form of decision-making shorthand and reminds us of what is worth protecting and promoting.

c. *Conflict.* Human sentiment gives us reason to participate in conflict and highlights perceived differences between and among persons. The task of leadership in conflict is to frame practices that encourage the development of human sentiments that embody goods worthy of protecting and promoting.

4. Conflict Origins.

Ethics, leadership, and conflict originate in differences between and among narrative ground standpoints that naturally suggest social and personal goals and require power for their enactment. Odysseus displayed such a narrative foundation; his actions required power and implementation.

The origins of conflict that constitute the story of the *Odyssey* begin with the Battle of Troy described in the *Iliad*. This great battle begins, of course, with the struggle over Helen. The origin of this classic confrontation is not in dispute. However, the contrary interpretations of the implications of the origin generate and propel the conflict. Contrasting assumptions on the part of Paris of Troy, son of Priam, the king of Troy, and Menelaus, king of Mycenaean Sparta and husband of Helen, are in profound discrepancy. Additionally, the *Odyssey* ends with another conflict origin as Odysseus discovers suitors seeking the hand of his wife, Penelope. The suitors and Odysseus find themselves at prodigious odds. Again, there is no dispute over the origin of the conflict, but the standpoint on and the interpretation of the situation give birth to this final conflict.

Differing narratives give character to divergent understandings of the communicative environment in Ithaka. Odysseus and the suitors are competitive interlocutors whose narrative beginnings give assent to quite dissimilar interests and goals that mold juxtaposed power interests. The narrative of a king and the narrative base of suitors benefiting from Odysseus's supposed demise are in sizeable disparity, giving rise to a significant conflict.

a. *Ethics*. Narratives that ground our worldviews matter, framing our interests and goals. Conflict emerges from differing narratives that shape ethical goods that one seeks to protect and promote; the origin of a conflict situated within a given narrative offers insight into what matters for both parties.

b. *Leadership*. The task of leadership is to work within narratives and understand the narrative framework of others. One finds what matters when narratives clash. Leadership is not value neutral. Leadership emerges out of a public narrative that reflects the mission and vision of a given place, informing us about what matters.

c. *Conflict*. The basic definition of postmodernity in practical terms is the clash of narrative structures. We cannot agree on one narrative or one standard that evaluates all narratives. The task of leadership in conflict is to frame the importance of narratives that embody a public mission and vision, bypassing the temptation to pursue one's own personal preferences.

5. Welcome and Difference.

Ethics, leadership, and conflict recognize the importance and the challenges of difference, which gives rise to differing communities and cultures. The story of The Odyssey is a voyage from one distinct locality to another, announcing differences in goods that are protected and promoted.

Our identities emerge from the interplay of welcome and difference. A dwelling furnishes us an assurance of welcome and encourages differentiation through our public actions. Odysseus is a king with a mandate for both welcome and difference. His culture welcomed him into a role defined by Greek virtues of courage, honor, friendship, and justice (Isle, 2006, p. 16). It is not these virtues, but the unique manner in which these virtues are lived in action with others, that differentiates Odysseus from others.

We are witnesses to the power of welcome and differentiation throughout the story of the *Odyssey*. One of the distinctive moments that announcing the union of welcome and difference involves Telemachos' decision to look for his father. As Telemachos seeks to welcome Odysseus, he must separate himself from his former self—the son must become an adult. The shift from youth to adulthood is a classic transition within the Western world and necessitates both welcome and differentiation. Leaders must respond to their environments, to the demands of their context. If one refuses to answer such a call, leadership is impossible as one declines to attend to a welcome that permits differentiation of one's identity. Such a repudiation of the welcome of responsibility is an invitation to conflict, which beckons others to seek to fill the void left by inaction.

a. *Ethics.* Moments in existence offer a welcome; it is as if we were called into response. Rejection of the welcome is an ethical infraction toward existence and a disregard for those for whom we are responsible. Ethics is a form of "response-ability" (Buber, 1947/1993).

b. *Leadership.* Odysseus, Telemachos, and Penelope offer three different insights into the praxis of leadership. They hold in common one major action assumption—each person, in a unique manner, answers the welcome of responsibility and in so doing shapes an identity of leadership substance.

c. *Conflict.* As our heroes respond with responsibility to the circumstances before them, conflict follows. The welcome of leadership is akin to interruption in normative behavior, offering a change in routine direction. The task of leadership in conflict is to frame a response to a welcome that emerges in a given context, and, as a by-product, to frame one's identity as a leader.

6. The Primacy of Relationships.

Ethics, leadership, and conflict in relational contexts necessitate discerning the differences between selfishness and individualism and between jealousy and envy in order for the revelatory to emerge. The Odyssey revolves around such relational discernment.

The *Odyssey* continues a relational set of commitments that begins in the *Iliad*. The Battle of Troy inaugurates relational questions and an emphasis on bonds between persons, which endure through the actions of the main characters, Odysseus, Telemachos, and Penelope, and through the actions of numerous supporting actors throughout the novel who provide relational support. Additionally, the significance of conflict augments relational connections in the case of Poseidon and Polyphemos as they work to offer retribution against Odysseus. And, of course, the relational connections between Odysseus and his son initiate fatal consequences for the suitors standing in wait for Penelope.

Relationships are vital for a meaningful life. Our ties to one another can move us in constructive or destructive directions as we protect and promote something that matters. In leadership, one must limit the temptation for one relationship to trump. In most cases, one has multiple obligations and responsibilities. If one does not protect meaningful relationships, then the significance of life diminishes, but one cannot forget the advice of Georg Simmel: engage in multiple relational ties. Breadth of relational perspective lessens the hazard of a leader's judgments falling into the abyss of provincialism. The task of leadership in conflict is to frame the importance of multiple relational ties, from a local context to a larger professional organization, which permits one to judge from the vantage point of multiple perspectives.

a. *Ethics*. Relationships matter. They carry much of the meaning of our lives. However, in a leadership position, one must protect and promote not one, but numerous relationships. Ties to the many lessen the danger of promoting one's own insular group.

b. *Leadership*. We counter the assumption that a leader should be so objective that relational engagements are alien considerations. We suggest otherwise; relationships matter a great deal. The crucial point is not to deny the significance of relationships, but to bring more, not fewer, persons into the importance of relational commitment.

c. *Conflict*. Because relationships matter, they invite conflict—relationships become something worthy of protecting and promoting. Our suggestion, once again, is not to eliminate relationships, but to work from a perspective that includes an ever-expanding web of relationships that call for responsibility. The task of leadership in conflict is to frame the importance of relationships in a manner that assists many and avoids the temptation of nurturing only a proximate few.

7. Emotional Intelligence.

Ethics, leadership, and conflict require enactment of emotional labor and emotional intelligence, which requires work and practice. Such practices require doing and reflection through emotional awareness. The cunning of Odysseus is defined by his emotional intelligence and emotional awareness.

Odysseus used emotional intelligence in most of his conflict encounters. He generally followed the course of action called for by the situation and his role. He commonly and successfully battled the impulse to release expressions that were merely self-serving. Odysseus's emotional intelligence moved his attention from self-centered hubris to the interplay of role and responsiveness to immediate demands. In the story of the *Odyssey*, Odysseus consistently keeps his identity a secret. Even when he finally returns home, Odysseus is careful to hide his identity; he fears placing others in danger as well as decreasing his chances for reclaiming his kingdom. His wife and father are the last to learn his identity.

Odysseus had used the term "nobody" to refer to himself when he was on the island of Cyclops. He had struggled with Polyphemos, the son of Poseidon. Throughout that experience, Odysseus was shrewd and cunning, taking his men from imprisonment to freedom. Eventually, Odysseus overcame Polyphemos and escaped with his men. However, as the ship pulled away from the shore and onto safety, Odysseus displayed an uncharacteristic act—in an expression of pure hubris he yelled at the top of his lungs information about his true identity. The result was tragic as Polyphemos then called for his father's help and intervention. His trip home met difficulty again; this time by a lack of cunning manifested in a response void of emotional intelligence. Odysseus moved the focus from doing what was necessary, understood through emotional intelligence, to a hubris that took the focus off the demands before him.

a. *Ethics.* Whenever one loses direction, attentiveness to the immediate demands of the situation no longer guide action; instead, one is likely to assume a self-focus, which loses an ethics of alterity that attends to the strangeness of contexts and others. One must learn from what one does not know, from extreme difference, from attending to that which is not known but calls forth our identity in the action of response.

b. *Leadership.* One of the principal demands of leadership is to stay focused on the difficulties of an immediate experience understood within a larger framework of public direction. Leadership ceases the moment attention moves to the person in the role of leader and leaves behind the task of responding to unique emerging characteristics comprehended within a backdrop of mission and vision.

c. *Conflict.* The pursuit of a vision and responsive engagement with the proximate context will inevitably generate conflict. Not all want to go in the same direction. Foolish conflict emerges when direction and immediacy are lost from becoming too fascinated with oneself. The task of leadership in conflict is to frame the importance of learning from difference, attending to alterity, and avoiding the temptation of a self-inflated sense of importance.

8. Internal Dialogue.

Ethics, leadership, and conflict require thoughtful enactment and reflection emerging from an internal dialogue. When there are potential disagreements, one must sort out possibilities in a conflict map in order to engage the unknown. The journey of Odysseus was a journey into and through ambiguity, requiring ongoing reflective discernment.

Thinking, not speaking, is the first step in constructive conflict engagement. Thinking begins in an internal dialogue well before one makes a given position public. Penelope displayed internal dialogue as she struggled with ongoing intrapersonal conflict in a manner that was thoughtful and cunning. Consider the macro events that made Penelope's intrapersonal conflict an everyday confrontation. First, her husband was at war for ten years. Then his journey home took an additional ten years. During that time, Penelope struggled with basic questions: Is Odysseus dead? Is he still alive? Will he ever come home? How do I keep this kingdom together in his absence? To complicate this trial, Penelope witnesses her son becoming a man and leaving to search for his father. She has to wonder once again, Will he return? Even when Odysseus returns and informs her of his true identity, she waits to greet him. Penelope works internally with the question: Is this situation for real or are the gods playing a trick on me? She consistently thinks before she acts.

a. *Ethics.* The pragmatic first step of conflict engagement is to test what one thinks internally before uttering that information to another. Internal dialogue is a practical skill that enhances self-knowledge and augments the number of tests an idea will receive before one takes it to the public domain. A self-challenge may eliminate a large set of future problems with others.

b. *Leadership.* The task of leadership is to solve and manage problems, not create them. Internal dialogue does not guarantee that one will never cause unneeded conflict, but the acts of self-thought and self-challenge diminish the odds of such a mistake.

c. *Conflict.* Conflict invited by thoughtless uttering of an idea or position that was never initially considered in self-thought cannot be eliminated. Perhaps such imprudent conduct is a working definition of being human. However, the goal should be to minimize such outbursts, and certainly one should not encourage them. One needs to think before one speaks. The task of leadership in conflict is to frame both the necessity and the habit of self-talk that challenges one's own ideas before they become part of public conversation.

9. Opinions.

Ethics, leadership, and conflict require attentiveness to thoughtful opinions, a wariness of unreflective attribution, and even more caution in reliance upon emotivism. Leaders such as Odysseus gather information in the social environment; they do not simply rely on their own perceptions.

Perhaps the most graphic and public display of contrary opinions is the act of war, which is the central story line of the *Iliad* and the ongoing backdrop for the *Odyssey.* There are numerous instances in the *Odyssey* where multiple opinions within the public domain divide persons. One of the displays of opinions in contention takes place between Penelope and Telemachos; the son takes a very different position on the presence of the suitors than does the mother. Telemachos wants the suitors gone, and Penelope does not dismiss them. One can see why Telemachos is confused. Penelope must keep the suitors at bay, even as they seek to convey to her the most negative fears about her husband's fate. The suitors want Penelope to admit that Odysseus is long since dead. Penelope then promises the suitors that she will choose one after she has completed knitting the funeral shroud for her father-in-law, Laertes. Her opinion is contrary to that of her son; we contend that her opinion was a defense maneuver meant to secure more time for Odysseus, but we are not certain. The poet leaves hearers to their own opinions about Penelope's actions.

Homer does not offer us one reason for Penelope's behavior. The audience and now the reader must ascertain the "why" of her actions. It is as if Homer is courting multiple opinions about Penelope's actions. Penelope appears cunning, a heroine, skilled, waiting for Odysseus, and perhaps "hedging her bets" to us—yet, not so to Telemachos or to the determined and confused suitors. The story demands that we engage in attribution if we want to know the "reason" for her behavior. However, the poet keeps us in ambiguity, leaving us to wonder which opinion is correct. Homer contributes a lesson in leadership—there is seldom one reason. The interplay of multiple opinions constructs what we conventionally term reason. Life is more complex than a "yes" or "no." Homer gives us insight into leadership as the ability to be nimble in opinion gathering, knowing that a pragmatic truth most likely rests not in one opinion, but among a variety of different positions.

a. *Ethics.* Opinions guide and motivate us. Gathering an opinion with as much evidence as possible is pragmatically ethical. Additionally, assuming that truth rarely rests with one master opinion is the heart of ethical pragmatics.

b. *Leadership.* Leaders must decide. Seldom are significant decisions driven by undisputed confidence if one understands the complexity of opinions in the public domain. Leaders must take stands without discounting the position of another; one might even reconsider that position later. Keeping multiple opinions in the public domain permits the possibility of a later change of direction.

c. *Conflict.* The natural result of following an opinion can easily generate conflict. The manner in which one responds to opinions temporarily discarded is as important as the opinions followed. Keeping multiple ideas alive within the public domain is essential; it permits changes of course and acknowledges the positions of others. The task of leadership in conflict is to frame both the necessity of following a direction, a given opinion, while simultaneously not destroying positions contrary to the one pursued.

10. Undue Familiarity.

Ethics, leadership, and conflict suggest the importance of knowing when to enact a given conflict style. Knowing the "why" and "how" of conflict engagement counters unreflective routine. Such leadership activity manifests itself in the social order with existential trust. Odysseus's cunning ultimately added trust to the environment, announcing, through action, his ability to lead.

A fundamental component of leadership success rests with flexibility in conflict styles. Odysseus is an exemplar of such variability. He is a follower, a comrade-in-arms, a commander, a guest, a prisoner, a lover, a beggar, and a king. He engages a large number of conflict options from avoidance to competition to acts of aggression. His decisions about which conflict style to use are driven by the context, not by his identity as a king.

When Odysseus arrives home, Athene meets him. His conflict style is determined by care and caution in response to the demands before him; he discloses his true identity only after Athene divulges to him who she actually is. He then takes on the manner and look of a shepherd. He is watchful of his identity; his primary responsibility is to protect his son, wife, and kingdom. To do so he must carefully weigh the moment he announces his true identity, for with that announcement, his conflict style will be put into motion at dangerous levels of contention. The context informs him of the conflict style he must use and the personal manner he must assume as he carries out his responsibilities of leadership.

a. *Ethics.* Odysseus is consistent throughout his journey. He is thoughtful about the question, "Whom and what am I to protect and promote in this context at this time?" With the exception of a few moments of hubris, he was able to balance his commitment to short and long-term responsibilities in the journey back to leadership at Ithaka.

b. *Leadership.* Perhaps one of the most important moments in the test of leadership is to know when not to take the primary seat or first place of honor. When a person temporarily gives up the cloak of leadership in order to guide and direct later, we witness an overt use of leadership attentive to a longer-term horizon.

c. *Conflict.* One's selected style of conflict, driven by one's reading of a given context, gives rise to different echelons and types of struggles. Conflict driven by both the context and one's public persona constitutes leadership. The task of leadership in conflict is to frame one's manner and conflict style in response to the context and one's short and long-range responsibilities.

11. Anachronistic Responses.

Ethics, leadership, and conflict require us to be careful about anachronistic responses that are out of place and out of time and invite us to fulfill our roles with integrity as we meet existence on its own terms. Odysseus was an exemplar of leadership as he met the unpredictable.

We discover few anachronistic responses for Odysseus. He is skilled and adept at permitting the context to shape his response. We find this quality in Telemachos and in Penelope as well. We are given a clear impression by the *Odyssey* that anachronistic responses are not helpful in leadership. In order to lead, one must rely on what is needed, not what is unduly familiar and common.

The final segment of the story of the *Odyssey* includes Hermes taking souls who did not die in courageous or noble fashion to Hades. The center of noble leadership in Homer's work is having the courage to respond to the demands of the context. From Homer's perspective, Hermes would lead those who failed in leadership to Hades for one major crime. Leaders cannot afford to ignore the demands before them. Living in abstraction is contrary to leadership. His emphasis on attentiveness to the particular attracted Aristotle (trans., 2011) as he developed *Nicomachean Ethics* in response to Homer's story.

a. *Ethics.* This work, *Conflict between Persons: The Origins of Leadership*, has stressed the importance of enacting particular practices. Ethics, however, requires differentiation between repetition and practice. The danger of **repetition** is that it can become so habitual that it is thoughtless. **Practice** necessitates thoughtful examination. The practicing of ethical communicative action yields thoughtful application.

b. *Leadership*. Leaders respond to particular circumstances. As the situation changes, the rejoinder must be unique and responsive to the given context. Anachronistic responses are not only too familiar, but they are too reactive. We contend that reaction emerges from thoughtlessness, with responsiveness called forth by a particularity of context and the task that a leader must frame.

c. *Conflict*. Conflict emerges from both appropriate and inappropriate responses to a unique situation. An appropriate response to a conflict does not ensure success, but its counter most likely will invite unproductive clashes between persons. Thoughtful meeting of conflict begins with recognizing that each conflict must be respected in its own contextual uniqueness. The task of leadership in conflict is to frame an exclusive response for each and every conflict.

12. Performative Trust.

Ethics, leadership, and conflict require interactive sensitivity and concern for others, our environment, and the context and our impact upon them. One watches actions to discern whether performative trust defines a given leader. The leader's responsibility is for all; it is impersonal responsibility. Odysseus's leadership announced reliability and the assurance of trust. His leadership illustrated performative trust in action.

Odysseus did not habitually rely on the trappings of leadership. His leadership did not rest in pomp and ceremony. Instead, his leadership emerged out of performative trust. His actions and practices spoke louder than his desire of recognition as king. He did his own fighting, thinking, and improvising. Those who followed him could witness performative practices that were appropriate to the situation and the moment.

When Odysseus was with the Phaenkians and King Alkinoös, there was a feast at which Odysseus played the part of a grateful guest, but when there was a shift to competitive games and he was taunted to show his prowess by Laodamas, he did so and won handily. However, when there was a shift back to the feast, he moved his men out and back to the ship. He practiced leadership as a guest, as a competitor, and by knowing when to exit the stage.

a. *Ethics*. Practicing ethics requires one to be responsive to context and to role with the former shifting the latter. Role tied to ethics resists reification with responsiveness to fluctuations within a given communicative environment. An ethic resists imposition; it is responsive to exteriority and its demands.

b. *Leadership*. Leadership is not something found in a manual; it requires learning, performing, and practicing. Being in a leadership role is not the same as performing leader-like practices. Performative trust bestowed by others is the criterion from which leaders gather their influence.

c. *Conflict.* Conflict that results from practices of performative trust offers confidence in a given communicative environment. Conflict reveals what is important to protect and promote and gives energy to leadership when such goods are threatened. The task of leadership in conflict is to frame practices responsive to a particular communicative environment, announcing performative trust about goods that call forth action of protection and promotion.

13. Destructive Conflict.

Ethics, leadership, and conflict must decrease the tendency for divisive conflict, encouraging appropriate forms of resistance and inviting professional civility that invites productivity to propel an organization. Odysseus understood the destructive nature of unchecked destructive conflict and continually resisted its divisive power.

This chapter addresses the final stages of the *Odyssey*. We discover the destructive manner in which suitors treat Odysseus verbally and physically. The suitors' reaction to this man who looks like a beggar is disparaging. Odysseus offers a powerful reminder of what revenge can look like. He even provides a warning to Amphinomos, who was kind to Odysseus in his role as a beggar. Amphinomos, however, does not heed the suggestion and, like the other suitors, meets an untimely end. Clearly, not every person who distributes destructive conflict meets a tragic end; however, such communicative behavior does not generate friends. It is possible for the abused to gather status and strength and eventually retaliate.

The principal heuristic rule in conflict is to avoid creating unnecessary conflict with one's style. Clearly, destructive conflict illuminates this communicative error. Bullies, problematic others, and all who encourage divisive conflict generate pain for others and diminish the quality of a communicative environment. Such persons hurt the place in which they live instead of assisting others in ways that promote the quality of the places one works and dwells.

a. *Ethics.* A basic assumption of this work is that conflict should be over issues that matter. Partaking in unnecessary conflict is a pragmatic ethical violation. We do not need to create unnecessary conflict; genuine issues will continue to divide us and call for creative responses. Actions that invite destructive conflict seldom get us anywhere; such imposing movements are propelled more by amusement than by building and renovating a constructive communicative dwelling.

b. *Leadership.* Leaders learn from conflicts that offer new insights. Destructive conflict offers clarity on whom not to promote or place in control of an important project. Destructive conflict permits leadership to discern the potential, or lack thereof, for particular persons to build a given communicative environment.

c. *Conflict.* Conflict is a reminder of what is important to oneself and to the other. Without conflict, we learn little about what matters to another. Discovering that another enjoys engaging in destructive conflict is not gratifying, but it is realistic and important information to acquire. Such action damages the constructive soil needed to nurture a communicative environment. As we witness destructive practices, we need to offer communicative alternatives that protect and promote the places that make our interaction together possible. The task of leadership in conflict is to frame the learning emerging from conflict.

Four Ending Notes:

1. *Conflict matters.* It informs and reminds us about what is significant between and among persons.
2. *Conflict and generosity.* We and others require a munificence of spirit that is more interested in learning than in winning.
3. *Conflict and sociality.* Disputes remind us of our sociality; we must discern creative ways to work with those who protect and promote goods different from our own.
4. *Conflict and truth.* We end this book with the wisdom of Mahatma Gandhi. He reminds us of the importance of difference, even as we seek to protect and promote that which we believe really matters.

> *But how is one to realize this Truth . . . By single-minded devotion (abbyasa) and indifference to every other interest in life (vairagya)—replies the Bhagavad Gita. In spite, however, of such devotion, what may appear as truth to one person will often appear as untruth to another person. But this need not worry the seeker . . . there is nothing wrong in everyone following Truth according to one's lights. Indeed it is one's duty to do so. Then if there is a mistake on the part of any one so following Truth, it will automatically be set right . . . [if] one takes to the wrong path one stumbles, and is thus redirected to the right path. (Gandhi, 1972, p. 42; Arnett, 1980, p. 37)*

Leaders must follow a direction with conviction and simultaneously have the courage to walk in the midst of diversity and conflict, the communicative dwelling place for pragmatic research and development of the next great idea.

Leadership frames, moving behavior to clear, public action situated within clarity of story. We end with a quote from *Communication Ethics in Dark Times: Hannah Arendt's Rhetoric of Warning and Hope*, underscoring the necessity of story in the public comprehension of meaningful behavior:

> *Arendt's rhetoric is defiant . . . and a call to responsibility, reminding all of the importance of the ground of tradition upon which one discovers a counter-rhetoric to modernity . . . . Existence requires us to understand that which we meet, whether or not we concur with what is before us. Deliberation entails contemplative consideration before, during, and after the doing of a given action. Story-centered action moves behavior and ideas into narrative coherence, which carries meaning and shapes what Arendt called "vita activa." (Arnett, 2013, p. 259).*

REFERENCES

Arendt, H. (1993). *Between past and future*. New York, NY: Penguin Books. (Original work published 1954)

—. (1998). *The human condition*. Chicago, IL: University of Chicago Press. (Original work published 1958)

Aristotle. (Trans., 2011). *Aristotle's* Nicomachean ethics. (R. C. Bartlett & S. D. Collins, Trans.). Chicago, IL: The University of Chicago Press.

Arnett, R. C. (1980). *Dwell in peace: Applying nonviolence to everyday relationships*. Elgin, IL: The Brethren Press.

—. (2013). *Communication ethics in dark times: Hannah Arendt's rhetoric of warning and hope*. Carbondale: Southern Illinois University Press.

Bellah, R., Madsen, R., Sullivan, W. M., Swidler, A., & Tipton, S. M. (1985). *Habits of the heart: Individualism and commitment in American life*. New York, NY: Perennial Library.

Bryn Mawr College. (2013). "Biography of Richard Lattimore (1906–1984)." Accessed March 29, 2013, from http://www.brynmawr.edu/classics/history/lattimore.html

Buber, M. (1993). *Between man and man*. London: Routledge. (Original work published 1947)

Cairns, F. (1989). *Virgil's Augustan epic*. Cambridge: University of Cambridge Press.

Fisher, W. R. (1989). *Human communication as narration: Toward a philosophy of reason, value, and action*. Columbia: University of South Carolina Press.

Forster, N., Cebis, M., Majteles, S., Mathur, A., Morgan, R., Preuss, J., Vinod, T. & Wilkinson, D. (1999). The role of story-telling in organizational leadership. *Leadership & Organization Development Journal, 20*, 11–17.

Fritz, J. M. H. (2013). *Professional civility: Communicative virtue at work*. New York, NY: Peter Lang.

Gandhi, M. (1972). *Gandhi: Selected writings* (R. Duncan, Ed.). New York, NY: Harper and Row Publishers.

Gibson, J. W., Tesone, D. V., & Buchalski, R. M. (2000). The leader as mentor. *Journal of Leadership & Organizational Studies, 7*, 56–67.

Homer. (Trans. 1991). *Odyssey* (R. Lattimore, Trans.). New York, NY: HarperCollins Publishers, Inc. (Original translation published 1967)

Isle, M. (2006). *Aristotle: Pioneering philosopher and founder of the lyceum*. New York, NY: Rosen Publishing Group, Inc.

Joseph R. McCarthy. (2013). In *Encyclopaedia Britannica Online*. Retrieved from http://www.britannica.com/EBchecked/topic/353904/Joseph-R-McCarthy.

Kant, I. (2006). On the common saying: That may be right in theory but does not work in practice. In P. Kleingeld (Ed.), *Toward perceptual peace and other writings on politics, peace, and history* (D. L. Colclasure, Trans.). New Haven, CT: Yale University Press. (Original work published 1793)

Lasch, C. (1984). *The minimal self: Psychic survival in troubled times*. New York, NY: W. W. Norton & Company, Inc.

Latemore, G., & Callan, V. J. (1999). Odysseus for today: Ancient and modern lessons for leaders. *Asia Pacific Journal of Human Resources, 36*, 76–86.

MacIntyre, A. (2007). *After virtue: A study of moral theory* (3rd ed.). Notre Dame, IN: University of Notre Dame Press. (Original work published 1981)

Nelson, M. (2008). Odysseus and Aeneas: A classical perspective on leadership. *The Leadership Quarterly, 19*, 469–477.

Pearce, W. B. (1989). *Communication and the human condition*. Carbondale: Southern Illinois University Press.

Pearce, W. B., & Cronen, V. (1980). *Communication, action, and meaning: The creation of social realities*. Santa Barbara, CA: Praeger.

Pearce, W. B., & Littlejohn, S. W. (1997). *Moral conflict: When social worlds collide*. Thousand Oaks, CA: Sage.

Philology. (2013). In *Encyclopaedia Britannica Online*. Retrieved from http://www.britannica.com/EBchecked/topic/456678/philology.

Virgil (Trans. 1909). *Virgil's Aeneid: Part 13 Harvard classics* (J. Dryden, Trans.). New York, NY: P. F. Collier & Sons.

Appendix

GAIL T. FAIRHURST BIBLIOGRAPHY

Abu Baker, H. B., Jian, G. & Fairhurst, G. T. (2014). Where do I stand? The interaction of leader-member exchange and performance ratings. *Asian Business & Management, 13,* 143-170.

Barge, J. K., & Fairhurst, G. T. (2008). Living leadership: A systemic, constructionist approach. *Leadership, 4,* 227–251.

Cooren, F., & Fairhurst, G. T. (2002). The leader as the practical narrator: Leadership as the art of translating. In D. Holman & R. Thorpe (Eds.), *Management and language: The manager as a practical author* (pp. 85–103). London: Sage Publications.

Cooren, F., & Fairhurst, G. T. (2004). Speech timing and spacing: The phenomenon of organizational closure. *Organization, 11,* 793–824.

Cooren, F., & Fairhurst, G. T. (2009). Dislocation and stabilization: How to scale up from interactions to organizations. In L. L. Putnam & A. Nicotera (Eds.), *Building theories of organization: The constitutive role of communication* (pp. 117–152). New York, NY: Routledge.

Cooren, F., Fairhurst, G. T., & Huët, R. (2011). Why matter always matters in organizational communication. In P. Leonardi & B. Nardi (Eds.), *Materiality in organizing: Social interaction in a technical world* (pp. 296–314). Ann Arbor: University of Michigan Press.

Courtright, J. A., Fairhurst, G. T., & Rogers, L. E. (1989). Interaction patterns in organic and mechanistic systems. *Academy of Management Journal, 32,* 773–802.

Fairhurst, G. T. (1981). Test of a model of message-attitude-behavior relations. *Western Journal of Speech Communication, 45,* 252–268.

_____. (1981). Two methodological traditions. In K. Reardon (Ed.), *Persuasion: Theory and context.* Thousand Oaks, CA: Sage Publications.

_____. (1985). Male-female communication on the job: Literature review and commentary. In. M. McLaughlin (Ed.), *Communication yearbook 9.* Thousand Oaks, CA: Sage Publications.

_____. (1990). Changing the information culture at Pearson Company. In B. D. Sypher (Ed.), *Case studies in organizational communication* (pp. 223–234). New York, NY: Guilford Press.

_____. (1993). Echoes of the vision: When the rest of the organization talks total quality. *Management Communication Quarterly, 6,* 331–371.

_____. (1993). The leader-member exchange patterns of women leaders in industry. *Communication Monographs, 60,* 1–31.

_____. (2000). Paradigm skirmishes in the review process. In S. Corman & M. S. Poole (Eds.), *Finding the common ground: Reconciling metatheoretical perspectives in organizational communication* (pp. 120–127). New York, NY: Guilford Press.

_____. (2001). Dualisms in leadership communication. In L. L. Putnam & F. M. Jablin (Eds.), *The new handbook of organizational communication* (pp. 379–439). Newbury Park, CA: Sage Publications.

_____. (2001). [Review of the book *Values at work: Employee participation meets market pressure at Mondragon,* by G. Cheney]. *Communication Theory, 11,* 242–245.

_____. (2004). Organizational relational control research: Problems and possibilities. In L. E. Rogers & V. Escrudo (Eds.), *Relational communication: An interactional perspective to the study of process and form* (pp. 197–218). Mahwah, NJ: Erlbaum.

_____. (2004). Textuality and agency in interaction analysis. *Organization, 11,* 335–353.

_____. (2005). Reframing the art of framing: Problems and prospects for leadership. *Leadership, 1,* 165–185.

_____. (2007). *Discursive leadership: In conversation with leadership psychology.* Thousand Oaks, CA: Sage Publications.

_____. (2007). Liberating leadership: A response. In F. Cooren (Ed.), *Interacting and organizing: Analyses of a board meeting* (pp. 53–76). Mahwah, NJ: Lawrence Erlbaum.

_____. (2007). 'Standing by' numbers and statistics in organizational discourse analysis. *Communication Methods and Measures, 1,* 47–54.

_____. (2008). Communication. In Y. Gabriel (Ed.), *Organizing words.* Oxford: Oxford University Press.

_____. (2008). Discursive leadership: A communication alternative to leadership psychology. *Management Communication Quarterly, 21,* 510–521.

_____. (2008). Interaction analysis. In S. R. Cleggs & J. Bailey (Eds.), *International encyclopedia of organization studies.* Los Angeles, CA: Sage Publications.

_____. (2008). Organizational discourse. In W. Donsbach (Ed.), *The international encyclopedia of communication* (pp. 3455–3450). Malden, MA: Blackwell.

_____. (2009). Considering context in discursive leadership research. *Human Relations, 62,* 1–27.

_____. (2011). Communicating leadership metaphors. In M. Alvesson & A. Spicer (Eds.), *Metaphors we lead by* (pp. 180–193). New York, NY: Routledge.

_____. (2011). Discursive leadership. In A. Bryman, D. Collinson, K. Grint, B. Jackson, & M. Ulh-Bien (Eds.), *The Sage handbook of leadership* (pp. 439–505). London: Sage Publications.

_____. (2011). Leadership and the power of framing. *Leader to Leader, 61,* 43–47.

_____. (2011). *The power of framing: creating the language of leadership.* San Francisco, CA: Jossey-Bass.

_____. (2012). Linda Putnam's contributions towards the building of cross-disciplinary relationships. *Management Communication Quarterly, 26,* 492–497.

_____. (2012). [Review of the book *Discourse perspectives on organizational communication,* by J. Aritz & R. Walker (Eds.)]. *Journal of Pragmatics, 44,* 1378–1380.

Fairhurst, G. T., & Antonakis, J. (2012). A research agenda for relational leadership. In M. Uhl-Bien & S. Ospina (Eds.), *Advancing relational leadership theory: A conversation among perspectives* (pp. 433–459). Charlotte, NC: Information Age Publishing.

Fairhurst, G. T., & Chandler, T. A. (1989). Social structure in leader-member interaction. *Communication Monographs, 56,* 215–239.

Fairhurst, G. T., Church, M. L., Hagen, D. E., & Levi, J. T. (2011). Leadership discourses of difference: Executive coaching and the alpha male syndrome. In D. Mumby (Ed.), *Reframing difference in organizational communication studies: Research, pedagogy, and practice* (pp. 77–100). Thousand Oaks, CA: Sage Publications.

Fairhurst, G. T., & Connaughton, S. (In press). Leadership: A communication perspective. *Leadership.*

_____. (In press). Leadership. In L. L. Putnam & D. Mumby (Eds.), *The new handbook of organizational communication*. Thousand Oaks, CA: Sage Publications.

Fairhurst, G. T., & Cooren, F. (2004). Organizational language-in-use: Interaction analysis, conversation analysis, and speech act schematics. In D. Grant, C. Hardy, C. Oswich, N. Phillips, & L. Putnam (Eds.), *The Sage handbook of organizational discourse* (pp. 131–152). London: Sage Publications.

_____. (2009). Charismatic leadership and the hybrid production of presence(s). *Leadership, 5,* 1–22.

Fairhurst, G. T., Cooren, F., & Cahill, D. (2002). Discursiveness, contradiction, and unintended consequences in successive downsizings. *Management Communication Quarterly, 15,* 501–540.

Fairhurst, G. T., & Grant, D. (2010). The social construction of leadership: A sailing guide. *Management Communication Quarterly, 24,* 171–210.

Fairhurst, G. T., Green, S., & Courtright, J. A. (1995). Inertial forces and the implementation of a socio-technical systems intervention. *Organization Science, 6,* 168–195.

Fairhurst, G. T., Green, S. G., & Snavely, B. K. (1984). Managerial control and discipline: Whips and chains. In R. Bostrom (Ed.), *Communication yearbook 8* (pp. 558–593). Beverly Hills, CA: Sage Publications.

Fairhurst, G. T. & Hamlett, S. R. (2003). The narrative basis of leader-member exchange. In G. Graen (Ed.), *LMX, the series* (vol. 1) (pp. 117–144). Greenwich, CT: Information Age Publishing.

Fairhurst, G. T., Jordan, J. M., & Neuwirth, K. (1997). Why are we here? Managing the meaning of an organizational mission. *Journal of Applied Communication Research, 25,* 243–263.

Fairhurst, G. T., & Putnam, L. L. (In press). Discourse analysis. In L. L. Putnam & D. Mumby (Eds.), *The new handbook of organizational communication*. Thousand Oaks, CA: Sage Publications.

Fairhurst, G. T. & Putnam, L. L. (1985). Women and organizational communication: Research directions and new perspectives. *Women and Language, 9,* 1–5.

_____. (1999). Reflections on the organizational-communication equivalency question: The contributions of James Taylor and his colleagues. *The Communication Review, 3,* 1–9.

_____. (2004). Organizations as discursive constructions. *Communication Theory, 14,* 1–22.

Fairhurst, G. T. & Reuther, C. (2000). A feminist reinterpretation of chaos theory as applied to the glass ceiling. In P. Buzzanell (Ed.), *Feminist approaches to organizational communication* (pp. 236–252). Thousand Oaks, CA: Sage Publications.

Fairhurst, G. T., Rogers, L. E., & Sarr, R. A. (1987). Manager-subordinate control patterns and judgments about the relationship. In M. McLaughlin (Ed.), *Communication yearbook 10* (pp. 395–415). Beverly Hills, CA: Sage Publications.

Fairhurst, G. T., & Sarr, R. A. (1996). *The art of framing: Managing the language of leadership*. San Francisco, CA: Jossey-Bass.

Fairhurst, G. T., Schenck-Hamlin, W., Neal, W. P., & Haskins, W. (1975). Teaching persuasion: A comprehensive approach. *Journal of the Wisconsin Communication Association, 8,* 65–75.

Fairhurst, G. T. & Schuster, C. M. (1976). Is that what you meant? I didn't know that. In V. Wall (Ed.), *Small group communication*. Columbus, OH: Collegiate Publishing.

Fairhurst, G. T., & Shellenbarger, S. (1983). Target adaptiveness in messages designed to control poor performance. *Ohio Speech Journal, 21.*

Fairhurst, G. T., & Snavely, B. K. (1982). The impact of sex status differences and numerical underrepresentation on communication apprehension. *Ohio Speech Journal, 20*, 60–68.

_____. (1983). A test of the social isolation of male tokens. *Academy of Management Journal, 26*, 353–361.

_____. (1983). Majority and token minority group relationships: Power acquisition and communication. *Academy of Management Review, 8*, 292–300.

Fairhurst, G. T., & Uhl-Bien, M. (2012). Organizational discourse (ODA): Examining leadership as a relational process. *Leadership Quarterly, 23*, 1043–1062.

Fairhurst, G. T., & Wendt, R. F. (1993). The gap in total quality. *Management Communication Quarterly, 6*, 441–451.

Fairhurst, G. T., & Zoller, H. Z. (2008). Resistance, dissent, and leadership in practice. In S. P. Banks (Ed.), *Dissent and the failure of leadership* (pp. 135–148). Northhampton, MA: Edward Elgar Publishing.

Gavin, M. B., Green, S. G., & Fairhurst, G. T. (1995). Managerial control strategies for poor performance and the impact on subordinate perceptions of justice. *Organizational Behavior and Human Decision Processes, 63*, 207–221.

Green, S. G., Fairhurst, G. T., & Snavely, B. K. (1986). Chains of poor performance and supervisory control. *Organizational Behavior and Human Decision Processes, 38*, 7–27.

Jian, G., Schmisseur, A., & Fairhurst, G. T. (2008). Organizational discourse and communication: The progeny of Proteus. *Discourse & Communication, 2*, 299–320.

_____. (2008). The debate about organizational discourse and communication: A rejoinder. *Discourse & Communication, 2*, 353–355.

Putnam, L. L., Fairhurst, G. T., & Banghart, S. G. (2016). Contradictions, dialectics, and paradoxes in organizations: A constitutive approach. *Academy of Management Annals, 10*, 65-171.

Putnam, L. L., & Fairhurst, G. T. (2001). Discourse analysis in organizations. In L. L. Putnam & F. M. Jablin (Eds.), *The new handbook of organizational communication* (pp. 78–136). Newbury Park, CA: Sage Publications.

Schmisseur, A., Jian, G., & Fairhurst, G. T. (2009). Business discourse and the field of organizational communication. In F. Bargiela-Chiappini (Ed.), *The handbook of business discourse* (pp. 256–268). Edinburgh: Edinburgh University.

Sheep, M. L., Fairhurst, G. T., & Khazanchi, S. (2017). Knots in the discourse of innovation: Investigating multiple tensions in a reacquired spin-off. *Organization Studies, 38*, 463-488.

Snavely, B. K., & Fairhurst, G. T. (1984). The male nursing student as a token. *Research in Nursing and Health, 7*, 287–294.

Wendt, R. F., & Fairhurst, G. T. (1994). Looking for the vision thing: The search for a transforming leader in American presidential campaigns. *Communication Quarterly, 42*, 180–195.

Wilhelm, A., & Fairhurst, G. T. (1997). I heard it through the grapevine: Dealing with rumors, politics, and total quality management. In B. Sypher (Ed.), *Case studies in organizational communication* (vol. 2) (pp. 240–248). New York, NY: Guilford Press.

Zoller, H. Z., & Fairhurst, G. T. (2007). Resistance leadership: The overlooked potential in critical organization and leadership studies. *Human Relations, 60*, 1331–1360.

GLOSSARY[1]

A priori: Knowledge prior to experience (3).

Accessing: The ability of emotional intelligence that generates emotions that assist in judgment (7).

Accommodating: Conflict style where one concurs with the position of another (10).

Action: The telling of an act that is understood within a story (14).

Active listening: A type of listening that occurs when one attempts to understand the other's message, focusing on the content of the message, not a particular judgment about the message (11).

Active mental groping: A form of sexual harassment that involves the harasser's imagination that seems projected upon the communicative environment. Sometimes, but not always, the harasser's behavior can be observed by others (13).

Aesthetic appreciation: A form of sexual harassment that involves the harasser complimenting the victim on his or her physical appearance (13).

Affect: A fundamental element of one's emotional experience (7).

Aggregate: A group or body of units or parts that are loosely associated with one another (5).

American Dream: A narrative of hope for social advancement that includes individual advancement and care for a community (4).

Anachronism: An idea or action that is still being used but no longer addresses the needs of the current moment—an idea or action that is out of place and out of time (4; 11).

Anachronistic lament: An unwillingness or inability to re-consider routine, even when previous actions no longer contribute to success (11).

Anger: An emotion characterized by antagonism toward someone or something that is "wrong" (7).

Anticipatory socialization: A socialization process that begins before one formally enters the organization, beginning with the application, the interview, and preparation for engaging a new social setting (13).

Appreciative inquiry: An exploration of the existential fact that we live in an era of moral conflict, resulting in the colliding of social worlds (1).

Appreciative listening: A type of listening that occurs for pleasure or enjoyment (11).

Argument: The use of logic, reason, and evidence marshaled with intent to persuade (3).

Attending to existence: A wake-up call that demands that we notice the distinctiveness of the communicative environment (11).

Attentive hearing: A pivot point that launches engaged listening (11).

Attentiveness: A component of relational sensitivity that focuses on what is before us and a rejection of the impulse to demand repeatedly that the world conform to our wishes (12).

---

[1] There are many alternative definitions for the terms listed in this glossary. The definitions provided here are the ones these authors have chosen to employ in this work. Some of these terms are quoted directly from the literature and are referenced in the indicated chapters. Please reference the indicated chapters for citation information. Note: Numbers in (parentheses) indicate chapter where term is discussed.

Attribution theory: Individuals are motivated to evaluate a situation in order to understand why an outcome/event occurred (9).

Avoiding: Conflict style where individuals intentionally remove themselves from the dispute situation (10).

Backing: Additional research that supports the warrant (3).

Becoming aware: Perception that focuses on the specific person, responding in a unique fashion to the other (6).

Becoming orientation: An organizational discourse orientation where the organization is in a continual process of becoming (2).

Behavior: Isolated conduct not understood within a story that frames the action (14).

Behavioral profiles: Action tendencies produced by various emotions (7).

Believable frames: An ingredient of framing that responds to a communicative context in a fashion that others deem appropriate (11).

Between: An ontological reality that offers an opportunity for creativity of discovery in a conversational space not possessed by one party or another (6).

Blind loyalty: The responsibility for action is taken out of one's hands because one is just following the routine (3).

Broken covenant: The recognition that all organizations and relationships are flawed (10).

Bullying: A form of divisive conflict that focuses on aggressive behavior that attempts to inflict harm or discomfort on another (13).

Categorical imperative: Ongoing test of practical reason to act in accordance with what should be universal law (3).

Change agent: Persons who influence others within an organization (11).

Claim: The statement being argued, otherwise known as a thesis to the argument (3).

Closed family: A type of family that maintains tight connections, exhibiting skepticism about difference and experiences outside of the family unit (5).

Coercive power: A form of power that uses fear and punishment to control the behavior of another (4).

Cognition: A mental state that assists with interpreting emotional responses (7).

Collaborating: Conflict style that is a form of invitational rhetoric and permits both parties to reach a resolution that offers a win/win situation (10).

Collective agreement: The concurrence of a large number of people within a group that moves a story to a narrative that can offer guidance for communicative action (4).

Collectivist cultures: Cultures that adopt relational, process-oriented strategies (5).

Common center: A commitment that brings people together while preserving the interspaces between persons (5).

Common sense: The unique task a community gathers around to protect and promote (9).

Communication: A component of conflict definitions that includes the distribution of symbols, acts, and exchanges of messages (3).

Communication competence: The ability to flexibly adapt one's communication style depending on the needs of the other and a given location (12).

Communication ethics: The interplay of philosophy of communication (why) and applied communication (how) (1).

Communicative gestalt: The interplay of figure and ground, understanding the whole as greater than the sum of its parts that is necessary for understanding both ethics and conflict (1).

Communicative leadership: A form of leadership that understands why ethics is often an engine for conflict, identifies the communicative implications of both the parts and the whole, recognizes the goods that matter to oneself and others, and accepts responsibility for building communicative dwellings that seek to learn from difference and conflict (1).

Communicative meaning: Temporal clarity that manifests through differentiating between pertinent information and irrelevant content (10).

Community: A place constituted by a commitment to a common center worthy of protecting and promoting (5).

Community of affinity: People who are relationally drawn to one another without a common center other than immediate pleasure (5).

Community of memory: People brought together through an enduring commitment to shared stories (5).

Community of otherness: People brought together through a recognition of the diversity of individuals who contribute to a common center (5).

Competing: Conflict style that insists on being right, moving the focus of attention to winning alone (10).

Competitive power: A form of power that engages another person in a power struggle in which only one party will eventually benefit (4).

Comprehensive listening: Type of listening that allows us to understand the complexity of the message of a speaker (11).

Compromising: Conflict style that allows for us to find a solution that is perceived as fair by both parties, but neither party is fully satisfied (10).

Concrete other: Someone who comprehends the unique needs of the other, his or her motives, and what he or she searches for and desires (12).

Conflict: The combination of perceptions, goals, and values combined with communicative interactions and context, involving a complex interplay of all the senses (3).

Conflict management: A dialogic approach to reason, uncovering the assumptions of what can be considered fair and reasonable (3).

Conflict map: A public blueprint that consists of four elements: (1) the *persons* who are included in the conflict, (2) the *context* of the conflict, (3) an understanding of the larger *background* of the conflict, and (4) the *ethical significance/importance* attached to the content of the conflict (8).

Conflict mapping: A first step in intervening to manage a particular conflict (8).

Conflict resolution: The evaluation of facts to determine what is reasonable in a given conflict (3).

Conflict style: A responsive option called forth by the uniqueness of a situation (10).

Consciousness: Evidence based on judgments that arise from internal senses, sensations, and passions—for example, from seeing or feeling (9).

Constructivism: A cognitive theory of human communication that examines how people produce and perceive messages in society. Constructivism focuses on how the mind constructs reality in relation to the external world (1).

Constructivist: One who views communication as a *cognitive* process of *knowing* the world (1).

Context: The dwelling where ideas and actions are tested that is both local and inclusive of the larger environment (2). A component of conflict definitions that examines elements that give rise to conflict, such as limited or scarce resources, which are regulated by one's culture and differing cultural communities (3).

Context insensitivity: Disregard for context that leads to decision making in the abstract and disregards the particular moment and situation (2).

Context sensitivity: Attending to particular contexts where one's words and actions congruently match the needs of a communicative environment and lead towards decisions that are experiential and situated in continuous study (2; 5).

Continuous benchmarking: A communicative tool that assists in determining the implementation success of one's own vision (2).

Contradictions: The unintended communicative consequences that lessen the ability of others to trust the congruence between word and deed (2).

Conventional communication: Attends to the norms of a given place (2).

Conversation analysis: Insight into what is occurring in a particular place at a given time (2).

Coordinated management of meaning: A theory that discusses the ongoing complexity of bringing diverse perspectives of meaning together (6).

Core framing: A central element of leadership that focuses on instilling trust (12).

Craftsman: One who is concerned with careful and thoughtful building and renovation (1).

Critical listening: A type of listening that evaluates a message for purposes of accepting or rejecting an argument (11).

Critical theory: Theory concerned with the transformative process for individuals and society with the goal of emancipating people, meanings, and values (13).

Cross-theoretical thinking: Textured insight that takes one out of a provincial and normative imposition of ideas upon a communicative environment and provides a pragmatic cosmopolitan scholarly perspective (2).

Cultural discourse: The knowledge and uniqueness of a specific place, suggesting that each communicative environment has its own unique possibilities (2; 12).

Culture: A system of ideas/beliefs about social life, which relies upon conventions, assumptions, and a sense of common identity (5).

Cunning: A skill that hinges upon a creative blend of past experience and an attentive sensing of what is called for by a unique environment (14).

Customer orientation: A form of displaced conflict that blames the other (11).

Data: The facts and evidence that compose the baseline of an argument (3).

Deductive evidence: A broad category of evidence that is either demonstrative or moral (9).

Demonstrative evidence: Evidence that is arrived at through intellection and based on scientific reasoning (9).

Dialogue: Words shared between persons that give insight into the unexpected, thereby shaping our relational lives. Dialogue originated from the Greek work *dialogos* (*dia* means "through" and *logos* means "the word") (6).

Discourse: General and enduring systems of thought that frame and limit communicative resources available to communicating actors. The study of talk and text in social practices, joining persons and context (2).

Discourse ethics: The importance of participating in the public domain and examining questions about abjuration of public access (1).

Discriminative listening: A type of listening that distinguishes between sounds (11).

Displaced conflict: Conflict directed toward the wrong person or group of people (11).

Displaced dissent: Employees who focus their irritation and frustration on persons not responsible for the conflict generation for the dispute (11).

Divisive conflict: Conflict that seeks to provoke unnecessary struggles at another's expense (13).

Doxa: Platonic word, meaning of opinion (9).

Emotion: Rationales for meeting interpersonal dispute that can constructively propel us and sometimes move us in problematic directions (7).

Emotional alert: A form of metacommunication that calls for thoughtful and reflective engagement of emotions (7).

Emotional awareness: The ability to interpret and label one's emotions about a particular situation (7).

Emotional intelligence: The ability to monitor one's own and others' feelings, to discriminate among them, and to use this information to guide one's thinking and action (7).

Emotional labor: A practice where workers are expected to display certain emotions to satisfy the organization's role expectations (7).

Emotional resilience: The ability to adapt to various conditions, as one secures a sense of purpose and balance in mental and physical well being (7).

Emotivistic judgment: Judgment made without any concern for the particular details that might alter or texture an emotive decision (9).

Emotivism: Decision making by personal preference (6; 9).

Empathic listening: A type of listening that provides emotional support for the person offering information (11).

Empiricism: Extreme sensory to rationalism that relies upon concrete experiences that construct categories in our mind (3).

Encounter: The stage of organizational socialization where one initially enters an organization and tries to make sense of that place (13).

Enlightened self-interest: Selfishness that embraces individual success and aids others (6).

Entry stage: A stage of uncertainty reduction theory that centers on evaluation of physical characteristics that are governed by social norms (8).

Environmental communication: A practical field of study that applies communication principles to engaging conflicts over wilderness, farmland, and endangered species (5).

Envy: A form of social comparison where one demands to have a talent that one simply does not possess (1; 6).

Ethical assumptions: The guiding meaning, direction, and conviction that simultaneously generate conflict when we meet persons with alternative ethical positions (1).

Ethical codes: Necessary and important discourse practices that aid existential trust within an organization (10).

Ethnocentrism: A denial of diversity where one's particular view of a unique environment is deemed the only true perspective, inviting conflict propelled by arrogance and ignorance (5).

Ethos: An Aristotelian term that describes the persuasive power of a speaker's credibility derived from his or her character (2).

Evidence: Support for decisions and communicative practices in personal and professional life (9).

Evidence-based opinions: Unique perspectives that emerge between one's knowledge and a particular situation (9).

Exception framing: A communicative tool that takes us beyond the obvious when responding to rhetorical interruptions and moves us beyond conventional expectations (2).

Existential messages: Reminders of the necessity to respond to changes in a given moment (11).

Existential mistrust: Communicative atmosphere of suspicion and judgment that results in destruction of confidence in existence (10).

Existential moods: Moods that come from being in the world and not only propel us into action but also shift our understanding of existence (7).

Existential trust: Trust in existence or the ground on which one stands (10).

Exit stage: Stage of uncertainty reduction theory where one decides if he or she should pursue future interactions or abandon pursuit of the relationship (8).

Expert power: A form of power that combines knowledge and specialized skills (4).

Exploitative power: A form of power that focuses on consuming power by making demands on another (4).

Expressive communication: Communication that is a reflection of one's own position (2).

External causes of behavior: A component of attribution theory related to particular circumstances beyond the control of the individual (9).

Face: A claimed sense of favorable social self-worth that a person wants others to have of her or him (5).

Face-approval: The practice of others recognizing one's positive face (5).

Face-autonomy: Practices that convey independence and freedom from the interference of others (5).

Face maintenance: A practice of upholding a positive sense of face in social interactions (5).

Face negotiation theory: A theory that describes how individuals from different cultures negotiate face and deal with conflict (5).

Face saving: The practical skill of protecting one's identity (5).

Facework: The actions oriented toward one's own face as well as the actions oriented toward the other's face (5).

Family: A communicative environment where love trumps liking (5).

Fantasy: A conflict response that involves the abstract (8).

Focus of attention: The thoughtfulness to the needs and demands of a particular context in a given moment (10).

Foreplay harassment: A form of sexual harassment that moves beyond touching with the harasser attempting to initiate more involved activities (13).

Forethought: Carefully considering what matters; antithetical to thoughtlessness and babble (2; 3).

Forgiveness: Suggestion to invite existential trust that reduces impulses for psychological aggression and allows one to move forward, permitting relationships to accrue depth and maturity (10).

Formal rationality: A category of rationality that is the rational calculation of means to ends based on rules, regulations, and the law (3).

Framing: A communication activity that includes active grouping of ideas with an objective of constructing a particular meaning (2).

Framing coordination: An ingredient of relational sensitivity that focuses on working with others in a manner that continues to coordinate a given initiative (12).

Free speech: Protecting each person's vote and voice, learning from contrary public positions, and supporting public space composed of competing and contending opinions (1).

Friendship: An ongoing human association voluntarily developed and privately negotiated (13).

Friendship of pleasure: Relationships that are centered on immediate enjoyment (6).

Friendship of utility: Relationships that focus on the expectation of usefulness (6).

Friendship of virtue: Relationships that require reciprocal good will (6).

Fundamental attribution error: The tendency to overemphasize the internal and underestimate the external causes of another's behavior (9).

Generalized other: The collective thoughts, ideas, or attitudes of a group, community, or society that guides how individuals behave in various contexts (12).

Gestalt: What we apprehend in the foreground depends upon its background (1).

Goals: Representations of desired end states toward which people strive (4).

Good will: A condition of the value of happiness defined through the categorical imperative (10).

Gossip: A form of divisive conflict that focuses on idle talk or rumor, especially about personal or private affairs of others (13).

Grounded in action orientation: A form of organizational discourse where the organization exists only insofar as it is relatable to the moment-by-moment goings on of organizational activity (2).

Guilt: An emotion that arises from regret of treating another unjustly, connecting behavior to a narrative of importance (7).

Harassment: A form of divisive conflict where one tries to use one's power to belittle another by monopolizing, offending, and controlling behavior in the interaction (13).

Hearing: An act of attending to sound with the ear where the information does not call forth a responsive participation and engagement (11).

High-context communication: Internal contexting that makes it possible for human beings to perform the exceedingly important function of automatically correcting for distortions or omissions in the messages (3).

Historical moment: Questions that require understanding and interpretation in response to particular circumstances (4).

Historicity: The overlapping of historical moments (4).

History: Insight into the chronology and significance of past events (4).

Hope: The vigorous and tenacious meeting of what is before us, making the best of both the good and the bad and demanding justice rather than a naïve belief in progress (5; 10).

Human sentiment: The moral weight of a given perspective (3).

Hurt: An emotive signal that entails reaction to what another says or does (7).

"I": The part of the self that gives order and expresses feelings (6; 8).

"I" statements: A self-focused message that reflects ownership of an emotion rather than enacting an accusatory response upon another (7).

Identity: Constructed through performative acts that are socially shared and historically situated (12).

Imagination: Conflict response that pushes off a concrete reality, something that actually exists (8).

Imagined interactions: The silent, internal process of envisioning conversations with others (8).

Impersonal: An alternative to limiting ethics and caring to those who meet one's relational approval that demands that we assist all (12).

Individualism: An assumption that it is possible for one to stand above human history, ignoring all social and relational ties that both propel and restrain us and additionally give us identity (6).

Individualistic cultures: Cultures that adopt outcome-oriented strategies (5)

Inner speech: A dialogue with the self and the process of a thought being realized in words (8).

Integrative power: A form of power that encourages people to share resources with the objective of enhancing creative productivity for all (4).

Intellection: Evidence based on mathematical axioms, for example, 2 + 2 = 4 (9).

Interactional communication theory: Perceiving meaning that is continually changing, evolving, and adapting to the context (11).

Intercultural facework competence: Diverse knowledge and a commitment to interpret the conflict communication process from various lenses (5).

Interests: Orientations that give a sense of direction (4).

Internal causes of behavior: A component of attribution theory that refers to the character flaws of a given individual (9).

Internal conflict: Individual reflection on ongoing events that transpire before, during, and after an interpersonal conflict (8).

Internal dialogue: A pragmatic caution that permits us to think before we speak to another, consider before we act, and learn from intrapersonal conflict before entering interpersonal disputes (8).

Internal-reflective deliberation: A necessary first step for public deliberation (8).

Interspaces: The necessary distance between opinions and persons in the public domain (1; 5).

Intrapersonal communication: Physiological and psychological processing of messages that happens within individuals at conscious and nonconscious levels as they attempt to understand themselves and their environment (8).

Intrapersonal communicology: The premise that the experience of a message is intersubjective and that it does not constitute independent data processed through the mechanism of the mind (8).

Intuitive evidence: A broad category of evidence that comes from pure intellection, consciousness, and common sense (9).

Irony: Meaning that has the potential to undermine the clarity of the communicative environment (12).

Jealousy: A form of invidious social comparison in which the other human being has a skill set similar to one's own, with one major difference—the other person is much better at the doing, the engagement, and the use of that skill set (1; 6).

Language: A component of framing that places information in categories with classifications that amass evidence, making it accessible to memory (2).

Leader member exchange (LMX): Model of leadership that that permits persons to transformationally move beyond their limited self-interests (2).

Leaning into conflict: Constructively meeting a conflict head on, refusing to displace a genuine conflict (11).

Legitimate power: A form of power that is linked to an official role, which grants authority and power to appropriately use any of the forms of power (4).

Listening: A participatory cognitive process involving steps such as sensing, processing, and responding but also as a perceived behavior (11).

Looking on: Perception that involves perceiving the other in relationship within a larger context (6).

Low-context communication: A communication style that focuses on the explicit content of the message, with very little, if any, interpretation supplied by the listener (3).

Managed smile: An emphasis on relational exchanges that includes those seeking to dominate others with a smile and those subjugated to the demand to appear constantly upbeat (12).

Manipulative power: A form of power that seeks control without the other's awareness (4).

Matter: Important features (people, places, objects, ideas, surroundings) that can invite conflict between persons (3).

"Me": The part of the self that brings the influence of others into consciousness (6; 8).

Meaning management: A communicative skill that must be practiced that is central to defining the communicative success of a leader (2).

Mental modeling: Thoughtful advance preparation, offering readiness for the unexpected (2; 3).

Metacommunication: A reflective perspective on the significance of meaning that can be a warning to self and other—communication about communication (7).

Metamorphosis: A phase of the organizational socialization process when one moves from being a novice to a more seasoned participant in an organization, giving one the ability to predict events and direction with greater accuracy (13).

Metaphorical language: An ingredient of framing that opens up imagination and avoids the dangers of taking the words unduly literally (11).

Miracle questions: A communicative tool that takes people and an organization well beyond its normative expectations (2).

Mission statements: Common corporate reporting tools that guide an organization's actions and offer information on what an organization has historically accomplished (4).

Mixed messages: A part of any communicative experience where there is contradiction between what we say and what we do (2; 7).

Moods: States that are more general than emotions, which can last for longer periods of time (7).

Moral evidence: Evidence based on experience, analogy, testimony, and calculations of chances (9).

Moral imperative: The exercise of internal dialogue and individual autonomy (8).

Moral positioning: Perspective larger than one's own vision that frames what matters in leadership (10).

Moral sources: The faculties, levels, or aspects of our being that give rise to the identity of an individual person (5).

Multi-valued orientation: An orientation that a variety of options are available for addressing the conflict situation (10).

Mutual-face: The practice of protecting the relationship that exists between various individuals that is also associated with integrating, obliging, and compromising styles (5).

Narratives: Public and personal stories that a particular group of people corporately agree upon to give meaning and structure to speech, writing, and visual communication (4).

Nature of the action: A component of conflict definitions that examines expressed struggles, dissonance, tension, and frustration (3).

Nihilism: A perspective that undercuts all authority (1).

Noble self: An interpersonal style that is insensitive to others and context and is obsessed with personal goals (12).

Nutrient power: A form of power that cultivates relationships and is used to assist others (4).

Object orientation: A style of organizational discourse where the organization is treated as an already formed object to which actors relate (2).

Observing: Perception that attends to details about another, acknowledging the characteristics of the person (6).

Open family: Type of family that allows new experiences to emerge (5).

Opinion: Beliefs that should rely on public evidence, thoughtful examination of the context, and reflection upon potentially unintended consequences (9).

Optimism: The practice of demanding that the world conform to our needs and demands (5; 10).

Organizational culture: The background of a specific communicative environment that offers guidance through signs that acknowledge values, heroes, rites, and rituals (11).

Other-face: The practice of protecting another's need for inclusion that is associated with integrating, obliging, and compromising styles of communication (5).

Paradigm: A unified set of coordinates or boundaries that guide inquiry (3).

Perceiving: The ability of emotional intelligence that permits one to identify emotion in oneself and others (7).

Performative trust: The interplay of the impersonal and relational sensitivity played out in our communicative practices (12).

Person role-role incompatibility: Organizational stress that arises when the organizational roles of two or more persons clash or collide (11).

Personal stage: A stage of uncertainty reduction theory that consists of sharing attitudes, beliefs, and values (8).

Person-centered trust: People's abstract positive expectations that they can count on partners to care for them and be responsive to their needs now and in the future (10).

Person-person incompatibility: Organizational stress that occurs when the personal styles of two employees conflict (11).

Person-role duality: Classifications that create difficult role stress within the workplace (11).

Person-role incompatibility: Organizational stress that emerges when role requirements do not align with the person's style (11).

Physiological changes: Biological responses that accompany emotional reactions (7).

Pleasure: An unimpeded activity of our natural state (9).

Postmodernity: The post-World War II era marked by the transition from one encompassing grand metanarrative to various petite narrative structures (1).

Power: A resource that makes productivity possible (4).

Practical rationality: A category of rationality that engages everyday affairs with a methodical attainment of a definitely given and practical end by means of an increasingly precise calculation of adequate means (3).

Pragmatism: A philosophical tradition that focuses on thought that guides our communicative actions through experiences ever attentive to the uniqueness of a given moment (1; 8).

Praxis: Theory-informed practices that thoughtfully direct communicative leadership (2; 4).

Presentation of self: Interactions where individuals tend to treat the others present on the basis of the impressions they give now about the past and the future (7).

Priming: The communicative act of repetitive reflection, permitting mental readiness to assist in framing on the spot (8).

Proactive framing: Mental models that influence leadership decision making prior to the event (2).

Problematic opinion: Opinions that emerge from unreflective emotive venting (9).

Problematic other: An individual who engages in toxic practices in the workplace and moves from one place to another creating similar problems (10; 13).

Producer orientation: The refusal to displace the conflict onto the wrong topic or person by putting the responsibility on oneself (11).

Professional civility: A communicative virtue that protects and promotes professions, productivity, place, and persons (13).

Prospective goals: Objectives we anticipate doing (4).

Public domain: A space that permits diverse persons and ideas to be heard and engaged (1).

Public evidence: Claims that are tested in the public sphere, socially accepted, and the basis of thoughtful opinions (9).

Public opinion: Trends and patterns that shape the decision-making process (9).

Public opinion poll: Snapshot of what the entire population is thinking regarding a particular issue (9).

Public sphere: The undifferentiated public domain in which civic conversation, in general, occurs (9).

Qualifiers: The conditions under which the argument is considered, which are then used to enhance the claim and strengthen the overall argument (3).

Quasistatistical sense organ: An intuitive response to assist in discerning the general direction of public opinion (9).

Random family: A type of family that unpredictably encourages all new types of experiences to the point of risking a sense of belonging (5).

Rationalism: Categories in one's mind that guide the thinking process and presuppose universal truth can be located as one ignores the particularities of given context or environment (3).

Rationality: An instrumental activity that has its roots in Aristotle's view of logos (logical appeal) and in the systematic process of the scientific method. Rationality focuses on logical consistencies absent of emotional appeal and in accordance with one's reason (3).

Reason: A logical approach that supports conclusions and offers explanation of facts (3).

Rebuttals: Counter arguments used by both parties that state why a particular argument is not true in specific circumstances (3).

Referent power: A form of power associated with those who have significant influence over us due to their prestige and our attraction and relational connections to them (4).

Regulating: the ability of emotional intelligence that allows one to offer and receive criticism appropriately (7).

Relational attentiveness: An awareness of the significance of others (6).

Relational maintenance: The practice of attending to relational sensitivity and the social nature of our lives (6).

Relational sensitivity: A disposition toward acknowledging the importance of the other and recognizing what the other protects and promotes (12).

Relationship: A component of conflict definitions that examine the connections between persons and their interdependence central to the conflict process and eventual outcomes (3; 6).

Retrospective framing: Mental models that influence leadership decision making after an event has concluded (2).

Retrospective goals: Objectives that become reality as we reflect upon what actually happened despite a contrary original hope (4).

Revelatory space: The communicative region between self and other that gives rise to information that would likely go unnoticed without communicative interaction with another (6).

Reward power: A form of power that permits a person to gain access to material resources for work to be accomplished (4).

Rhetorical reflection: An interpersonal style that requires altering one's own personal goals in order to adapt to another person (12).

Rhetorical sensitivity: People who display rhetorical sensitivity consider their own position, their partners' perspectives, and the various constraints presented by the situation and the context (12).

Role: A perceptual dwelling that situates what is heard and frames a responsible space from which one listens (11).

Role ambiguity: Uncertainty about responsibilities associated with a particular function (11).

Role clarity: The process of framing one's role for others and for oneself (2).

Role conflict: The clashing of two or more role responsibilities (11).

Role identity: A standpoint that shapes one's sense of meaning and guides one's behavior (11).

Sapir-Whorf hypothesis: A theory that language and thought are intimately connected (5).

Scope: A component of conflict definitions that focus on incompatible interests, goals, needs, desires, values, and beliefs (3).

Scripts: Mental representations of conversational events; for example, the manner in which we order a meal in a restaurant or conduct a job interview (11).

Self-face: The practice of protecting one's need for inclusion in relationships that is positively associated with being dominant and emotionally expressive in a Western culture (5).

Selfishness: A communicative act that assists another and oneself in a relational exchange (6).

Self-talk: A component of intrapersonal communication that creates meaning for the self (8).

Sensations: Bodily responses that indicate the weightiness of issues that demand our attention (3).

Sequences of interaction: The temporal and the embedded nature of communicative leadership (2).

Sexual abuse: A form of sexual harassment that includes the type of touch such as strokes, brushes, and squeezes and the location of touch on the body (13).

Silent speech: The unity of word and deed that does not eliminate conflict, but decreases the chances of falling into unnecessary conflict due to heedless speech and action (8).

Simplified frames: An ingredient of framing that keeps the conversation close to the context and permits clarity of implications (11).

Six relational perceptions: The views that emerge in the meeting of two people: (1) my image of myself; (2) my image of the Other; (3) my image of the Other's image of me; (4) the Other's image of the Other; (5) the Other's image of me; and (6) the Other's image of my image of the Other (6).

Social comparison: A natural human process that can either motivate one to improve performance or encourage one to undercut another (6).

Social construction: A form of social interaction where we negotiate, reinforce, and shift meaning (1).

Social constructionist: One who views communication as a social process of creating the world (1).

Socialization: A communicative public roadmap of how we should work constructively with one another (13).

Social touching: A form of sexual harassment that includes behaviors where the harasser arranges to be close to the victim, permitting opportunities to touch the victim (13).

Society: A gathering of multiple families, aggregates, communities, and cultures, offering an opportunity to nourish diversity and variability (5).

Space of subjectivity: A dwelling that takes the information, the context, all the partners in the conversation, and the relationship seriously and is constituted by the "by," "for," and "about" of communication (6).

Spiral of silence theory: The perspective that people feel an increased pressure to conceal their opinions when they are in the minority (9).

Spontaneous framing: Practices that arise from inner dialogue that has already challenged ideas and positions prior to testing them in the public domain of leadership (8).

Standpoint: An achieved and collective position, not an ascribed position or individual opinion (10).

Stimuli: Emotion-producing phenomena that may disrupt or enrich one's goals (7).

Story-centered leadership: A form of leadership where behavior is embedded within a story before it is understood as meaningful action (14).

Strategic communication: Attentiveness to a single event, functioning as an illustration or pathway to a larger and more important destination (2).

Subjectivism: An extreme appeal to personal experience (1).

Substantive rationality: A category of rationality that involves values that guide people in their daily lives (3).

Symbolic interaction theory: A theory that examines different images of "I" and "me" where communicative interaction becomes the main shaper of self-concept in relationship to the other (6; 12).

Systems perspective: Awareness that the whole is greater than the sum of the parts and comprehension of the uniqueness of each component (10).

Tainted ground: A perspective that one holds so tenaciously that one may reject any position that contrasts with one's own (1).

Taking Conflict Personally (TCP): A shift in attention from the conflict to the self (11).

Theoretical rationality: A category of rationality that permits one to use precise and abstract concepts to make sense of reality (3).

Theory: A public map that announces a perceptual frame that guides one's investigation (8).

Thought: Language in reflection (2).

Thoughtful opinion: Opinion that requires public evidence, examination of the context, and reflection upon potentially unintended consequences (9).

Total Quality Management (TQM): A philosophy brought forth by W. Edwards Deming that focuses on achieving efficiency, solving problems, imposing standardization and statistical control, and regulating design (2).

Transactional framing: Framing that is responsive to the unexpected within a unique context and moment (2).

Transactional goals: Objectives that emerge in the give and take of life (4).

Transactional model of communication: A model that examines the interconnected relationships of self and other (6).

Trust: People's abstract positive expectations that they can count on partners to care for them and be responsive to their needs now and in the future (10).

Turning points: Instances in the socialization process that allows individuals to become further connected to the organization (13).

Two-valued orientation: An orientation that one viewpoint is right and all other viewpoints are wrong (10).

Ugly American: A person who demands that another culture be like one's own (5).

Ultimate threat: A form of sexual harassment that makes the victim believe that not obliging the harasser will result in serious consequences (13).

Uncertainty reduction theory: An examination of the role of ambiguity in relational development between strangers that contends persons seek to lessen uncertainty in interpersonal relationships (8).

Understanding: The ability of emotional intelligence that involves analyzing emotions and recognizing how they are connected to our actions (7).

Unity of contraries: Learning to perform two opposing relational acts simultaneously (12).

Vision-based framing: A mental model that assists in understanding what goes unnoticed in everyday looking (2).

Visions: Leadership responses to challenges that limit an organization (2).

Warrant: A bridge that offers a logical rationale uniting data and claim (3).

Web of relationships: Relational connections that support and shape individual identity (6).

Weightiness: A sensation that permits one to tacitly comprehend tension in the environment even when its origin may be difficult to comprehend (3).

BIOGRAPHY GLOSSARY

James Truslow Adams (1878–1949) was an American historian and writer. He is the author of *Epic of America* and was the recipient of the Pulitzer Prize for History in 1922 for *The Founding of New England* ("Winners of the Pulitzer Prize for history," 2013) (Chapter 4).

Theodor Wiesengrund Adorno (1903–1969) was a German philosopher who was a part of the Frankfurt School. In 1934, Adorno moved from Germany to England to escape the Nazi occupation. He then moved to the United States in 1938 until 1949 when he returned to Germany. Adorno taught at the University of Oxford and Princeton University and was the co-director of the University of California at Berkeley's Research Project on Social Discrimination from 1941 until 1948. After returning to Germany, Adorno worked with Max Horkheimer to rebuild the Institute for Social Research and the Frankfurt School of critical thought ("Thomas Wiesengrund Adorno," 2013) (Chapter 5).

Hannah Arendt (1906–1975) was born in Hannover, Germany and studied at the Universities of Marburg, Freiburg, and Heidelberg. In 1941, she came to the United States with her husband, Heinrich Blücher, to escape the Nazi reign. She became an American citizen in 1951. Her most well-known works include *Origins of Totalitarianism* (published in 1951, critiquing anti-Semitism, imperialism, and racism), *The Human Condition* (published in 1958, introducing her conception of the *vita activa*), and her most controversial work, *Eichmann in Jerusalem: The Banality of Evil* (published in 1963, reporting the trial of Adolf Eichmann in 1961 for the *New Yorker*) ("Hannah Arendt," 2013) (Chapter 1; Chapter 3; Chapter 4; Chapter 5; Chapter 6; Chapter 9; Chapter 10; Chapter 12; Chapter 14).

Mikhail Bakhtin (1895–1975) was a Russian philosopher and literary theorist. His work focuses on cultural history, linguistics, literary theory, and aesthetics ("Mikhail Bakhtin," 2013) (Chapter 6).

Gregory Bateson (1904–1980) was a British-born anthropologist whose primary study areas included cultural symbolism, rituals, and issues related to learning and communication ("Gregory Bateson," 2013) (Chapter 2).

Robert Bellah (1927–2013) is an American sociologist. Bellah studied at Harvard University, receiving his B.A. in 1950 and his Ph.D. in 1955. Bellah's works seek to "reconcil[e] traditional religious societies with social change" ("Robert Neelly Bellah," 2013) (Chapter 5; Chapter 10; Chapter 14).

Wayne Booth (1921–2005) was an American literary critic and teacher associated with the Chicago School of literary criticism ("Wayne C. Booth," 2013) (Chapter 12).

Martin Buber (1878–1965) was a Jewish philosopher whose work focused on dialogue. His most well-known work, *I and Thou*, was published in 1923 and explored dialogue between self and other ("Martin Buber," 2013) (Chapter 1; Chapter 4; Chapter 5; Chapter 6; Chapter 7; Chapter 10; Chapter 12; Chapter 13; Chapter 14).

Kenneth Burke (1897–1993) was an American literary critic and rhetorician. He is best known for his theory of Dramatism, where "language and human agency combine" ("Kenneth Burke," 2013) (Chapter 10; Chapter 11).

Judith Butler (b. 1956) is an American philosopher. She studied philosophy at Yale University, graduating with her B.A. in 1978, her M.A. in

1982, and her Ph.D. in 1984. She has taught at Wesleyan University, George Washington University, Johns Hopkins University, and the University of California at Berkeley. Her work explores issues of gender and sex, cultural theory, queer theory, and feminism ("Judith Butler," 2013) (Chapter 12).

Edward Hallett Carr (1892–1982) was a British political historian whose works focused on Russian history. From 1941 until 1946, he was the assistant editor for the *Times*, one of the United Kingdom's oldest and more influential newspapers ("E. H. Carr," 2013) (Chapter 4).

Miguel de Cervantes (1547–1616) was the Spanish poet, playwright, and novelist who created the character of Don Quixote. *Don Quixote* has been translated into over sixty languages and is considered one of the most important works of all time. The character, Don Quixote, has become a symbol of the "impractical pursuit of idealistic goals" ("Don Quixote," 2013) (Chapter 6; Chapter 11).

Charlie Chaplin (1889–1977) was a British actor, director, and film producer, regarded as one of the most influential figures of motion-picture history. *Modern Times*, released in 1936, included music and sound, but no spoken words—Chaplin wished to preserve the silent film. *Modern Times* is regarded as "the last great silent film" and was a social critique of "talkies" ("Modern Times," 2013) (Chapter 7).

Charles Darwin (1809–1882) was an English naturalist who developed the theory of evolution by natural selection, or survival of the fittest. In 1859, Darwin first made his theory public with the publication of *On the Origin of Species* ("Charles Darwin," 2013) (Chapter 7).

W. Edwards Deming (1900–1993) was an American statistician and educator whose "advocacy of quality-control methods in industrial production aided Japan's economic recovery after World War II and spurred the subsequent global success of many Japanese firms in the late 20th century" ("W. Edwards Deming," 2013). Total Quality Man-

agement is a philosophy brought forth by Deming that focuses on achieving "efficiency, solving problems, imposing standardization and statistical control, and regulating design" ("Total Quality Management (TQM)," 2013) (Chapter 2).

John Dewey (1859–1952) was an American philosopher who founded the philosophical movement of pragmatism and led the progressive movement in United States education. He received a Ph.D. in philosophy from Johns Hopkins University and taught at the University of Michigan ("John Dewey," 2013) (Chapter 1; Chapter 8).

Don Juan is a "symbol of libertinism" who has become as familiar as Don Quixote, Faust, and Shakespeare's Hamlet. Don Juan has continued to appear in works by Mozart, Molière, Prosper Mérimée, Alexandre Dumas père, Thomas Shadwell, Lord Byron, and George Bernard Shaw ("Don Juan," 2013) (Chapter 6).

Umberto Eco (b. 1932) is an Italian novelist, semiotician, and critic. His most well-known novels include *The Name of the Rose* (Eco, 1980/1983) and *Foucault's Pendulum* (Eco, 1988/1989). His most well-known works on communication and semiotics include *A Theory of Semiotics* (Eco, 1976) and *Semiotics and the Philosophy of Language* (Eco, 1984). Additionally, he is the author of three pictorial collections: *On Beauty* (Eco, 2004/2011), *On Ugliness* (Eco, 2007/2011), and *The Infinity of Lists* (Eco, 2009/2011) (Chapter 5).

Adolf Eichmann (1906–1962) was an Austrian citizen who joined the Nazi party in 1932. Eichmann rose within Nazi ranks and ultimately was given the responsibility of overseeing and organizing the logistics and transportation of the Jewish people within occupied Europe. Eichmann was arrested in Buenos Aires, Argentina, in 1960 and then taken to Israel for trial, where he was ultimately sentenced to death by hanging in 1962 ("Adolf Eichmann," 2013) (Chapter 1).

Faust first emerged in 1587 in *Faustbuch*, which was written by an unknown author. Faust has continued to appear in the works of Christopher Marlowe, Gotthold Lessing, Hector Berlioz, Charles Gounod, Adelbert von Chamisso, Christian Grabbe, Nikolaus Lenau, Heinrich Heine, Paul Valéry, Johann Wolfgang von Goethe, and Thomas Mann ("Faust," 2013) (Chapter 6).

Adam Ferguson (1723–1816) was a philosopher of the Scottish Enlightenment whose work focused on civil society and explored "common sense" philosophy ("Adam Ferguson," 2013) (Chapter 6; Chapter 12).

Walter Fisher (b. 1931) is an Emeritus Professor at the University of Southern California. His work, *Human Communication as Narration: Toward a Philosophy of Reason, Value, and Action*, led to his conception of the narrative paradigm, which presents humans as primarily story-telling creatures ("Walter Fisher," 2013) (Chapter 3; Chapter 4; Chapter 14).

Mary Parker Follett (1868–1933) was an American author and sociologist. Follett studied interpersonal relations and personnel management. Her work continues to influence the study and practice of business administration ("Mary Parker Follett," 2013) (Chapter 4; Chapter 10).

Michel Foucault (1926–1984) was a French philosopher who has had a significant influence post-World War II. He studied psychology and philosophy at the École Normale Supérieure, with scholarly focuses on power and power-knowledge ("Michel Foucault," 2013) (Chapter 2).

Viktor Frankl (1905–1997) was an Austrian psychiatrist who developed the "'third school' of Viennese psychotherapy," after Sigmund Freud (first school) and Alfred Adler (second school). The search for meaning was central to Frankl's theory ("Viktor Frankl," 2013) (Chapter 7; Chapter 11).

Paulo Freire (1921–1997) was a Brazilian educator whose most well-known work was *Pedagogy of the Oppressed* (1970). Freire is recognized for his innovative teaching style that empowered marginalized populations ("Paulo Freire," 2013) (Chapter 6).

Hans-Georg Gadamer (1900–2002) was a German philosopher, whose most well-known work, *Truth and Method*, was published in 1960. Gadamer worked from the insights of Wilhelm Dilthey, Edmund Husserl, and Martin Heidegger. He is most well known for his understanding of philosophical hermeneutics ("Hans-Georg Gadamer," 2013) (Chapter 4; Chapter 6).

Mahatma Gandhi (1869–1948) was the leader of the Indian nationalist movement and is considered the father of India. He is known for his nonviolent protest tactics ("Mohandas Karamchand Gandhi," 2013) (Chapter 14).

Erving Goffman (1922–1982) was a Canadian-American sociologist whose work focused on face-to-face communication and social interaction ("Erving Goffman," 2013) (Chapter 2; Chapter 5; Chapter 7).

Jürgen Habermas (b. 1929) is a German philosopher of social and political thought. He received a Ph.D. in philosophy at the University of Bonn in 1954, and studied at the Universities of Göttingen and Zürich. Habermas was the student of Theodor Adorno and Max Horkheimer ("Jürgen Habermas," 2013) (Chapter 1; Chapter 3; Chapter 4; Chapter 5; Chapter 6; Chapter 9; Chapter 13).

Georg Wilhelm Friedrich Hegel (1770–1831) was a German philosopher whose works focused on dialectics and history's progression in terms of thesis, antithesis, and synthesis ("Georg Wilhelm Friedrich Hegel," 2013) (Chapter 3).

Martin Heidegger (1889–1976) was a German philosopher whose work explored ontology and metaphysics. He was a student of Edmund Husserl at the University of Freiburg, where he later taught from 1919 until 1923. Heidegger then became a professor at the University of Marburg, where he taught Hannah Arendt. He is most well known for *Being and Time* published in 1927. From 1933 until 1934, Heidegger served as the elected rector of the University of Freiburg where he delivered "The Self-Assertion of the German University," his most controversial speech due to Heidegger's membership and seeming support for the Nazi Party ("Martin Heidegger," 2013) (Chapter 7).

Homer was an Ancient Greek poet who lived during the 8th or 9th century BCE and was the author of the epic poems the *Iliad* and the *Odyssey* ("Homer," 2013) (Chapter 9; Chapter 14).

Max Horkheimer (1895–1973) was a German philosopher and the director of the Institute for Social Research at the University of Frankfurt from 1930 until 1941 and then again from 1950 until 1958. Horkheimer developed critical theory and was part of the Frankfurt School of philosophical thought ("Max Horkheimer," 2013) (Chapter 5; Chapter 13).

David Hume (1711–1776) was a philosopher of the Scottish Enlightenment. His works addressed epistemology, history, economics, empiricism, and skepticism. Hume's most well-known work is *A Treatise of Human Nature* ("David Hume," 2013) (Chapter 3; Chapter 7).

Friedrich Heinrich Jacobi (1743–1819) was a German philosopher who critiqued rationalism and explored the philosophy of feeling. Jacobi was the president of the Bavarian Academy of Science from 1807 until 1812 ("Friedrich Heinrich Jacobi," 2013) (Chapter 1).

William James (1842–1910) was an American philosopher and psychologist. He was the leader of pragmatism within philosophy and functionalism within psychology ("William James," 2013) (Chapter 1; Chapter 6).

James Joyce (1882–1941) was an Irish novelist born in Dublin. His most well-known novels include *Dubliners*, published in 1914; *A Portrait of an Artist as a Young Man*, published in 1916;

Ulysses, published in 1922; and *Finnegans Wake*, published in 1939. Joyce is known for "his experimental use of language and exploration of new literary methods," including stream of consciousness writing ("James Joyce," 2013) (Chapter 6).

Immanuel Kant (1724–1804) was a German Enlightenment philosopher whose works centered on epistemology, ethics, metaphysics, and aesthetics. His most well-known works include *Critique of Pure Reason* published in 1781, *Critique of Practical Reason* published in 1788, and *Critique of Judgment* published in 1790 ("Immanuel Kant," 2013) (Chapter 3; Chapter 7; Chapter 8; Chapter 10; Chapter 12; Chapter 14).

Martin Luther King, Jr. (1929–1968) was a social activist, Baptist minister, and leader of the Civil Rights Movement. King is known for protesting African-American segregation with nonviolent rebellion tactics such as marches and sit-ins. He received the Nobel Peace Prize in 1964. In 1968, King was assassinated by James Earl Ray in Memphis, Tennessee at the Lorraine Motel, the current site of the National Civil Rights Museum ("Martin Luther King, Jr.," 2013) (Chapter 5).

Elisabeth Kübler-Ross (1926–2004) was an American psychiatrist who was born in Switzerland. Her work focused on the study of terminally ill patients, death, and dying. Her most well-known work, *On Death and Dying*, published in 1969, outlined the five stages of grief ("Elisabeth Kübler-Ross," 2013) (Chapter 7).

Thomas S. Kuhn (1922–1996) was an American historian and philosopher. He attended Harvard receiving a B.A. (1943) and M.A. (1946) in physics and his Ph.D. (1949) in history of science. He taught at Harvard from 1951 until 1956, the University of California at Berkeley from 1956 until 1964, Princeton from 1964 until 1979, and MIT from 1979 until 1991. His most well-known book, *The Structure of Scientific Revolutions*, was published in 1962 ("Thomas S. Kuhn," 2013) (Chapter 3; Chapter 11).

Jacques Lacan (1901–1981) was a French psychologist known as an "original interpreter" of Sigmund Freud ("Jacques Lacan," 2013) and founder of the Freudian School of Paris (1964–1980). In 1932, Lacan received a medical degree and began practicing psychiatry and psychoanalysis in Paris ("Jacques Lacan," 2013) (Chapter 3).

Christopher Lasch (1931–1994) was an American academic and social critic. He is most well known for his 1979 best-seller *The Culture of Narcissism*. Lasch received his M.A. in 1955 and his Ph.D. in 1961, both from Harvard University. He taught at the University of Iowa, Northwestern University, and the University of Rochester ("Christopher Lasch," 2013) (Chapter 10; Chapter 12; Chapter 14).

Richmond Lattimore (1906–1984) received a B.A. from Dartmouth in 1926, a B.A. from Oxford in 1932, and a Ph.D. from the University of Illinois in 1934. Lattimore worked as a faculty member teaching Greek Studies at Byrn Mawr College and as a visiting professor at the University of Chicago (1947), Columbia (1948/1950), Johns Hopkins (1958), the University of Toronto (1966), and the University of California at Los Angeles (1974). Lattimore was a recipient of both the Rockefeller Post-War Fellowship and the Fulbright Research Fellowship for study in Greece. In 1984, Lattimore was elected as an Academy of American Poets Fellow. Apart from his translation of Homer's *Odyssey*, his works include translations of *The Complete Greek Tragedies*, *Homer's Iliad*, and *The Poetry of Greek Tragedies* (Bryn Mawr College, 2013) (Chapter 14).

Owen Lattimore (1900–1989) was accused by Senator McCarthy of being a Soviet spy in 1950. Owen was exonerated later that year, but a Senate Internal Security subcommittee renewed the investigation. In 1952, Owen was indicted for perjury in connection with testimony that he had given during the subcommittee's investigation; however, all charges were dropped in 1955 by the Justice Department ("Owen Lattimore," 2013) (Chapter 14).

Emmanuel Levinas (1906–1995) was a French philosopher born in Lithuania. Levinas studied under Edmund Husserl and Martin Heidegger at the universities of Strasbourg and Freiburg, focusing his work on the critique and proper placement of ontology. During World War II, he served in the French army and spent five years as a prisoner-of-war after being captured by German troops in 1940. After the war, Levinas became the director of the École Normale Israélite Orientale until 1961, where he also taught ("Emmanuel Levinas," 2013) (Chapter 1; Chapter 12).

Sinclair Lewis (1885–1951) was an American novelist and social critic who, in 1930, was the first American recipient of the Nobel Prize for Literature ("Sinclair Lewis," 2013) (Chapter 6).

Alasdair MacIntyre (b. 1929) is a Scottish-born philosopher. He is well known for incorporating Aristotelian ethics, history, and politics into philosophical thought. He studied at the University of London, Manchester University, and the University of Oxford, and he has taught at Boston University, Oxford, Duke University, and the University of Notre Dame among others. MacIntyre immigrated to America in 1970 ("Alasdair MacIntyre," 2013) (Chapter 1; Chapter 3; Chapter 4; Chapter 9; Chapter 12; Chapter 14).

Bernie Madoff (b. 1938) is a former hedge-fund manager and chairman of the NASDAQ. In March 2009, he pleaded guilty to fraud, money laundering, and managing a Ponzi scheme, for which he received a 150-year prison sentence ("Bernie Madoff," 2013) (Chapter 9).

George Herbert Mead (1863–1931) was an American philosopher who was influential to social psychology and pragmatism. He studied at Oberlin College and Harvard University before teaching at the University of Michigan and the University of Chicago. Mead never published; his students edited four volumes of Mead's work, which were published posthumously ("George Herbert Mead," 2013) (Chapter 6; Chapter 8; Chapter 12).

John Stuart Mill (1806–1873) was a British philosopher and economist who advocated utilitarianism. The basic assumption of utilitarianism, founded by Jeremy Bentham, contends that actions prompting happiness for the greater community are right and those that deny happiness are wrong. Mill's writings addressed liberty, logic, utilitarianism, political economics, and political philosophy ("John Stuart Mill," 2013) (Chapter 1).

Friedrich Nietzsche (1843–1900) was a German philosopher and cultural critic, writing on religion, philosophy, and morality. Nietzsche is associated with nihilism, the will to power, Übermensch (superman), and his famous announcement that "God is dead," made after the secularization of the Enlightenment ("Friedrich Nietzsche," 2013) (Chapter 1).

Charles Sanders Peirce (1839–1914) was an American scientist and philosopher. Peirce's work centers on logic and pragmatism ("Charles Sanders Peirce," 2013) (Chapter 8).

Robinson Crusoe is a fictional seaman and the protagonist of Daniel Defoe's (1660–1731) *Robinson Crusoe*. The character is known for his "self-reliance" as he survives on his own for 28 years on an uninhabited island ("Robinson Crusoe," 2013) (Chapter 6).

Edward Sapir (1884–1939) was an American anthropologist and linguist who is well known for his careful study of Native American languages and for ethnolinguistics, the examination of the relationship between culture and language ("Edward Sapir," 2013) (Chapter 5).

Jean-Paul Sartre (1905–1980) was a French writer and existentialist philosopher. He was the author of both novels and plays. Sartre received the Nobel Prize for Literature in 1964, but declined the award. His work centered on questions of human freedom ("Jean-Paul Sartre," 2013) (Chapter 11).

Georg Simmel (1858–1918) was a German sociologist and philosopher. He taught at the University of Berlin from 1885 until 1914 when he began to teach at the University of Strasbourg, where he taught until his death in 1918. His work explores social interaction, which later led to the development of qualitative analysis in sociology ("Georg Simmel," 2013) (Chapter 6; Chapter 7; Chapter 10).

B. F. Skinner (1904–1990) was an American psychologist who studied behaviorism. Skinner is the author of *Walden Two*, published in 1948, which offers an alternative utopia to Henry David Thoreau's *Walden* ("B. F. Skinner," 2013) (Chapter 10).

Adam Smith (1723–1790) was a Scottish philosopher and economist. Smith is most well known for the economic system explicated in *An Inquiry into the Nature and Causes of the Wealth of Nations*, published in 1776 ("Adam Smith," 2013) (Chapter 3; Chapter 5; Chapter 6).

William Graham Sumner (1840–1910) was an American sociologist and economist. Sumner taught at Yale University from 1872 until 1909. His work was based in a Social Darwinist perspective ("William Graham Sumner," 2013) (Chapter 5).

Charles Taylor (b. 1931) is a Canadian philosopher. He is known for his work in the "examination of the modern self" through works such as *Sources of the Self: The Making of the Modern Identity*, which was published in 1989 ("Charles Taylor," 2013) (Chapter 5).

Dylan Thomas (1914–1953) was a Welsh writer of poetry and prose. He is recognized for his "comic exuberance, rhapsodic lilt, and pathos" ("Dylan Thomas," 2013) (Chapter 7).

Alexis de Tocqueville (1805–1859) was a French political writer. Tocqueville visited America with the task of writing his observations of the American prison system. The emerging work, *Democracy in America*, however, provided a critique and analysis of American life ("Alexis de Tocqueville," 2013) (Chapter 4; Chapter 5; Chapter 6; Chapter 12).

J. R. R. Tolkien (1892–1973) was an English writer and author of the *Lord of the Rings* series and *The Hobbit*. The character Gollum appears in both, and in each, he is obsessed with maintaining possession of the ring, the central symbol in the novels ("J. R. R. Tolkien," 2013) (Chapter 12).

Stephen Toulmin (1922–2009) was an English philosopher and educator. He was educated at Cambridge University and taught at Oxford. He became the department head at the University of Leeds from 1955 until 1959 and the director of the Nuffield Foundation from 1960 until 1964. He moved to the United States in the 1960s, where he taught at Brandeis University, Michigan State University, University of California at Santa Cruz, University of Chicago, Northwestern University, and University of Southern California ("Stephen Edelston Toulmin," 2013) (Chapter 3; Chapter 9).

Ivan S. Turgenev (1818–1883) was a Russian writer whose works included novels, poems, and plays. In addition to *Fathers and Sons*, which popularized nihilism, his most famous works include *Rudin* published in 1856, *Home of the Gentry* published in 1859, and *On the Eve* published in 1860. Turgenev is well known for depicting realistic representations of life among Russian peasants ("Ivan Sergeyevich Turgenev," 2013) (Chapter 1).

Virgil (70 BCE–19 BCE) was an Ancient Roman poet and author of the epic poem, the *Aeneid*, which is partially based off of Homer's epics ("Virgil," 2013) (Chapter 9; Chapter 14).

Eric Voegelin (1901–1985) was a German-born American political scientist. Voegelin received a Ph.D. from the University of Vienna in 1922. He became a naturalized American citizen in 1944 after escaping Nazi-occupied Austria. He taught at Harvard, Bennington College, the University of Alabama, and Louisiana State University ("Eric Voegelin," 2013) (Chapter 11).

L. S. Vygotsky (1896–1934) studied philosophy and linguistics at the University of Moscow and became influential in post-revolutionary Soviet psychology. His most well-known work, *Thought and Language*, was published in 1934 and explored the relationship between signs and speech development ("L. S. Vygotsky," 2013) (Chapter 1; Chapter 8).

Max Weber (1864–1920) was a German philosopher and political economist who is most well known for *The Protestant Ethic and the Spirit of Capitalism*, published in 1904 and 1905, and his work on bureaucracy ("Max Weber," 2013) (Chapter 3).

Max Wertheimer (1880–1943) was a Czech psychologist who was instrumental in founding Gestalt psychology. Wertheimer received his Ph.D. from the University of Würzburg in 1904. His research was grounded in perception, with his work on Gestalt psychology beginning in 1910 ("Max Wertheimer," 2013) (Chapter 1).

Benjamin Lee Whorf (1897–1941) was the student of Edward Sapir and was an American linguist. Whorf is known for his study of Hebrew, Hopi, and Mexican and Mayan languages and dialects. Whorf's work concentrated on the relationship between language and thinking ("Benjamin Lee Whorf," 2013) (Chapter 5).

INDEX

Communication
    based upon reciprocity, danger of, 216
    as conflict component, 50
*Communication, Action, and Meaning: The Cre-
    ation of Social Realities*, 27
*Communication and Community: Implications of
    Martin Buber's Dialogue*, 85
Communication competence, 278
    and rhetorical sensitivity, 212
Communication ethics
    and conflict. *See* Communication ethics and
        conflict
    background and foreground action, 5–8
    conflict and, 4, 8–12
    definition, 17
Communication ethics and conflict
    and communicative leadership, 17–18
    communicative gestalt, 4–8
    construction perspective on. *See* Social con-
        struction
    engine for dispute, 3–4
    interplay of, 256–257
    link between
        acts of oppression, 7
        ethical positions. *See* Ethical positions
        leadership. *See* Communicative
            leadership
        postmodernity, 9
        pragmatic communicative gesture,
            3–4, 8
        public space. *See* Public space
        tainted ground, 8
    Odyssey (story), 256–257
Communicative action. *See* Action
Communicative building, 15–16
Communicative dwellings, 14, 17, 79, 176
    and construction, 15–16
    importance of, 79
    of welcome. *See* Welcome, dwellings of
Communicative environment, 194
    of existential trust, 180–181
        broken covenant, 181–182
        exit strategy, 183
        forgiving, 181
        optimism and hope, 181–182
    hearing. *See* Hearing

listening in. *See* Listening
necessity of good will, 184
organizational culture and, 195
struggle for, 183
transformation in, 194–195
Communication Yearbook, 164
Communicative gestalt, 3–6, 8
Communicative goals, 32
Communicative goods, 26
Communicative interaction, 108
Communicative leadership, 24–25
    emotional intelligence, 37
    framing of. *See* Framing
    importance of content, 70
    insight and wisdom into, 27
Communicative meaning, 177
Communicative obligation, 15
Communicative responsibility, 13–14
Communicative space, 175–176
Communicator behaviors and uncertainty
    cause-effect relationships between
        axioms, 144
        theorems, 144
Community
    of affinity, 85
    with common center, 85–86
    communicative movement from family to, 84
    definition of, 84
    of memory, 86
    and optimism, 86
    of otherness, 85
*Compass of Friendship, The: Narratives, Identities,
    and Dialogue*, 102
Competing style of conflict, 178
Competitive power, 69
Comprehensive listening, 197
Compromising (conflict style), 178
Concrete other, 213
Conflict
    and argument, difference between, 41
    avoidance, 178–179
    and communication ethics. *See* Communi-
        cation ethics and conflict
    communicative environment of, 42
    conceptualizations, 49
    confederates, 194

Context
    as conflict component, 50
    framing, 92
    insensitivity, 33
Context sensitivity, 33
    and communicative leadership, 91
Continuous benchmarking, 33
Continuous response measurement (CRM), 165
Contradictions, emotional alerts, 130
Conventional communication
    ethical implications of, 36
    scholarship, 180
Conversation analysis, 27
Coordinated management of meaning, 108
Core framing tasks, 36, 220
Craftsman, 15
Creative engagement and conflict maps, 139
Creative Group, The, 230
Credibility, mutual framing, 112. *See also* Web of
    relationships
Critical listening, 198
Critical theory, 236–237
Crisis Leadership: Planning for the Unthinkable, 191
Cross-theoretical thinking, 30
Cultural discourses, 36, 220
Culture, 79, 86–87
    components of, 87
    definition of, 87
    individualistic and collectivist, 88
    and language, 88
    and society, 89–90
    symbolic nature of, 87
Culture of Narcissism, The, 182
"Culture of poverty," 87
Cunning, 154, 246–247, 254, 257–258, 262–265
Curiosity, pragmatic importance of, 81
Customer orientation, 201

D
Darwin, Charles, 121
Data, in argument, 48
De Anima, 51
On Death and Dying, 123
Deductive evidence, 161
Deming, W. Edwards, 31
Democracy in America, 86, 105

Demodokos, 250–251
Demonstrative evidence, 161
Depression, 123, 161–162
Destructive conflict, 198, 228, 238, 269. *See also*
    Divisive conflict
    danger of, 228
    Odyssey (story), 268–269
Dewey, John, 15, 140–141, 212
Dialectical tensions, 82, 102, 229
Dialogue, 110
    conceptualizations of, 109–110
    internal. *See* Internal dialogue
Dimensions, framing content, 71
Disappointment, illustration of pouting chim-
    panzee, 121
Discipline and discourse, 34–35
Discourse, 27
    background and foreground, 71
    ethics, 13–14, 237
    orientations, 30
    thought structures of, 33–34
Discriminative listening, 197
*Discursive Leadership: In Conversation with Lead-
    ership Psychology*, 27, 34
Discursiveness, Contradiction, and Unintended
    Consequences in Successive Downsiz-
    ings, 28, 29
Disgust, 121
Displaced conflicts, 194, 200
    conflict toward wrong person, 194
    management strategies, 200
    over tangential issues, 200
    Taking Conflict Personally concept, 200
Displaced dissent, 200
Dissimilarities, ethical backgrounds, 1, 7–8
Divisive conflict, 228–229, 233
    communicative acts constituting
        bullying, 228–229
        gossip, 229–231
        harassment, 233–235
    vs. friendship, 229
    generation, 229
    impact on credibility, 229–230
Dominant groups, 7, 89
Don Juan (literary character), 106
Don Quixote (literary character), 105

Initiative in framing, 55
Inner dialogue, 139
Inner speech, 139–141, 143
Innovative responsiveness, 194
Integrative power, 69
Intellection, 161
Intentional malevolent action, 102
Interactional communication, 195
    theory, 195
Interactive sensitivity, 210–214
Intercultural facework competence, 91
Interests
    conflict negotiations, 60, 61, 63
    narrative expressions, 63–65
Internal causes of behavior, 159
Internal conflict, 42, 64, 137–149
Internal dialogue, 137, 139–141
    and American pragmatism, 140
    challenges, 139
    and communicative leadership, 148–149
    importance of, 139–140
    and intrapersonal communication, 143–144
    and *Odyssey* (story), 263–264
Internal-reflective deliberation, 140
Interpersonal conflict, 42, 230
    and emotion, 119
    and internal dialogue, 137, 141
Interpersonal relationships, 212, 232
    and attribution theory, 63, 159
    and goals, 64
Interpretation, emotional alerts, 130
Interspaces, 13–15, 84
Intrapersonal communication, 139, 142–143
    and internal dialogue, 139–141
    study of, 142
    traction of area of, 142
Intrapersonal Communication Processes, 142
Intrapersonal communicology, 143
Intrapersonal conflict, 127, 143
    advantages, 138
    sources of, 143
Intuitive evidence, 161
Irony, 215
"I" statements, 125
Ithaka, 248, 249, 252

J
Jacobi, Friedrich Heinrich, 11
James Joyce Bridge, Dublin, 100
James, William, 102–103, 140
Jealousy, 103
    contemporary example, 103
    definition, 103
    and envy, 101, 103–104, 107, 112, 200, 261
    practical advice for addressing, 104
Job hopping, 2
Job movement, 2
Job shifting, ethical dissatisfaction, 2–3
Jobs, Steve, 119
Johnson & Johnson Company, 219
Journal of Communication, 164
Joyce, James, 99–100

K
KaBOOM! Inc., 69
Kalypso, 249–250, 254
Kant, Immanuel, 44, 45, 53, 127, 139–140, 142, 148, 175, 177, 184, 218, 220
Kayakers
    in class 5 rapids, 202
    in class I rapids, 201
Kerrigan, Nancy, 103
King, Martin Luther, 78
Kübler-Ross, Elisabeth, 122
Kuhn, Thomas S., 47, 178–179, 193

L
Lacan, Jacques, 46
Language
    action and, 31–32, 88
    and culture, 141
    and framing, 31–32
    development of self, 141
    metaphorical, 203
    performative terms, 219
Larger environments, communication, 92
Lasch, Christopher, 182
Lattimore, Owen, 247
Lattimore, Richmond, 247–248
Leader-Member Exchange Patterns of Women Leaders in Industry: A Discourse Analysis, The, 28–29

philosophical roots of, 163
polls, 157–158
and public evidence, relationship between, 161
and thoughtfulness, 162
Public space, 13–16, 163–164
Public sphere, 14, 155, 160–163
Public trial of people, 52–53
Public virtues and narratives, 62

Q

Qualifiers, 48
Quasistatistical sense organ, 165

R

Racial harassment, 234
Rafting, 201–202
Random families, 83
Rationalism, 43
Rationality
    categories of, 46–47
    as instrumental activity, 46
    role in interpersonal and political contexts, 46
Reason
    definition, 43
    performative modality, 43–47
    relation to love, 46
Rebuttals, in argument, 48
Referent power, 68
Regulating, emotional intelligence, 129
Relational attentiveness, 100, 111, 113
Relational disregard, 102–103
Relational friendship webs, 102
Relational maintenance, conflict engagement, 100, 111, 113, 178, 184
Relational perception
    and communicative leadership, 112–113
    and perceptual thoughtlessness, 109
    and revelatory space, 101, 108–112
    perceptual meeting of two people, 108
    uniqueness of others, 109
Relational processes of interaction, 28
Relational sensitivity, 210–211, 214–215, 217, 220
    attentiveness requirements, 211
    communicative leadership, 220–221

Relational webs of connection
    and friendship, 102
    importance of, 101–102
    power of, 101–102
Relationship
    as conflict component, 50
    displaced conflict in, 202
    Odyssey (story), 261
Repetition versus practice, 266
Resistance to the problematic, organizational socialization, 228, 235–237
Responding to existence, communicative environment, 193–195
Responsive listening, 193, 196–198
Responsiveness, framing of opinions, 167
Retrospective framing, 33
Retrospective goals, 63
Revelatory space, 101, 107–111
    and genuine dialogue, 111
    of perception, 108
    space of the between, 108–112
Reward power, 68
Rhetorical reflection, 211
Rhetorical sensitivity, 209–212, 215, 217, 220
    and communication competence, 212–213
    and interactive sensitivity, 211
    attentiveness to, 211
    elements of, 211
    impersonal responsibility, 214–215
    importance of, 211
    interacting with concrete other, 213
    interacting with generalized other, 213
    interpersonal styles and, 211
    notion of reciprocity, 210
    paying attention to everything, 215
Ricoeur, Paul, 12
Right action, 9
Robinson Crusoe (Protagonist), 106
Role ambiguity, 199
Role clarity, 30
Role, communicative interaction, 198
Role conflict, 199
Role of framing, communicative rule, 238
Role identity, 198
Role-role incompatibility, 199

Roles and responsibilities, conflict perspectives, 194, 198–200
Roosevelt, Franklin D., 157
Routine messages, 33

S
Sadness, 120–121, 123
Sapir, Edward, 88
Sapir-Whorf hypothesis, 88
Sartre, Jean-Paul, 202
Schultz, Howard, 41
Scope, conflict component, 49
Scott, Alexandra, 210
Scottish Enlightenment, 50–51, 107, 160
Scripts, conversational events, 195
Second Life (SL) contexts, 125
Self development, 141
Self-face, 90
Self-identity, 125
Self-questioning, communicative process of. *See* Internal dialogue
Self-talk, 43, 141–143, 148, 264
Selfishness, 107, 156
    versus emotivism, 156
    and individualism, 107
Semiotics and the Philosophy of Language, 82
Sensations, 50
    and conflict, link between, 50–51
Sensitivity in conflict, 210–211
Sentiment. *See* Human sentiment
Sequences of interaction, 27
Sexual abuse, 234
Sexual harassment
    Carlson against Fox News Channel, 234–235
    communicative approach to managing, 234
    six-step process for assessing, 234
    training, 235
Shame, 121, 123
A Short History of Ethics: A History of Moral Philosophy from the Homeric Age to the Twentieth Century, 65
Silent speech, 137
Simmel, George, 89, 101, 103–104, 112, 122, 124, 178, 261
Simplified frames, 203

Sisyphos, 253
Situation and context, 167
Six relational perceptions, 108
Skinner, B. F., 186
Smith, Adam, 41, 89, 107
Smith, Jacqueline, 78
Social communicative interaction, 15
Social comparison, 101, 103–104, 107
Social construction, 15–16, 79
    changes in, 15–16
    dwelling of public space, 15–16
    gender differences in, 28–29
    importance of, 15
Social Construction of Reality, 15
Social constructionists, 15–16
    constructivists, difference between, 15–16
Social Constructionist Movement in Modern Psychology, 16
Social media gaffes, 164
Social media platforms, 125, 164
Social Network, The, 146
Social structures, changing, 11
Social touching, 234
Socialization, 235
    anticipatory, 235
    communicative public roadmap, 235
    professional civility, 236
Society, 79, 89–90
    definition, 89
    hierarchical structures within, 237
Socrates, 46, 162
Sources of the Self, The, 81
Space of subjectivity, 109
Space of between, conversational space, 109
Spiral of silence theory, 164
Spontaneous framing, 32, 149
Stalin, Joseph, 7
"Stand for the Silent," 227
Standpoint theory, 184
Stimuli, 121, 212
Stories, conflict context, 204
Story-centered leadership, 245–246
Story, learning for leadership, 61
Story, practices, and meaning, 61, 70–71
Strategic communication, 36
A Study of History, 9

Virtue ethics framework, 236
Vision, communicative leadership, 71
Vision-based framing, 33
Visions
    definition, 33
    ways to offer, 33–34
Visual perspectives, 80
Voegelin, Eric, 194
Vygotsky, 15, 140–141

W
Walden Two, 186
Warrant, in argument, 48
Watson, Tom, 145
Watt, Ian, 105–106
Web of relationships, 100–102, 107, 112, 262
Weber, Max, 46–47
Webs of human relationships. *See* Relational
        webs of connection
Weightiness, 50–51
Welcome and difference interplay, 260–261

Welcome, dwellings of, 91–92
    aggregate, 84
    community. *See* Community
    culture. *See* Culture
    family. *See* Family
    importance of, 77–78
    social construction of, 79
Wertheimer, Max, 5
Whorf, Benjamin Lee, 88
Workplace bullying, 231
Workplace harassment
    communicative approach to managing,
        233–235
    definition, 233
World War II, 9, 31, 35, 52

Y
Youghiogheny River, fatalities on, 201
Yousafzai, Malala, 227

Z
Zuckerberg, Mark, 146–147